REVIEW OF DISABILITY AND REHABILITATION RESEARCH

NIDRR GRANTMAKING PROCESSES AND PRODUCTS

Committee on the External Evaluation of NIDRR and Its Grantees

Jeanne C. Rivard, Mary Ellen O'Connell, and David H. Wegman, *Editors*

Board on Human-Systems Integration

Division of Behavioral and Social Sciences and Education

NATIONAL RESEARCH COUNCIL
OF THE NATIONAL ACADEMIES

THE NATIONAL ACADEMIES PRESS
Washington, D.C.
www.nap.edu

THE NATIONAL ACADEMIES PRESS **500 Fifth Street, N.W.** **Washington, DC 20001**

NOTICE: The project that is the subject of this report was approved by the Governing Board of the National Research Council, whose members are drawn from the councils of the National Academy of Sciences, the National Academy of Engineering, and the Institute of Medicine. The members of the committee responsible for the report were chosen for their special competences and with regard for appropriate balance.

This study was supported by Grant No. ED-OSE-09-C-0048 between the National Academy of Sciences and the U.S. Department of Education. Any opinions, findings, conclusions, or recommendations expressed in this publication are those of the author(s) and do not necessarily reflect the views of the organizations or agencies that provided support for the project.

International Standard Book Number-13: 978-0-309-22229-7
International Standard Book Number-10: 0-309-22229-X

Additional copies of this report are available from the National Academies Press, 500 Fifth Street, N.W., Lockbox 285, Washington, DC 20055; (800) 624-6242 or (202) 334-3313 (in the Washington metropolitan area); Internet, http://www.nap.edu.

Printed in the United States of America

Suggested citation: National Research Council. (2012). *Review of Disability and Rehabilitation Research: NIDRR Grantmaking Processes and Products*. Committee on the External Evaluation of NIDRR and Its Grantees. J.C. Rivard, M.E. O'Connell, and D.H. Wegman, Eds. Board on Human-Systems Integration, Division of Behavioral and Social Sciences and Education. Washington, DC: The National Academies Press.

THE NATIONAL ACADEMIES

Advisers to the Nation on Science, Engineering, and Medicine

The **National Academy of Sciences** is a private, nonprofit, self-perpetuating society of distinguished scholars engaged in scientific and engineering research, dedicated to the furtherance of science and technology and to their use for the general welfare. Upon the authority of the charter granted to it by the Congress in 1863, the Academy has a mandate that requires it to advise the federal government on scientific and technical matters. Dr. Ralph J. Cicerone is president of the National Academy of Sciences.

The **National Academy of Engineering** was established in 1964, under the charter of the National Academy of Sciences, as a parallel organization of outstanding engineers. It is autonomous in its administration and in the selection of its members, sharing with the National Academy of Sciences the responsibility for advising the federal government. The National Academy of Engineering also sponsors engineering programs aimed at meeting national needs, encourages education and research, and recognizes the superior achievements of engineers. Dr. Charles M. Vest is president of the National Academy of Engineering.

The **Institute of Medicine** was established in 1970 by the National Academy of Sciences to secure the services of eminent members of appropriate professions in the examination of policy matters pertaining to the health of the public. The Institute acts under the responsibility given to the National Academy of Sciences by its congressional charter to be an adviser to the federal government and, upon its own initiative, to identify issues of medical care, research, and education. Dr. Harvey V. Fineberg is president of the Institute of Medicine.

The **National Research Council** was organized by the National Academy of Sciences in 1916 to associate the broad community of science and technology with the Academy's purposes of furthering knowledge and advising the federal government. Functioning in accordance with general policies determined by the Academy, the Council has become the principal operating agency of both the National Academy of Sciences and the National Academy of Engineering in providing services to the government, the public, and the scientific and engineering communities. The Council is administered jointly by both Academies and the Institute of Medicine. Dr. Ralph J. Cicerone and Dr. Charles M. Vest are chair and vice chair, respectively, of the National Research Council.

www.national-academies.org

COMMITTEE ON THE EXTERNAL EVALUATION OF NIDRR AND ITS GRANTEES

David H. Wegman (*Chair*), Department of Work Environment, University of Massachusetts, Lowell (Emeritus)
Thomas J. Armstrong, Center for Ergonomics, University of Michigan
Burt S. Barnow, Trachtenberg School of Public Policy and Public Administration, George Washington University
Leighton Chan, Rehabilitation Medicine Department, Clinical Center, National Institutes of Health
Peter C. Esselman, Department of Rehabilitation Medicine, University of Washington, Seattle
Walter R. Frontera, School of Medicine, University of Puerto Rico
Glenn T. Fujiura, Department of Disability and Human Development, University of Illinois at Chicago
Bruce M. Gans, Kessler Institute for Rehabilitation, West Orange, New Jersey
Ian D. Graham, Knowledge Translation, Canadian Institutes of Health Research
Lisa I. Iezzoni, Mongan Institute for Health Policy, Massachusetts General Hospital, Boston
Alan M. Jette, School of Public Health, Boston University
Thubi H.A. Kolobe, Department of Rehabilitation Sciences, University of Oklahoma Health Sciences Center
Pamela Loprest, Urban Institute, Washington, DC
Kathryn E. Newcomer, Trachtenberg School of Public Policy and Public Administration, George Washington University
Patricia M. Owens, Government Accountability Office, Minisink Hills, Pennsylvania
Robert G. Radwin, Department of Biomedical Engineering, University of Wisconsin

Jeanne C. Rivard, *Senior Program Officer and Co-Study Director* (from September 2010)
Mary Ellen O'Connell, *Co-Study Director* (from September 2010)
Molly Follette Story, *Study Director* (through September 2010)
Laudan Y. Aron, *Senior Program Officer* (until April 2010)
Tina Winters, *Associate Program Officer*
Matthew D. McDonough, *Research Associate*
Mary Beth Ficklin, *Research Associate*
Eric Chen, *Senior Program Assistant*
Gary Fischer, *Senior Program Assistant*
Jatryce Jackson, *Senior Program Assistant*

Acknowledgments

This study was sponsored by the National Institute on Disability and Rehabilitation Research (NIDRR). The committee would first like to express its appreciation to Doris Werwie, NIDRR evaluation lead, for supplying the committee with extensive background materials about NIDRR, for compiling special databases and reports on grantee performance to assist in the committee's expert review of grantee outputs, and for offering ongoing coordination and assistance with the committee's requests for additional information or data. The committee would also like to extend its appreciation to Ruth Brannon, director of NIDRR's Research Sciences Division; Timothy Muzzio, director of NIDRR's Program, Budget, and Evaluation Division; and Phillip Beatty, associate director, Research Sciences Division, for spending extensive time with the committee staff in describing the operation of NIDRR's priority-writing, peer review, and grant management processes. We would also like to acknowledge William Schutz, program specialist, for his assistance in compiling data for the committee; Leslie Caplan, rehabilitation specialist, for coordinating with the committee so it could observe peer review panels in action; and Mary Darnell, NIDRR's contracting officer's representative. Appreciation is extended as well to Sue Swenson, NIDRR acting director, and Connie Pledger, director of the Interagency Committee on Disability Research (ICDR), for helping to clarify for the committee the role of the ICDR in relation to NIDRR and in the larger research system. Finally, the committee appreciates the time dedicated by the NIDRR staff who agreed to participate in confidential interviews to share their special knowledge and perspectives on NIDRR's key processes.

We would also like to thank all of the participants in the evaluation who lent us their time and valuable perspectives. They include the representatives of federal agencies, professional associations, and advocacy organizations who responded to our survey of NIDRR stakeholder organizations and the NIDRR peer reviewers who contributed their perspectives on NIDRR's peer review processes. Among this group of evaluation participants, much appreciation is extended to the 30 principal investigators (PIs) of the NIDRR grants we reviewed. Their participation required a substantial amount of time and effort, especially in the case of large center grants that produce many outputs. The PIs identified and submitted outputs for the committee's review and completed a set of questions concerning each output. For many PIs, this effort involved coordination with other team members who had been involved in their projects. In addition, the committee asked the PIs to respond to a separate set of questions regarding how they managed their grants and what other projects had been generated from their grants and outputs. Finally, the PIs were also asked to comment on key NIDRR processes (priority setting, peer review, and grant monitoring) that may influence their work. Some grantees extended themselves as well by setting up special demonstrations of their outputs via teleconference or websites.

We also wish to thank a number of individuals who, in two early public sessions, presented important contextual information for our consideration in planning the evaluation. In addition to Ruth Brannon and Doris Werwie, these included Alexa Posny, assistant secretary, Office of Special Education and Rehabilitative Services; and Lynnae Ruttledge, acting director of NIDRR (as of April 2010) and commissioner of the Rehabilitation Services Administration. They also included NIDRR grantees Richard Burkhauser of Cornell University, Judith Cook of the University of Illinois at Chicago, John Whyte of Moss Rehabilitation Institute, Wayne Gordon of Mt. Sinai University, and Gregg Vanderheiden of the University of Wisconsin–Madison, and federal agency representatives Pamela O'Neil of the National Science Foundation, Alan Willard of the National Institutes of Health, and Jeffrey Dowd of the U.S. Department of Energy.

We are also grateful to the following individuals who contributed their time in critically reviewing our preliminary evaluation plan and providing input into the final plan: Carol Weiss of Harvard University, Joseph Wholey of the University of Southern California, Adele Harrell (retired) of the Urban Institute, Deborah Boehm-Davis of George Mason University, and Pascale Carayon of the University of Wisconsin.

Appreciation is extended as well to those who played a key role in early stages of the evaluation: Laudy Aaron for her efforts in planning and forming the committee, and Molly Story, whose knowledge and experience in disability and rehabilitation research laid a strong foundation for our work as the first study director.

Among the National Research Council (NRC) staff, special thanks are due to Barbara Wanchisen, who provided oversight of and support for the study; Matt McDonough, research associate, and Tina Winters, associate program officer, who provided research and program expertise in developing drafts of key sections of the report; and senior program assistants Gary Fischer, Jatryce Jackson, and Eric Chen who provided administrative and logistic support over the course of the study. We wish to extend our appreciation as well to Christine Mirzayan Science and Technology Policy Graduate Fellow Mary Beth Ficklin for her special analyses, NRC consultants Eleanor Johnson and Jessica Scheer for their qualitative analyses and contributions to the writing of the report, and Rona Briere for her extensive assistance in editing many drafts of the report. Finally, we thank the executive office reports staff of the Division of Behavioral and Social Sciences and Education, especially Eugenia Grohman and Yvonne Wise, who provided valuable help with the editing and production of the report, and Kirsten Sampson Snyder, who managed the report review process.

Finally, the committee members wish to thank the staff of their institutions who assisted and supported their work on this study, and in particular Tana Gaylene of the Rehabilitation Medicine Department Clinical Center, National Institutes of Health.

This report has been reviewed in draft form by individuals chosen for their diverse perspectives and technical expertise, in accordance with procedures approved by the NRC's Report Review Committee. The purpose of this independent review is to provide candid and critical comments that will assist the institution in making its published report as sound as possible and to ensure that the report meets institutional standards for objectivity, evidence, and responsiveness to the study charge. The review comments and draft manuscript remain confidential to protect the integrity of the deliberative process. We wish to thank the following individuals for their review of this report: Peter Axelson, director of research and development, Beneficial Designs, Inc., Minden NV; Stephen H. Bell, senior fellow and principal scientist, Abt Associates, Inc., Bethesda, MD; Alicia L. Carriquiry, professor of statistics, Iowa State University; Judith A. Cook, professor and director, Center on Mental Health Services Research and Policy, Department of Psychiatry, University of Illinois at Chicago; Susan E. Cozzens, professor of public policy and director, Technology Policy and Assessment Center, School of Public Policy, Georgia Institute of Technology; Michael Feuerstein, professor of Departments of Medical and Clinical Psychology and Preventive Medicine And Biometrics, Uniformed Services University of the Health Sciences, Bethesda MD; Lex Frieden, professor of biomedical informatics and professor of rehabilitation, University of Texas, Health Science Center at Houston, and professor of rehabilitation, Baylor College of Medicine; David B. Gray, professor of occupational therapy and neurology, Program in

Occupational Therapy, Washington University School of Medicine; Richard Hurtig, professor and Starch faculty fellow, Department of Communication Sciences and Disorders, University of Iowa; William Zev Rymer, John G. Searle professor and vice president for research, Rehabilitation Institute of Chicago; David Stapleton, Center for Studying Disability Policy, Mathematica Policy Research, Inc.; and Jack M. Winters, professor of biomedical engineering and co-director of Falk Neurorehabilitation Engineering Research Center, Marquette University.

Although the reviewers listed above provided many constructive comments and suggestions, they were not asked to endorse the content of the report, nor did they see the final draft of the report before its release. The review of this report was overseen by John Bailar of the University of Chicago and William Howell of Arizona State University. Appointed by the NRC, they were responsible for making certain that an independent examination of this report was carried out in accordance with institutional procedures and that all review comments were carefully considered. Responsibility for the final content of this report rests entirely with the committee and the institution.

David H. Wegman, *Chair*
Jeanne C. Rivard, *Co-Study Director*
Mary Ellen O'Connell, *Co-Study Director*
Committee on the External Evaluation of NIDRR and Its Grantees

Contents

Summary 1

1 Introduction 17

2 Evaluation Scope and Methods 34

3 NIDRR's Priority-Setting Processes 56

4 NIDRR's Peer Review Process 83

5 Grant Management 128

6 Summative Evaluation 158

Appendixes

A Grant Summaries 207
B Rating Sheets/Questionnaires 305
C Acronyms 330
D Committee and Staff Biographical Sketches 334

Summary

The National Institute on Disability and Rehabilitation Research (NIDRR) is one of the principal federal agencies supporting applied research, training, and development to improve the lives of individuals with disabilities. NIDRR's mission is to generate new knowledge and promote its effective use in improving the ability of persons with disabilities to perform activities of their choice in the community, as well as to expand society's capacity to provide full opportunities and accommodations for its citizens with disabilities. Located within the Office of Special Education and Rehabilitative Services in the U.S. Department of Education (ED), NIDRR has an annual budget for grants and contracts of approximately $109 million, awarded through 14 separate program mechanisms that result in 1- to 5-year awards ranging in size from less than $100,000 to several million dollars. NIDRR has the largest budget of the three primary federal agencies with disability and rehabilitation as part of their mandate but also has the broadest mandate. NIDRR aims to reach all disability types and age groups, and its mission is tied to long-term outcomes such as independence, community participation, and employment.

Assessing the outcomes of research is a complex undertaking that can variably take into account the stated goals of the research, the contribution to the relevant field of research, the impact on the well-being of a particular population, or other related issues. The Government Performance and Results Act has led to a particular emphasis on establishing specific performance measures assessing the outputs of research programs.

NIDRR takes pride in proactively establishing program performance measures focused on the quality of its grantee outputs, developing accountability data systems to track the results of those measures, and developing internal management systems to facilitate quality research. In 2009, NIDRR requested that the National Research Council form a committee to conduct a "process evaluation" of aspects of its grantmaking and a "summative evaluation" of the quality of grantee outputs. In addition, the committee was charged with assessing the methods it developed for conducting the summative evaluation and making recommendations for the conduct of future evaluations.[1] The requested study was the most recent effort in a series of NIDRR-funded activities aimed at assessing and improving the agency's performance.

PROCESS EVALUATION

NIDRR posed three questions specific to the process evaluation aimed at assessing the process used for priority writing, practices for peer review of grant applications, and the planning and budgetary processes used by grantees. The development of priorities determines the areas of emphasis for research and the specific topics to be targeted by potential applicants, while peer review is a fundamental component of the grant selection process. Although it is not possible to establish a clear causal link, these NIDRR processes, as well as planning and budgetary processes used by grantees, can influence the quality of the work produced by grantees.

To address these questions, the committee reviewed existing documents (e.g., legislation, *Federal Register* notices, NIDRR and ED policies and procedures) and interviewed NIDRR management to obtain a more thorough and cohesive understanding of these processes. The committee gained additional insight into NIDRR's peer review process by listening to teleconferences held by three panels as they conducted their reviews of different grant competitions. In addition, the committee collected original data through surveys of NIDRR staff, stakeholder organizations (other federal agencies, professional associations, and advocacy organizations), NIDRR peer reviewers, and principal investigators of NIDRR grants.

Priority Setting

To what extent is NIDRR's priority-writing process conducted in such a way as to enhance the quality of the final results?

As used in the study question, the term "priority-writing process" encompasses many aspects of priority setting, including gathering input from

---

[1] This aspect of the committee's charge was summarized in a letter report provided to NIDRR in July 2011 and is also addressed in Chapter 6 of this report.

multiple sources (e.g., the field, stakeholder organizations, grantees, other agencies, and persons with disabilities and their families), identifying potential topics and determining priorities for funding, writing the proposed priorities and having them cleared for release, and publishing notices inviting applications (NIAs) on these priorities. The term "priority setting" is used synonymously with "priority writing" in this report to clarify that the focus of the committee's evaluation included this larger priority-setting process.

The committee concluded that NIDRR's long-range planning and priority-setting processes are successful in producing grants that are aligned with its mission and that stakeholders value as unique. Nonetheless, areas for improvement were identified. First, the committee concluded that NIDRR needs to do more to inform and engage stakeholders with respect to its long-range planning and priority-setting processes. Although the results of the stakeholder survey were generally positive, the transparency of the processes, responsiveness to stakeholder feedback, and use of NIDRR grantee products could be improved. Second, priority setting not only reflects the agency's intent to influence the advancement of research in targeted areas but also offers specific funding opportunities for potential grant applications to the agency. The announced priorities should therefore be developed and communicated in a manner that attracts the best researchers to participate in disability and rehabilitation research. Attracting the largest pool of applications from which to select grantees increases the chances for the highest quality outputs. When establishing its priorities, the agency needs to consider continuity from one funding cycle to another, as well as identify future research challenges and societal needs. The committee offers recommendations in four areas to strengthen NIDRR's long-range planning and priority-setting processes.

Formation of an Advisory Council

NIDRR has a broad and diverse mission that makes it challenging to set priorities that are responsive to the current state of the science and the needs of the stakeholder community. Currently, NIDRR relies on staff, the portfolio of existing projects, recent findings from completed grants, and the current research literature, as well as guidance from federal partners, for input to the priority-setting process. NIDRR's statute directs it to establish a standing Rehabilitation Research Advisory Council to advise the director of the agency on research priorities and the development of the agency's Long-Range Plans. While NIDRR has formed ad hoc advisory bodies to support the development of its Long-Range Plans, a standing body has never been formed. Given NIDRR's mandate, the council should be tasked with providing advice on both disability and rehabilitation research.

Recommendation 3-1[2]: NIDRR should fulfill the statutory mandate to form and utilize a standing disability and rehabilitation research advisory council to advise on the priority-setting process and provide input for priority setting.

Most federal funding agencies, including the National Institutes of Health (NIH), the National Science Foundation (NSF), and the National Institute for Occupational Safety and Health (NIOSH), use standing advisory bodies. A standing advisory body is likely to add stability and continuity to both NIDRR's long-range planning and its priority setting. The committee recognizes that NIDRR, like other federal research agencies, will face challenges in capturing the broad diversity of perspectives held by its many stakeholders. However, the committee feels strongly that, like other federal research agencies, NIDRR can meet these challenges.

Strategic Planning

NIDRR's multiple stakeholders include persons with disabilities and their families, the scientific community, professional associations, and advocacy organizations representing a variety of disability groups. In the face of this diversity, it is important for the agency to have a consistent mechanism for gathering information and input to inform the strategic planning process beyond the input that will be possible through an advisory council. NIDRR utilizes input from multiple sources, such as its stakeholders, other federal agencies, the Interagency Committee on Disability Research (ICDR), the current literature, and state-of-the-science conferences. However, the processes for gathering input and developing proposed Long-Range Plans have varied from one plan to another. Negative comments from the field generated by the last draft Long-Range Plan, coupled with the plan's subsequent delay, which caused NIDRR to operate under the prior plan for several years beyond its intended time frame, suggest a breakdown in NIDRR's priority-setting process. The lack of a permanent director also hampers and delays the agency's priority-setting process.[3]

Recommendation 3-2: NIDRR should use a structured, consistent, and inclusive strategic planning process to develop its Long-Range Plans and priorities.

NIDRR might consider the long-range planning and priority setting processes of other funding agencies, including NIH, NSF, and NIOSH, which

[2] The committee's recommendations are numbered according to the chapter of the report in which they appear.

[3] At the time of this writing, a permanent NIDRR Director had been recently hired.

have sought to integrate long-range planning and priority-setting processes through specific initiatives such as the NIH Roadmap, the NSF Strategic Plan, and the National Occupational Research Agenda.

Establishment of a Standard Calendar

For many program mechanisms, NIDRR has not established a regular schedule for drafting and approving priorities and NIAs and disseminating them to the field. ED has a lengthy review and approval process for obtaining clearance for the release of priorities and NIAs. The variability in the length of the clearance process may be an important factor, among others, that impacts the timing of the release of NIAs. The irregular or delayed release of NIAs may affect NIDRR's ability to provide individuals sufficient notice of grant opportunities or an optimal amount of time to complete applications. An irregular schedule may discourage the best investigators from submitting applications. Additionally, certain program mechanisms (such as Model Systems) include collaboration between institutions. Irregular posting and shortened response times hamper the ability of applicants to identity and recruit appropriate collaborators. These factors are likely to limit the number of investigators who apply and adversely affect the quality of the applications they submit. Additionally, young investigators less familiar with NIDRR are more likely to pursue grants from other agencies.

Recommendation 3-3: NIDRR should utilize a standard calendar for the setting of priorities, publication of notices inviting applications, submission of applications, and peer review meetings to improve the efficiency of the process.

NIDRR has made efforts to standardize the schedule for NIAs. The committee suggests that program mechanisms competed on a yearly basis have a consistent annual schedule for the submission and review of applications. For multiyear grants, the committee recommends that NIDRR establish a long-range operational plan listing projected future grant application submission dates, pending funding availability in that fiscal year.

Soliciting Applications

Like other federal agencies, NIDRR makes its NIAs available at Grants.gov in addition to publishing them in the *Federal Register*. The agency also uses a contractor to notify former grantees and others who, via their webpage, express an interest in receiving NIAs. NIDRR would benefit from more active efforts to solicit interest in its funding announcements.

Recommendation 3-4: NIDRR should expand its efforts to disseminate notices inviting applications to new potential applicants, including developing a communication strategy to ensure that the notices reach new audiences.

To expand dissemination, notices should be sent to the disability and rehabilitation professional and research organizations that make up NIDRR's stakeholder network and to university departments and offices of sponsored research. The latter could perhaps be accomplished through collaboration with other federal research programs that regularly send funding notices to universities.

Peer Review

To what extent are peer reviews of grant applications done in such a way as to enhance the quality of final results?

NIDRR's peer review process encompasses recruiting and training reviewers, conducting the review, and approving the awards. As with priority setting, it is challenging to link the peer review process directly to specific results because the quality of the portfolio, grants, and outputs emerging from the process is the product of multiple complex factors. It is clear, however, that the peer review process used by NIDRR contributes significantly to the success of the grant award program and the quality of the outputs produced.

The responses to the committee's peer review survey were largely positive, including peer reviewers' responses related to their experiences with NIDRR's peer review process and how it compares with the processes used by other federal research agencies. While the committee concluded that NIDRR's peer review process is generally good, there are opportunities for improvement that would likely enhance the process and the quality of final results. The committee offers three recommendations to this end.

Enhancements to the Peer Review Process

The committee concluded that NIDRR's peer review process is hampered by a limited pool of potential reviewers. NIDRR's competition managers take great care to assemble and facilitate qualified review panels and spend considerable time recruiting and screening potential reviewers. Competition managers regularly must manage potential conflicts of interest and rule out qualified reviewers. Despite these staff efforts, however, the committee found evidence that a number of panels are smaller than NIDRR's recommended size, reviewers are added so close to the meeting date that they have inadequate time to prepare, and reviewers lacking necessary scientific expertise may be participating in reviews.

The formation of formal "cohorts" of reviewers with particular areas of expertise would reduce the recruiting burden on NIDRR staff in locating reviewers needed for individual competitions with specific targeted expertise. In addition, reviewers surveyed by the committee reported that the quality of the training they received was inconsistent; enhancing this training would be a simple and effective way to improve the quality of the review process. Finally, considerable variation exists among competitions in the way NIDRR staff facilitate panel discussions. The result is variation in the quality of the discussions; such inconsistency also can result in confusion and negatively influence overall quality.

Recommendation 4-1: NIDRR should further strengthen the peer review infrastructure by expanding the pool of high-quality reviewers; establishing standing panels, or formal cohorts of peer reviewers with specialized knowledge and expertise as appropriate for the program mechanisms; enhancing reviewer training; and improving the consistency of NIDRR staff facilitation of panel meetings and the quality of feedback provided to grantees.

Reducing Reviewer Burden

Participating in NIDRR's peer review process is a significant burden for a large percentage of reviewers. Many reviewers spend more time than they would like preparing, and the review days are long and intense. This significant time commitment makes it less likely that qualified and experienced reviewers will participate. Reviewers surveyed also reported sometimes having insufficient time to review proposals, which could affect the quality of the review discussions. The committee concluded that the review process is so burdensome to peer reviewers as to threaten the quality of the process.

Recommendation 4-2: NIDRR should streamline the review process in order to reduce the burden on peer reviewers.

Use of Consumer Peer Reviewers

To address its mission, NIDRR makes concerted efforts to include both scientists with disabilities and consumers without scientific expertise in the peer review process. Consumers can represent the experiences and views of their particular disability communities and can evaluate applications for relevance to their community's needs and concerns.

All reviewers, including researchers and consumers, should have the appropriate expertise to review those elements of proposals to which they are assigned. If consumers are to review scientific aspects of proposals, they should have the relevant expertise, or NIDRR should consider providing them with relevant methodological training. NIDRR should review and monitor the role of consumers and researchers in peer review to ensure that quality is not compromised.

Recommendation 4-3: NIDRR should continue to have consumer representation in the peer review process and establish procedures to guide the participation of those without scientific expertise.

Many federal research programs involve consumers without scientific expertise in peer review. NIDRR may want to examine such practices at NIH, Congressionally Directed Medical Research Programs, Juvenile Diabetes Research Foundation, and other agencies to inform its own approach to including nonresearchers in peer review.

Grant Management

What planning and budgetary processes does the grantee use to promote high-quality outputs?

The committee assessed grantee planning and budgetary processes in the larger context of NIDRR's structure and processes supporting grant management. To perform this assessment, the committee (1) reviewed existing documentation on the grant management and monitoring processes of ED and NIDRR, (2) gathered information from principal investigators about the processes they use for managing grants, and (3) interviewed NIDRR staff to obtain their perspectives on how grant monitoring facilitates grantees' efforts to manage their grants for successful results.

NIDRR appears to have developed a good plan for upgrading its routine monitoring of grants and for identifying and monitoring grants that are at risk of noncompliance with ED or NIDRR requirements and performance expectations. On the whole, grantees appear to appreciate aspects of NIDRR's grant management processes that facilitate their own grant management strategies. While grantees generally commented that NIDRR's grant management processes were effective in facilitating their own grant management processes, they offered some suggestions for improvement that would help them further. NIDRR staff also offered suggestions for improvement, focused on strengthening their capacity to monitor grants and help grantees stay on course in implementing their grants and meeting performance expectations. Among other suggestions, they expressed the need for smaller grant caseloads, additional travel funds for on-site monitoring of grants that require higher levels of technical assistance, more training for new project officers to promote consistency and quality in the monitoring process, and a freer flow of communication between project officers and NIDRR planning staff with respect to financial information.

Recommendation 5-1: NIDRR should continue to focus efforts on improving its grant monitoring procedures and specific elements of its overall grant management system that impact grantee-level planning, budgets, and the quality of outputs.

From its interviews with grantees, the committee also learned that some grants focused on developing technology innovations may not accord well with a management template that calls for strict up-front planning and adherence to original designs and timetables. Similarly, a grant funding a large multisite study may require more or different supervision, monitoring, and technical assistance than a more focused or limited study. Grantees expressed the need for greater flexibility in grant management so they can stay on the cutting edge of technology or adapt more easily to changing needs of multisite research projects.

Recommendation 5-2: NIDRR should review the requirements placed upon technical innovation grants and large multisite studies to ensure that planning, reporting, supervisory, and technical assistance requirements fit their particular circumstances.

To what extent are the results of the reviewed research and development outputs used to inform new projects by both the grantee and NIDRR?

To assess how research and development outputs inform new projects, the committee (1) reviewed information from NIDRR management about how they use the results of their grantees' research and (2) reviewed information from grantees about new projects that have been generated from their grants. The committee concluded that research and development outputs are used to generate new projects by grantees to a great extent and lead to substantial numbers of new collaborations with other researchers and organizations, as well as transfers of data, instruments, or models to other projects, and commercialization of technology products.

SUMMATIVE EVALUATION

The summative evaluation, designed to inform NIDRR's performance monitoring and reporting, involved assessing the quality of outputs produced by a sample of 30 NIDRR grantees.[4] These grants were drawn from nine NIDRR program mechanisms: Burn Model System, Traumatic Brain Injury Model System, Spinal Cord Injury Model System, Rehabilitation Research and Training Center, Rehabilitation Engineering Research Center, Disability and Rehabilitation Research Project-General, Field Initiated Project, Small Business Innovation Research II, and Switzer Fellowship. The committee reviewed four different types of outputs, as defined by NIDRR: publications; tools, measures, and intervention protocols; technology products and devices; and informational products.

The committee developed and used four criteria to assess quality: (1) technical quality; (2) advancement of knowledge or the field; (3) likely or demonstrated impact (on science, persons with disabilities and their families, provider practice, health and social systems, social and health policy, and the private sector/commercialization); and (4) dissemination according to principles of appropriate knowledge translation.

A total of 148 outputs produced by the 30 grantees were rated on each criterion, using a 7-point scale, where 1 indicated poor quality, 4 indicated good quality, and 7 indicated excellent quality. Ratings on each of the four criteria were distributed fairly symmetrically along the scale, with the largest proportion of scores falling at the midpoint of 4 and with most being slightly skewed toward the higher end of the scale. Although close to 75 percent of the outputs rated fell in the "good to excellent" range of the quality scale (i.e., mean ratings of 4 or greater on the 7-point quality scale), 25 percent of the outputs fell in the lower quality range (1 or "poor" to 3 or "below good") across all four criteria. The committee offers NIDRR two recommendations for assisting grantees in continuously improving the quality of their outputs.

First, the quality of outputs is the product of multiple complex factors that involve the priority-setting process, the funding level, the peer review process, the quality of the proposed science/research and the grantees, and ultimately the quality of the research findings. For grantees that are not performing optimally, NIDRR may conduct ongoing formative reviews with experts to identify strategies for improvement, increase its grant monitoring activities, and require additional grantee reporting. Grantees generally report that NIDRR's oversight and reporting functions foster successful grants and high-quality outputs by assisting them in adhering to their budget and timeline, providing an external quality assurance mechanism for their project management, and prompting them to maintain their focus on project goals for high-quality products.

[4]The committee performed a random sampling of grants at the level of program mechanism. Five mechanisms were excluded in consultation with NIDRR.

Recommendation 6-1: Although close to 75 percent of outputs were rated as "good to excellent" (i.e., 4 or higher on the 7-point quality scale), NIDRR should make it clear that it expects all grantees to produce the highest quality outputs.

The intent of this recommendation is for NIDRR to encourage all of its grantees to publish in peer-reviewed journals, present at national meetings, publish/disseminate materials, and bring technology solutions to market while producing these outputs at the highest levels of quality. To this end, NIDRR should push forward by establishing clear and consistent expectations for grantees to publish in higher-impact journals as one indicator of higher quality. For outputs other than publications, NIDRR should establish standards for quality to be achieved and adopt appropriate metrics to assess adherence to these standards. One way of setting the quality bar higher would be to encourage grantees to use standardized reporting forms and checklists[5] for reviewing the technical quality of their own work before subjecting it to external review.

Second, despite limitations in the use of bibliometrics,[6] they are a valuable and objective set of measures that can be used in combination with other assessment strategies. NIDRR has conducted bibliometric analyses in the past, but has not routinely incorporated use of these metrics into its performance measurement process.

Recommendation 6-2: NIDRR should consider undertaking bibliometric analyses of its grantees' publications as a routine component of performance measurement.

Bibliometric analyses would take advantage of an existing data source for periodic measurement of the scientific impact of NIDRR grantee publications, and would provide an indicator of the extent to which these grant outputs are being disseminated and used. This type of metric is being recommended for use in combination with other measures, just as it was used in the committee's evaluation along with expert review and supplemental evidence of the impact an article may have had on science, persons with disabilities and their families, provider practice, health and social systems, social and health policy, and the private sector/commercialization.

---

[5] See http://www.equator-network.org/ for examples.

[6] Common bibliometric measures include the impact factor of journals in which articles are published and the number of times an article is cited in other articles.

SELF-ASSESSMENT OF THE COMMITTEE'S METHODS FOR OUTPUT REVIEW AND RECOMMENDATIONS FOR FUTURE EVALUATIONS

The committee developed and implemented an evaluation process for assessing the outputs of NIDRR's grantees and identifying the various levels of quality and characteristics of those outputs. The committee spent considerable time selecting and refining the criteria used to assess the quality of outputs. While some variation was evident in the independent scoring among the committee members, it was rarely extreme, particularly after group discussions. However, as summarized below, the committee encountered several challenges and obstacles during the course of its work that limited the generalization of its findings and restricted what could be said about the totality of outputs generated by all NIDRR grantees.

Defining Future Evaluation Objectives

The primary focus of the committee's summative evaluation was on assessing the quality of outputs produced by grantees; the evaluation did not include in-depth examination or comparison of the larger contexts of the funding programs, grants, or projects within which the outputs were produced. However, the committee was asked to formulate an overall rating for each grant based on the outputs reviewed and the information available about the grant from the Annual Performance Report (APR). Results at the grant level were subject to limitations resulting from the general lack of information about how the outputs did or did not interrelate; whether, and if so how, grant objectives were accomplished; and the relative priority placed on the various outputs. In addition, for larger, more complex grants, such as center grants, a number of expectations for the grants, such as capacity building, dissemination, outreach, technical assistance, and training, are unlikely to be adequately reflected in the committee's approach, which focused exclusively on specific outputs. The relationship of outputs to grants is more complex than this approach could address.

Recommendation 6-3: NIDRR should determine whether assessment of the quality of outputs should be the sole evaluation objective.

Strengthening the Output Assessment

The committee was able to develop and implement a quantifiable expert review process for evaluating the outputs of NIDRR grantees that was based on criteria used in assessing research programs in both the United States and other countries. With refinements, this method could be applied to the evaluation of future outputs even more effectively. Nonetheless, in implementing this method, the committee encountered challenges and issues related to the diversity of outputs, the timing of evaluations, sources of information, and reviewer expertise.

Diversity of Outputs

There were acknowledged limitations in conducting the summative evaluation, such as the inability to generalize the results because of the small sample size, the need for more testing of the quality rating scale developed, and possible biases that could have arisen from sampling and measurement methods. In spite of these limitations, the quality rating system used for the committee's summative evaluation worked well for publications in particular, which made up 70 percent of the outputs reviewed. Using the four criteria outlined above, the reviewers were able to identify and describe varying levels of quality and the characteristics associated with each. However, the committee's quality criteria were not as easily applied to outputs such as websites, conferences, and interventions; these outputs require more individualized criteria for assessing specialized technical elements, and sometimes more in-depth evaluation methods. Applying one set of criteria, even though broad and flexible, could not guarantee sufficient or appropriate applicability to every type of output.

Timing of Evaluations

The question arises of when best to perform an evaluation of outputs. Evaluation of outputs during the final year of an award may not allow sufficient time for the outputs to have full impact. For example, some publications will be forthcoming at this point, and others will not have had sufficient time to have full impact. The trade-off of waiting a year or more after the end of a grant before performing the evaluation is the likelihood that staff involved with the original grant may not be available, recollection of grant activities may be compromised, and engagement or interest in demonstrating results may be reduced. However, publications can be tracked regardless of access to the grantee. Outputs other than publications, such as technology products, could undergo an interim evaluation to enable examination of the development and evolution of outputs.

Sources of Information

In addition to reviewing outputs directly, committee members considered information from two other sources in rating the quality of outputs: information submitted through the grantee's APR and information provided in a supplemental questionnaire developed by the committee. It is important to note that both of these sources involved grantee self-reports, which could be susceptible to social desirability bias. Moreover, the APR is designed as a grant *monitoring* tool rather than as a source of information for a program *evaluation*. Because the information supplied on the APR and the questionnaire was not always sufficient to inform the quality ratings, additional methods are needed to ensure complete information for such reviews.

Reviewer Expertise

The committee was directed to assess the quality of four types of prespecified outputs. While the most common output type was publications, NIDRR grants produce a variety of other outputs, including tools and measures, technology devices and standards, and informational products. These outputs vary widely in their complexity and the investment needed to produce them. The criteria used by the committee to assess the quality of outputs were based on the cumulative literature reviewed and the committee members' own research expertise in diverse areas of disability and rehabilitation research, medicine, and engineering, as well as their expertise in evaluation, economics, knowledge translation, and policy. However, the committee's combined expertise did not include every possible content area in the broad field of disability and rehabilitation research.

> **Recommendation 6-4: If future evaluations of output quality are conducted, the process developed by the committee should be implemented with refinements to strengthen the design related to the diversity of outputs, timing of evaluations, sources of information, and reviewer expertise.**

Improving Use of the Annual Performance Report

The APR data set provided to the committee by NIDRR at the outset of the evaluation was helpful in profiling the grants for sampling and in listing all of the grantees' projects and outputs. In addition, the narrative information provided in the reports was useful to the committee in compiling descriptions of the grants; however, they varied with respect to the quality of the information they contained.

> **Recommendation 6-5: NIDRR should consider revising its APR to better capture information needed to routinely evaluate the quality and impacts of outputs, grants, or program mechanisms. They might consider efforts such as consolidating existing data elements**

or adding new elements to capture the quality criteria and dimensions used in the present summative evaluation.

Recommendation 6-6: NIDRR should investigate ways to work with grantees to ensure the completeness and consistency of information provided in the APR.

CONCLUSION

In summary, the committee concluded that NIDRR grants have produced valuable research, tools, and other outputs for advancing the field of disability and rehabilitation research in line with the agency's mandate. Improvements to NIDRR's priority-setting, peer review, and grant management processes, as well as consideration of alternative evaluation goals and strategies, would further enhance the quality of these processes, their results, and the agency's efforts to improve the lives of individuals with disabilities.

1

Introduction

The National Institute on Disability and Rehabilitation Research (NIDRR) is located within the Office of Special Education and Rehabilitative Services in the U.S. Department of Education. NIDRR is one of multiple federal agencies that invest in disability and rehabilitation research, but it has a broader mandate than those other agencies. Established by the 1978 amendments to the Rehabilitation Act of 1973,[1] NIDRR's mission "is to generate new knowledge and promote its effective use to improve the abilities of people with disabilities to perform activities of their choice in the community, and also to expand society's capacity to provide full opportunities and accommodations for its citizens with disabilities" (National Institute on Disability and Rehabilitation Research, 2006c, p. 8,167). The agency pursues this mission by funding research and related activities focused on maximizing the full inclusion, social integration, employment, and independent living of individuals of all ages with disabilities (National Institute on Disability and Rehabilitation Research, 2009a).

NIDRR prides itself on being proactive in establishing program performance measures and developing accountability data systems to track the progress of its grantees. An electronic annual reporting system is used to collect data from grantees on many aspects of grant operation and outputs. Various formative and summative evaluation approaches have been used to assess the quality of the performance and results of the agency's research portfolio and its grantees. Prompted by the need to provide more data on

[1]NIDRR was originally called the National Institute on Handicapped Research in the 1978 amendments to the act; its name was changed to its present form by the 1986 amendments.

its program results, in 2009 NIDRR requested that the National Research Council (NRC) conduct an external evaluation of some of the agency's key processes and assess the quality of outputs produced by NIDRR grantees (National Institute on Disability and Rehabilitation Research, 2009a). This report presents the results of that evaluation.

This chapter introduces the report by first explaining the charge to the committee that conducted the evaluation. It then provides background information on NIDRR, including its unique legislative mandate, the types of research it funds and its grant funding mechanisms, its role related to the Interagency Committee on Disability Research, and its budget and staff. The third section summarizes approaches NIDRR has used in the past to evaluate its grantees and distinguishes them from the methods used by the committee. The final section provides an overview of the remaining chapters of the report.

CHARGE TO THE COMMITTEE

This ad hoc committee, with oversight by the NRC's Board on Human-Systems Integration, was charged with developing and implementing a framework and evaluation design for the purpose of (1) reviewing NIDRR's priority-writing and grant review processes ("process evaluation") and (2) assessing the quality of grantee outputs for a sample of grants representing the NIDRR portfolio ("summative evaluation"). Additionally, the committee was charged with assessing the design and implementation of its summative evaluation process and making recommendations for additional evaluations that might follow this effort. The evaluation was to be conducted over a period of 2 years between October 2009 and September 2011. The results of this evaluation are intended to provide NIDRR with a better understanding of the quality of its grantees' outputs and how the agency can best manage an important and evolving research portfolio that meets its strategic goals and objectives while regularly assessing and improving its performance as required by the Government Performance and Results Act (GPRA) of 1993 (U.S. Office of Management and Budget, 2009a). The specific questions guiding the evaluation were as follows:

Process Evaluation

1. To what extent is NIDRR's priority-writing process conducted in such a way as to enhance the quality of the final results?
2. To what extent are the peer reviews of grant applications done in such a way as to enhance the quality of the final results?
3. What planning and budgetary processes does the grantee use to promote high-quality outputs?

Summative Evaluation

4. To what extent are the final outputs from NIDRR grants of high quality?
5. To what extent are the results of the reviewed research and development outputs used to inform new projects by both the grantee and NIDRR?

This external evaluation was designed and conducted independently by the NRC committee. However, it was funded by NIDRR, and the contract stipulated in advance certain features and parameters for the design of the summative evaluation component (study questions 4 and 5) as follows:

- **Level of analysis**—The level of analysis was specified to be grantee outputs. The outputs to be assessed included four types as defined by NIDRR: (1) publications; (2) tools, measures, and intervention protocols; (3) technology products and devices; and (4) informational products.
- **Sampling of grants**—The sample for the evaluation was to include a minimum of 30 grants. The selection criteria were to include representation across all program mechanisms and grants in their last year of funding.
- **Number of outputs to be reviewed**—Two outputs were to be reviewed for each project being carried out under each grant selected for the evaluation. The number of projects depended on the size of the grant and varied from 1 for small investigator-initiated grants to 10 for large center grants.

For NIDRR, the ultimate objective of the output review was to gain an understanding of what was being produced by the time grants came to an end with respect to value added for the disability community and new knowledge produced for the field. Because the focus of the summative evaluation was primarily on the quality of outputs produced by the sampled grants, it is important to clarify what was not included in the committee's charge. The charge did not include a larger focus on how the grants were implemented with respect to their original objectives and whether the objectives were achieved, how the outputs of the various projects were linked and how they developed over time, and how the quality of outputs differed across the various NIDRR program mechanisms. The charge also did not include an assessment of the long-term impact of outputs on persons with disabilities. However, suggestions are made by the committee on the importance of these types of evaluation foci in Chapter 6 of the report.

BACKGROUND ON NIDRR

NIDRR's purpose is to

> . . . provide for research, demonstration projects, training, and related activities to maximize the full inclusion and integration into society, employment, independent living, family support, and economic and social self-sufficiency of individuals with disabilities of all ages . . .; promote the transfer of rehabilitation technology to individuals with disabilities through research and demonstration projects . . .; ensure the widespread distribution, in usable formats, of practical scientific and technological information . . .; identify effective strategies that enhance the opportunities of individuals with disabilities to engage in employment . . .; and increase opportunities for researchers who are members of traditionally underserved populations, including researchers who are members of minority groups and researchers who are individuals with disabilities (The Rehabilitation Act of 1973, as amended).

NIDRR's Unique Role

The multidimensional challenges faced by individuals with disabilities in employment, housing, public accommodations, education, transportation, communication, recreation, health services, institutionalization, voting, and public services, as outlined in the Rehabilitation Act of 1973 as amended, necessitate a comprehensive, holistic approach to NIDRR's mission (National Institute on Disability and Rehabilitation Research, 2009a). Across NIDRR's agenda, the central focus is on the whole person with a disability, whose ability to function and quality of life are dependent on the complex interactions among personal, societal, and environmental factors.

NIDRR is one of three major disability-focused research sponsors in the federal government,[2] but it plays a unique role in that its target population includes all disability types and all age groups. (See the Rehabilitation Act of 1973 as amended for a complete list of NIDRR's mandated responsibilities.) While other federal research entities fund prevention, cure, and acute rehabilitation research, NIDRR also invests in rehabilitation research that is tied more closely to longer-term outcomes, such as independence, community participation, and employment (National Institute on Disability

---

[2]One of the other major sponsors is the National Center for Medical and Rehabilitation Research (NCMRR), which is located within the National Institute of Child Health and Human Development of the U.S. Department of Health and Human Services. NCMRR funds research aimed at developing scientific knowledge to enhance the health, productivity, independence, and quality of life of people with disabilities. The other major sponsor is the Department of Veterans Affairs, which, through its Veterans Administration Rehabilitation Research and Development Service, funds extramural basic and biomedical research and an intramural research program in 13 rehabilitation centers.

and Rehabilitation Research, 2009b). The World Health Organization's International Classification of Functioning, Disability and Health (ICF) (World Health Organization, 2001) provides context for understanding NIDRR-supported research and development. The ICF classifies disability and health along a continuum from body function and structure to activities and participation, while accounting for environmental and personal factors. In these terms, NIDRR funds primarily research and development grants that are aimed at increasing functional abilities to facilitate greater self-determination and participation of individuals with disabilities in the home, community, school, and workplace as defined in the ICF (National Institute on Disability and Rehabilitation Research, 2009b).

NIDRR's Research Domains

Table 1-1 summarizes the various types of research that NIDRR funds in five outcome domains: (1) employment, (2) participation and community living, (3) health and function, (4) technology for access and function, and (5) disability demographics (National Institute on Disability and Rehabilitation Research, 2009a, pp. 3-6). Although most grants address more than

TABLE 1-1 NIDRR Research Domains and Topics

Research Domain	Number of Awards as of January 2009	Research Topics
Employment	16 (7%)	• Career planning; job entry, advancement, and retention; transitions in moving from financial dependency to self-sufficiency or from underemployment into work that is consistent with the individual's strengths, abilities, and interests. • Methods for integrating the unique needs of employers and disability populations to improve employment outcomes across the life span, such as methods, costs, and results of services by rehabilitation programs or supported employment, including studies of natural supports at work as they relate to employment outcomes. • The role of personal assistance services in the workplace and the application of rehabilitation technology, universal design principals, environmental adaptations, and engineering solutions to enhance personal function and address barriers confronted in employment by people with disabilities.

continued

TABLE 1-1 Continued

Research Domain	Number of Awards as of January 2009	Research Topics
Participation and Community Living	39 (17%)	• Development and evaluation of strategies for services, interventions, products, and modifications to the built and social environments that would allow individuals with all types of disabilities to live and participate in their communities. • Development of new and improved theories about and measures of participation and community living that will enable the impact of specific strategies and interventions to be determined more accurately.
Health and Function	93 (39%)	Individual level: • Ongoing research and clinical efforts to produce a wide variety of programs, interventions, and products aimed at enhancing the health and function of individuals with disabilities. • Study of new technologies that can improve the diagnosis and measurement of disabling conditions and study of devices to support enhanced function. • Research that can help prevent secondary conditions from developing among people with disabilities and explore the implications of nonmedical interventions, such as exercise, in this context. Systems level: • Study of system-level policies and practices that exacerbate or ameliorate disability-related disparities in access to health care services. • Accurate assessment of the health status of individuals with disabilities to increase understanding of the impact of the health care delivery system on their health and wellness. • Studies to classify specific interventions in medical rehabilitation so as to better define and measure the effectiveness of the multitude of rehabilitation interventions.

TABLE 1-1 Continued

Research Domain	Number of Awards as of January 2009	Research Topics
Technology for Access and Function	81 (34%)	Individual level: • Focuses primarily on assistive technology devices that enhance the physical, sensory, and cognitive abilities of people with disabilities and assist them in participating and functioning more independently in the home, at work, in recreational settings, and at cultural and community events. Systems level: • Focuses on applying technology research and development in ways that enhance community integration, independence, productivity, competitiveness, and equal opportunity by mitigating or eliminating barriers found in large social systems, such as public transportation, telecommunications, information technology, and the built environment. • Exploration of how recent, breakthrough advances in biomaterials research, composite technologies, information and telecommunication technologies, nanotechnologies, micro electro-mechanical systems (MEMS), sensor technologies, and the neurosciences can be incorporated into future rehabilitation-related technology research.
Disability Demographics	8 (3%)	• Studies to generate new information that can be used by individuals with disabilities, service providers, policy makers, and others working to identify and eliminate disparities in employment, participation and community living, and health and function. • Studies that mine data to address the full range of social, health, and economic facets of disability and that compare findings across data sources. • Research to understand the variances in levels of participation by individuals with disabilities and to evaluate strategies or interventions that may help bridge the gap between preference and feasibility in an existing environment. • Establishment of a center on disability demographics and statistics.
Total Number of Awards as of January 2009	237	

SOURCE: National Institute on Disability and Rehabilitation Research (2009a, pp. 3-6).

one domain, the second column of the table notes the number of grants in NIDRR's portfolio as of January 2009 whose primary research domain was in each of these five areas.

NIDRR Grant Mechanisms

NIDRR has eight primary mechanisms for awarding grants defined by the Catalog of Federal Domestic Assistance (CFDA) (National Institute on Disability and Rehabilitation Research, 2009a, pp. 7-29). Using these primary mechanisms, funds are distributed through 14 separate program mechanisms, which are described below.

1. **Disability and Rehabilitation Research Project (DRRP; CFDA #84.133A).** DRRPs are awarded through six separate program mechanisms:

   - *Disability and Business Technical Assistance Center (DBTAC)*, which comprises a network of 10 regional centers and one Coordination Outreach and Research Center that provide information and referral, technical assistance, public awareness, and training on all aspects of the Americans with Disabilities Act (ADA).[3]
   - *Traumatic Brain Injury Model System (TBIMS)*, whose aim is to demonstrate the benefits of a coordinated system of neurotrauma and rehabilitation care and to conduct innovative research on all aspects of care for those who sustain traumatic brain injuries. The mission of the TBIMS program is to improve the lives of persons who experience traumatic brain injury by creating and disseminating new knowledge about the course, treatment, and outcomes relating to their condition.
   - *Disability and Rehabilitation Research Project-General (DRRP)*, which funds projects with special emphasis on research, demonstrations, training, dissemination, utilization, and technical assistance. Projects may include combinations of these activities. These projects may develop methods, procedures, and rehabilitation technology to assist in achieving the full inclusion and integration into society, employment, independent living, family support, and economic and social self-sufficiency of individuals with disabilities, especially individuals with the most severe disabilities, or to improve the effectiveness of services authorized under the Rehabilitation Act.
   - *Knowledge Translation (KT)*, whose projects range from investigating models, methods, strategies, and mechanisms that could

---

[3] Although still funded as DBTACs, these centers are currently referred to as ADA National Network Centers.

contribute to the successful knowledge translation of disability and rehabilitation research and products to synthesizing, disseminating, and promoting the use of existing knowledge and products to improve the lives of individuals with disabilities.

- *Burn Model System (BMS)*, which comprises centers that establish innovative projects for the delivery, demonstration, and evaluation of comprehensive medical, vocational, and other rehabilitation services to meet the wide range of needs of individuals with burns.
- *Section 21*, which focuses on research capacity building for minority entities such as historically black colleges and universities and institutions serving primarily Hispanic, Asian, and American Indian students and nonminority entities with an interest in improving understanding about the needs and outcomes of individuals with disabilities from minority populations. Program activities include assisting minority entities with networking that supports enhanced collaboration between minority and nonminority entities and the exchange of expertise and advanced training across program areas.

2. **Rehabilitation Research and Training Center (RRTC; CFDA #84.133B).** RRTCs conduct coordinated and integrated advanced research aimed at alleviating or stabilizing disabling conditions, promoting maximum social and economic independence of people with disabilities, or improving rehabilitation methodology or service delivery systems. RRTCs operate in collaboration with institutions of higher education and providers of rehabilitation services and serve as national centers of excellence in rehabilitation research.
3. **Rehabilitation Engineering Research Center (RERC; CFDA #84.133E).** RERCs conduct programs of advanced engineering and technical research designed to apply technology, scientific achievement, and psychological and social knowledge to solve rehabilitation problems and remove environmental barriers. RERCs are affiliated with institutions of higher education or nonprofit organizations.
4. **Switzer Fellowship (CFDA #84.133F).** The Switzer program gives individual researchers an opportunity to develop new ideas and gain research experience. Fellows design and work for 1 year on an independent research project.
5. **Field Initiated Project (FIP; CFDA #84.133G).** The FIP program provides funding to individual researchers to address rehabilitation issues in promising and innovative ways. FIPs are of two types—Field Initiated Projects-Research (FIR) and Field Initiated Projects-Development (FID).
6. **Spinal Cord Injury Model System (SCIMS) (CFDA #84.133N).** SCIMS centers study the course of recovery and outcomes following the delivery of a coordinated system of care for individuals with spinal cord injuries.

The centers under this program provide comprehensive rehabilitation services to individuals with such injuries and conduct spinal cord research, including clinical research.

7. **Advanced Rehabilitation Research Training (ARRT; CFDA #84.133P).** The ARRT program provides funding to institutions of higher education to recruit qualified postdoctoral candidates with clinical, management, basic, or engineering research experience and prepare them to conduct independent research on disability and rehabilitation issues.
8. **Small Business Innovation Research (SBIR; CFDA #84.133S).** SBIR grants, administered by NIDRR as a part of the larger mandatory SBIR program, help support the production of new assistive and rehabilitation technology. This two-phase program takes a rehabilitation-related product from development to market readiness. Phase I grants are designed to demonstrate proof of concept, while Phase II grants develop products envisioned in Phase I grants.

In addition to these program mechanisms, contracts are awarded to provide technical support for NIDRR's internal management, research, and knowledge translation activities.

Interagency Collaboration

Efforts have been made to develop and coordinate a coherent program of disability and rehabilitation research across the many federal agencies involved in such research. Yet coordination is difficult to accomplish because of differences in agency missions and organizational cultures (e.g., medical model versus social or environmental model), competitive budget processes, weak to nonexistent incentives for coordination and collaboration, and separately constructed long-range strategic plans within each agency (Institute of Medicine, 2007).

The Rehabilitation Act of 1973 authorized the Interagency Committee on Disability Research (ICDR), a federal interagency committee chaired by the NIDRR Director. The ICDR is mandated to promote coordination and cooperation among the many federal departments and agencies conducting disability and rehabilitation research programs. The committee comprises presidential designees, including the following (or their designees): the Director of NIDRR, the Commissioner of the Rehabilitation Services Administration, the Assistant Secretary for the Office of Special Education and Rehabilitative Services, the Secretary of Education, the Secretary of Veterans Affairs, the Director of the National Institutes of Health, the Director of the National Institute of Mental Health, the Administrator of the National Aeronautics and Space Administration, the Secretary of Transportation, the Assistant Secretary of the Interior for Indian Affairs, the Director of the Indian Health Service, and the Director of the National Science Foundation. The role of ICDR is to identify and provide opportunities for information sharing and partnerships on various initiatives in which the agencies are engaged. The ICDR works to cross-fertilize ideas and promote dialogue, but does not prescribe activities to its members.[4] Its activities are organized and undertaken through the structure of five subcommittees addressing medical rehabilitation, employment, technology, education, and disability statistics.

NIDRR Budget

The Rehabilitation Act states that NIDRR's Director will lay out funding priorities and covered activities in a 5-year plan that will be published in the *Federal Register* and that the plan will dedicate at least 90 percent of NIDRR funds to extramural research. Additionally, Section 21 of the Rehabilitation Act mandates that 1 percent of NIDRR appropriations be set aside to address traditionally underserved populations. Finally, the SBIR Development Act of 2000 requires agencies with research and development budgets in excess of $100 million, such as NIDRR, to set aside a certain percentage of their funds for SBIR. The current set-aside is 2.5 percent of the research and development budget.

NIDRR's 2009 budget for grants and contracts was $109 million. Of this total, $99,904,000 (U.S. Department of Education, 2009) was dedicated to grants, with the remainder going to contracts and project support. Figure 1-1 illustrates NIDRR's distribution of its funds for grants across all of the program mechanisms in 2009 (National Institute on Disability and Rehabilitation Research, 2009a).

NIDRR's annual budget for research and development grants has remained fairly constant in nominal terms during the last decade. As stated above, the budget for grants in 2009 was nearly $100 million; in 2008 and 2007 it was approximately $97 million (U.S. Department of Education, 2008, 2009). Previously, a report of the Institute of Medicine (2007) showed that the agency's overall funding had been fairly steady since 2002. Although inflation has been reasonably low in recent years, steady funding in nominal terms implies a reduction in the research that can be conducted.

NIDRR Staff

NIDRR's most recent organizational chart (National Institute on Disability and Rehabilitation Research, 2011) shows an acting Director,[5] an

[4] S. Swenson and C. Pledger, personal communication, April 2011.

[5] At the time of this writing, a permanent NIDRR Director had been recently hired.

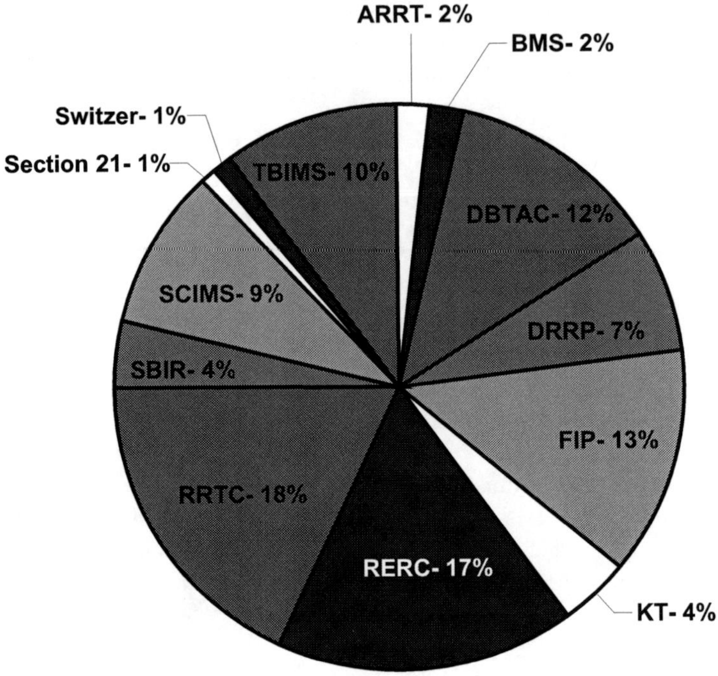

FIGURE 1-1 Distribution of NIDRR funds across program mechanisms, fiscal year 2009.
NOTE: ARRT = Advanced Rehabilitation Research Training, BMS = Burn Model System, DBTAC = Disability and Business Technical Assistance Center, DRRP = Disability and Rehabilitation Research Project-General, FIP = Field Initiated Project, KT = Knowledge Translation, RERC = Rehabilitation Engineering Research Center, RRTC = Rehabilitation Research and Training Center, SBIR = Small Business Innovation Research, SCIMS = Spinal Cord Injury Model System, TBIMS = Traumatic Brain Injury Model System.
SOURCE: National Institute on Disability and Rehabilitation Research (2009a, p. 32).

acting Deputy Director, and two main divisions—Research Sciences and Program, Budget, and Evaluation. Both divisions have directors and supervisors. In the Research Sciences Division, 14 positions are classified as rehabilitation specialists; these are the project officers who interact directly with grantees and perform grant monitoring functions. The organizational chart shows four of these positions to be vacant. The Program, Budget, and Evaluation Division has 10 other staff positions.

HISTORY OF NIDRR ASSESSMENTS

Assessments of NIDRR have included a 2005 performance assessment under the GPRA and Annual Performance Assessment Expert Reviews conducted in 2005 and 2006.

NIDRR Performance Assessment Under GPRA

In compliance with the GPRA (U.S. Office of Management and Budget, 2009b), NIDRR developed the following performance measures to assess its key outcomes (National Institute on Disability and Rehabilitation Research, 2009a, pp. 78-79):

- The percentage of NIDRR-supported fellows, post-doctoral trainees, and doctoral students who publish results of NIDRR-sponsored research in refereed journals
- The number of accomplishments (new or improved tools, methods, discoveries, standards, interventions, programs, or devices) developed or tested with NIDRR funding that has been judged by expert panels to be of high quality and to advance the field
- The percentage of NIDRR-funded grant applications that receive an average peer review score of 85 or higher
- The percentage of NIDRR grants that assess the effectiveness of interventions, programs, and devices using rigorous methods
- The number of new or improved NIDRR-funded assistive and universally designed technologies, products, and devices, transferred to industry for potential commercialization
- The average number of publications per award based on NIDRR-funded R&D activities in refereed journals
- The percentage of NIDRR competitions announced by October 1
- The percentage of NIDRR grant awards issued within 6 months of the competition closing date
- The percentage of NIDRR-funded research projects identified as having an employment focus (This is a measure required by the Department of Education, Office of Special Education and Rehabilitative Services, not a GPRA measure)

Under the GPRA requirements at the time,[6] NIDRR's 2005 Program Assessment Rating Tool (PART) review showed excellent scores on Pro-

[6] PART was developed and used by the Office of Management and Budget to assess the performance of federal programs and to identify actions that could improve results (http://www.whitehouse.gov/omb/performance_past [October 24, 2011]). Expectations for performance measurement are currently being amended by the GPRA Modernization Act of 2010 (http://www.whitehouse.gov/omb/performance/gprm-act [October 24, 2011]).

gram Purpose and Design (100 percent), Strategic Planning (90 percent), and Program Management (90 percent). However, Program Results and Accountability was rated ineffective (42 percent).[7]

NIDRR's Annual Performance Assessment Expert Reviews

NIDRR's Annual Performance Assessment Expert Review process was implemented in 2005 and 2006 to evaluate the agency's portfolio of grants in three areas: (1) health and function, (2) employment, and (3) technology. The objectives of the review were to provide an independent assessment of the quality and relevance of NIDRR-funded research and the extent to which the research outputs and outcomes were contributing to the agency's long-term performance goals and measures; the quality and relevance of the agency's management of research directions and award decisions; and the strengths and weaknesses of the three research portfolios, including recommendations to ensure the accomplishment of NIDRR's goals and objectives (National Institute on Disability and Rehabilitation Research, 2006a, 2006b, 2007). To conduct the review, NIDRR assembled three panels of expert reviewers, one to review each portfolio.

As with the present evaluation, grantee outputs were reviewed as part of the portfolio evaluation. Grantees submitted up to five accomplishments, defined as "outputs" or "outcomes," that they considered to be the most important that occurred or matured during the current reporting period. "Outputs" included publications or presentations of significant findings; products, including tools, devices, and written products; and services completed as part of training or capacity building. "Outcomes" could be either short term (referring to documented changes or advances in knowledge, understanding, or skills) or intermediate (referring to documented changes in policy, practice, behavior, or systems capacity). The accomplishments were scored on a scale of 1 to 3, with 1 being "little-to-no contribution to the field," 2 being a "substantial contribution," and "3" being an "outstanding contribution." A rating of 0 was used for "unable to determine."

Key findings from the three reports include the following:

- **Health and function (October 2006)** (National Institute on Disability and Rehabilitation Research, 2007) (included multiple program mechanisms): The panel commended NIDRR on its long-standing productive portfolio in health and function research, and recognized the agency's success in building infrastructure and capacity

[7] ExpectMore.gov: National Institute on Disability and Rehabilitation Research, page 8 of 15 (http://www.whitehouse.gov/omb/expectmore/detail/10001041.2005.html [April 30, 2010]).

for disability and rehabilitation research. The panel noted several achievements of grantees, but felt limited in making judgments based on information covering only 1 year or less of multiyear awards. The panel rated 67 percent of the grantee accomplishments in this area as substantial or outstanding.

- **Employment (September 2005)** (National Institute on Disability and Rehabilitation Research, 2006a) (included the RRTC, DRRP, and FIP program mechanisms): Overall, the panel concluded that the portfolio contained very high-quality research ideas. However, the panel expressed four concerns: "(1) the apparent lack of scientific rigor behind the identified outputs, (2) the lack of sufficient information on the methodologies used by grantees, (3) the lack of evidence supporting many of the claims made by grantees in their Supplemental Information Reports, and (4) the lack of peer-reviewed publications" (p. 4). The panel was unable to rate the grantee accomplishments given the limited information it received.
- **Technology (October 2005)** (National Institute on Disability and Rehabilitation Research, 2006b) (included the RERC, DRRP, and FIP program mechanisms): The panel identified significant accomplishments in each cluster area. However, given NIDRR's level of investment, the panel stated that the overall number of high-quality research and development outputs and outcomes that advanced scientific knowledge was inadequate. The panel also noted that many of the claims made in the reports it reviewed lacked sufficient supporting evidence. The panel rated 54 percent of the grantee accomplishments as substantial or outstanding.

Methods used in the summative component of the present evaluation were somewhat similar to those used in the Annual Portfolio Assessment Expert Reviews with regard to the assessment of accomplishments, but can be distinguished from the latter in several ways. First, this committee reviewed only the category of "outputs." Second, the committee focused on the quality of outputs. Therefore, instead of assigning one rating for the extent to which the outputs contributed to the field as was done in the Annual Portfolio Assessment Expert Reviews, the committee examined and rated each output in a multidimensional way using four criteria: technical quality, advancement of knowledge or the field, likely or demonstrated impact, and dissemination. Third, the committee itself served as the expert panel of reviewers. Finally, the committee assessed the methods used in its summative evaluation and made recommendations for improving future evaluations of outputs from NIDRR research. A full description of the methods used to assess outputs is presented in Chapter 6.

ORGANIZATION OF THE REPORT

Chapter 2 describes the scope of the committee's evaluation and the methods used. Chapters 3, 4, and 5, respectively, present results of the evaluation of NIDRR's priority-setting, peer review, and grant management processes. The chapters summarize NIDRR's policies and procedures with regard to these key processes and present the committee's findings based on information gathered from such sources as interviews with NIDRR staff; questionnaires completed by grantees; and surveys of NIDRR stakeholder organizations, other federal agencies, and NIDRR peer reviewers. Chapter 6 summarizes the findings of the evaluation of grantee outputs, based on a sample of 30 grants, and presents the assessment of the committee's summative evaluation process. Conclusions and recommendations for improving NIDRR's key processes and the quality of grantee outputs and for conducting future evaluations are included at the end of Chapters 3 through 6.

The report's appendixes provide background information. Appendix A contains summaries of the 30 grants whose outputs were evaluated by the committee; these summaries include descriptions of the outputs reviewed. Appendix B contains the questionnaires and rating sheets used in the committee's process and summative evaluations. Appendix C lists the acronyms used in this report. Finally, Appendix D contains biographical sketches of the committee members and NRC staff who participated in the study.

REFERENCES

Institute of Medicine. (2007). *The future of disability in America*. Washington, DC: The National Academies Press.

National Institute on Disability and Rehabilitation Research. (2006a). *Annual portfolio assessment expert review pilot employment portfolio panel summary report*. Available: http://www.naric.com/nidrr/APAER_Employ_Final-Revised1-4-06.pdf [March 21, 2011].

National Institute on Disability and Rehabilitation Research. (2006b). *Annual portfolio assessment expert review pilot technology portfolio panel summary report*. Available: http://www.naric.com/nidrr/APAERTechnologyReport-FinalRevised-1-4-06.pdf [March 21, 2011].

National Institute on Disability and Rehabilitation Research. (2006c). Department of Education: National Institute on Disability and Rehabilitation Research—Notice of Final Long-Range Plan for Fiscal Years 2005–2009. *Federal Register, 71*(31), 8,166-8,200.

National Institute on Disability and Rehabilitation Research. (2007). *Annual performance assessment expert review health and function research*. Available: http://www.ncddr.org/new/announcements/apaer/hf/HF-APAER2006RptPub7-5-07.pdf [March 21, 2011].

National Institute on Disability and Rehabilitation Research. (2009a). *Briefing book for The National Academies*. Unpublished document. Washington, DC: National Institute on Disability and Rehabilitation Research.

National Institute on Disability and Rehabilitation Research. (2009b). Department of Education: National Institute on Disability and Rehabilitation Research—Notice of Proposed Long-Range Plan for Fiscal Years 2010–2014. *Federal Register, 74*(10), 2,564-2,569.

National Institute on Disability and Rehabilitation Research. (2011). *NIDRR organizational chart*. Unpublished document. Washington, DC: National Institute on Disability and Rehabilitation Research.

The Rehabilitation Act of 1973, as amended. Pub. L. No. 93-112. Available: http://www2.ed.gov/policy/speced/reg/narrative.html [January 21, 2011].

U.S. Department of Education, Office of Special Education, Rehabilitative Services, Rehabilitation Services Administration. (2008). *Annual report on federal activities under the Rehabilitation Act, Fiscal Year 2008*. Washington, DC: U.S. Department of Education.

U.S. Department of Education, Office of Special Education, Rehabilitative Services, Rehabilitation Services Administration. (2009). *Annual report on federal activities under the Rehabilitation Act, Fiscal Year 2009*. Washington, DC: U.S. Department of Education.

U.S. Office of Management and Budget. (2009a). *Government Performance and Result Act*. Available: http://www.whitehouse.gov/omb/mgmt-gpra/gplaw2m.html [March 20, 2009].

U.S. Office of Management and Budget. (2009b). *Assessing program performance*. Available: http://whitehouse.gov/omb/part/ [March 20, 2009].

World Health Organization. (2001). *ICF: International Classification of Functioning, Disability and Health*. Geneva, Switzerland: World Health Organization.

2

Evaluation Scope and Methods

This chapter begins by explaining the scope of the committee's evaluation. It then describes the methods used for the evaluation. Both the scope of the evaluation and potential limitations of its findings are discussed to clarify the extent to which the findings can be generalized and used by the National Institute on Disability and Rehabilitation Research (NIDRR) to enhance its priority-setting, peer review, and grant management processes.

SCOPE OF THE EVALUATION

This section explains the parameters of the committee's evaluation through a conceptual framework that guided the evaluation. It also defines "quality" as operationalized for this study.

Conceptual Framework

In designing the evaluation, the committee used NIDRR's published logic model (National Institute on Disability and Rehabilitation Research, 2006) as a starting point. In this model, NIDRR's investments in grants aimed at capacity building, research and development, and knowledge translation are intended to produce discoveries; theories, measures, and methods; and interventions, products, devices, and environmental adaptations (i.e., short-term outcomes). These outputs should promote the adoption and use of knowledge leading to changes in policy, practice, behavior, and system capacity (i.e., intermediate outcomes) for the ultimate benefit of persons with disabilities in the domains of employment, participation and community living, and health and function (i.e., long-term outcome arenas). NIDRR holds itself accountable primarily for the generation of knowledge in the short-term outcome arena, and it is this arena that was the focus of the committee's external evaluation.

The committee examined how NIDRR's grant funding is prioritized for these investment areas, the processes used for reviewing and selecting grants, and the quality of the research and development outputs, as depicted in the conceptual framework in Figure 2-1. The committee developed this framework to guide the evaluation effort. The boxes labeled Q1 to Q5 (i.e., NIDRR's process and summative evaluation questions 1 to 5; see Chapter 1), were the direct foci of the evaluation. The figure also includes other inputs, contextual factors, and implementation considerations as they are likely to influence the processes and short-term outcomes. The figure shows that the measurable elements of the short-term outcomes are what NIDRR considers to be the array of grant outputs (Q4) generated by grantees, which are expected to inform and generate new projects (Q5). Also shown are the expected long-term outcomes, which include an expanded knowledge base; improved programs and policy; and reduced disparities for people with disabilities in employment, participation and community living, and health and function. However, these long-term outcomes were beyond the scope of the committee's evaluation.

In summary, the scope of the evaluation encompassed key NIDRR processes of priority setting, peer review, and grant management (process evaluation) and the quality of grantee outputs (summative evaluation). It is important to point out that the scope of the summative evaluation did not include a larger explicit focus on assessing the overall performance of individual grants or NIDRR portfolios (e.g., Did grants achieve their proposed objectives? Did the various research and development portfolios operate as intended to produce the expected results?). Although capacity building is a major thrust of NIDRR's center and training grants, the present evaluation did not include assessment of outputs related to capacity building (e.g., number of trainees moving into research positions), which would have required methods different from those used for this study.

Definition of "Quality"

The evaluation focused on the quality of NIDRR's priority-setting, peer review, and grant management processes and on the quality of the outputs generated by grants. A review of the literature on evaluation of federal research programs reveals that the term "quality" is operationalized in a variety of ways. For example, the National Research Council (NRC) and Institute of Medicine (IOM) (2007) developed a framework and suggested

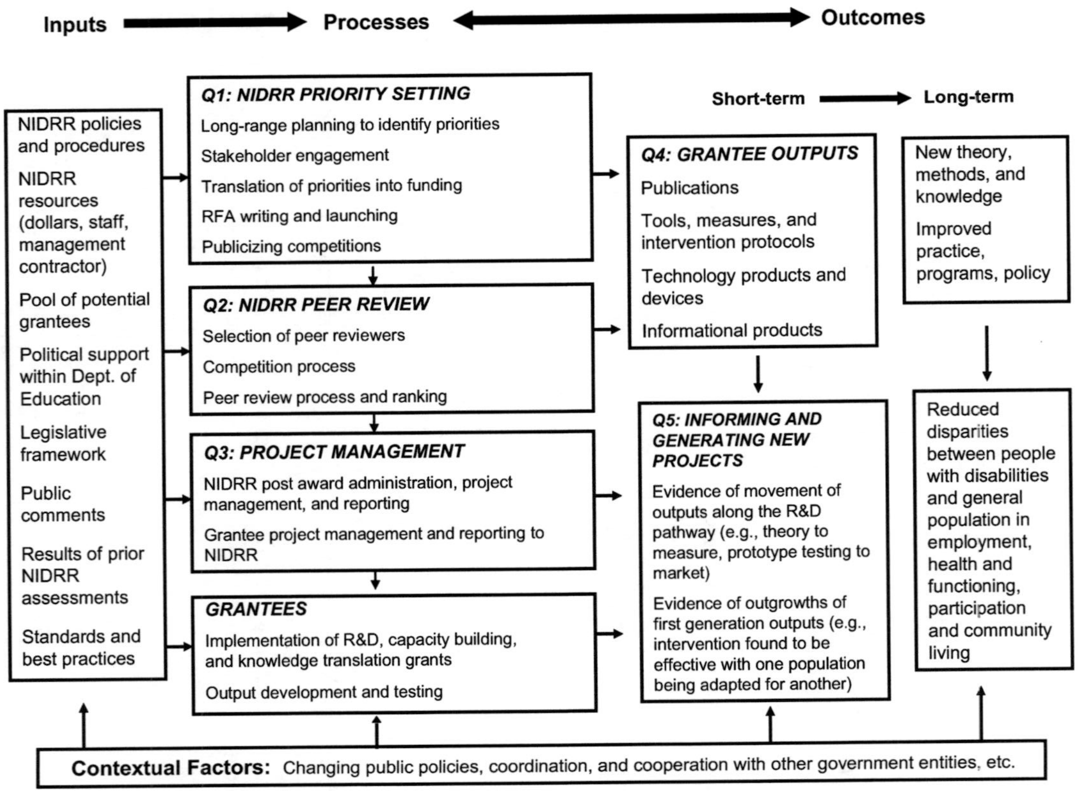

FIGURE 2-1 Conceptual framework for the committee's external evaluation of NIDRR and its grantees.

measures for assessing multiple research programs across the National Institute for Occupational Safety and Health. That approach refers to various quality-related criteria for assessing "outputs" and "intermediate outcomes." In another example, within a return-on-investment framework (Panel on Return on Investment in Health Research, 2009), the Canadian Academy of Health Sciences developed a menu of indicators that can be used for evaluating research programs. "Quality criteria" were included as an indicator of "advancing knowledge," along with "activity" (also called "outputs") and "outreach" (also called "transfer"). A third example is a framework and web-based survey approach developed by RAND (Ismail et al., 2010; Wooding and Starkey, 2010; Wooding et al., 2009) for measuring outputs and impacts of research programs for the Arthritis Research Campaign (UK), which was also applied to the Medical Research Council (UK) and the Canadian Institute of Health Research-Institute of Musculoskeletal Health and Arthritis. The survey contains a series of questions for grantees that are focused on stages of research and development and possible impacts. A final example is an approach, developed in Taiwan for assessing a wide range of the country's federal research programs, that refers to quality-related criteria as "performance attributes" in the areas of academic achievement, technology output, knowledge services, and technology diffusion (Chien et al., 2009).

Annex 2-1 at the end of this chapter shows the various quality criteria and dimensions used across these studies, as well as those compiled by an external advisory group convened by NIDRR in August 2008 to assist the agency in laying the groundwork for the current External Evaluation of NIDRR and its Grantees. Referring specifically to the four output categories used by NIDRR (i.e., publications, tools, technology products, and information products), the advisory group provided responses to the following questions: What criteria could be used by an external peer review panel to rate the quality of NIDRR grantee research outputs? What are some of the dimensions of quality? The first column in the table in Annex 2-1 summarizes the advisory group's suggested criteria and dimensions for assessing the quality of NIDRR outputs and relates these to the criteria used in the other studies referred to above.

The list of criteria is intended to be exhaustive to illustrate the types of criteria and dimensions that have been used in U.S. and international studies of federal research programs and that the committee drew on in developing the criteria used in this evaluation. Most of these criteria and dimensions were incorporated into the summative evaluation, as described in Chapter 6 of the report and as can be seen in the output quality rating form used for the evaluation (see Appendix B).

In keeping with the literature and other approaches to evaluating federal research programs, the committee used a broad concept of "quality" encompassing attributes that lead to the selection of grants and eventual grant results that (1) meet technical and professional standards of science and technology; (2) will advance the knowledge base or the field of research, policy, or practice; (3) are likely to have or have had demonstrated impacts on science, consumers, provider practice, health and social systems, social and health policy, and the private sector/commercialization; and (4) are disseminated according to principles of appropriate knowledge translation.

METHODS

The committee used a cross-sectional design that incorporated both quantitative and qualitative methods to address the two sets of questions in the process and summative evaluation phases of the study. The process evaluation phase involved reviewing existing documentation and collecting testimonial data to examine how NIDRR, through its policies and procedures and in practice, develops its research and funding priorities, reviews and evaluates submitted proposals, makes decisions and awards grants based on these reviews, and manages grant-supported activities. The summative evaluation phase involved the use of expert panels to assess the quality of grant outputs. The following sections present the study methods that were used to address the two sets of questions for these two phases. Data collection took place between July 2010 and February 2011.

Sources of Information, Data Collection, and Analysis

Process Evaluation

To address questions related to NIDRR's priority-setting, peer review, and grant management processes, the committee reviewed existing documentation (e.g., legislation, *Federal Register* notices, NIDRR and U.S. Department of Education [ED] policies and procedures) and interviewed NIDRR and ED management to obtain a more thorough and cohesive understanding of these processes.[1] The committee gained additional insight into NIDRR's peer review process by listening to teleconferences held by three panels as they conducted their reviews of different competitions. The committee also collected original data from the following key informant groups.

NIDRR staff and contractors NIDRR management provided the committee with a list of the agency's administrative and program management staff who had sufficient knowledge, experience, and responsibilities in the

[1]The committee conducted interviews with NIDRR and ED management in four sessions during summer 2010 and one session in spring 2011.

priority-setting, peer review, and grant management processes to respond to the committee's interview questions. The committee interviewed 16 NIDRR staff from this list in person to gather information on their roles in and perspectives on these processes. Two-thirds of the interviewees were project officers or direct supervisors of project officers; the remaining held administrative positions. The interview questions were open-ended, and the interviews were recorded and transcribed. The committee also interviewed by telephone a manager from a NIDRR contractor that assists the agency with the logistics of convening peer review panels to obtain the contractor's perspective on the peer review process.

NIDRR stakeholder organizations The committee obtained a list of 130 organizations that operate in NIDRR's arena from (1) NIDRR, which provided the names of professional and advocacy organizations the agency considers to be stakeholders, and (2) the Interagency Committee on Disability Research (ICDR), which provided the names of federal agencies that are statutory members of the ICDR or nonstatutory members that have participated in ICDR special committees. The committee sent all 130 organizations invitations to participate in an online survey; the invitations were addressed specifically to the executive directors of the professional and advocacy organizations and to the named representatives of the federal agencies. Invited respondents were asked to either complete the survey themselves or forward it to a member of their organization who would be knowledgeable about the organization's relationships with NIDRR. The invitations were sent in an e-mail letter that provided a link to the online survey and a password for logging on to the secure website. If respondents were unable to access the survey online or preferred another method, the committee offered to send them the survey in hard-copy form or to conduct it by telephone. The survey contained a series of closed- and open-ended questions inquiring about the organizations' role in the NIDRR planning and priority-setting process, respondents' perspectives on the process, benefits their agencies derived from NIDRR grants or outputs, and suggestions for enhancements to the priority-setting process. Of the 130 organizations, 72 responded to the survey (a response rate of 55 percent). According to Baruch and Holtom (2008), who examined 175 organizational studies, 55 percent is an acceptable response rate for a survey targeting executive directors.

NIDRR peer reviewers The committee sent invitations to complete a survey to all individuals (a total of 156) who served on NIDRR peer review panels during fiscal year 2008-2009. The invitations were sent in an e-mail letter that provided a link to the online survey and a password for logging on to the secure website. If respondents were unable to access the survey online or preferred another method, the committee offered to send it to them in hard-copy form or to conduct the survey by telephone. The survey contained a series of closed- and open-ended questions inquiring about their experiences with and perspectives on the NIDRR peer review process, how it compares with the peer review processes of other federal research agencies, and suggestions for enhancements to the process. Four potential respondents were deleted from the list because their e-mail addresses were invalid even after a concentrated search. Of the 152 individuals successfully invited, 121 responded to the questionnaire (a response rate of 80 percent).

Principal investigators (PIs) of NIDRR grants The committee invited 30 PIs whose grants were randomly selected for review in the summative phase of the evaluation (see the section below on methods for the summative evaluation) to respond in writing to a special set of questions focused on NIDRR's priority-setting, peer review, and grant management processes. One set of questions focused specifically on NIDRR's third major study question, which related to planning and budgetary processes used by grantees to promote high-quality outputs. Twenty-eight of the 30 grantees opted to respond to this set of process questions.

Analysis of Process Data

The committee analyzed quantitative data from the online surveys of stakeholders and peer reviewers descriptively to examine frequencies and measures of central distribution. For process data gathered from NIDRR staff, grantees, stakeholder organizations, and peer reviewers (i.e., responses to open-ended questions that were based on individuals' opinions or perspectives), standard qualitative analysis techniques (Miles and Huberman, 1994; Patton, 2002) were used. These techniques involved a three-phase process of coding the data to identify common topics, categories, and themes. The first phase in the iterative process of coding each data source involved an initial examination or "read-through" of the complete data set. The initial examination resulted in a preliminary list of topic codes, which were then used to code the data. The second phase of the process involved reviewing the coded data in order to refine and finalize the list of codes. During this effort, analysts generally combined two or more codes into one of the existing codes or into a new overarching code. Multiple variations were attempted before a final list of codes was determined and a final coding of the data was completed. The final phase of the process involved reviewing the finalized coded data and drawing out categories and themes.

While researchers sought to perform each analytic phase similarly for each source of data, differences in the nature and volume of data from the different sources necessitated some variation:

- Grantees, peer reviewers, and stakeholders—Open-ended data were collected from these sources in the form of their written answers to specific questions. The coding of these data was done initially by question, and codes were then compared and combined across the questions.
- NIDRR staff—Qualitative data were collected from NIDRR staff through personal interviews that were audio recorded and transcribed. The questions concerning NIDRR processes of priority setting, peer review, and grant management were phrased in general terms, and respondents were then prompted to provide additional details or clarification. Preliminary coding was done on the first five transcribed interviews, then refined as additional interviews were analyzed. Code lists were significantly refined through the iterative process described above.

It is important to recognize the limitations of qualitative analyses of responses elicited to open-ended survey questions. First, the data set does not generally represent the viewpoints of all respondents because it is common for 15 to 35 percent not to respond to the open-ended questions (Ulin et al., 2005). Second, among those who do respond, a varying number of the responses either are not written in a coherent manner; do not represent complete thoughts; or are vague generalities, lacking detail or specificity. Third, it is common for respondents with critical comments or suggestions to respond more often than those with neutral or positive comments (Gendall et al., 1996).

Finally, Miles and Huberman (1994) encourage using counts of the number of times that certain codes or topics are observed in the data because these counts come into play when describing results, such as the frequency or consistency of observations. In the NIDRR staff (N = 16 respondents) and grantee (N = 28 respondents) data sets collected for this evaluation, counts were used in a highly limited manner because the frequencies were very low in these small data sets. Where data sets were larger (stakeholders = 72 respondents and peer reviewers = 121), counts were used in reporting results of the qualitative analyses for greater transparency, but the committee acknowledges that in most cases, the number of specific observations for certain topics also is quite low. Despite these limitations, the committee believes that the collected data and qualitative analyses add background, context, and insight to many issues raised by respondents. In addition, they can lend support to this report's conclusions and recommendations when similar issues emerge across respondent groups or across both qualitative and quantitative data sources.

Summative Evaluation

The summative study questions focused on the quality of outputs generated by NIDRR grantees and the potential for the outputs to lead to further research and development. Chapter 6, which summarizes the results of the summative evaluation, also describes in detail the sampling, measurement, and data collection methods used to conduct the assessment of outputs. Therefore, these methods are described only briefly here.

The committee and NRC staff sampled 30 grants from NIDRR's portfolio, and the committee as a panel of experts reviewed outputs of these 30 grants. These grants were drawn from nine of NIDRR's program mechanisms: Burn Model System, Traumatic Brain Injury Model System, Spinal Cord Injury Model System, Rehabilitation Research and Training Center, Rehabilitation Engineering Research Center, Disability and Rehabilitation Research Project, Field Initiated Project, Small Business Innovation Research II, and Switzer Fellowship. The primary focus of the committee's summative evaluation was on assessing the quality of research and development outputs produced by grantees. The review focused on four different types of outputs, as defined in NIDRR's Annual Performance Report: (1) publications (e.g., research reports and other publications in peer-reviewed and nonpeer-reviewed journals); (2) tools, measures, and intervention protocols (e.g., instruments or processes created to acquire quantitative or qualitative information, knowledge, or data on a specific disability or rehabilitation issue or to provide a rehabilitative intervention); (3) technology products and devices (e.g., industry standards/guidelines, software/netware, inventions, patents/licenses/patent disclosures, working prototypes, product(s) evaluated or field tested, product(s) transferred to industry for potential commercialization, product(s) in the marketplace); and (4) informational products (e.g., training manuals or curricula; fact sheets; newsletters; audiovisual materials; marketing tools; educational aids; websites or other Internet sites produced in conjunction with research and development, training, dissemination, knowledge translation, and/or consumer involvement activities).

In assessing the quality of outputs, the committee used the following four criteria, stemming from its definition of quality (as discussed earlier): (1) technical quality, (2) advancement of knowledge or the field, (3) likely or demonstrated impact (on science, consumers, provider practice, health and social systems, social and health policy, and the private sector/commercialization), and (4) dissemination according to principles of appropriate knowledge translation. The committee analyzed data from the summative evaluation using frequency distributions and reported ratings of the quality of outputs in the aggregate by quality criteria assessed.

Table 2-1 summarizes the data collection and measurement methods described above.

TABLE 2-1 Summary of Data Collection and Measurement Methods

Study Question	Measures/Instruments	Data Sources	Data Collection Methods
Process Evaluation (July to September 2010)			
1. To what extent is NIDRR's priority-writing process conducted in such a way as to enhance the quality of the final results?	• Existing data: – Rehabilitation Act of 1973, as amended, and other related regulations (Education Department General Administrative Regulations, Department of Education Handbook for the Discretionary Grant Process) – NIDRR briefing documents (descriptive and procedural) – Current and proposed NIDRR Long-Range Plans – Notices inviting applications (NIAs) and application kits by program mechanism (2009 and 2010) (relevant to funded priorities) – NIDRR assessments: U.S. Office of Management and Budget Performance Assessment Rating Tool (2005); Annual Performance Assessment Expert Panel Reviews (pilot reports for 2006, 2007) – NIDRR External Advisory Group report	NIDRR and *Federal Register*	Extraction of relevant detail from documentation
	• Questions for process evaluation interviews tailored for NIDRR management and staff • Web-based survey (form tailored for NIDRR stakeholders)	NIDRR personnel, stakeholder organizations	Semistructured face-to-face interviews Web-based survey (self-administered)

continued

TABLE 2-1 Continued

Study Question	Measures/Instruments	Data Sources	Data Collection Methods
2. To what extent are peer reviews of grant applications done in such a way as to enhance the quality of the final results?	• Existing data: As above for question #1, plus: – NIDRR descriptive and procedural documents on peer review: Application Technical Review Plan; peer reviewer instructions – NIAs and application kits by program mechanism (2009 and 2010) (relevant to criteria for rating grants) – Analysis of peer review tracking database (Synergy, 2008)	NIDRR and *Federal Register*	Extraction of relevant detail from documentation
	• Questions for process evaluation interviews tailored for NIDRR management and staff • Web-based survey (form tailored for peer reviewers)	NIDRR personnel, peer reviewers	Semistructured face-to-face interviews Web-based survey (self-administered)
3. What planning and budgetary processes does the grantee use to promote high-quality outputs?	• Questions for process evaluation interviews tailored for NIDRR management and staff • Grantee questionnaire	NIDRR personnel, grantees (principal investigators [PIs])	Semistructured face-to-face interviews Self-administered questionnaire

Summative Evaluation (October 2010 to January 2011)			
4. To what extent are the final outputs from NIDRR grants of high quality?	• Existing data: NIDRR Annual Performance Report database to describe and summarize the outputs	NIDRR	Extraction of data from APR
	• Grantee outputs and supplemental questionnaire with items classifying and describing the types of outputs, features of the outputs that reflect the quality criteria, and future research and development as an outgrowth	Grantees (PIs)	Self-administered questionnaire
	• Quality of outputs: committee member rating sheet, based on criteria such as: – Technical quality – Advancement of knowledge or the field – Likely or demonstrated impact – Dissemination	Committee's peer review scores	Peer review of outputs and other materials (APR, grantee questionnaire)
5. To what extent are the results of the reviewed research and development outputs used to inform new projects by both the grantee and NIDRR?	• Questions for process evaluation interviews	NIDRR personnel	Semistructured face-to-face interviews
	• Grantee questionnaire: same questionnaire as in #4 above for items related to the generation of new research and outputs	Grantees (PIs)	Self-administered questionnaire

Potential Limitations

Although the committee used the most rigorous methods possible to conduct its process and summative evaluations, the evaluation results may have been affected by a number of potential limitations. First, based on the study scope as described above, the committee was limited to directly evaluating only grant outputs. Evaluation of grants was performed only as a second step through synthesis of the results of the output evaluation. Additionally, several grant program mechanisms were not evaluated because the timing of their funding cycles did not accord with the timing of this study.

Second, *measurement validity* is concerned with the degree to which the study indicators accurately portray the concept of interest (Newcomer, 2011). For the process evaluation, the committee gathered information from different sources (existing documentation, interviews, observation, surveys), but the interviews relied on the accuracy of the memories and perceptions of individuals, which could be susceptible to recall or social desirability biases. For example, the NIDRR staff who were interviewed may have felt pressed to provide positive input on the processes being reviewed. However, NRC staff who conducted the interviews believe all NIDRR staff members were candid in their comments.

To assess the quality of outputs for the summative evaluation, the committee used sound criteria that were based on the cumulative literature reviewed and its members' own research expertise in diverse areas of disability and rehabilitation research, medicine, engineering, and the social sciences, as well as their expertise in evaluation, economics, knowledge translation, and policy. However, the accuracy of the committee's assessment of the quality of outputs could have been affected by a number of factors. For example, the committee's combined expertise did not include every possible content area in such a broad field as disability and rehabilitation research. Because of the diversity of the field, the grants and outputs were extremely varied, so applying one set of criteria, even though broad and flexible, could not guarantee accurate applicability to every output. For example, websites, conferences, training curricula, therapeutic interventions, and educational outreach services ideally would require additional evaluation methods tailored to those types of outputs. The limitations and challenges encountered in conducting the output assessment are discussed in more detail in Chapter 6.

Third, *measurement reliability* is concerned with the extent to which a measurement can be expected to produce similar results on repeated observations of the same condition or event (Newcomer, 2011). The expert review methods used to assess the quality of grantee outputs could pose a threat to measurement reliability in that they relied on subjective assessments of different expert reviewers. To address this limitation, the committee members frequently discussed how they were applying the criteria and interpreting the anchors of the rating scale so they could calibrate their ratings. They rated the outputs independently and then discussed their results and determined overall ratings that reflected consensus scores. Results of an interrater reliability analysis are presented in Chapter 6.

Fourth, with regard to the process evaluation, it is possible that the respondents choosing to respond to the online surveys of stakeholders and peer reviewers may have differed from those who declined to participate. However, the response rates were respectable on both surveys (80 percent on the peer reviewer survey and 55 percent on the stakeholder survey), and the results of those two surveys also appeared to be balanced and not biased.

Finally, results of the summative evaluation cannot be generalized because of the small sample size and the small number of outputs reviewed from each grant. A total of 30 grants were reviewed across nine program mechanisms from a pool of 111 grants. Another threat to the generalizability of the findings stems from the fact that most of the grants reviewed ended in 2009. Because of the length of time it takes to publish research articles, grantees may have been unable to share their most important work with the committee. Other potential biases in the summative evaluation methods are described in Chapter 6.

Review of the Evaluation Plan

Before the committee implemented its evaluation plan, the plan was reviewed by leading experts in the field who provided suggestions for strengthening the methods to be used. In addition, the evaluation plan was reviewed and approved by the Institutional Review Board of the National Academies, under the category of Expedited Review, as meeting all criteria related to data confidentiality, security, and final disposition; informed consent; and potential risks and benefits to human subjects.

CONCLUSION

In conclusion, the committee used a conceptual framework (see Figure 2-1) developed around NIDRR's study questions and a definition of quality drawn from the literature as the foundation for its evaluation. The study was conducted with a cross-sectional design using quantitative and qualitative methods. The process evaluation included a review of existing documentation, interviews, online surveys, and written questionnaires. The summative evaluation included an expert panel review of outputs from randomly selected grantees. While the nature of the evaluation itself and the methods used suggest several potential limitations to the study findings, the committee strove to address these limitations where possible and acknowledge cases in which doing so was not possible.

REFERENCES

Baruch, Y., and Holtom, B.C. (2008). Survey levels and trends in organizational research. *Human Relations, 61*(8), 1139-1160.

Chien, C.F., Chen, C.P., and Chen, C.H. (2009). Designing performance indices and a novel mechanism for evaluating government R&D projects. *Journal of Quality, 19*(2), 119-135.

Gendall, P., Menelaou, H., and Brennan, M. (1996). Open-ended questions: Some implications for mail survey research. *Marketing Bulletin, 7*, 1-8.

Ismail, S., Tiessen, J., and Wooding, S. (2010). *Strengthening research portfolio evaluation at the Medical Research Council: Developing a survey for the collection of information about research outputs.* Santa Monica, CA: RAND Corporation.

Miles, M.B., and Huberman, A.M. (1994). *Qualitative data analysis* (2nd ed.). Thousand Oaks, CA: Sage.

National Institute on Disability and Rehabilitation Research. (2006). Department of Education: National Institute on Disability and Rehabilitation Research—Notice of Final Long-Range Plan for Fiscal Years 2005–2009. *Federal Register, 71*(31), 8,166-8,200.

National Institute on Disability and Rehabilitation Research. (2008, August). *Meeting report of the NIDRR External Evaluation Advisory Group.* Washington, DC: National Institute on Disability and Rehabilitation Research.

National Research Council and Institute of Medicine. (2007). *Mining safety and health research at NIOSH: Reviews of research programs of the National Institute for Occupational Safety and Health.* Committee to Review the NIOSH Mining Safety and Research Program. Committee on Earth Resources and Board on Earth Sciences and Resources. Washington, DC: The National Academies Press.

Newcomer, K.E. (2011). *Strategies to help strengthen validity and reliability of data.* Unpublished presentation. George Washington University, Washington, DC

Panel on Return on Investment in Health Research. (2009). *Appendices—Making an impact: A preferred framework and indicators to measure returns on investment in health research.* Ottawa, Canada: Canadian Academy of Health Sciences.

Patton, M.Q. (2002). *Qualitative research & evaluation methods.* Thousand Oaks, CA: Sage.

Synergy Enterprises, Inc. (2008). *Draft task 4 analysis.* Washington, DC: National Institute on Disability and Rehabilitation.

Ulin, P., Robinson, E., and Tolley, E. (2005). *Qualitative methods in public health: A field guide for applied research.* San Francisco: Jossey-Bass.

Wooding, S., and Starkey, T. (2010). *Piloting the RAND/ARC Impact Scoring System (RAISS) tool in the Canadian context.* Cambridge, England: RAND Europe.

Wooding, S., Nason, E., Starkey, T., Haney, S., and Grant, J. (2009). *Mapping the impact: Exploring the payback of arthritis research.* Santa Monica, CA: RAND Corporation.

ANNEX 2-1
SUMMARY OF QUALITY CRITERIA AND DIMENSIONS

TABLE A2-1 Summary of Quality Criteria and Dimensions

Criteria/Dimensions	NIDRR External Advisory Group (U.S.)	National Institute for Occupational Safety and Health (NIOSH) (U.S.)	Canadian Academy of Health Sciences (CAHS) Indicators (Canada)	RAND (UK, Canada)	Chien et al. (Taiwan)
Stage of Development of the Research and of the Output (depending on type of research)				x	
• Research (e.g., basic, clinical services, health services delivery, output development)					
• Output: What stage of output development was carried out during the grant? (e.g., prototype development, initial testing, regulatory approval, on the market, trialing in a new context)					
• Movement along research and/or development pathway					
Peer Recognition of Output					
• Number of peer-reviewed articles (e.g., using such measures as "journal impact factor" for assessing relative quality, or counting publications in high-quality journals/publishers)	x	x	x	x	x
—Number of original research articles		x			
—Number of review articles		x			
• Number of research reports	x	x	x		x
• Number of conference papers published	x		x		x
• Number of citations in peer-reviewed articles (e.g., using such measures as "crown indicator," "highly cited publication counts," "H-index")	x	x	x	x	
• Citations assimilated into clinical guidelines				x	

• Quantity of citations indicates “breakthrough” results		x		x	
• Measures of esteem (number of awards and honors received)	x		x	x	
• Number of patents awarded	x	x		x	x
• Number of Web downloads or hits	x	x	x		
• Number of reprints or books sold	x				
Multiple and Interdisciplinary Audience Involvement in Output Development					
• Multiple consumer input/collaboration in all stages (other researchers, clinicians, policy makers, manufacturers, intellectual property brokers) and evidence of their involvement	x	x			
• Appropriate targeting of audience	x				
Output Meets Acceptable Standards of Science and Technology					
• Appropriate methodology for answering research questions	x				
• Output is well defined and implemented with integrity	x				
• Well-documented conclusions, supported by the literature	x	x			
• Ability for the document to stand alone	x				
• Meets human subjects protection requirements	x				
• Meets ethical standards	x				
• Applies concepts of universal design and accessibility	x				
• Research done on the need for and development of the instrument or device	x				
• Measurement instruments tested and found to have acceptable type and level of validity	x				
• Measurement instruments tested and found to have acceptable level of reliability	x				

continued

TABLE A2-1 Continued

Criteria/Dimensions	NIDRR External Advisory Group (U.S.)	National Institute for Occupational Safety and Health (NIOSH) (U.S.)	Canadian Academy of Health Sciences (CAHS) Indicators (Canada)	RAND (UK, Canada)	Chien et al. (Taiwan)
• Pilot testing conducted with consumers and adaptations made as indicated	x				
• Theoretical underpinnings and evidence base (e.g., level of evidence per American Psychological Association, American Medical Association) used and well documented	x				
Output Has Potential to Improve Lives of People with Disabilities					
• Valued by consumers	x				
• Evidence of beneficial outcomes (i.e., How does the output improve abilities of people with disabilities to perform activities of their choice in the community and also expand society's capacity to provide full opportunities and accommodations?)	x				
Output Usability					
• Builds upon person-environment interaction and human-system integration paradigm	x				
• Ability to reach target population	x				

• Adheres to principles of knowledge translation	x	
• Readability; information translated into consumer language that is easy to understand and implement	x	x
• Can be used effectively, repeatedly as intended by design	x	
• Feasibility	x	
• Accessibility	x	
• Acceptability	x	
• Generalizability	x	
• User-friendly	x	x
• Ease of use (for measures: ease of scoring and administration)	x	
• Flexibility	x	
• Scalability (for measures)	x	
• Adoptability	x	
• Affordability and repair cost (for devices)	x	
• Cost/benefit	x	
• Financing available	x	
• Compatibility and durability	x	
• Sustainability	x	
• Safety issues considered	x	
Output Utility and Relevance		
• Addresses high-priority area	x	x
• Addresses NIDRR mission, International Classification of Function, Disability and Health (ICF) model, and Rehabilitation Act	x	
• Addresses a practical problem	x	
• Importance of contribution to the field (i.e., results expand the knowledge base, advance understanding, define issues, fill a gap)	x	x

continued

TABLE A2-1 Continued

Criteria/Dimensions	NIDRR External Advisory Group (U.S.)	National Institute for Occupational Safety and Health (NIOSH) (U.S.)	Canadian Academy of Health Sciences (CAHS) Indicators (Canada)	RAND (UK, Canada)	Chien et al. (Taiwan)
• Significance and magnitude of impact within and outside of field (i.e., Does output help build internal or extramural institutional knowledge? Does output transcend boundaries? Does output produce effective cross-agency, cross-institute, internal/external collaboration?)	x	x	x	x	x
• Transferability (number of technology output transfers, number of companies transferred to, technology transfer sustained, source of citations in other fields)	x	x	x	x	x
• Focuses on innovation or emerging technologies	x				
• Ability to stimulate new research, new knowledge, or new products	x	x			
• Perceived as useful to practitioners; has changed practice	x	x			
• Perceived as useful to consumers	x				
• Outputs are actually used in the field (e.g., adoption of guidelines/protocols/interventions; acceptance of outputs via publications/conference proceedings; manufacture license; product available in marketplace; percentage of target audience that has adopted; example of implementation in the field)	x	x		x	x
• Outputs provide evidence to support state-level changes to policies and/or practices	x				
• Output recommendations have been implemented by policy makers	x	x		x	

• Requests for expert testimony, participation in national advisory roles	x			x	
Dissemination of Outputs	x				
• Evidence of efforts to disseminate (e.g., dissemination plan and activities)	x				
• Timely dissemination	x				
• Depth and breadth (e.g., percentage of target group that has used/adopted and duration of use)	x	x			
• Dissemination of research in practice literature and conferences for transfer potential	x			x	
• Use of multimedia and emerging technology (RAND survey asks about specific sources for different audiences)	x			x	
• Mode of dissemination matches target audience	x				
• Counts of products distributed (e.g., manuals, newsletters, curricula)	x	x			
• Evaluation plan and consumer reviews	x				
• Scope of training: topics covered, number of training events, hours of training, participant hours, participant characteristics	x				
• Technical assistance/consultation provided	x				x
• Number of sponsored conferences and workshops, with documented sponsorship, number and composition of attendees, products of the event, assessment of the event	x	x			x
• Dissemination of research through databases	x	x	x	x	

SOURCE: Generated by the committee based on cited sources.

3

NIDRR's Priority-Setting Processes

This chapter addresses the following key study question:

Key Question #1. To what extent is NIDRR's priority-writing process conducted in such a way as to enhance the quality of the final results?

As used in the study question, the term "priority-writing" process encompasses many aspects of priority setting, including gathering input from multiple sources (e.g., the field, stakeholder organizations, grantees, other agencies, and persons with disabilities and their families), identifying potential topics and determining priorities for funding, writing the proposed priorities and having them cleared for release, and publishing notices inviting applications (NIAs)[1] on these priorities.[2] The term "priority setting" is used synonymously with "priority writing" in this report to clarify that the focus of the committee's evaluation was on this larger priority-setting process.

Priority setting not only reflects the National Institute on Disability and Rehabilitation Research's (NIDRR's) intent to influence the advancement of research in targeted areas but also offers specific funding opportunities for potential grant applications to the agency. The announced priorities should therefore be developed and communicated in a manner that attracts the best researchers and encourages participation in disability and rehabilita-

[1] A "notice inviting applications" (NIA) is NIDRR's announcement to the field of the opening of a grant competition. It is similar to the terms "request for proposals" and "request for applications" used by other agencies.

[2] "Priority" in this context means the topic of the grant competition for which scientists submit applications to investigate.

tion research. Attracting the largest pool of applications from which to select grantees increases the chances for the highest-quality outputs. When establishing its priorities, the agency needs to consider continuity from one funding cycle to another, as well as identify future research challenges and societal needs.

In the context of this committee's work, it is challenging to link priority setting directly to specific output quality. The quality of NIDRR's research portfolio, grants, and outputs is the product of multiple complex factors, including the priority-setting process, funding levels, the peer review process, and the scientific quality of the grantees. It is clear, however, that NIDRR's priority-setting process has a positive impact on the quality of the final outputs. In this chapter, the committee reviews and assesses that process and makes recommendations for its improvement.

The chapter has three major sections. The first describes NIDRR's priority-setting process based on existing documentation and interviews with NIDRR executives. The second presents an assessment of the process, based on data gathered from NIDRR staff, grantees, and stakeholder organizations. The final section offers the committee's conclusions and recommendations with respect to NIDRR's priority-setting process.

DESCRIPTION OF NIDRR'S PRIORITY-SETTING PROCESS

The following description is based on existing documentation, such as legislation, the *Federal Register*, NIDRR and the U.S. Department of Education (ED) policies and procedures, NIDRR's Long-Range Plan (LRP), and NIAs, as well as interviews with NIDRR and ED management.[3]

Legislative Foundation

The Rehabilitation Act (1973, as amended) authorizes the formula grant programs of vocational rehabilitation, supported employment, independent living, and client assistance. Title II[4] of the act—Research and Training—authorizes the majority of NIDRR's research activities, while Section 21 of the Act and the Small Business Innovation Research (SBIR) Development Act (2000) require NIDRR to reserve small portions of its budget for those two specific program mechanisms. Section 202 of Title II states that NIDRR's Director will lay out funding priorities and covered activities in a 5-year plan

[3]The committee conducted interviews with NIDRR and ED management in four sessions during summer 2010 and one session in spring 2011.

[4]The other six titles are Title I, Vocational Rehabilitation Services; Title III, Professional Development and Special Projects and Demonstrations; Title IV, National Council on Disability; Title V, Rights and Advocacy; Title VI, Employment Opportunities for Individuals with Disabilities; and Title VII, Independent Living Services and Centers for Independent Living.

that will be published in the *Federal Register*. The plan will utilize at least 90 percent of NIDRR funds for extramural research. Chapter 1 provides a description of NIDRR's program mechanisms.

The Long-Range Plan

Title II, section 202(h), of the Rehabilitation Act states that, starting in October 1998 and every subsequent fifth October, the NIDRR Director will develop and publish in the *Federal Register* for public comment a draft LRP outlining NIDRR's priorities, explaining the basis for those priorities, and providing a broad framework for the funding of research aimed at achieving the priorities. Every fifth subsequent June, after consideration of public comments, the final LRP with revisions will be submitted to the appropriate members of Congress. The LRP is required to

- Identify any covered activity that should be conducted under section 202 (NIDRR) and section 204 (Research and Other Covered Activities) respecting the full inclusion and integration into society of individuals with disabilities, especially in the area of employment;
- Determine the funding priorities for covered activities to be conducted under section 202 and section 204; and
- Specify appropriate goals and timetables for covered activities to be conducted under this section and section 204.

The LRP is the foundation that guides the development of grant priorities.

In developing the 5-year LRP, the Director must consider input from the Commissioner of the Rehabilitation Services Administration, the Commissioner of the Administration on Developmental Disabilities, the National Council on Disability, the Interagency Committee on Disability Research (ICDR), consumers, organizations representing people with disabilities, researchers, service providers, and other appropriate entities. Additionally, Title II, section 205, states that, subject to the availability of appropriations, a 12-member standing disability and rehabilitation research advisory council should advise the Director on the development and revision of each LRP; however, NIDRR has never formed such a council.

According to NIDRR management, the agency's use of long-range plans extends back to the development of the first such plan, which spanned 1981 to 1985. Based on information gathered from 4,000 agencies and organizations, this plan laid out a comprehensive landscape of research and development needs and topics across all disability and age groups. More recently, the LRP for 1999 to 2003 was developed in 1998 by key management staff following the reauthorization of the Rehabilitation Act. The content of the plan was drawn from staff member contributions, and commissioned papers helped inform the process. The major innovations in the 1999 to 2003 LRP included the "paradigm of disability" (which emphasizes the contextual nature of disability as a product of individual and societal factors) and the five research domains (Employment Outcomes, Health and Function, Technology for Access and Function, Independent Living and Community Integration, and Associated Disability Research Areas). This plan also encouraged participatory action research, which generated a great deal of positive feedback. According to NIDRR management, the agency was able to accomplish the vast majority of the research goals outlined in this LRP. During the next presidential administration (in 2000), however, the LRP was criticized for not being written in outcome-oriented terms.

The development of the next LRP, covering 2005 to 2009, differed somewhat from that of the prior LRP. Agency staff utilized considerable outside assistance to gather input from the public. These efforts included hiring a contractor to support teleconferences linking NIDRR staff with centers around the country and forming a steering committee. Subteams of the staff wrote sections of the plan corresponding to the research domains and capacity building. The major innovation in the LRP for 2005 to 2009 was a logic model that supported and provided a structure for more outcome-oriented work.

The development of the LRP for 2010 to 2014 was impacted by the change in presidential administrations, the departure of NIDRR's Director, and a shorter time frame in which to develop the plan. Input was solicited through a national teleconference, but the development of this plan was driven more by department leadership. During the public comment phase of the plan's development, close to 100 comments were received, many of which were critical of the increased focus on employment included in this plan. As a result, the plan was put on hold, and NIDRR is still operating under the LRP for 2005 to 2009.[5] At the time of this writing, a new LRP was under development but had not yet been published for public comment. In addition, after several years of the position being filled only on a temporary basis, a new permanent Director has recently been hired.

Priority-Setting Stages in the Grant Competition Process

To meet the objectives laid out in the LRP, NIDRR formulates priorities for research grants and development projects aimed at generating new knowledge and products, along with supporting knowledge translation and capacity-building activities (National Institute on Disability and Rehabilitation Research, 2006). The priority-setting process generally starts 2 years before funding announcements are published and involves several stages (see

[5] NIDRR's 1999-2003 LRP, 2005-2009 LRP, and information about the development of the 2010-2014 LRP can be found on the Publications and Products page of NIDRR's website, http://www2.ed.gov/rschstat/research/pubs/index.html [January 4, 2012].

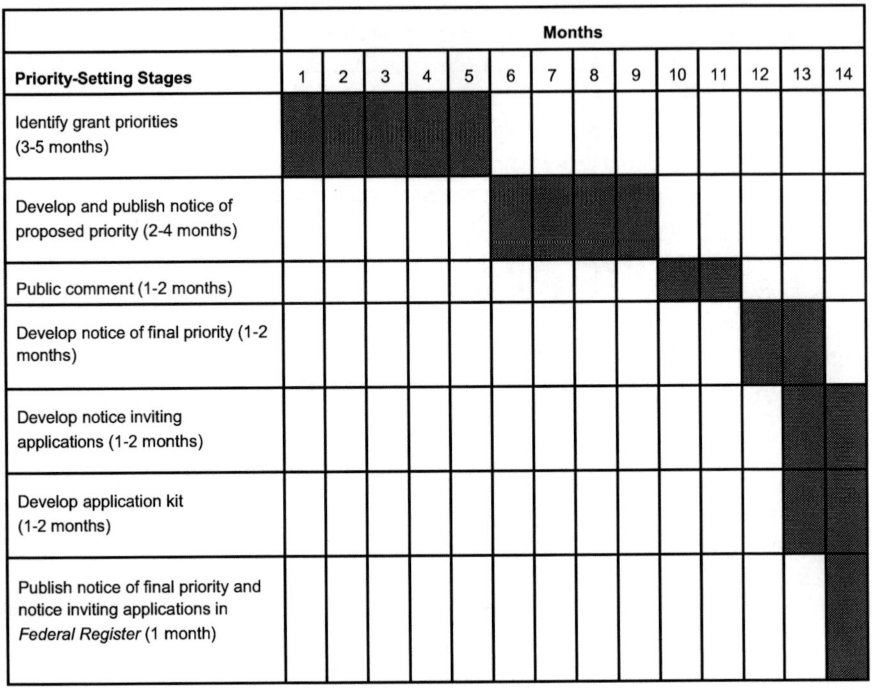

FIGURE 3-1 Timeline for NIDRR's priority-setting process.
SOURCE: Committee developed from National Institute on Disability and Rehabilitation Research (2009).

Figure 3-1 for an illustration of the general timeline). According to NIDRR management, while NIDRR has standard procedures for the various stages of priority setting, described below, the length of time required for new proposed priorities to obtain ED approval and clearance varies.

Identification of Grant Priorities

In planning its priorities for funding, NIDRR considers changes to its budget, as well as the funding level of expiring grants, and determines the amount of money that will be available for new grant competitions (National Institute on Disability and Rehabilitation Research, 2009). Looking at current priority areas, NIDRR determines whether grantees have been productive, and whether more work remains to be done or a topic has been exhausted. NIDRR management stated that new priority areas may be added if there is additional funding, if new technology or science suggests new areas for research, if experts from the field suggest a new area, or if the administration suggests new priorities.

To inform the identification and development of potential priority topics, NIDRR's Research Sciences Division (RSD) considers the LRP, other strategic and performance goals, the portfolio of existing projects, recent findings from completed grants, and the current research literature, as well as key guidance documents from federal partners, professional associations, and consumer organizations (National Institute on Disability and Rehabilitation Research, 2006, 2009). Contractors may be asked to conduct specific literature searches and factor in feedback from the field in response to prior grant cycles. New priority areas may also be generated by NIDRR-funded state-of-the-science conferences. The ICDR helps facilitate information sharing and partnerships that can contribute to the identification of new priority areas. In addition, the NIDRR Director and the Assistant Secretary of the Office of Special Education and Rehabilitative Services often identify potential priority topics of high importance (National Institute on Disability and Rehabilitation Research, 2009).

NIDRR staff, as key sources of input into potential priority topics, continually monitor the literature in their areas of expertise to stay current, to identify potential areas for funding, to determine field capacity, and also to identify active researchers who might serve as peer reviewers of proposals. When resources are available to support travel, staff also stay current with the state of the science through attending meetings of organizations such as the Rehabilitation Engineering and Assistive Technology Society of North America, the American Congress of Rehabilitation Medicine, the American Public Health Association, the Gerontological Society of America, or the National Council of Rehabilitation Educators.

As priority topics are being considered, NIDRR assesses their alignment with the following criteria (National Institute on Disability and Rehabilitation Research, 2009, p. 58). Research priorities must

- Reflect and incorporate state-of-the-science in a specific area
- Fulfill a demonstrated need for new knowledge
- Build upon prior research-based knowledge and advance the stage of knowledge development in specific areas
- Have real-world relevance to individuals with disabilities
- Prioritize meeting the needs of individuals with disabilities from minority backgrounds
- Support the NIDRR mission
- Reflect the thinking and guidance of the current LRP

Considering all of the possible priority topics, emerging opportunities, and ongoing needs, NIDRR management then asks staff to utilize their knowledge of the relevant literature and the field in developing succinct, one-paragraph descriptions of the most promising potential topics, along with rationales and recommendations for which topics should be selected. The descriptions address the following areas (National Institute on Disability and Rehabilitation Research, 2009):

- Incidence and prevalence of the condition to be targeted
- Problem or need addressed, in terms of improved policy, practice, behavior, or system capacity
- How the priority topic builds upon the state of the science in this topic area
- NIDRR's historical investment in this topic area, key findings from NIDRR investments in this area, and how the proposed priority topic builds upon these investments
- How the priority topic relates to the work of NIDRR's relevant federal partners, or other organizations that fund research
- Real-world relevance of this topic to people with disabilities
- How this priority topic addresses the needs of individuals with disabilities from minority backgrounds
- How the priority topic fits under NIDRR LRP goals, objectives, and strategies

The written descriptions of the potential topics are discussed with the NIDRR Director who then approves topics to be published as priorities and presents these to the Assistant Secretary of the Office of Special Education and Rehabilitative Services. The process of identifying funding priorities generally takes 3 to 5 months or longer.

Notices of Proposed Priority

Once priority topics have been indentified, the second stage in NIDRR's priority-setting process is to draft and publish notices of proposed priority (NPPs). According to NIDRR management, NIDRR staff follow a template in drafting selected topics into NPPs, which are NIDRR's first notice to the research community about each grant solicitation. The NPP explains the nature of the problem and describes the requirements of the priority (e.g., for Burn Injury Model System grants, establish a multidisciplinary system that begins with acute care and encompasses rehabilitation services specifically designed to meet the needs of individuals with burn injuries). NIDRR's style of NPPs has shifted over time from more to less prescriptive.

Each NPP is reviewed and cleared at multiple levels within NIDRR, the Office of Special Education and Rehabilitative Services, and ED (including the Office of the General Counsel, the Budget Office, the Deputy Secretary, and the Executive Secretary) (National Institute on Disability and Rehabilitation Research, 2009). The NPPs must also be reviewed and approved by the Office of Management and Budget. According to NIDRR management, multiple rounds of comments and revisions are not uncommon. The resulting NPP is published in the *Federal Register*. During a response period, the public may submit comments on the proposed priority. The NPP development and clearance process often takes 2-4 months, while the public comment period lasts for 1-2 months, which includes the period of time for NIDRR to respond to public comments.

Notices of Final Priority

After the close of the public comment period, NIDRR staff review comments on the NPP, respond to the comments, and develop a notice of final priority (NFP) (National Institute on Disability and Rehabilitation Research, 2009). The draft NFP is reviewed and cleared at several levels within NIDRR, the Office of Special Education and Rehabilitative Services, and ED, much as is done with the NPP. Again, multiple revisions are not uncommon. Development of the NFP generally takes 1-2 months, and when approved it is published in the *Federal Register.*

Notices Inviting Applications and Application Kits

Concurrently with the NFP, NIDRR drafts the NIA and develops an application kit for each priority (development of these materials generally takes 1-2 months) (National Institute on Disability and Rehabilitation Research, 2009). The NIA contains information about the grant competition, such as submission deadlines, dollar amounts, and the procedure for submitting an application. The NIA goes through the same clearance process as the NFP and is published with the NFP in the *Federal Register*. NIAs are also published on Grants.gov. In addition, NIDRR uses a contractor to notify former grantees and others who, via the contractor's webpage, express an interest in receiving NIAs.

Application kits contain application forms, the NFP and NIA, regulations, and the peer review criteria. The application kits are available on Grants.gov and NIDRR's website. The standard period between publication of the NFP and NIA and the application deadline is 60 days, although NIDRR management stated that the period may be shortened to 45 days or less when needed to enable awards before the end of the fiscal year.

For each competition, NIDRR convenes a preapplication technical assistance meeting for potential applicants (National Institute on Disability and Rehabilitation Research, 2010; also noted by NIDRR management). Upon request, staff members are also available for individual consultation. The staff can discuss only the application process with potential applicants, however—not application content. NIDRR does not track whether those who participate in assistance events go on to apply for grants. Every NIDRR competition has received at least one application, which is all that is required to conduct the peer review process. However, not every competition has resulted in a grant being funded. (Chapter 4 provides information on the number of competitions between 2006 and 2009.)

RESULTS OF THE ASSESSMENT OF NIDRR'S PRIORITY-SETTING PROCESS

This section summarizes the results of interviews and surveys of NIDRR staff, grantees, and other stakeholder organizations concerning their views of NIDRR's priority-setting process. See Chapter 2 for a description of the data collection and analysis methods used by the committee.

Perspectives of NIDRR Staff

In personal interviews, 16 NIDRR staff members were asked open-ended questions about their roles in the priority-setting process, their perspectives on the quality of the process, and suggestions for improvement. Two-thirds of the interviewees were project officers or direct supervisors of project officers; the remaining held administrative positions. The perspectives of staff coalesced around the processes of identifying priorities, moving priorities into the funding announcement phase, and disseminating priorities to the field.

Identification of Priority Topics

As stated earlier in the chapter, potential priority topics are identified through several sources. Staff comments focused on several of these sources. With regard to the roles of project officers, some play a very active part in proposing priority topics, conducting the literature reviews for proposed priorities, and writing the proposed priorities. Other project officers commented that their role in priority setting is fairly minimal. This difference appears to be based on individuals' areas of expertise and allocation of time among their other duties (e.g., monitoring grants; organizing and leading peer review activities; managing program areas, such as Field Initiated Project [FIP] grants or Traumatic Brain Injury center or research grants). Staying well informed and current with the relevant literature entails a substantial time commitment on the part of project officers. This demand was noted as particularly challenging considering that staffing levels at NIDRR have fallen over the years.

Another source of potential priority topics is the results of previously funded grants. The Annual Performance Reports submitted by grantees are used to feed into priority setting more now than in the past. Staff mentioned that this is an example of how NIDRR's processes have become more standardized and data driven. However, it was suggested that more systematic information should be collected on the stages of grant development, movement rates, and life cycles. Such information could potentially inform successive generations of priorities that would build on each other.

Staff also commented on other forces that influence the selection of priority topics. The broad scope of NIDRR's mission, which includes all disabilities and all ages, relative to its limited budget sets a base of competing priorities to meet the needs of multiple target populations. While NIDRR is striving toward more scientific rigor in the research it funds, tensions still arise among differing paradigms that call for varying levels of scientific rigor to achieve research and development goals. There are also tensions at play between proponents of the continuance of large center grant priorities and those of smaller, flexible, more problem-focused or field-driven priorities. It was suggested that NIDRR should gather information from the field more regularly to inform priority setting and that NIDRR could benefit from the use of a national advisory board with more diverse disability research expertise to inform its priority-setting process.

Moving Priorities into the Funding Announcement Phase

Several comments were made about the challenges inherent in moving proposed priorities through the various organizational clearance levels to the final grant announcement phase. This process sometimes causes delays as questions about proposed priorities arise at different levels, and new justifications for or changes to proposed priorities must be made. More barriers are encountered with smaller, innovative grants than with the larger center grants. Delays in the clearance process impact the regularity of the timing of grant announcements and competitions.

Dissemination and Response

Staff commented that once grants have been announced, the specialty nature of certain priorities (e.g., for Model System grants) limits the number of researchers eligible to apply, whereas programs with field-driven priorities (e.g., FIP grants) have larger applicant pools. Concern was expressed that grant announcements are not reaching the largest intended audience and that there needs to be broader dissemination of priorities through listservs and routine dissemination to universities.

Perspectives of NIDRR Grantees

As part of the questionnaire dealing primarily with outputs that grantees submitted to the committee for review, grantees were asked to share their perspectives on NIDRR's priority-setting process. Comments on this topic were received from 14 of the 30 grantees that were involved in the output assessment.

Some comments applauded NIDRR's periodic formulation of 5-year LRPs, suggesting that significant field and community input increases the likelihood that the priorities established and resulting outputs can have the greatest potential impact. Consistent with a point made earlier in this chapter, it was commented that priorities are less prescriptive now than in the past, making it possible to explore areas of importance that would not otherwise have been addressed. It was also noted that NIDRR is able to fund studies that would not have been funded by other agencies in the early stages. As a result, important developmental studies can be incubated before other agencies will assume and extend them.

Some concern was expressed about the nature of priorities, which may shift from cycle to cycle. Grantees suggested that this can inhibit certain lines of research from continuing, affect the quality of research, and reduce the potential pool of applicants. Difficulties also were noted with respect to certain changes that have occurred in the course of grants (e.g., requirements for dissemination) that, although ultimately good, affected grantee activities and budgets.

These respondents also commented on some areas in which they thought priorities should be focused, including treatment and intervention studies in the rehabilitation process, which have received little attention; economic empowerment; and individual fellowship grants (similar to the National Institutes of Health [NIH] F series for predoctoral and postdoctoral training) for capacity building in many research areas covered by NIDRR that do not map neatly to NIH priorities. One respondent suggested that NIDRR should continue to focus on projects that go beyond what is encompassed by the medical rehabilitation research funded by NIH.

Perspectives of NIDRR Stakeholder Organizations

Because stakeholder input is a fundamental aspect of priority setting, the committee gathered information on stakeholder perspectives on NIDRR's long-range planning and priority-setting processes by surveying three key stakeholder groups. First, in NIDRR's most immediate network of stakeholders are other federal agencies with which it interacts and collaborates in order to achieve its mission. Second, professional associations are key stakeholders that represent the professional base of providers and researchers that work in the field. Third, the intended ultimate beneficiaries of NIDRR research and development activities are persons with disabilities and their families. Advocacy organizations were surveyed to gather the perspectives of consumers, who are defined in this report as individuals with disabilities and their family members and/or authorized representatives.

Responding representatives of stakeholder organizations were asked closed- and open-ended questions about their role in the NIDRR planning and priority-setting processes, their perspectives on the processes, benefits their organization derived from NIDRR grants or outputs, and suggestions for enhancements to the priority-setting process.

Methods

As discussed in Chapter 2, the committee sent invitations to participate in the survey to executive directors of 130 professional and advocacy organizations identified by NIDRR as stakeholders and to organizations that are statutory members of the ICDR or nonstatutory members that have participated in ICDR special committees, as identified through a list provided by the ICDR. Seventy-two agencies responded to the survey with a response rate of 55 percent, an acceptable response rate for a questionnaire targeting executive directors (Baruch and Holtom, 2008). Of the 72 organizations responding to the survey, 26 percent described themselves as professional associations, 31 percent as advocacy organizations, and 43 percent as federal agencies. The questionnaire is included in Appendix B.

Responses to the quantitative survey items, summarized first, illuminate these stakeholder organizations' relationships with NIDRR, how they were involved in NIDRR's priority-setting process and their perspectives on the process, and the extent to which NIDRR grants are perceived as beneficial and their products are used. Responses to the open-ended questions are summarized next, organized by the major topics that emerged.

Summary of Quantitative Responses

Relationships with NIDRR Many of the respondents have interacted with NIDRR in multiple ways, but not all have the same level of familiarity with the agency. On a 5-point scale from 1 (not at all) to 5 (very much), 28 percent of the stakeholder organizations stated that they were "somewhat" familiar with NIDRR, 31 percent that they were "more than somewhat" familiar, and 40 percent that they were "very much" familiar. More than half of the organizations reported having interacted with the agency in the following ways: using the NIDRR website or related information sources to search for information, tools, or resources for working with consumers (61 percent) or to search for information about grants (56 percent); speaking with NIDRR representatives about professional issues (63 percent); and attending NIDRR trainings sessions, workshops, or conferences (58 percent). With regard to collaboration, 51 percent reported having participated in general planning and special-purpose meetings convened by NIDRR, 38 percent having collaborated with NIDRR as a member of a consortium or professional association, and 29 percent having coordinated activities with NIDRR to support joint priorities and/or avoid duplication of effort.

Involvement in and perspectives on NIDRR priority setting Stakeholders were asked about their involvement in NIDRR's priority-setting process through submission of comments and review of the LRP and/or funding priorities. A majority (63 percent) of the responding organizations stated that they had had opportunities to review and comment on NIDRR's LRP or funding priorities. Approximately one-third of respondents reported that their organization had submitted comments to NIDRR.

Table 3-1 presents stakeholders' perspectives on the extent to which they think that NIDRR's long-range planning and priority-setting processes reflect important attributes of priority setting. Results include 72 respondents. However, no attribute was rated by all respondents, so the number of total responses (shown in the shaded first column of the table) for each attribute is less than 72. A relatively large number of respondents indicated that they did not know how to rate some of the attributes, which in part reflects the 28 percent of respondents stating that they were only somewhat familiar with NIDRR and the 37 percent stating that they had not had an opportunity to review or comment on NIDRR's LRP or funding priorities (see above). The number of "don't know" responses for each attribute is shown in the shaded column to the right of the "Total Responses" column. The number of valid responses for each attribute—responses that rated the attribute on the scale—is shown in the unshaded column to the right of the "don't know" responses. The "don't know" responses plus the valid responses equal the total responses for each attribute. The proportion of valid responses that characterized NIDRR's priority setting at the various points along the five-point scale for each attribute is shown to the right of the "Valid Responses" column.

The attribute "relevant to your organization" had the highest number of favorable responses, with 67 percent of organizations responding "more than somewhat" or "very much." The next two highest ratings were for the attributes "responsive to emerging issues in disability and rehabilitation/ research" (51 percent) and "publicized" (48 percent). The priority-setting attribute that respondents thought NIDRR's process least reflected was "responsive to stakeholder organization feedback"; only 29 percent responded "more than somewhat" or "very much" on this attribute, and 26 percent responded "less than somewhat." A large number (28 out of 70, or 40 per-

TABLE 3-1 Distribution of Ratings of the Extent to Which NIDRR's Process Reflects Important Attributes of Priority Setting (72 respondents)

			Scale					
Priority-Setting Attributes	Total* Responses	Number of "Don't Know" Responses	Number of Valid Responses	Not at All (%)	Less Than Somewhat (%)	Somewhat (%)	More Than Somewhat (%)	Very Much (%)
Transparent	70	18	52	4	10	46	29	11
Publicized	71	15	56	2	14	36	32	16
Relevant to your organization	68	10	58	2	10	21	31	36
Responsive to emerging issues in disability and rehabilitation/research	71	15	56	—	13	36	31	20
Welcoming of stakeholder organization feedback	70	22	48	—	6	50	23	21
Responsive to stakeholder organization feedback	70	28	42	—	26	45	19	10

*The total number of responses for each attribute is less than the overall sample size of 72 because no attribute was rated by all respondents.
SOURCE: Generated by the committee based on data from the stakeholder questionnaire.

cent) of respondents answered they did not know for this attribute, a larger proportion than for the other attributes.

Another question on the survey asked how NIDRR's long-range planning and priority-setting processes compare with those of other federal research agencies. With only 37 (42 percent) organizations responding to this question, 40 percent stated that the processes were about the same, 38 percent that NIDRR's processes were stronger, and 22 percent that they were weaker.

Extent to which grants are perceived as beneficial and products are used
To assess the extent to which NIDRR's priority-setting process enhances the quality of final products, the survey asked stakeholders whether they perceive NIDRR grants as beneficial and whether they use the resulting products. Responses are summarized in Table 3-2. As in Table 3-1, the results in Table 3-2 include 72 respondents, as indicated in the shaded "Total Responses" column at the left of the table. Within the 72 responses, the numbers of "don't know" and "not applicable" responses are indicated in the next two shaded columns to the right of the "Total Responses" column. The number of remaining valid responses to the questions is indicated in the unshaded column to the right of the "Not Applicable Responses" column. The proportion of valid responses that characterized NIDRR grants as beneficial and NIDRR products as useful along the five-point scale is shown to the right of the "Valid Responses" column.

The first row of Table 3-2 shows that 39 percent of respondents from stakeholder organizations indicated that the grants NIDRR funds are "somewhat" advancing the field in a direction that is beneficial for their organization and the members and consumers they represent, while 41 percent stated that the grants are "more than somewhat" to "very much" beneficial.

The survey also asked stakeholder organizations to rate the extent to which grant products (e.g., publications, websites, training materials, tools, devices, measures, interventions) are used. Thirty-three percent of respondents reported that the products of NIDRR-funded grants are used "somewhat," while 28 percent stated they are used "more than somewhat" to "very much."

The relatively large number of "don't know" responses across several items was somewhat surprising in a sample of NIDRR-identified stakeholder organizations. A post hoc analysis of the results by type of stakeholder organization (professional association, advocacy organization, federal agency) showed that the "don't know" responses could not be attributed systematically to any one type of stakeholder organization, although respondents from professional associations tended to give somewhat greater proportions of this response on several items. Results of the survey may indicate that further work is needed to inform and engage stakeholders with respect to the process. However, it is also possible that the large number of "don't know" responses is due to high turnover in the leadership positions the survey was targeting. Professional associations, advocacy organizations, and federal agencies often experience high turnover in their executive positions, so it is possible that some of these respondents were less than familiar with NIDRR because they were relatively new to their job.

Summary of Qualitative Responses

Four open-ended questions asked respondents to elaborate on their responses to the quantitative questions and additionally to offer suggestions for enhancing NIDRR's long-range planning and priority-setting processes:

- Please use the space below to comment on the above, or any other types of interactions, your organization has had with NIDRR.
- What types of grants have served your organization, and the members and consumers that you represent?
- What are the three most important NIDRR-funded products used by your organization?
- What three things might NIDRR do to enhance its long-range planning and priority-setting processes?

One or more of the four open-ended questions were answered by 76 percent of respondents. As discussed in Chapter 2, responses to these questions were analyzed using standard qualitative methods. The results of the analysis were organized into five major topics: (1) the types of interactions the stakeholder organizations have had with NIDRR, (2) the uniqueness and strengths of NIDRR's mission and research, (3) ways of enhancing collaboration with federal agencies, (4) strengths and needs related to outreach and dissemination, and (5) policies and practices related to priority setting. A summary of the stakeholders' narrative responses is presented below under each of these topic headings.

Types of interactions with NIDRR Respondents from five federal agencies remarked that they have had strong collaboration with NIDRR over the years on such activities as coordinating research priorities, co-funding grants, participating in working groups on topics of mutual interest, and sharing information and expertise. Respondents from nine federal agencies stated that they participated in the work of the ICDR. Respondents from seven federal agencies stated that they have participated in other types of working groups, panels, and meetings to give NIDRR feedback about research priorities and LRPs. For example, representatives from two federal agencies commented on the strength of their collaboration with NIDRR:

TABLE 3-2 Distribution of Ratings of the Extent to Which NIDRR's Grants Are Perceived as Beneficial and Their Products Are Used (72 respondents)

				Scale					
	Total Responses	Number of "Don't Know" Responses	Number of "Not Applicable" Responses	Number of Valid Responses	Not at All (%)	Less Than Somewhat (%)	Somewhat (%)	More Than Somewhat (%)	Very Much (%)
Question									
Are grants beneficial?	72	14	3	55	4	16	39	27	14
Are products used?	72	13	2	57	9	30	33	14	14

SOURCE: Generated by the committee based on data from the stakeholder questionnaire.

> The synergy of the two agencies working together for 30 years may be a study of braiding funding and staff which is unique to the Federal Government. Sharing similar values and principles that reflect our individual Departments and what the field reflects is unusual.

> We have extensive scientific and strategic interaction with NIDRR. We have coordinated research priorities with NIDRR plans and given presentations at each other's venues. We and NIDRR officials have served on each other's technical working groups, [and] shared technical information and expertise that is relevant for both groups.

Respondents from 3 professional associations and advocacy organizations remarked that they have met with NIDRR staff to prepare materials to be used in advocating with Congress for NIDRR funding. Respondents from 6 of these organizations stated that NIDRR staff have attended their meetings and forums to inform members about program mechanisms and research priorities.

Uniqueness and strengths of NIDRR's mission and research Respondents from 7 federal agencies emphasized the benefits of NIDRR's specialized mission as the touchstone for all of the agency's program mechanisms and grants. They commented that NIDRR's unique mission among all federal agencies requires grantees to use the state-of-the-art International Classification of Functioning, Disability and Health (ICF) as a framework for all research, training, and demonstration projects. They emphasized the benefits of NIDRR's specialized scope of research, which includes people of all ages with psychiatric disabilities and comparative effectiveness research focused on health services for persons with disabilities. Respondents from 12 of the other stakeholder organizations and 8 federal agencies identified specific program mechanisms beneficial to their organization: Burn Model System (BMS), Traumatic Brain Injury Model System (TBIMS), Spinal Cord Injury Model System (SCIMS), FIP, Rehabilitation Research and Training Center (RRTC), Rehabilitation Engineering Research Center (RERC), and Disability and Rehabilitation Research Project-General (DRRP). Respondents from 7 professional associations and advocacy organizations applauded the funding of grants aimed at increasing accessibility for people with disabilities, as exemplified by grants related to communication for the deaf and hard-of-hearing; the availability of assistive technology; and physical and programmatic access to health care, education, housing, and employment. Respondents from 12 of these same organizations also emphasized the benefits of grants focused on community participation, such as employment and delivery of services to people with disabilities who are seeking employment; information technology issues that prevent these people from getting jobs; outcome research related to community participation, personal assistants, and aging with developmental disabilities; and education and workforce development.

Ways of enhancing collaboration with federal agencies Respondents from four professional associations and advocacy organizations commented on the need to develop stronger collaborations with currently collaborating federal agencies and entities and to expand the number of new potential collaborators (e.g., more coordination of priorities with NIH institutes and the Department of Veterans Affairs). Respondents from two federal agencies suggested that NIDRR make more effective use of ICDR members in the strategic planning and priority-setting processes—for example, by delivering presentations to the group with specific review requests to members. Three federal agency respondents commented on the need to expand the depth and breadth of collaboration with agencies and co-funding of research projects with new agencies. Four federal agency respondents suggested that an important quality improvement initiative would be for NIDRR staff to become more knowledgeable about the relevant research efforts and products of other agencies so they could seek opportunities and avoid duplication of effort. Respondents from eight other stakeholder organizations suggested establishing quality improvement initiatives related to priority setting by, for example, investigating how other federal agencies establish priorities, communicating the details of the process, and incorporating feedback.

Strengths and needs related to outreach and dissemination Although respondents from four of the stakeholder organizations stated that they were unaware of available products of NIDRR grants, respondents from 8 professional and advocacy organizations and from 11 federal agencies commented that NIDRR's website and other linked sources (e.g., National Rehabilitation Information Center [NARIC], the Center for International Rehabilitation Research Information and Exchange, the Repository of Recovery Resources, and RERC and RRTC grant websites) provide easy access to information, resources, technical assistance, and research results in topic areas such as: asistive technology use, evidence-based information on employment, disability statistics, guidelines for accessible digital media and guidelines, information on health promotion for persons with disabilities, and technical assistance related to the Americans with Disabilities Act.

Several suggestions also were made for ways to enhance NIDRR's outreach and dissemination activities to inform the agency's planning and priority setting. For example, respondents from 5 federal agencies recommended expanding and refining NIDRR's outreach plan by including experts from a wider variety of disciplines and heads of research and evaluation departments of other federal agencies. For greater outreach, 4 federal agency respondents suggested increasing stakeholders' awareness of NIDRR accomplishments by initiating a new public relations campaign using "brag-sheets" and disseminating information about companies and vendors that use products based on the results of NIDRR-funded projects. Seven professional association and advocacy organization respondents commented on the need to develop more user-friendly ways for NIDRR to receive feedback from stakeholders (e.g., provide summaries of larger planning documents, develop electronic capacity to insert comments directly into LRPs undergoing public review and comment). In addition, 12 respondents from these same stakeholder organizations encouraged NIDRR to make more effective use of the disability communities through enhanced communication approaches, such as webinars and presentations at existing annual meetings.

Policies and practices related to priority setting Finally, four federal agency respondents suggested that NIDRR should review and adapt its current policies and practices that guide the long-range planning and priority-setting processes to include standardized timelines and a review of progress halfway through the 5-year LRPs. One federal agency respondent proposed a specific set of guidelines for priority setting that would

> (a) point to a national vision for research that is aspirational; (b) capture the imagination and support of the disability community at-large; (c) [be] based on the best available evidence and information; (d) require projects to produce measurable outcomes and results; (e) promote initiatives that are supported over an appropriate timeframe; (f) [be] multidisciplinary in nature; and (g) stimulate a collaborative approach to solutions among stakeholders.

Respondents from three other federal agencies suggested in general that NIDRR should increase funding for planning and priority setting. With regard to how grants are structured, respondents from four professional associations and advocacy organizations remarked that NIDRR should refine the inclusion of policies and practices in funded studies and projects to ensure that grantees planning to include people with disabilities as collaborators or partners actually follow through in doing so. In this same vein, one federal agency respondent commented that the "diversity" criteria NIDRR uses to score applications should be critically reviewed so as to consider requirements for including consumers in the planning and implementation phases of all projects.

CONCLUSIONS AND RECOMMENDATIONS

NIDRR has a legislatively based process for formulating 5-year LRPs and for establishing its funding priorities. In proposing priority topics, NIDRR has specific criteria that must be met and subjects potential priorities to key questions. It also has written procedures for staff to follow in proposing priorities that will be recommended to the Office of Special

Education and Rehabilitative Services for funding. Processes for gathering initial input on LRPs and priorities appear to be inclusive but vary from cycle to cycle. However, formal public comments on proposed LRPs and priorities are consistently obtained via the *Federal Register*. NIDRR has not established a standing disability and rehabilitation research advisory council, which is included in its legislation. As of the time of this writing, the agency is still operating under the LRP for 2005 to 2009 because of critical input from formal public comments and the long-term absence of a permanent Director. However, a permanent Director was recently hired.

Seventy-one percent of stakeholder organizations surveyed were "more than somewhat" or "very much" familiar with NIDRR. Attributes of NIDRR's priority-setting process that were most endorsed included relevance of the process to their organization, responsiveness to emerging issues in disability and rehabilitation research, and degree to which the process is publicized. Respondents thought NIDRR's priority-setting process least reflected the attribute of responsiveness to stakeholder organization feedback. In open-ended remarks, stakeholder organizations emphasized the benefits of NIDRR's specialized mission and scope of research, its specific program mechanisms, and funding of grants aimed at increasing accessibility and community participation for people with disabilities. Respondents commented on the need to develop stronger collaborations with federal agencies and entities. Although stakeholder organizations commented on the benefits of NIDRR's website and linked sources, suggestions were made for ways to enhance the agency's outreach and dissemination activities. Respondents suggested that NIDRR should review and adapt its current policies and practices that guide the long-range planning and priority-setting processes to include standardized timelines.

The committee offers recommendations regarding NIDRR's priority-setting process in four areas: formation of an advisory council, strategic planning, establishment of a standard calendar, and expanded dissemination of NIAs.

Formation of an Advisory Council

NIDRR has a broad and diverse mission that makes it challenging to set priorities that are responsive to the current state of the science and the needs of the stakeholder community. Currently, NIDRR relies on staff, the portfolio of existing projects, recent findings from completed grants, and the current research literature, as well as guidance from federal partners, for input to the priority-setting process. Title II, section 205, of the Rehabilitation Act instructs NIDRR, subject to the availability of appropriations, to establish a 12-member standing disability and rehabilitation research advisory council to support its priority setting. While NIDRR formed a steering committee to support the development of the LRP for 2005 to 2009, a standing body has never been formed.

Recommendation 3-1[6]: NIDRR should fulfill the statutory mandate to form and utilize a standing disability and rehabilitation research advisory council to advise on the priority-setting process and provide input for priority setting.

In the committee's view, it is somewhat anomalous that NIDRR does not have a standing advisory body. Most federal funding agencies, including NIH, the National Science Foundation (NSF), and the National Institute for Occupational Safety and Health (NIOSH), benefit from the use of standing advisory bodies. A standing advisory body is likely to add stability and continuity to both NIDRR's long-range planning and priority-setting processes.

Additionally, a disability and rehabilitation research advisory council would be an efficient way to obtain expertise from the scientific community, as well as input from members of NIDRR's diverse constituency of stakeholder organizations and consumers. As documented in the survey data presented in this chapter, a number of relevant stakeholder organizations, including professional associations, advocacy associations, and federal agencies, are less familiar with NIDRR than they might be expected to be. An advisory council could provide another way for these stakeholder organizations to interact meaningfully with NIDRR.

Furthermore, an advisory council would represent an important, regular forum through which consumers could interact with NIDRR. According to Title II, at least half of the council members are to be consumers. Consumer participation on the council should help build and strengthen productive partnerships between NIDRR and the populations it serves. Participation would allow consumers to have direct input into the advice that guides NIDRR's work, which is vital for those affected by the research the agency funds (Ahmed and Palermo, 2010). Such input could benefit NIDRR in many ways. Consumer input could educate scientists about the research being conducted. As the Director's Consumer Liaison Group of the National Cancer Institute (2011) states, consumer input can "improve research outcomes by identifying new approaches, promoting innovation, recognizing unforeseen risks or barriers, and identifying unintended consequences." According to the NIH Director's Council of Public Representatives, through participation on the advisory board, consumers may have the ability to represent their communities to research funders such as NIDRR

---

[6]The committee's recommendations are numbered according to the chapter of the report in which they appear.

(National Institutes of Health, 2011). At the same time, they can gain a more informed understanding of NIDRR and the research being conducted. This understanding in turn can be used to better inform their communities about NIDRR's work.

Title II states that, in addition to including six consumers, the membership of the council should represent the community of rehabilitation professionals and the community of rehabilitation researchers. Additional populations that NIDRR regularly tries to engage include national, state, and local rehabilitation agencies and facilities; administrators and practitioners in agencies serving persons with disabilities; other federal agencies; educators of rehabilitation professionals and their students; and the general public (National Institute on Disability and Rehabilitation Research, 2011). The committee recognizes that NIDRR, like other federal research agencies, will face challenges in capturing the broad diversity of perspectives held by this large collection of different populations. However, the committee feels strongly that, like other federal research agencies, NIDRR can meet these challenges.

Strategic Planning

The delay in NIDRR's LRP for 2010 to 2014, resulting from the negative reaction to the plan by the field as well as the absence of a Director to guide the process, suggests a breakdown in the LRP process. As the LRP is the foundation of priority setting, the priority-setting process is likewise affected. Long-range planning and priority-setting processes may be enhanced in ways that are likely to help NIDRR avoid such a breakdown in the future.

In its review of NIDRR's long-range planning process, the committee was never presented by NIDRR with a document explaining the steps in the process from start to finish. Instead, the process has varied from the creation of one LRP to the next. It is the Committee's viewpoint that LRP processes are better conceived as a documented series of logical stages. The methods used to gather input from stakeholders also have varied during the development of each plan. In addition, NIDRR documentation (discussed above) indicated that input into the creation of NPPs is drawn from such sources as experts in the field, the current literature, and state-of-the-science conferences. The committee applauds these efforts but notes that this input is somewhat informal and the process is not systematic. The first formal input is not received until after potential topics have been narrowed down and the NPPs have been published for comment in the *Federal Register*. The committee believes more could be done to involve stakeholders earlier in the process of identifying potential priority topics.

Recommendation 3-2: NIDRR should use a structured, consistent, and inclusive strategic planning process to develop its Long-Range Plans and priorities.

To begin implementing this recommendation, NIDRR should first formalize and document the structure of its long-range planning process. The advisory council recommended above could assist in this effort. Once the structure of the process has been documented, NIDRR will be able to follow it consistently in the development of future LRPs. Subsequent changes to the process, and the rationale behind them, should be documented as well.

NIDRR should also establish a regular form of interaction with stakeholders in the long-range planning process, and might also make efforts to expand the stakeholder groups that are included in the process. The recommended advisory council might assist in regularizing and expanding the inclusivity of the process. With regard to priority setting, NIDRR should seek more formal input from the field on potential priority topics earlier in the process and pursue maximum participation from stakeholders. While incorporating a broad range of stakeholder views can be a slow, arduous process, the added structure and consistency, along with the regular influence of an advisory council, will allow the process to be as efficient as possible.

One source NIDRR might consider in planning a more structured, consistent, and inclusive process is the Canadian Institutes of Health Research's Knowledge Translation module on Deliberative Priority Setting (Campbell, 2010). Included in Campbell's work, derived from an extensive literature review, is a description of seven ideal elements of agenda-setting and/or priority-setting processes:

- planning of the process, including anticipating the needs, barriers, and challenges for all the remaining steps and identifying the leadership that will guide the process;
- stakeholder identification, analysis, and engagement, which involves purposefully identifying the proper stakeholders to include in the process, understanding both the opportunities and risks associated with including stakeholders, and formulating appropriate engagement strategies;
- knowledge management, which ensures that all stakeholders have the same information, and any stakeholders with less technical expertise are supported such that they can understand all the information;
- interpretive workshops, which involve gathering with stakeholders to define criteria, establish weights, and then apply the criteria to identify the most relevant issues or topics;

- translation of the issues or topics identified in the workshops into actionable research agendas and priorities;
- publication and validation, which involve making the draft long-range plans and/or proposed priorities available to all stakeholders to ensure alignment with the goals of the communities and clarity of the expected outcomes; and
- revision or an appeal mechanism, the presence of which is necessary to allow stakeholders to communicate disagreement with draft long-range plans and/or proposed priorities constructively and through which such concerns can be comprehensively addressed.

The document also contains an extensive literature review on different types of priority-setting processes.

Additionally, NIDRR might consider the long-range planning and priority setting of other funding agencies, including NIH, the National Science Foundation, and the National Institute for Occupational Safety and Health, which have sought to integrate long-range planning and priority-setting processes through specific initiatives such as the NIH Roadmap, the NSF Strategic Plan, and the National Occupational Research Agenda.

Establishment of a Standard Calendar

For many program mechanisms, NIDRR has not established a regular schedule for drafting and approving priorities and NIAs and disseminating them to the field. In exploring this issue further, the committee reviewed *Federal Register* publication dates of NIAs for all of the program mechanisms over the last 5 years. There appeared to be no regular timing pattern of the publication of NIAs either within or across program mechanisms. The Department of Education has a lengthy review and approval process for obtaining clearance for the release of priorities and NIAs. The variability in the length of the clearance process may be an important factor, among others, that impacts the timing of the release of NIAs. The irregular or delayed release of NIAs may affect NIDRR's ability to provide individuals sufficient notice of grant opportunities or an optimal amount of time to complete applications. An irregular schedule may discourage the best investigators from submitting applications. Additionally, certain program mechanisms (such as Model Systems) include collaboration between institutions. Irregular posting and shortened response times hamper the ability of applicants to identity and recruit appropriate collaborators. These factors are likely to limit the number of investigators who apply and adversely affect the quality of the applications they submit. Additionally, young investigators less familiar with NIDRR are more likely to pursue grants from other agencies.

Recommendation 3-3: NIDRR should utilize a standard calendar for the setting of priorities, publication of notices inviting applications, submission of applications, and peer review meetings to improve the efficiency of the process.

NIDRR has made efforts to standardize the schedule for NIAs for its various program mechanisms, such as FIP, SBIR, Advanced Rehabilitation Research Training (ARRT), and Switzer Fellowship. However, NIDRR has been unable to standardize the schedule for most of its program mechanisms. Even within the constraints of its lengthy review process for publishing NIAs, a standardized calendar should be developed. The committee suggests that program mechanisms competed on a yearly basis have a consistent annual schedule for the submission and review of applications. For multi-year grants, the committee recommends that NIDRR establish a long-range operational plan listing projected future grant application submission dates, pending funding availability in that fiscal year. With a submission timeline, NIDRR could establish when NPPs would have to be published for public comment and also when NFPs would have to be published. In addition to better supporting applicants, establishing a standard calendar would reduce some of the burden on NIDRR staff caused by the current unanticipatable priority-setting timeline. Delays in priority setting also often cause delays and/or shortened timelines in the peer review process (see Chapter 4). A standard calendar could potentially help address those delays as well.

Expanded Dissemination of Notices Inviting Application

While creating and utilizing a standard calendar is likely to increase the number of researchers already familiar with NIDRR who will apply for grants, the committee thinks more effort needs to be made to expand this pool. NIDRR publishes NIAs in the *Federal Register* and on Grants.gov, and also uses a contractor to notify former grantees and others who, via the contractor's webpage, express an interest in receiving NIAs. Given the vast number of scientists whose work is relevant to disability and rehabilitation research, however, NIDRR would benefit from more active efforts to solicit interest in its funding announcements.

Recommendation 3-4: NIDRR should expand its efforts to disseminate notices inviting applications to new potential applicants, including developing a communication strategy to ensure that the notices reach new audiences.

Increasing the pool of applicants may ultimately increase the quality of the work NIDRR funds. A logical means of expanding dissemination is through sending notices to the disability-relevant professional organizations and agencies and disability and rehabilitation research organizations that make up NIDRR's stakeholder network. NIDRR should also make efforts to expand the network to organizations not yet familiar with the agency. Additionally, NIDRR should begin sending notices to university departments and offices of sponsored research. This could perhaps be accomplished through collaboration with other federal research programs that regularly send funding notices to universities. Increasing the number of potential applicants may also contribute to increasing the pool of reviewers, addressed by Recommendation 4-1 in the next chapter.

REFERENCES

Ahmed, S.M., and Palermo, A.-G.S. (2010). Community engagement in research: Frameworks for education and peer review. *American Journal of Public Health, 100*(8), 1,380-1,387.

Baruch, Y., and Holtom, B.C. (2008). Survey levels and trends in organizational research. *Human Relations, 61*(8), 1,139-1,160.

Campbell, S. (2010). *Deliberative priority setting*. Ottawa, Canada: Canadian Institutes of Health Research.

National Cancer Institute. (2011). *About the Director's Consumer Liaison Group*. Available: http://dclg.cancer.gov/about [June 4, 2011].

National Institute on Disability and Rehabilitation Research. (2006). Department of Education: National Institute on Disability and Rehabilitation Research—Notice of Final Long-Range Plan for Fiscal Years 2005–2009. *Federal Register, 71*(31), 8,166–8,200.

National Institute on Disability and Rehabilitation Research. (2009). *Briefing book for The National Academies*. Unpublished document. Washington, DC: National Institute on Disability and Rehabilitation Research.

National Institute on Disability and Rehabilitation Research. (2010). *Overview of the NIDRR's peer review process (what happens between OPP's priority review and OPP's slate review)*. Unpublished document. Washington, DC: National Institute on Disability and Rehabilitation Research.

National Institute on Disability and Rehabilitation Research. (2011). *Target populations for NARIC*. Unpublished document. Washington, DC: National Institute on Disability and Rehabilitation Research.

National Institutes of Health. (2011). *About Council of Public Representatives*. Available: http://copr.nih.gov/secondary/about/ [June 4, 2011].

The Rehabilitation Act of 1973, as amended. Pub. L. No. 93-112. Available: http://www2.ed.gov/policy/speced/reg/narrative.html [January 21, 2011].

The Small Business Innovation Research Development Act, Public. L. No. 97-219, 106 Stat. 2965 (2000).

4

NIDRR's Peer Review Process

This chapter addresses the following key study question:

Key Question #2. To what extent are peer reviews of grant applications done in such a way as to enhance the quality of final results?

The National Institute on Disability and Rehabilitation Research's (NIDRR's) peer review process encompasses recruiting and training reviewers, conducting the review, and approving the awards. In the context of this study, as with the priority-setting process (Chapter 3), it is challenging to link the peer review process directly with specific output quality because the quality of grant outputs is the product of multiple complex factors, including the priority-setting process, funding levels, the peer review process, and the scientific quality of grantees. However, it is clear that the peer review process used by NIDRR contributes significantly to the success of the grant award program and the quality of the resulting outputs. Moreover, as described in *The Future of Disability* (Institute of Medicine, 2007), significant efforts to enhance the quality of NIDRR's portfolio by strengthening the peer review process were implemented during the past decade.

This chapter begins by describing NIDRR's peer review process. It then presents results of the committee's assessment of the process. Finally, the chapter offers the committee's conclusions and recommendations on this aspect of its evaluation.

DESCRIPTION OF NIDRR'S PEER REVIEW PROCESS

This description of NIDRR's peer review process was compiled from existing documentation, such as legislation, the *Federal Register*, NIDRR and the U.S. Department of Education (ED) policies and procedures, NIDRR's Long-Range Plan (LRP), and notices inviting applications (NIAs). In addition, the committee interviewed NIDRR and ED management to obtain a more thorough and cohesive understanding of the process.[1]

Legislative and Departmental Foundation

Title II, section 202, of the Rehabilitation Act (1973, as amended) states that NIDRR will perform scientific peer review of all applications for research, training, and demonstration projects. The peer review is to "be conducted by scientists or other experts in the rehabilitation field, including knowledgeable individuals with disabilities, and the individuals' representatives" (p. 98). Federal employees are not allowed to be peer reviewers. NIDRR is to provide training for peer reviewers as is deemed necessary and appropriate.

Title 34 of the Code of Federal Regulations (Disability and Rehabilitation Research Projects and Centers Program, 2009) states, "The purpose of peer review is to insure that activities supported by NIDRR are of the highest scientific, administrative, and technical quality, and include all appropriate target populations and rehabilitation problems" (p. 217). Applications for awards of $60,000 or more must be reviewed by a peer review panel, with the exception of applications related to evaluation, dissemination of information, or conferences.

In addition, NIDRR follows the peer review requirements of ED. In accordance with ED's *Handbook for the Discretionary Grant Process* (ED Handbook), NIDRR annually reviews and updates its procedures in ED's Application Technical Review Plan (a description of the processes for identifying and involving reviewers, resolving conflicts of interest, working with the review panels, and selecting applications for funding) and maintains Grant Program Competition Files (a collection of all information, decisions, and documentation related to a competition) (U.S. Department of Education, 2009).

Key Personnel in NIDRR's Peer Review Process

Key personnel in NIDRR's peer review process include the competition manager, the panel monitor, and the agency's peer review contractor.

[1] The committee conducted interviews with NIDRR and ED management in four sessions during summer 2010 and one session in spring 2011.

Competition Manager

Once an application kit[2] has been published, NIDRR assigns a competition manager—a NIDRR staff member who is responsible for all aspects of the review process (generally the individual who wrote the description of the priority area; see Chapter 3) (National Institute on Disability and Rehabilitation Research, 2010b, 2010c). The competition manager arranges for the participation of additional NIDRR staff as necessary, recruits reviewers, confirms receipt of all applications, and performs a final screen of eligibility and responsiveness. In accordance with the Education Department General Administrative Regulations (EDGAR) (2008),[3] NIDRR generally errs on the side of inclusivity, ruling out applications that are ineligible or nonresponsive and allowing peer reviewers to judge the merit of all remaining applications.

Panel Monitor

According to NIDRR management, the competition manager may also be the panel monitor. Duties of the panel monitor include managing the logistics of panel review with assistance from NIDRR's peer review contractor (see below), monitoring the progress of individual reviews, and overseeing the panel discussion. Competitions involving multiple panels typically employ additional panel monitors from NIDRR, but may include panel monitors drawn from across the Office of Special Education and Rehabilitative Services (OSERS).

Contractor Support

NIDRR uses a contractor to provide support for the grant application and review process (Synergy Enterprises, Inc., 2008). The peer review contractor performs an initial screen of the eligibility and responsiveness of applications prior to the competition manager's final screen, provides logistical support for the panel discussions, administers the postmeeting survey of the reviewers, compiles reports as requested, and provides other support as required. Additional detail on the role of the peer review contractor is provided later in the chapter.

---

[2] An application kit is a package containing application forms, the notice of final priority, the NIA, salient regulations, and the peer review criteria for a competition.

[3] Available: http://www2.ed.gov/policy/fund/reg/edgarReg/edgar.html [November 22, 2011].

Stages in NIDRR's Peer Review Process

NIDRR's grant selection and peer review process consists of 12 stages:

1. Determine peer review criteria
2. Peer review kick-off meeting
3. Recruiting of peer reviewers
4. Preapplication meeting with potential applicants
5. Peer reviewer orientation
6. Prepanel correspondence
7. Panel discussion
8. Site visits
9. Prefunding meeting
10. Preparation and finalization of slate
11. Slate review
12. Slate approval and award

The process takes approximately 4-6 months. The stages of the process are described below.

Determine Peer Review Criteria

Selection criteria applied by peer reviewers to assess and rate applications are drawn from Title 34 of the Code of Federal Regulations and matched to the requirements of the competition. Each competition includes 100 possible points allocated across the criteria and subcriteria. With the exception of Spinal Cord Injury Model System (SCIMS), for which the point allocation is prespecified, the distribution of points across the selected criteria is determined by NIDRR staff. Criteria related to the quality of the proposed research or development are always allocated a substantial percentage of the points (National Institute on Disability and Rehabilitation Research, 2010c). Past performance as a NIDRR grantee is not considered in the criteria for peer review, but is considered during the prefunding meeting (discussed below). The ED Handbook instructs reviewers to consider only the merit of the application itself. Additional knowledge of the field or the applicant is not to influence the review. Annex 4-1 at the end of this chapter provides more detail on the grant selection criteria, as well as an example of the selection criteria for a Disability and Rehabilitation Research Project-General (DRRP) competition.

Kick-Off Meeting

After publication of an application kit the competition manager convenes a kick-off meeting with the contractor. During the kick-off meeting,

NIDRR staff determine the dates of panel discussions and other key dates leading up to the competition and discuss the division of labor for recruiting peer reviewers (National Institute on Disability and Rehabilitation Research, 2010c).

Recruiting of Peer Reviewers

NIDRR establishes peer review panels of five to seven members to review each submitted grant application (National Institute on Disability and Rehabilitation Research, 2006, 2009a, 2009b). The panel size depends on the size of the grants to be reviewed and the expertise needed. NIDRR uses standing panels—consisting of seven reviewers who serve as peer reviewers for up to 3 consecutive years following their initial appointment—for Field Initiated Project (FIP) competitions.[4] Ad hoc panels are formed for all other competitions (National Institute on Disability and Rehabilitation Research, 2010b). According to NIDRR management, for Advanced Rehabilitation Research Training (ARRT), Small Business Innovation Research (SBIR), and Switzer Fellowship competitions, NIDRR draws on reviewers who have previously been supported by these program mechanisms and who have relevant knowledge and expertise in these program areas.

The competition manager tailors the composition of each review panel to competition requirements to ensure that the panel includes the expertise needed for the review (National Institute on Disability and Rehabilitation Research, 2010b). Competition managers identify potential reviewers through the Peer Review System (PRS), a searchable database containing information and resumes for thousands of potential peer reviewers maintained at the OSERS level, as well as through literature searches, networking at conferences, and personal connections (National Institute on Disability and Rehabilitation Research, 2010b). As part of the recruiting process, the competition manager screens potential reviewers for conflicts of interest and often is forced to rule out many qualified individuals. NIDRR management stated that it is not uncommon for competition managers to make 50 or more recruitment calls in order to find five reviewers. Additionally, conflicts of interest can develop after the initial screening, requiring that reviewers be replaced (sometimes at the last minute). Furthermore, delays in the approval and publication of NIAs often leave NIDRR staff with shortened timelines in which to recruit peer reviewers and hold the panel discussion.

NIDRR also strives to include qualified individuals with disabilities or their authorized representatives on review panels, as well as individuals from underrepresented populations. Since the number of individuals with disabili-

[4] ED has strict rules related to conflict of interest, which impact the formation of NIDRR standing panels. FIP competitions are large enough to be exempt from the particular ED rules on conflict of interest.

ties who have the scientific credentials to conduct reviews is quite small, it can be difficult to represent the views of the various disability constituencies. At times, NIDRR will include individuals with disabilities without scientific expertise on review panels to lend the perspective of consumers[5] if particularly relevant constituencies would otherwise not be included.

NIDRR also produces a general list of all reviewers who have served in a given year (National Institute on Disability and Rehabilitation Research, 2009b). Per ED policy, the list does not identify the specific competitions in which the reviewers participated and is made available upon request (U.S. Department of Education, 2009).

Preapplication Meeting with Potential Applicants

Several weeks after an NIA is published in the *Federal Register*, NIDRR arranges and publicizes a conference call to provide guidance on the peer review process and technical assistance to potential applicants (National Institute on Disability and Rehabilitation Research, 2010c; also noted by NIDRR management). During the call, NIDRR staff provide guidance on the application process but do not provide advice related to the content of potential applications. NIDRR staff also generally make time for one-on-one consultation if it is requested.

Peer Reviewer Orientation

The competition manager conducts a competition-specific orientation session for all reviewers (National Institute on Disability and Rehabilitation Research, 2010b). The session is conducted via telephone within a few days of reviewers' receipt of applications and review materials. The session is set up by the peer review contractor and generally lasts 1 hour. It includes an overview of the review process, a review of the selection criteria to be used in evaluating each application, a review of the online system, a discussion of reviewers' responsibilities, tips for conducting a good review, and inquiries to determine whether any reviewer has developed a conflict of interest.

Prepanel Correspondence

After the training session and prior to the review, the competition manager and/or panel monitor will correspond with the reviewers (National Institute on Disability and Rehabilitation Research, 2010c; also noted by NIDRR management). The correspondence is intended to ensure that re-

---

[5] Consumers are defined in this report as individuals with disabilities and their family members and/or authorized representatives.

viewers have everything they need to complete the review, that they are progressing through their initial reading of the applications, and that they are entering their initial scores and comments into the e-Reader system.

Panel Discussion[6]

The technical review of applications consists of two parts: individual review of all applications, followed by panel review (National Institute on Disability and Rehabilitation Research, 2009a, 2009b). The panel review generally takes place via teleconference and e-Reader over 2-3 days. Individual written reviews from each member of the review panel and a summary of the panel review documenting an application's strengths and weaknesses are required before a grant can be awarded.

NIDRR has conducted review meetings exclusively via teleconference for more than 5 years. NIDRR management noted that in the past there was some resistance to conducting review meetings by teleconference as opposed to in person. However, NIDRR believes that the benefits of teleconferences, including reduced cost for the agency and reduced time commitment for reviewers (which has resulted in more experienced researchers agreeing to participate), far outweigh the drawbacks, such as a loss of rapport among reviewers and between NIDRR staff and reviewers. Additionally, NIDRR has noticed that reviewers with mobility impairments benefit greatly from teleconference reviews, although reviewers with vision and hearing disabilities find the teleconference reviews more challenging. NIDRR provides additional support as necessary in the form of interpreters, communication access realtime translation (CART) services, alternative-format materials, and other personal assistance to allow reviewers with disabilities to participate fully in the review.

Grant applications are mailed to reviewers at least 3 weeks in advance of the review whenever possible (U.S. Department of Education, 2009). Reviewers independently score and comment on each application using technical review forms, which are accessed and saved electronically via e-Reader. Scores (whole numbers only) are assigned to each factor of each criterion. Peer reviewers may adjust their own scores before or immediately following the review teleconference. A score of less than the maximum point value must be accompanied by a written rationale. A maximum score does not require a written rationale, but reviewers are encouraged to include comments. As described by NIDRR management, the number of applications

[6]Panel discussion procedures described here are a synthesis of information from written sources provided by NIDRR (National Institute on Disability and Rehabilitation Research, 2009a, 2009b); interviews with NIDRR management; and direct observation of panel discussions by committee members Thubi Kolobe and Pamela Loprest and co-study director Jeanne Rivard.

each panel reviews and the size of the applications vary greatly by program mechanism. On one end of the spectrum, center grant panel reviews (such as RRTC and RERC) generally include 2 or 3 applications with a maximum recommended length of 125 pages each (or 375 total pages maximum). Although center grant competitions usually receive only a few applications, each application is highly complex and technical. Additionally, many applications are longer than the maximum recommended length. On the other end of the spectrum, FIP applications are shorter (50 pages) and not as technical as center grant applications, but a single panel is likely to review 20 applications totaling 1,000 pages minimum.

In addition to the general review of all applications, each panel member is assigned to be either the primary or secondary reviewer for certain applications. The primary reviewer presents the application for discussion and writes a summary of the discussion. The secondary reviewer provides commentary on the application and assists the primary reviewer in writing the summary.

All panel members participate in the discussion of each proposal (National Institute on Disability and Rehabilitation Research, 2009a, 2009b). Each application is discussed in turn, with each reviewer, beginning with the primary reviewer, presenting the scores and rationales for each criterion. Differences in scores among reviewers are discussed. If panel members' scores are very different, the primary reviewer submits a description, taken from the discussion, of why this is the case.

During the teleconference, the panel monitor oversees the discussion; helps the panel maintain consistency from criterion to criterion and application to application; reviews scores, comments, and summaries for adequacy and accuracy; and provides information concerning policy, regulations, selection criteria, technical review forms, conflicts of interest, and confidentiality. The panel monitor does not participate in the substantive discussion of applications or related research issues.

NIDRR provides peer reviewers an honorarium of $200 a day, generally for 1 day of preparation and 3 days of reviewing.[7] NIDRR monitors the compensation for peer reviewers provided by other federal agencies and believes its rates are competitive.

Site Visits

Title II of the Rehabilitation Act requires a preaward 1-day site visit for those competitions in which an award or awards of more than $500,000 will be made. NIDRR management stated that the site visit is considered a

[7]Doris Werwie, personal communication, National Institute on Disability and Rehabilitation Research, April 14, 2011.

part of the peer review process, with a visit being conducted for the highest rated applicant. Multiple site visits may be made if the highest rated applicants are within one point of each other. Site visits are conducted shortly after the review and include one member of the review panel and one NIDRR staff member (National Institute on Disability and Rehabilitation Research, 2010c). Shortly before the visit, the NIDRR staff member submits questions to the applicant developed by the peer reviewers and by NIDRR staff. Applicants respond to the questions in writing prior to and during the visit.

Prefunding Meeting

Following peer review, NIDRR holds a prefunding meeting involving the NIDRR Director, the Deputy Director, the two division Directors, the agency's scientific advisor, the competition manager, and interested NIDRR staff to develop specific funding recommendations (National Institute on Disability and Rehabilitation Research, 2009a). At the meeting, the panel monitor and/or the competition manager presents the rank order of the applications as well as summary information on the peer review process, including information from the site visit if applicable, with emphasis on the peer reviewer comments (National Institute on Disability and Rehabilitation Research, 2010b). Additionally, applicants' proposed project activities, budgets, and past performance are discussed. From this discussion, program staff develop specific funding recommendations. According to NIDRR management, only in rare cases do the recommendations not follow the rank order established in peer review.

Preparation and Finalization of Slate Through Award

After the prefunding meeting, the competition manager transfers the recommendations for funding into a departmental format called a slate (National Institute on Disability and Rehabilitation Research, 2010c). The slate is then reviewed by Research Division management and approved by the NIDRR Director. It then must undergo an OSERS and ED clearance process, similar to proposed priorities (see Chapter 3). After approval of a slate by the Office of the Secretary of Education, NIDRR's Program, Budget, and Evaluation Division obligates the funds to the new grantee. Additionally, NIDRR provides comments and suggestions for improvement to unsuccessful applicants following a review.

NIDRR Competitions from Fiscal Years 2006 to 2009

NIDRR provided the committee with general data on the competitions held from fiscal years (FY) 2006 through 2009, including the number of competitions held for each program mechanism, applications received per competition, applications reviewed per competition, and awards made per competition (National Institute on Disability and Rehabilitation Research, 2010a). Table 4-1 summarizes these data. Each year over this 4-year time span, NIDRR held an average of 25 competitions and received an average of 492 applications. NIDRR reviewed between 48 percent (RERC 2006 competition) and 100 percent (13 different competitions) of applications received for each competition, and awarded grants to between 6 percent (Field Initiated Project-Development [FID] 2006 competition) and 83 percent (Burn Model System [BMS] 2007 competition) of applications reviewed for each competition. However, the numbers of submitted applications, reviewed applications, and awards appear to vary greatly across years within the various program mechanisms. FIPs for research or development (FIR and FID) are by far the most competitive of the mechanisms, having the smallest proportion of grants awarded relative to number of grants reviewed (6 percent to 11 percent over the 4 years). The BMS and Disability and Business Technical Assistance Center (DBTAC) mechanisms (two mechanisms for which competitions were held for only a year of the analyzed data) appear to be the least competitive. Five out of the six BMS applications that were reviewed received awards; half of the DBTAC applications reviewed received awards.

Data Collection and Analysis by the Peer Review Contractor

NIDRR's peer review contractor collects and manages the data from and about peer reviews, including the peer review scores themselves and peer reviewer feedback on the process. In 2008, NIDRR asked the contractor to analyze the scoring data it had collected for 18 of the competitions that occurred in 2007 (Synergy Enterprises, Inc., 2008). The contractor drew three notable conclusions. First, there appeared to be no bias as to the types of individuals and organizations that received NIDRR funding, although institutes of higher education were being funded slightly more often than other types of organizations. Second, some competitions, such as those under the DRRP and RERC program mechanisms, had a notably higher rate of ineligible applications. Finally, while all funded applications received an overall score of at least 77, the contractor observed a lack of consistency in the language used for the scoring criteria for each program mechanism and no consistency in the number of points assigned to each scoring criterion within a mechanism.

NIDRR's peer review contractor surveys peer reviewers for feedback following every panel using the OSERS Panel Review Logistics Evaluation Form (Synergy Enterprises, Inc., 2010). Peer reviewers are asked to provide feedback on the prereview and review process, logistical support provided by the contractor, special needs (only if any special accommodation was received), and suggestions for future reviews. Reviewers use a 5-point scale from poor (1) to excellent (5) to rate dimensions of the first three areas and provide comments on all areas.

NIDRR provided the National Research Council (NRC) with data and a summary of the data collected from 147 of the 163 panel members participating in fiscal year 2008 to 2009 peer reviews. Response forms indicated the 18 specific competitions to which they related, but reviewer names were not included. Of note, 5 panels included fewer reviewers than are recommended by NIDRR procedure. To supplement NIDRR's summary, NRC staff conducted a reanalysis of the data on the prereview and review process, special needs, and suggestions for future reviews.

Data on the prereview and review process cover five dimensions: (1) completeness of materials, (2) quality of materials, (3) time allowed for initial review, (4) assistance provided by staff, and (5) participation by staff. The average rating for all dimensions was between excellent (5) and very good (4) except for the dimension time allowed, which was rated between very good (4) and good (3). The average ratings of the process across competitions for all dimensions ranged between 3.3 and 5, again except for time allowed, for which the ratings ranged from 1.7 to 4.8 and for which six ratings were lower than the lowest rating (3.3) for any of the other four dimensions.

Comments on the prereview and review process also indicated that peer reviewers spent an average of 27 hours preparing for the reviews and an average of 20 hours participating. Combined preparation and participation time ranged from a low of an average of 15 hours to a high of an average of 60 hours. It should be noted that some peer reviewers both reported less time spent preparing and gave low ratings to time allowed for initial review, indicating they had less time to prepare than they wished.

The last question about the prereview and review process asked reviewers to indicate whether the total of preparation and participation time was more than, less than, or about as much time as they expected to spend. Fifty-five percent of reviewers indicated they spent about as much time as they expected, 42 percent that they spent more time than they expected, and 3 percent that they spent less time then they expected.

The section of the Panel Review Logistics Evaluation Form on special needs includes space to rate interpreter services, CART services, alternative-format materials, readers or scribes, and other personal assistance if any of these were requested. Only six reviewers used this section of the form; five rated alternative-format materials, readers or scribes, and other personal assistance as excellent, and one rated alternative-format materials as fair.

Finally, many reviewers provided suggestions for future reviews. The most common suggestion by far was to reduce reviewers' time commitment—

TABLE 4-1 NIDRR Competitions from Fiscal Years 2006 to 2009

	FY 2006				FY 2007			
Mechanism	No. of Competitions	Apps. Received	Apps. Reviewed (% of received)	Grants Awarded (% of reviewed)	No. of Competitions	Apps. Received	Reviewed (% of received)	Awarded (% of reviewed)
Section 21	—	—	—	—	—	—	—	—
Burn Model System (BMS)	—	—	—	—	2	8	6 (75%)	5 (83%)
Disability and Business Technical Assistance Center (DBTAC)	2	27	22 (81%)	11 (50%)	—	—	—	—
Disability and Rehabilitation Research Project-General (DRRP)	7	50	44 (88%)	8 (18%)	2	15	10 (67%)	2 (20%)
Knowledge Translation (KT)	3	12	7 (58%)	3 (43%)	—	—	—	—
Traumatic Brain Injury Model System (TBIMS)	1	2	2 (100%)	1 (50%)	1	25	22 (88%)	14 (64%)
Rehabilitation Research and Training Center (RRTC)	1	7	7 (100%)	1 (14%)	1	3	3 (100%)	1 (33%)
Rehabilitation Engineering Research Center (RERC)	4	25	12 (48%)	3 (25%)	8	40	32 (80%)	5 (16%)
Switzer Fellowship	1	55	48 (87%)	8 (17%)	1	35	31 (89%)	8 (26%)
Field Initiated Project-Research (FIR)	1	137	129 (94%)	12 (9%)	1	125	118 (94%)	16 (14%)
Field Initiated Project-Development (FID)	1	149	143 (96%)	8 (6%)	1	100	97 (97%)	9 (9%)
Spinal Cord Injury Model System (SCIMS)	1	34	32 (94%)	15 (47%)	—	—	—	—
Advanced Rehabilitation Research Training (ARRT)	1	7	7 (100%)	1 (14%)	1	8	8 (100%)	3 (38%)
Small Business Innovation Research I (SBIR-I)	1	90	90 (100%)	12 (13%)	1	25	16 (64%)	6 (38%)
Small Business Innovation Research II (SBIR-II)	1	22	22 (100%)	7 (32%)	1	12	12 (100%)	5 (42%)

SOURCE: Generated by the committee based on National Institute on Disability and Rehabilitation Research (2010a).

FY 2008				FY 2009			
No. of Competitions	Apps. Received	Reviewed (% of received)	Awarded (% of reviewed)	No. of Competitions	Apps. Received	Reviewed (% of received)	Awarded (% of reviewed)
1	13	8 (62%)	3 (38%)	—	—	—	—
—	—	—	—	—	—	—	—
—	—	—	—	—	—	—	—
7	32	31 (97%)	7 (23%)	2	19	16 (84%)	3 (19%)
2	13	9 (69%)	2 (22%)	1	3	3 (100%)	1 (33%)
2	13	12 (92%)	4 (33%)	—	—	—	—
8	36	18 (50%)	8 (44%)	7	23	23 (100%)	9 (39%)
8	28	22 (79%)	7 (32%)	3	8	8 (100%)	4 (50%)
1	33	27 (82%)	8 (30%)	1	68	50 (74%)	8 (16%)
1	97	93 (96%)	14 (15%)	1	124	108 (87%)	14 (13%)
1	74	72 (97%)	8 (11%)	1	131	106 (81%)	8 (8%)
—	—	—	—	—	—	—	—
1	9	9 (100%)	4 (44%)	1	15	13 (87%)	5 (38%)
1	61	57 (93%)	16 (28%)	1	111	76 (68%)	15 (20%)
1	16	16 (100%)	5 (31%)	1	28	15 (54%)	5 (33%)

for example, by reducing the length of proposals, the number of proposals per competition, and/or the number of criteria. Additional comments included observations about logistical support and recognition of good work done by NIDRR staff.

RESULTS OF THE ASSESSMENT OF NIDRR'S PEER REVIEW PROCESS

This section first describes observations of peer review panels by committee members and NRC staff. It then reports on perspectives of NIDRR staff and grantees on the peer review process, including challenges and suggestions for change. Finally, it relates peer reviewers' experiences, perspectives, and suggestions for enhancing NIDRR's peer review process. This information was gathered from (1) observations of three peer review panels, (2) interviews with NIDRR staff members, (3) surveys of NIDRR grantees, and (4) surveys of peer reviewers identified as having reviewed in fiscal year 2008 to 2009.

In designing this assessment, NRC staff reviewed such sources as the NSF Committee of Visitors peer review model (National Science Foundation, 2011), the National Institutes of Health (NIH) *2007-2008 Peer Review Self-Study* (National Institutes of Health, 2008), and the RAND report *Evaluating Grant Peer Review in the Health Sciences* (Ismail et al., 2009).

Observations of NIDRR Peer Reviews

Two committee members and one NRC staff member individually observed (via teleconference) three peer review panels.[8] Two of the observed panels consisted of fewer members than are recommended by NIDRR procedure. Two of the panels dealt with conflict-of-interest issues, which resulted in smaller panels and one reviewer being added only a few days before the review. One panel was under pressure to complete its work before the end of the fiscal year, so all reviewers had less than 2 weeks to read the applications. ED's grant administration handbook (U.S. Department of Education, 2009) suggests that applications be mailed at least 3 weeks in advance of the review whenever possible. One panel reviewed six applications, one panel five applications, and the third panel three applications. One panel included two consumers, one of whom was also a researcher. One panel was scheduled for 3 days and the other panels for 2 days.

Committee and NRC staff members observed that the review process had a high degree of integrity. The panel members observed were generally appropriately knowledgeable in the field of disability and rehabilitation

[8] Committee members Thubi Kolobe and Pamela Loprest and co-study director Jeanne Rivard observed peer review panels during summer 2010.

research, and the discussions and deliberations were thorough and probing. The panel members also displayed strength in the way they directly addressed disagreements in ratings.

Each panel was led by the competition manager/panel monitor, who ably guided the panel members through a thoughtful and consistent review following the peer review procedures outlined above. The competition manager was observed providing such help as reminding panel members they could not use other information outside of the proposals to rate the applications, should not deduct points from multiple criterion areas for the same flaw, should apply criteria consistently across applications, and needed to justify all scores adequately. While operating within the scope of NIDRR procedures, the panel monitors did differ in the specific ways they facilitated each meeting. One panel monitor, for example, asked reviewers to first share overall scores, then proceed to discussion of the criteria, while another asked the panel to begin with the criteria and build to the overall scores. The preference of the panel monitor thus appears to determine the precise manner in which the panel discussion is carried out.

Committee and NRC staff members observed that the workload for reviewers appeared to be quite burdensome. Many reviewers reported spending considerable time prior to the meeting reviewing and rating the applications. One reviewer said it took 7 hours to review one application. One of the teleconferences started each day at 10 AM and ended each of 3 days at 4 PM or 5 PM. Discussion of each application generally took 2 hours (although one application was reviewed in as little as 45 minutes). There was a 2-hour lunch break each day, but most reviewers used a significant part of that time to revise and finalize technical review forms and panel summary statements. Reviewers also reported spending time in the evenings between review days completing technical review forms and summary statements. Throughout the teleconferences, the reviewers referred to some degree of frustration and fatigue in scoring the last applications, especially if those applications were poorly organized.

The applications themselves were a burden on reviewers at times. NIDRR recommends that the project narrative section of the application be no longer than 125 double-spaced pages, but some narratives are longer. There is no page limit for other sections of the application, such as budget, assurances and certifications, resumes, and letters of support. Applications vary considerably in organization and clarity, with the best being organized clearly by criterion. Some reviewers had trouble finding content in poorly organized applications and lowered their scores accordingly. On several occasions, a reviewer needed to point out information missed by another reviewer to prevent an unjustified lower score. One reviewer suggested it would be a good idea for NIDRR to require that applications be organized following the order of the criteria.

The observers perceived that reviewers had a good overall understanding of the selection criteria with some exceptions, possibly due to the nature of those particular competitions. Criteria such as "importance of the problem," "responsiveness to the priority," and "research hypothesis" engendered some discussion between the panel members and the competition managers. Also, one panel noticed some redundancy in several criteria items addressing access and diversity.

Some concern was noted about the structure of the panel summary that is provided as feedback to applicants. It consisted mainly of a list of strengths and weaknesses but appeared to lack comprehensiveness to inform future applications and build capacity.

Perspectives of NIDRR Staff and Grantees

NIDRR staff and grantees were asked open-ended questions about their perspectives on the agency's peer review process. Sixteen NIDRR staff members were interviewed in person and shared information about their roles in the process, their perspectives on its quality, and their suggestions for its improvement. Two-thirds of the interviewees were project officers or direct supervisors of project officers; the remaining held administrative positions. In addition, 28 grantees were asked to share their perspectives on NIDRR's peer review process through one item on the grantee questionnaire that was completed during the summative evaluation. Narrative data were analyzed using standard qualitative analysis techniques (see Chapter 2 for a description of the methods). Following are the major findings that emerged from an analysis of the data provided by NIDRR staff and grantees.

Quality and Consistency

Most of the NIDRR staff interviewed participated in NIDRR's peer review process as competition managers and/or panel monitors. Respondents indicated that the process is very strong and that the hard-working nature of their colleagues contributed to the quality of the process. Some stated that ED's grant administration handbook is an important facilitator of successful and consistent peer reviews. However, a need was identified for standard operating procedures and better training to promote greater consistency in monitoring competitions, such as FIP, involving multiple panels. NIDRR is aware of such questions about consistency, and recently has started debriefing competition managers and panel monitors after reviews for multipanel competitions to help promote consistency.

Challenges for Staff

Peer reviews were described as extremely time-consuming for staff in terms of both recruiting reviewers and running the panels. The small size of the field makes it difficult to find reviewers. A searchable database assists in recruiting reviewers, but it is somewhat dated, and its content has a broad focus designed to meet larger ED needs. It was suggested that a database more tailored to NIDRR's needs would be useful. To alleviate the recruiting burden, it was also suggested that the creation of more standing panels, as well as more up-front support from the peer review contractor, would be helpful. To respond to challenges in having adequate representation of minorities and individuals with disabilities on panels, more active recruitment was suggested within and outside of the disability field to build capacity.

Reviewer Burden

Several interviewees noted how burdensome reviews are for the reviewers. One remarked, "There is something like 32 items and subitems that have to be scored individually. And our applications are long and so it is a strenuous process for reviewers." Another commented, "I think every other review I will have somebody leave the review saying I can't review for NIDRR again. Not because they didn't enjoy the process. Not because they didn't enjoy reading the applications but because it was too time consuming, too burdensome." Another interviewee suggested that peer reviewers are undercompensated, even compared with reviewers for other ED programs, and suggested that their honorarium be increased.

Staff remarked that the agency is tackling the identified problems with the peer review process through a continuous quality improvement effort. The need has been identified to improve electronic systems for assembling panels, tracking reviewers and expertise, and managing meetings and ratings. At the time of the interviews, this issue was particularly critical because a new online system for managing scores had been found to be unusable and was being replaced temporarily by an e-mail-based system.

Peer Review Scoring System

Grantees commented primarily on the scoring system. It was stated that, having improved over time and being well managed by staff members, NIDRR's peer review process was good. The main element of the process the grantees suggested could be improved was the scoring system. Grantees' suggestions for changes to the system included placing more emphasis in scoring on the effort to accelerate translation and use and on the implications for policy change and for system design or service delivery interventions; amending the process so the lowest score for a proposal would be discarded; using a scoring system similar to that used by NIH, with greater emphasis on innovation; and awarding more points to applications that explain how the project's costs are reasonable when considered against the likely benefit of its outputs to the nation.

Perspectives of NIDRR Peer Reviewers

Peer reviewers surveyed were asked a series of closed- and open-ended questions inquiring about (1) their experiences with and perspectives on the NIDRR peer review process, (2) how the process compares with those of other federal research agencies, and (3) their suggestions for improving the process. Invitations to participate in the survey were sent to all individuals (a total of 156) who served on NIDRR peer review panels during FY 2008-2009. NIDRR provided the reviewers' names and contact information, but not the competitions they reviewed. Four potential respondents were deleted from the list because their e-mail addresses were invalid even after a concentrated search. Of the 152 reviewers successfully invited, 121 responded to the survey (response rate of 80 percent). Not all of the respondents elected to answer the 2 open-ended questions; 58 percent responded to the first question and 82 percent to the second.

The committee analyzed quantitative data from the closed-ended survey items descriptively to determine frequencies and measures of central distribution. The narrative data were analyzed using standard qualitative analysis techniques as described in Chapter 2. Results of the quantitative and qualitative analyses of responses to the 10 closed-ended and 2 open-ended questions follow.

Panel Participation Rates and Types of Program Mechanisms

From 2005 through 2010, respondents served on a median number of 3.5 review panels, with a range of 1 to18 panels (16 individuals served on 1 panel and 1 individual on 18 panels). The most common types of program mechanisms reviewed were FIR (by 69 percent of respondents), FID (52 percent), RRTC (37 percent), DRRP (28 percent), SBIR-I (23 percent), SBIR-II (13 percent), and RERC (17 percent). Fewer than 6 percent of peer reviewers served on panels for BMS, TBIMS, and SCIMS. Between 9 and 12 percent of reviewers served on panels for fellowship and training grants (Switzer Fellowship and ARRT).

Ratings of the Quality of NIDRR's Peer Review Process

Peer reviewers were asked to rate key elements of the NIDRR peer review process using a scale of 1 to 5, where 1 = poor, 3 = adequate, and 5 =

excellent. Table 4-2 presents the percentage of reviewers who rated the key elements along a 5-point scale. The table is arranged in order of most favorably rated (largest percentage rated 4 and 5) to least favorably rated (largest percentage rated 1 and 2). Results include 121 respondents, although a few respondents did not rate each element (with the exception of thoroughness of the deliberation), so the number of respondents for each element is less than 121. Additionally, 2 respondents answered "don't know" on level of experience, 3 responded "not applicable" on guidance in writing reviewer comments, and 1 responded "don't know" and another "not applicable" on quality of the training. These responses are also excluded from the number of respondents in the table. The key element of consistency in the overall quality of the peer reviews across panels was rated only by reviewers who had served on three or more panels, so the number of respondents for that element purposely excludes 3 "don't know" responses, 17 "not applicable" responses, and 7 reviewers who left the item blank.

Nine of the 13 elements were rated as "more than adequate to excellent" (4 to 5) by 61 percent or more of respondents. These included support and facilitation of the review panel by NIDRR staff (78 percent), integrity of the peer review process overall (76 percent), thoroughness of the deliberation (73 percent), use of reviewers' time during the panel meeting (72 percent), level of expertise of the peer review panel members (68 percent), guidance in writing reviewer comments (64 percent), quality of the training to prepare for the review (64 percent), consistency in the overall quality of the peer reviews across panels (61 percent), and appropriateness of the evaluation criteria to applications under review (61 percent). Peer reviewers surveyed by the peer review contractor (as summarized in a previous section) likewise gave highly favorable ratings to assistance and participation provided by staff in the review process and to reviewer orientation.

Although close to half of the respondents rated the remaining items as favorable (4 to 5 on the rating scale), 25 percent of respondents rated the elements adequacy of time for review of materials before the meeting and appropriateness of scoring system to applications under review as poor to less than adequate (1 to 2 on the rating scale). Peer reviewers surveyed by the peer review contractor likewise gave their least favorable ratings to time allowed for initial review.

An additional survey question asked the 94 reviewers who had served on multiple panels since January 1, 2005, whether, generally speaking, the quality of NIDRR's peer review process had changed over time. Two reviewers responded "don't know," and 3 reviewers responded "not applicable." Of the remaining 89 reviewers who responded to this survey question, 24 percent indicated that quality had increased, 50 percent that it had remained about the same, and 26 percent that it had decreased.

On related survey items dealing with the perceived burden of review-

TABLE 4-2 Peer Reviewers' Perceptions of Key Elements of NIDRR's Peer Review Process (121 respondents)

		1	2	3	4	5
Key Element	Number of Respondents	Poor (%)	(%)	Adequate (%)	(%)	Excellent (%)
Support and facilitation of the review panel by NIDRR staff	120	1	4	17	28	50
Integrity of the peer review process overall	117	2	2	20	41	35
Thoroughness of the deliberation (i.e., grant scoring and discussion) during the meeting	121	0	3	24	32	41
Use of reviewers' time during the panel meeting	118	1	8	19	41	31
Level of expertise of the peer review panel members	118	2	9	21	36	32
Guidance in writing reviewer comments	117	1	7	28	44	20
Quality of the training to prepare for the review	117	0	4	32	39	25
Consistency in the overall quality of the peer reviews across panels (if you have served on three or more panels)	94	2	16	21	42	19
Appropriateness of the evaluation criteria to applications under review	119	4	9	26	41	20
Appropriateness of scoring system to applications under review	120	4	21	21	39	15
Clarity of the criteria when applying them to applications	119	4	10	34	41	11
Ease of applying scoring system to applications	119	1	16	34	35	14
Adequacy of time for review of materials before the meeting	120	8	17	32	27	16

SOURCE: Generated by the committee based on data from the peer reviewer questionnaire.

ers' workload, 44 percent stated they had had more applications to review than they would like to have had on a given panel, and 44 percent stated that they had spent more time on each panel than they would like to have spent. On both of these items, however, more than 50 percent responded that the amount of time had been about right. Additionally, reviewers were asked about the quality of face-to-face meetings versus teleconferences. Fifty-one percent responded that face-to-face meetings were of higher quality, 40 percent that quality was the same, and 9 percent that teleconferences were of higher quality.

A final survey question about NIDRR's peer review process was posed to the subset of peer reviewers (55 percent) who had experience with other federal agency peer review processes. Results include 64 respondents, although a few respondents either responded "don't know" or did not rate each characteristic, so the number of respondents for each characteristic is less than 64. Table 4-3 shows that close to half of these respondents considered the selected characteristics of NIDRR's peer review process to be about the same as those of other federal agencies. More than one-quarter thought NIDRR's process was stronger to some degree; slightly less than a quarter considered NIDRR's process to be weaker. The committee noted that the 55 percent of respondents who had other federal agency review experience showed few differences from the other respondents when the two groups were stratified according to their perceptions of the key elements listed in Table 4-2. The order of the key elements from most to least favorable remained generally the same.

Perceptions of NIDRR's Peer Review Process

Peer reviewers responded to the following open-ended questions:

- Any additional comments you may have on NIDRR's peer review processes would be useful. Please use the space below. (This question followed a table asking respondents to rate key elements of NIDRR's peer review process.)
- What three things would you suggest to enhance NIDRR's peer review processes?

As noted in the discussion of analysis of process data in Chapter 2, responses to these questions were analyzed using standard qualitative methods. Two overarching themes emerged during the qualitative data analysis. Theme I, "Increase peer reviewer role satisfaction," focuses on the impact of the peer review process on respondents' perceived levels of role satisfaction. Theme II, "Develop quality improvement initiatives," focuses on

TABLE 4-3 Peer Reviewers' Perceptions of How the NIDRR Peer Review Process Compares with That of Other Agencies (64 respondents)

Characteristic	Number of Respondents	NIDRR's Are Much Weaker Than Those of Other Agencies (%)	NIDRR's Are Somewhat Weaker Than Those of Other Agencies (%)	NIDRR's Are About the Same (%)	NIDRR's Are Somewhat Stronger Than Those of Other Agencies (%)	NIDRR's Are Much Stronger Than Those of Other Agencies (%)
Quality of the review process	63	6	21	36	21	16
Transparency of the review process	61	8	13	46	17	16
Quality of the proposals reviewed	62	2	19	47	16	16
Fairness of the review process	62	7	16	47	15	15
Reliability of the ratings	60	8	20	44	15	13
Expertise of the panel members	62	7	19	50	6	18

SOURCE: Generated by the committee based on data from the peer reviewer questionnaire.

respondents' suggestions for enhancing the process. Both themes encompass aspects of peer review that affect the quality of final results.

Theme 1: Increase Peer Reviewer Role Satisfaction

Respondents identified six sources of role dissatisfaction during the premeeting phase of the peer review process that may negatively affect the quality of the results: (1) the time provided to read and review applications, (2) the number of applications to read and review per panel meeting, (3) the length of applications, (4) the lack of choice of format in which to view applications, (5) the compensation rate, and (6) the online software used to comment on and score applications. Comments on each of these factors are summarized below.

Increase the amount of time to review applications prior to the panel meeting Eleven respondents expressed strong concern about receiving applications too close to the meeting date and advised NIDRR to send applications more than a few weeks before the meeting; two respondents suggested 1 month before and five respondents suggested 2 months before. Four respondents contended that there was a link among three of the six sources of peer reviewer role dissatisfaction; as articulated by one, "either give reviewers more time to review, or reduce the number of applications each person has to review, and increase the compensation rate." The quantitative data support peer reviewers' comments on dissatisfaction with the amount of time allowed to review applications prior to a meeting. Ratings for adequacy of time for review of materials before the meeting received the largest percentage of poor to less than adequate ratings (25 percent).

Decrease the number of applications reviewed per panel meeting Eight respondents suggested that NIDRR needs to reduce the number of applications each panel reviews; four contended that excessive numbers of applications reduced the quality of the reviews, and two of these four believed the numbers discouraged busy, experienced reviewers from participating. The four suggested that decreased numbers would lead to more time spent on each application, as well as more detailed comments (cited by two of the four) and usable feedback (stated by one of the four). Potential solutions suggested included determining "the maximum number of applications to review according to the complexity of each [program] mechanism" (cited by three respondents) and enhanced prereview screening to eliminate very weak applications (also cited by three). These comments on the burdensome number of applications assigned to each reviewer echo the quantitative data, which revealed that 44 percent of respondents thought they received more applications than they would like to have reviewed.

Reduce the page length of applications Nine respondents stated that another way to reduce workload would be stricter page limits for applications. Four of the nine suggested a limit of 25 pages, and one suggested 50 pages; the remaining four did not mention a specific limit. Three of the nine respondents mentioned that NIH limits applications to 12 pages. One of the nine noted the additional need for page limits for appendices, without offering a specific limit.

Provide reviewers with a choice of formats in which to review applications Eight respondents suggested that reviewers should be able to choose the format of the applications they review based on their preferences, such as printed copies, on CD, or through a password-protected website. Respondents noted that PDF files would allow them to use the search function, and Word files would allow them to embed comments through the track changes feature.

Increase the compensation rate Eleven respondents were concerned about NIDRR's compensation rate. One respondent said, "there were simply too many applications to review for the amount of reimbursement provided." Four respondents were concerned that experienced reviewers might decline invitations to serve on panels because of the amount of time required and the relatively low compensation rates. Three respondents suggested that NIDRR increase compensation to match the rate paid by other federal agencies, while three suggested increasing compensation to better match the amount of time actually spent preparing and reviewing. One respondent suggested that increased compensation might encourage experienced researchers to participate.

Improve the online scoring software Fifteen respondents were concerned about the lack of user-friendly online software for completing reviews. Eleven of these respondents described the new G5 software as cumbersome, with "excessively convoluted navigations." One stated, "The G5 is inaccessible for reviewers with visual impairments . . . [and] my primary task should be to lend expertise to the analysis and scoring of the applications . . . the logistical problems detract from the integrity of the review process." Respondents provided specific suggestions for improving the software, such as placing one criterion and all subcomponents on a single screen (suggested by five respondents), allowing reviewers to enter critiques and scores for each application in one file (suggested by four), accepting both PDF and DOC formats (suggested by three), and adding a search/find command so reviewers can more easily edit or rescore an application (suggested by three).

Theme 2: Develop Peer Review Quality Improvement Initiatives

Respondents identified seven areas in which improvements would likely increase the integrity and quality of the peer review process and the quality of outputs: (1) expertise of peer reviewers, (2) premeeting orientation and training, (3) evaluation criteria used to score applications, (4) scoring process, (5) guidance and group facilitation provided by NIDRR staff, (6) panel discussions, and (7) feedback to applicants. Comments on each of these areas are summarized below.

Enhance the level of peer reviewer expertise Three respondents stated that the level of peer reviewer expertise has greatly improved over the years. However, six respondents held a mixed view of panel members' level of expertise and reported variation in reviewers' knowledge of the research process, areas of scientific methods and statistics (cited by four of the six), current literature on research and practice in rehabilitation medicine (cited by two of the six), or disability policy (cited by one of the six). Additionally, four of the six respondents mentioned having experienced instances in which insufficient expertise among primary or secondary reviewers significantly affected the review process. Three respondents commented on the urgent need to include a greater number of experienced researchers with disabilities to serve on panels, but also mentioned that inviting persons with disabilities who lack research expertise to serve as peer reviewers could impact the integrity of the review process.

Suggestions for addressing these issues included expanding peer reviewer recruitment (cited by seven respondents) to include more reviewers outside the NIDRR network (cited by three) and federally funded researchers (cited by one), increasing the responsibility of the secondary reviewer to balance out a potentially inexperienced primary reviewer (cited by one), asking reviewers to select applications for which they could serve as a primary or secondary reviewer (cited by one), and bringing in an ad hoc topic or methods expert if necessary for an application (cited by one).

While the open-ended comments related to expertise were mixed, on the quantitative item 68 percent of respondents rated level of expertise of the peer review panel members as more than adequate or excellent. Only 11 percent rated this element poor to less than adequate.

Improve the quality of premeeting orientation and training Ten respondents urged NIDRR to institute several quality improvement initiatives to increase the effectiveness of premeeting training. Seven of the 10 stated that both experienced and novice reviewers could benefit from additional training to help them better understand the qualities of excellent, average, and poor-quality applications. Suggestions included developing examples of excellent, average, and poor-quality applications (cited by five respondents), creating separate training sessions for novice reviewers and others who need additional training (cited by four); providing separate training for nonresearchers (cited by three); developing online training modules that would be available at all times for reviewers to use as needed (cited by two); providing training throughout the calendar year (cited by one); assigning mentors to first-time reviewers (cited by one); and providing brief biosketches of each panel member (cited by one).

Eight respondents suggested that training sessions and premeeting materials need to include more information about how to distinguish one criterion from another. Other suggestions included covering how to translate the scoring criteria to actual applications (cited by seven respondents), how to use the online software (cited by six), the purposes of the priority to be funded (cited by three), how the panel will be facilitated by NIDRR staff (cited by two), and the specifics of what each criterion measures (cited by one).

Despite these suggestions for improving training, the quantitative data suggest that NIDRR already has high-quality training. No respondents rated training as poor, only 4 percent rated it as less than adequate, 32 percent rated it as adequate and 64 percent rated it as more than adequate to excellent.

Improve the evaluation criteria used to score applications Thirteen respondents expressed varying degrees of frustration that the criteria are "ambiguous, overlapping, and redundant." One of the 13 captured the views of the other 12, suggesting that "the distinctions between criteria are too subtle and are very difficult for reviewers to distinguish one criterion from another." Five of the 13 respondents suggested that the redundant and ambiguous criteria could lead to inconsistent interpretation, wider discrepancies among reviewer ratings, and decreased ability to identify the best applications, all of which would diminish the quality of the review.

Six respondents stated that the criteria do not adequately evaluate innovation, feasibility, and scientific merit. One of the six found the criteria to be "less scientific and more political" in orientation. Three respondents suggested that the "plan of evaluation" criterion was overemphasized. Finally, two respondents described frustration that participation by both ethnic minorities and persons with disabilities was not adequately being measured by the "diversity" criterion.

To address the repetitive, ambiguous nature of the criteria, nine respondents advised NIDRR to "combine duplicative criteria" and to "specify what each criterion measures." To address the scientific inadequacy of the criteria, four respondents suggested better matching criteria and program mechanisms, two suggested developing new and innovative ways for applicants to demonstrate that diversity is considered in staffing configurations and reflected in contributions to diverse communities, and one suggested adding a new criterion—"impact on the field." One respondent suggested that reviewers should not evaluate budgets.

While the peer reviewers' comments highlighted flaws in the criteria, the quantitative data suggest the evaluation criteria are generally seen as adequate. Sixty-one percent of reviewers rated appropriateness of the evaluation criteria to applications under review as more than adequate to excellent, and 34 percent rated clarity of the criteria when applying them to applications as adequate.

Improve the scoring process used to rate applications on the criteria Ten respondents suggested there is considerable variation in how reviewers apply the scoring system to evaluate applications. Two of these respondents noted extreme cases of reviewers scoring all applications much higher or lower than all other panel members. One respondent attributed this discrepancy to the steep learning curve reviewers experience during their first meeting.

Additionally, eight respondents were critical of NIDRR's weighting of the criteria. One suggested that in some cases, primary issues are not given enough weight, one that minor details are given too much weight, and one that the weighting approach is not flexible enough to be adjusted across competitions. One respondent also expressed concern that "there are some criteria that are allotted a total of one point—that is really splitting hairs and is not significant."

To achieve greater scoring consistency among reviewers, five respondents advised NIDRR to "develop a standardized set of scoring procedures" and a set of training "materials using concrete examples of how to score applications appropriately." One respondent suggested that these materials would help reviewers translate the scoring criteria to the actual applications. Four respondents offered ways to improve the user-friendliness of the scoring system, such as by adopting a 0-10 scale for each criterion, beginning "with the lowest scoring applications to practice scoring as a group" (suggested by one respondent). Two respondents suggested that more weight be added to the criterion "implementation and outcomes," while another advised NIDRR to give more weight to the "significance of the project and the track record of the applicant" and less to researcher qualifications, as "most applications have qualified personnel."

Finally, two respondents expressed diametrically opposed views about the weight assigned to the "diversity" criterion. One stated that this criterion has too much weight such that the application's scientific rigor could be diluted, while the other stated that this criterion has far too little weight such that applications could be approved with only token representation of relevant communities. Common ground could possibly be reached by following the suggestion, described in the previous section, that NIDRR develop new and innovative ways to demonstrate diversity.

Address the inconsistent quality of the guidance and group facilitation provided by NIDRR staff Six respondents noted the high quality of guidance provided by NIDRR staff. However, 10 respondents thought the quality of staff guidance varied, with some staff being more knowledgeable about the process (cited by four respondents), more organized (cited by one), and more efficient (cited by one) than others. Nine respondents stated that the NIDRR panel monitors with whom they interacted lacked sufficient skills in guidance and facilitation. Two of these nine also noted confusing inconsistency in the direction given by different NIDRR staff members. For example, "some staff advocate for reviewers to start from zero and add points for positive features, whereas others say one should start from the maximum number of points and subtract for specific weaknesses or problems." Also, five of the nine respondents were concerned that staff lacked the knowledge base or skill set to recognize and manage reviewer bias.

Suggestions for improving the quality of guidance and facilitation provided by NIDRR staff included developing new training and materials on "managing situations where one reviewer dominates the discussion" (cited by four respondents), "including all reviewers in the discussion" (cited by two), "insisting on courteous behavior at all times" (cited by two), and encouraging discussion and allowing for disagreements (cited by two). While these are reasonable suggestions, it must be noted that support and facilitation of the review panel by NIDRR staff was the element rated most favorably by peer reviewers.

Reduce variation in the quality of the panel discussions Reviewers noted several factors that affect the quality of discussions, including the discussion venue, unprepared reviewers, weak applications, and reviewer bias. The most frequent issue raised by respondents was face-to-face meetings versus teleconferences (cited by 19 respondents). Fourteen respondents noted only the benefits of their preferred venue, while 5 others described the trade-offs. Three respondents were mindful of the current and future cost savings derived from using teleconferences but were against their exclusive use. One of the 3 advised NIDRR to use face-to-face meetings for "large Center applications and all 5-year award programs." Two respondents hoped that "video-conference calls would help to bridge the gap between the pros and cons of each venue."

Among these 19 respondents, many held differing views on the effectiveness of meeting by teleconference. Opinions ranged from "teleconferencing is very adequate" (cited by 6); to "it's possible to have an engaged teleconference, it's just more difficult" (cited by 1); to "teleconference reviews are a failed experiment" (cited by 6). The 19 respondents identified three pros of teleconferences, such as "The quality of the reviewers increase [sic] because there is no need for people to travel and significantly disrupt work and family schedules" (cited by 4). They also identified nine cons, such as "The quality and depth of the panel discussions has [sic] deteriorated since teleconferences have been substituted for in-person meetings" (cited by 9). Respondents also identified seven pros of face-to-face meetings, such as "Discussions are of a higher quality" (cited by 12). Respondents did not specifically mention any cons of face-to-face meetings, but they are implicit in several of the cited pros of teleconference meetings.

Additionally, four respondents reported frustration with unprepared reviewers. Three respondents expressed frustration at discussing very weak applications, which two suggested interfered with discussion of more worthy applications in greater depth. Three respondents were concerned about reviewer bias, one noting that "individual biases and not having the 'right' people at the table for the type of review being conducted unfortunately tend to influence the final outcome."

Five respondents offered ideas for better ensuring reviewer preparedness, including requiring all reviewers to write summaries of each application (cited by two) and requiring all reviewers to submit their comments and scores before the meeting (cited by one). One respondent advised NIDRR to disqualify weak applications, leaving reviewers to evaluate "only those applications that have potential for good scores." Two reviewers shared the idea that expanding the recruitment pool of peer reviewers would help combat bias and inject objectivity into the process. Three respondents suggested that forming more standing panels could increase the consistency and quality of individual competition reviews as panel members would have more experience. One of the three noted that standing panels could also improve quality across competition years as the same reviewers would evaluate resubmitted applications. Two respondents suggested limiting the number of discussion hours per day or scheduling more days but fewer hours, or possibly even holding panel meetings only during academic breaks (cited by one) as ways to improve quality and reduce reviewer fatigue.

Concerns about the quality of panel discussions were not as evident in the quantitative data. Seventy-three percent of respondents rated thoroughness of the deliberation as more than adequate or excellent, and 72 percent rated use of reviewers' time during the panel meeting as more than adequate or excellent. Only 3 percent of respondents rated thoroughness of the deliberation and 9 percent use of reviewers' time during the panel meeting as poor or less than adequate. Fifty-one percent of respondents thought panels generally took the right amount of time. Fifty-two percent suggested the quality of face-to-face reviews is better, 40 percent said quality is similar for face-to-face reviews and teleconferences, and 9 percent replied that teleconferences are of better quality than face-to-face reviews. As noted earlier in the chapter in the section on panel discussions, NIDRR is aware of the mixed opinions concerning the quality of reviews held by teleconference but believes the benefits outweigh the costs.

Improve the quality of feedback provided to applicants While one respondent stated that "reviewers' comments to applicants seem useful," four others shared the view that the "format and quality of the feedback to applicants lack depth and specificity." Two respondents suggested that improving the quality and consistency of feedback to applicants could contribute to building capacity in the field. Five respondents suggested that NIDRR develop strategies to increase the quality of the feedback provided to applicants. Two suggested providing comments from all or most of the panel members and a discussion summary, similar to the NIH procedure; one suggested that reviewers take turns being note takers; and one suggested standardizing the format of the feedback. On a related quantitative item, the majority of peer reviewers (64 percent) rated the guidance they received from NIDRR in writing review comments as good to excellent.

CONCLUSIONS AND RECOMMENDATIONS

The sources relevant to peer review who were engaged in this evaluation, including NIDRR staff, grantees, and peer reviewers, consistently described NIDRR's peer review process as generally good, although still in need of some improvement. Additionally, half of the NIDRR staff members interviewed thought the peer review process was very strong overall, although time-consuming and burdensome for both staff and peer reviewers. More than half of the grantees who commented on peer review noted significant recent improvement to the process, although certain aspects, such as the scoring system, could still be improved. Finally, of the 64 NIDRR peer reviewers surveyed who had experience with reviews for other federal research agencies, close to half considered the selected characteristics of NIDRR's peer review process to be about the same as those of other federal agency processes; more than one-quarter thought NIDRR's process was stronger to some degree; slightly less than a quarter considered NIDRR's process to be weaker than those of other agencies. The narrative comments of peer reviewers provide examples of some of the areas in which these respondents suggested improvements could be made to increase the role satisfaction of reviewers and improve the quality of the process.

The committee also recognizes that NIDRR's peer review process operates within the bounds of ED. As a result, some aspects of the process identified as potential weaknesses during the course of the review are controlled by ED, such as exclusion of grantees' past performance as a criteria in peer review, rules regarding the formation of standing panels, public identification of the competitions in which reviewers participate, and the ability of the ED-level database of potential reviewers to meet NIDRR's needs.

The evidence presented indicates that NIDRR's peer review process is generally good; nonetheless, there are significant opportunities for enhancements that would likely improve the quality of final project results. To address these concerns and strengthen NIDRR's peer review process, the committee offers recommendations for enhancing the peer review infrastructure, reducing reviewer burden, and using consumers on review panels.

Enhancements to the Peer Review

While recognizing the care with which NIDRR's competition managers assemble and facilitate review panels, the committee feels NIDRR's peer review process is hampered by a limited pool of potential reviewers. NIDRR staff spend considerable time recruiting and screening potential reviewers. Competition managers regularly must manage potential conflicts of interest and rule out qualified reviewers. Despite staff efforts to recruit adequate numbers of reviewers, some panels are smaller than NIDRR's recommended size; reviewers sometimes are added so close to the meeting date that they have inadequate time to prepare; and primary, secondary, and general reviewers lacking necessary scientific expertise may be participating in the reviews.

The committee concluded that improvements in the following areas of NIDRR's peer review process would likely enhance the quality of project outputs: use of standing panels or formal cohorts of peer reviewers with specialized knowledge and expertise as appropriate for the program mechanisms, reviewer training, consistency in facilitating panel meetings, and the quality of feedback provided to applicants. The formation of more standing panels or cohorts would reduce the recruiting burden on NIDRR staff and provide a pool of reviewers with more experience with the review process, both of which may lead to more consistent and higher-quality reviews. While some reviewers surveyed for this study reported receiving high-quality training, the committee believes that enhancing this training would be a simple and effective way to improve the quality of the review process. Finally, because panel monitors have different preferences as to how panels should be run and varying levels of experience in guiding panels, considerable variation exists across competitions. The committee believes that, even if all competition managers adhere to NIDRR rules, such inconsistency results in confusion and negatively influences the overall quality of the process.

Recommendation 4-1: NIDRR should further strengthen the peer review infrastructure by expanding the pool of high-quality review-

ers; establishing standing panels, or formal cohorts of peer reviewers with specialized knowledge and expertise as appropriate for the program mechanisms; enhancing reviewer training; and improving the consistency of NIDRR staff facilitation of panel meetings and the quality of feedback provided to grantees.

Expanding the pool of peer reviewers could be pivotal in helping to prevent conflicts of interest, a challenge that NIDRR consistently faces during the recruitment of peer reviewers. Examples of potential ways to increase the reviewer pool include formally reaching out to new groups of researchers, such as individuals who review for the National Center for Medical Rehabilitation Research (NCMRR), NIH, and the Agency for Healthcare Research and Quality (AHRQ). The committee recognizes that, in accordance with Title II of the Rehabilitation Act, federal employees are not allowed to be peer reviewers. In other peer review settings, however, federal employees are not necessarily prevented from serving as reviewers, depending on their agency's regulations. For example, with supervisor approval, NIH employees can serve as peer reviewers for other federal agencies as an official-duty activity, provided the competition involves no NIH funds (see http://www.niehs.nih.gov/about/od/ethics/duties/oda/index.cfm [November 21, 2011]). NIDRR should consider investigating whether, with similar restrictions. Title II could be amended to allow for federal peer reviewers.

NIDRR also should monitor how peer reviewers perform so that ineffective reviewers can be counseled on review procedures and/or not invited to serve on subsequent panels. The committee urges NIDRR to consult with other federal agencies that have similar peer review panels, such as NIH and NSF, for guidance on actions they have taken to ensure that reviewers are of high quality. Additionally, NIDRR should consider requesting that ED allow publication of reviewer names by competition, as is common practice in other federal agencies. This would improve the transparency of the process.

NIDRR has means for recruiting informal groups of peer reviewers based on their areas of expertise and experience with ARRT, SBIR, and Switzer grants. While the use of more formalized cohorts of these types of reviewers would be more challenging and require careful planning for other mechanisms, the committee encourages NIDRR to consider expanding the use of such cohorts to ease burdens on both reviewers and staff.

Peer reviewer training enhancements could include sharing reviews of successful grant applications, providing concrete examples of how to translate scoring criteria to applications, and requiring trainees to observe panels before they become official reviewers. Training enhancements should also take into account the different needs of inexperienced and experienced reviewers.

While support and facilitation of the review panel by NIDRR staff was one of the highest rated elements of the peer review process, comments from peer reviewers pointed to the need for greater consistency across panel managers. As indicated in staff interviews, NIDRR is aware of this need and has been focusing on improving the consistency in the manner in which peer review meetings are facilitated. However, it is the viewpoint of the committee that a more formal quality improvement initiative is needed to improve the consistency of managing the panel meetings.

The guidance provided to peer reviewers by NIDRR in writing review comments was rated quite highly by peer reviewers, but several commented that the quality of the feedback actually provided to grantees was lacking in depth and specificity, and was inconsistent. NIDRR should consider other approaches to consolidating comments from reviewers in order to provide applicants with comprehensive feedback that will inform future applications.

Finally, the standard calendar proposed in Recommendation 3-3 in Chapter 3 might also enhance the peer review process by providing staff with a longer and more regular period within which to recruit reviewers. A standard calendar could also benefit applicants, who would know when the peer review process was to take place and when decisions on awards would be likely.

Reducing Reviewer Burden

Participating in NIDRR's peer review process clearly is a significant burden for a large percentage of reviewers. Many reviewers spend more time than they wish in preparing, and review days are long and intense. This significant time commitment makes it less likely that qualified and experienced reviewers will participate. Indeed, the committee found the review process is so burdensome to peer reviewers as to threaten its quality. Reviewers surveyed also reported sometimes having insufficient time to review proposals, which could affect the quality of the review discussions.

Recommendation 4-2: NIDRR should streamline the review process in order to reduce the burden on peer reviewers.

NIDRR could reduce the burden on reviewers by implementing page length restrictions for applications (NSF and NIH use substantially shorter applications with strict page limits); simplifying the application format, scoring criteria, and software; and limiting the number of proposals to be reviewed by a single panel. Formats for applications should be standardized where possible. Additionally, the committee thinks NIDRR's requirement that reviewers write a rationale only when giving submaximum scores is a potential disincentive for reviewers to give such scores. NIDRR should consider options for addressing this issue, as well as for reducing the complexity of scoring. NIDRR is already taking actions to improve the software used to score proposals; these efforts should continue. In addition, NIDRR should consider improving the quality of reviews by giving reviewers more time to review proposals. Also, establishing standing panels and more formal cohorts, as well as enhancing training, as detailed in Recommendation 4-1, should reduce the burden perceived by reviewers. Finally, NIDRR may want to explore a blended model of in-person and teleconference meetings to reduce the burden imposed by teleconferences for some reviewers, as expressed in the survey.

Use of Consumer Peer Reviewers

To address its mission, NIDRR makes concerted efforts to include both scientists with disabilities and consumers without scientific expertise in the peer review process. Consumers can represent the experiences and views of their particular disability communities and can evaluate applications for relevance to their communities' needs and concerns (although it is important to note that one consumer cannot necessarily represent the views of consumers from a different community). Peer reviewers who are not consumers can learn from the people the research is intended to benefit. Additionally, consumers may gain a better understanding of NIDRR's research and peer review process through their participation and thus be able to inform their communities about NIDRR's work.

All reviewers, including researchers and consumers, should have the appropriate expertise to review those elements of proposals to which they are assigned. If consumers are to review scientific aspects of proposals, they should have the relevant expertise, or NIDRR should provide them with relevant methodological training suitable to their background and qualifications. NIDRR should review and monitor the role of consumers and researchers in peer review to ensure that quality is not compromised.

Recommendation 4-3: NIDRR should continue to have consumer representation in the peer review process and establish procedures to guide the participation of those without scientific expertise.

While the involvement of consumers without scientific expertise in conducting peer review and helping to shape the research agenda is critical, there is currently no scientific consensus as to how this involvement is best accomplished. Therefore, NIDRR should assess the participation of consumers without scientific expertise in its peer review process. A model of such an assessment was conducted by Andejeski and colleagues (2002) who examined the impact of nonscientist consumer participation in peer reviews of breast cancer research proposals on review panels that included 11-17 scientists and 2 lay consumers. The authors found little difference in proposal scores of the nonscientist consumers and the scientists. Pre- and post-panel opinion questionnaires concerning consumer involvement in the scientific review process showed significantly greater positive post-panel opinions of consumer involvement than negative opinions.

Furthermore, the use of consumers in peer review processes is extensive in many other agencies. Following are examples of models used by other agencies to involve consumers in peer review which NIDRR might wish to review and consider for future use. (These examples are not intended to be exhaustive.)

The Office of Congressionally Directed Medical Research Programs (CDMRP), located in the Department of Defense, fully integrates consumers and scientists on peer review panels. According to CDMRP (2011), consumers "add perspective, passion, and a sense of urgency that ensures the human dimension is incorporated in the program policy, investment strategy, and research focus." CDMRP employs a two-tiered system of review, involving first a scientific review by a peer review panel and then a programmatic review by an integration panel. Consumers are fully integrated in both panels.

Additionally, the National Institute of Mental Health (NIMH) at times includes consumers without scientific expertise in peer review. NIMH also uses a two-tiered peer review process. The first tier involves assessment of grant applications by review committees, which are comprised of scientist reviewers and sometimes reviewers who are members of the general public, including consumers (National Institute of Mental Health, 2011a). The NIMH website (2011b) states that, "The role of public reviewers is to bring critical perspectives from individuals and family members who have been directly affected . . . and to enhance the capability of the review committee to evaluate the 'real world' relevance and practicality of each research application." Public reviewers are instructed to focus their review on particular aspects of the grant applications, such as public health significance, feasibility, outreach, and protection of human subjects (National Institute of Mental Health, 2011a). Similarly, NIDRR might identify which of its review criteria are most relevant to consumers without scientific expertise, and then ask consumer reviewers to rate only these criteria. The second tier in the NIMH process involves review by the NIMH Advisory Council, which is also composed of both scientist and lay members.

Finally, the Juvenile Diabetes Research Foundation (2011) also utilizes a two-tiered system of review. The first tier is scientific review, during which "each individual project should be evaluated for its standalone scientific merit as well as its potential contribution to the whole program." This phase of the process involves panels made up only of scientists. The second tier is lay review, during which a lay review committee uses its consumer experience and the results of the scientific review to determine which applications are likely to have the greatest impact.

REFERENCES

Andejeski, Y., Bisceglio, I.T., Dickersin, K., Johnson, J.E., Robinson, S.I., Smith, H S., Visco, F.M., and Rich, I.M. (2002). Quantitative impact of including consumers in the scientific review of breast cancer research proposals. *Journal of Women's Health and Gender-Based Medicine*, *11*(4), 379-388.

Disability and Rehabilitation Research Projects and Centers Program, 34 C.F.R. pt. 350 (2009)

Education Department General Administrative Regulations, 34 C.F.R. pts. 74-86 and 97-99 (2008). Available: http://www2.ed.gov/policy/fund/reg/edgarReg/edgar.html [November 22, 2011] .

Institute of Medicine. (2007). *The future of disability in America*. Washington, DC: The National Academies Press.

Ismail, S., Farrands, A., and Wooding, S. (2009). *Evaluating grant peer review in the health sciences*. Cambridge, England: RAND Europe.

Juvenile Diabetes Research Foundation. (2011). *Information for reviewers*. Available: http://www.jdrf.org/index.cfm?page_id=103243 [June 4, 2011].

National Institute of Mental Health. (2011a). *Review process*. Available: http://www.nimh.nih.gov/research-funding/grants/review-process.shtml [October 12, 2011].

National Institute of Mental Health. (2011b). *Role of public participants in NIMH grant reviews*. Available: http://www.nimh.nih.gov/research-funding/grants/role-of-public-participants-in-nimh-grant-reviews.shtml [October 12, 2011].

National Institute on Disability and Rehabilitation Research. (2006). Department of Education: National Institute on Disability and Rehabilitation Research—Notice of Final Long-Range Plan for Fiscal Years 2005–2009. *Federal Register, 71*(31), 8,166-8,200.

National Institute on Disability and Rehabilitation Research. (2009a). *Briefing book for The National Academies*. Unpublished document. Washington, DC: National Institute on Disability and Rehabilitation Research.

National Institute on Disability and Rehabilitation Research. (2009b). *Peer reviewer instructions*. Unpublished document. Washington, DC: National Institute on Disability and Rehabilitation Research.

National Institute on Disability and Rehabilitation Research. (2010a). *2006-2009 applications received, applications reviewed, and applications funded*. Unpublished document. Washington, DC: National Institute on Disability and Rehabilitation Research.

National Institute on Disability and Rehabilitation Research. (2010b). *Application technical review plan*. Washington, DC: National Institute on Disability and Rehabilitation Research.

National Institute on Disability and Rehabilitation Research. (2010c). *Overview of the NIDRR's peer review process (what happens between OPP's priority review and OPP's slate review)*. Unpublished document. Washington, DC: National Institute on Disability and Rehabilitation Research.

National Institutes of Health. (2008). *2007-2008 peer review self-study*. Washington, DC: National Institutes of Health.

National Science Foundation. (2011). *Committee of Visitors (COV)*. Available: http://www.nsf.gov/od/oia/activities/cov/ [April 5, 2011].

Office of Congressionally Directed Medical Research Programs. (2011). *Consumer involvement*. Available: http://cdmrp.army.mil/cwg/default.shtml [June 4, 2011].

The Rehabilitation Act of 1973, as amended. Pub. L. No. 93-112. Available: http://www2.ed.gov/policy/speced/reg/narrative.html [January 21, 2011].

Synergy Enterprises, Inc. (2008). *Draft task 4 analysis*. Washington, DC: National Institute on Disability and Rehabilitation.
Synergy Enterprises, Inc. (2010). *Analysis of peer review process—Synergy survey*. Unpublished document. Washington, DC: National Institute on Disability and Rehabilitation.
U.S. Department of Education. (2009). *Handbook for the discretionary grant process*. Washington, DC: U.S. Department of Education.

ANNEX 4-1
SELECTION CRITERIA

Selection criteria are used by peer reviewers in assessing and rating applications submitted by researchers for funding. Title 34 of the Code of Federal Regulations (CFR)[9] provides guidance for NIDRR's peer review process, as well as selection criteria. Part 350 of the CFR outlines the selection criteria for the competitions administered through the DRRP primary mechanisms, including DRRP-General, DBTAC, KT, Section 21, BMS, and TBIMS, as well as for the program mechanisms ARRT, FIP, RERC, and RRTC. Part 356 provides selection criteria for Switzer Fellowship. Part 359 provides selection criteria for SCIMS. Part 75 provides selection criteria for SBIR. Each competition includes 100 possible points allocated across criteria and subcriteria. With the exception of Part 359, governing SCIMS, where the points are prespecified, the distribution of points across the selected criteria is determined by NIDRR staff. All criteria are displayed in Table A4-1.

The term "absolute priority" refers to those requirements that applicants must address to demonstrate their responsiveness to the requirements of the program mechanism (e.g., DRRP) or to the specific topic (e.g., telerehabilitation). The term "competitive priority" refers to requirements that can result in competitive preference, either by awarding extra points based on the extent to which the application meets the priority or by selecting an application that meets the priority over a similarly reviewed application that does not. An example is additional points being awarded to an application that includes effective strategies for employing and advancing in employment qualified individuals with disabilities.

Competitions under Parts 350 and 75 are not required to use all of the criteria, as certain criteria are not relevant to some competitions. NIDRR staff select the relevant criteria from the list provided in the CFR. As defined in the CFR, each criterion in Parts 350 and 75 contains subcriteria. As part

[9]The electronic Code of Federal Regulations can be accessed at: http://ecfr.gpoaccess.gov/cgi/t/text/text-idx?c=ecfr&tpl=%2Findex.tpl [January 4, 2012].

TABLE A4-1 Selection Criteria from Title 34, Code of Federal Regulations

	Title 34, Part 350			
	DBTAC	DRRP	KT	Burn
Title 34, Part 350				
Importance of the problem	x	x	x	x
Responsiveness to an absolute or competitive priority	x	x	x	x
Design of research activities	x	x	x	x
Design of development activities	x	x	x	x
Design of demonstration activities	x	x	x	x
Design of training activities	x	x	x	x
Design of dissemination activities	x	x	x	x
Design of utilization activities	x	x	x	x
Design of technical assistance activities	x	x	x	x
Plan of operation	x	x	x	x
Collaboration	x	x	x	x
Adequacy and reasonableness of the budget	x	x	x	x
Plan of evaluation	x	x	x	x
Project staff	x	x	x	x
Adequacy and reasonableness of resources	x	x	x	x
Title 34, Part 356				
Quality and level of formal education				
Previous work experience				
Recommendations				
Quality of a research proposal				
The research hypothesis, methodology, and design				
Resources, equipment, institutional support				

						Part 356	Part 359	Part 75
TBI	21	FIP	RRTC	RERC	ARRT	Switzer	SCI	SBIR
x	x	x	x	x	x			
x	x	x	x	x	x			
x	x	x	x	x	x			
x	x	x	x	x	x			
x	x	x	x	x	x			
x	x	x	x	x	x			
x	x	x	x	x	x			
x	x	x	x	x	x			
x	x	x	x	x	x			
x	x	x	x	x	x			
x	x	x	x	x	x			
x	x	x	x	x	x			
x	x	x	x	x	x			
x	x	x	x	x	x			
x	x	x	x	x	x			
						x		
						x		
						x		
						x		
						x		
						x		

continued

TABLE A4-1 Continued

	Title 34, Part 350			
	DBTAC	DRRP	KT	Burn
Title 34, Part 359				
Project design (20 points)				
Service comprehensiveness (20 points)				
Plan of operation (15 points)				
Quality of key personnel (10 points)				
Adequacy of resources (10 points)				
Budget/ cost effectiveness (10 points)				
Dissemination/ Utilization (5 points)				
Evaluation plan (10 points)				
Title 34, Part 75				
Need for project				
Significance				
Quality of the project design				
Quality of project services				
Quality of project personnel				
Adequacy of resources				
Quality of the management plan				
Quality of the project evaluation				

SOURCE: Generated by the committee based on the CFR, Title 34.

of recommending criteria for a competition, NIDRR staff also recommend which subcriteria are relevant. For each competition, points out of 100 are distributed across the chosen criteria. The points assigned to each criterion are then divided among the subcriteria for purposes of scoring. Box A4-1 contains an example of the selection criteria for a DRRP competition.

Part 350 also establishes additional considerations for FIP. Before funding is awarded, the Secretary of Education considers the extent to which applications that have been awarded 80 percent or more of the maximum possible points meet one or both of the following conditions: represent a unique opportunity to advance rehabilitation knowledge and/or complement current research or address such research in a promising new way. Part 75 does not include any additional considerations.

The criteria in Part 356 governing Switzer do not contain subcriteria. Based on peer review scores, the Secretary grades applicants as outstanding (5), superior (4), satisfactory (3), marginal (2), or poor (1). The Secretary

						Part 356	Part 359	Part 75
TBI	21	FIP	RRTC	RERC	ARRT	Switzer	SCI	SBIR
							x	
							x	
							x	
							x	
							x	
							x	
							x	
							x	
								x
								x
								x
								x
								x
								x
								x
								x

funds some or all of the applications that have been awarded a rating of superior or better (4-5). In making a final selection, the Secretary considers the extent to which outstanding or superior applicants present a unique opportunity to effect a major advance in knowledge, address critical problems in innovative ways, present proposals that are consistent with the NIDRR's Long-Range Plan, build research capacity within the field, or complement and significantly increase the potential value of already planned research and related activities.

Unlike the criteria in the other parts, Part 359 criteria governing SCIMS include point values (as can be seen in Table A4-1). The criteria in Part 359 do contain subcriteria for reviewers to consider, but the subcriteria are not scored; only the main criteria receive a score. In determining which applications to fund under this program, the Secretary also considers the proposed location of any project in order to achieve, to the extent possible, a geographic distribution of projects.

BOX A4-1
Example of Selection Criteria for Disability and Rehabilitation Research Project: Center on the Effective Delivery of Rehabilitation Technology by State Vocational Rehabilitation Agencies to Improve Employment Outcomes (CFDA Number 84.133A-4)

Requirement for DRRP Projects:
To meet this priority, the Disability and Rehabilitation Research Projects (DRRP) must—

(a) Coordinate on research projects of mutual interest with relevant NIDRR-funded projects, as identified through consultation with the NIDRR project officer;
(b) Involve individuals with disabilities in planning and implementing the DRRP's research, training, and dissemination activities, and in evaluating its work; and
(c) Identify anticipated outcomes (i.e., advances in knowledge or changes and improvements in policy, practice, behavior, and system capacity) that are linked to the applicant's stated grant objectives.

Specific Criteria for This Competition:
The following selection criteria are used to evaluate applications under the DRRP program. The maximum score for all of these criteria is 100 points. The maximum score for each criterion is indicated in parentheses.

(a) Importance of the problem. (8 points total).

(1) The Secretary considers the importance of the problem.
(2) In determining the importance of the problem, the Secretary considers the following factors:
(i) The extent to which the applicant clearly describes the need and target population (**4 points**).
(ii) The extent to which the proposed project will have a beneficial impact on the target population (**4 points**).

(b) Responsiveness to an absolute or competitive priority (8 points total).

(1) The Secretary considers the responsiveness of the application to an absolute or competitive priority published in the *Federal Register*.
(2) In determining the application's responsiveness to the absolute or competitive priority, the Secretary considers the following factors:
(i) The extent to which the applicant addresses all requirements of the absolute or competitive priority (**4 points**).
(ii) The extent to which the applicant's proposed activities are likely to achieve the purposes of the absolute or competitive priority (**4 points**).

(c) Design of research activities (40 points total).

(1) The Secretary considers the extent to which the design of research activities is likely to be effective in accomplishing the objectives of the project.

(2) In determining the extent to which the design is likely to be effective in accomplishing the objectives of the project, the Secretary considers the following factors:
(i) The extent to which the research activities constitute a coherent, sustained approach to research in the field, including a substantial addition to the state-of-the-art (**6 points**).
(ii) The extent to which the methodology of each proposed research activity is meritorious, including consideration of the extent to which—
(A) The proposed design includes a comprehensive and informed review of the current literature, demonstrating knowledge of the state-of-the-art (**5 points**).
(B) Each research hypothesis is theoretically sound and based on current knowledge (**5 points**).
(C) Each sample population is appropriate and of sufficient size (**8 points**).
(D) The data collection and measurement techniques are appropriate and likely to be effective (**8 points**).
(E) The data analysis methods are appropriate (**8 points**).

(d) Design of dissemination activities (8 points total).
(1) The Secretary considers the extent to which the design of dissemination activities is likely to be effective in accomplishing the objectives of the project.
(2) In determining the extent to which the design is likely to be effective in accomplishing the objectives of the project, the Secretary considers the following factors:
(i) The extent to which the methods for dissemination are of sufficient quality, intensity, and duration (**4 points**).
(ii) The extent to which the information to be disseminated will be accessible to individuals with disabilities (**4 points**).

(e) Plan of operation (6 points total).
(1) The Secretary considers the quality of the plan of operation.
(2) In determining the quality of the plan of operation, the Secretary considers the following factor:
(i) The adequacy of the plan of operation to achieve the objectives of the proposed project on time and within budget, including clearly defined responsibilities, and timelines for accomplishing project tasks (**6 points**).

(f) Collaboration (4 points total).
(1) The Secretary considers the quality of collaboration.
(2) In determining the quality of collaboration, the Secretary considers the following factor:
(i) The extent to which the applicant's proposed collaboration with one or more agencies, organizations, or institutions is likely to be effective in achieving the relevant proposed activities of the project **(4 points)**.

continued

BOX A4-1 Continued

(g) Adequacy and reasonableness of the budget (4 points total).

(1) The Secretary considers the adequacy and the reasonableness of the proposed budget.

(2) In determining the adequacy and the reasonableness of the proposed budget, the Secretary considers the following factors:

(i) The extent to which the costs are reasonable in relation to the proposed project activities (**2 points**).

(ii) The extent to which the budget for the project, including any subcontracts, is adequately justified to support the proposed project activities (**2 points**).

(h) Plan of evaluation (8 points total).

(1) The Secretary considers the quality of the plan of evaluation.

(2) In determining the quality of the plan of evaluation, the Secretary considers the following factors:

(i) The extent to which the plan of evaluation provides for periodic assessment of progress toward—

(A) Implementing the plan of operation (**4 points**); and

(B) Achieving the project's intended outcomes and expected impacts (**4 points**).

(i) Project staff (10 points total).

(1) The Secretary considers the quality of the project staff.

(2) In determining the quality of the project staff, the Secretary considers the extent to which the applicant encourages applications for employment from persons who are members of groups that have traditionally been underrepresented based on race, color, national origin, gender, age, or disability (**4 points**).

(3) In addition, the Secretary considers the following factors:

(i) The extent to which the key personnel and other key staff have appropriate training and experience in disciplines required to conduct all proposed activities (**3 points**).

(ii) The extent to which the commitment of staff time is adequate to accomplish all the proposed activities of the project (**3 points**).

(j) Adequacy and accessibility of resources (4 points).

(1) The Secretary considers the adequacy and accessibility of the applicant's resources to implement the proposed project.

(2) In determining the adequacy and accessibility of resources, the Secretary considers the following factors:

(i) The extent to which the applicant is committed to provide adequate facilities, equipment, other resources, including administrative support, and laboratories, if appropriate (**2 points**).

(ii) The extent to which the facilities, equipment, and other resources are appropriately accessible to individuals with disabilities who may use the facilities, equipment, and other resources of the project (**2 points**).

NOTE: After the substantive review by the committee, but before publication of this report, NIDRR changed the function of Part 350 subcriteria. Selection criteria from Part 350 continue to use subcriteria but no longer include a breakdown of main criteria point values across the subcriteria (similar to the criteria from Part 359).

SOURCE: NIDRR 2009 Application Kit for DRRP 84.133A-4, Center on the Effective Delivery of Rehabilitation Technology by State Vocational Rehabilitation Agencies to Improve Employment Outcomes.

5

Grant Management

This chapter addresses the following two key study questions:

Key Question #3. What planning and budgetary processes does the grantee use to promote high-quality outputs?

Key Question #5. To what extent are the results of the reviewed research and development outputs used to inform new projects by both the grantee and NIDRR?

These questions are addressed together in this chapter within the larger framework of grant management because the information gathered by the committee indicated they are interrelated. A firm foundation of grant management processes at the agency and grant levels (in terms of planning, quality assurance, reporting, and resource management) sets the stage for successful grant implementation and production of outputs, which in turn can influence the likelihood of informing new projects.

To correspond with the Key Question #3, the first section of this chapter describes how the National Institute on Disability and Rehabilitation Research (NIDRR) manages grants through its agency structure and processes, the planning and budgetary processes used by grantees in managing their grants to promote high-quality outputs, and how NIDRR's grant monitoring efforts facilitate grantees' planning and budgetary processes. Corresponding to Key Question #5, the second section summarizes information from grantees concerning how their research and development outputs have been used to inform new projects and collaborations, as well as how NIDRR uses the results of grantees' research. Conclusions are presented at the end of each section; the first section also includes recommendations to improve the grant management process.

GRANT MANAGEMENT PROCESSES

To address the planning and budgetary processes used by grantees, it is necessary to examine these grantee-level processes and associated requirements in the larger context of the structure and processes that support grant management at NIDRR and to obtain the perspectives of both NIDRR grantees and NIDRR staff. To these ends, the committee reviewed existing documentation on NIDRR's grant management and monitoring processes, interviewed NIDRR management to gather additional information about the processes,[1] collected information from principal investigators about the processes they use for managing grants, and interviewed NIDRR staff to obtain their perspectives on how grant monitoring facilitates grantees' efforts to manage their grants for successful results.

NIDRR's Grant Management Structure and Processes

NIDRR uses both the U.S. Department of Education (ED) and its own postaward grant management procedures and practices (U.S. Department of Education, 2009) to establish working partnerships with grantees and to monitor projects for performance and financial compliance. Grant management activities are supported by ED's web-based grant management system, called G5; by the Office of Special Education and Rehabilitative Services' (OSERS') web-based records management system, called TRIM; and by NIDRR's Annual Performance Report (APR) system. A postaward conference sets the stage for managing individual grants with regard to needs and expectations, and NIDRR uses various strategies to monitor grantee progress.

Setting the Stage for Individual Grant Management

The planning and budgetary processes used by grantees evolve directly from NIDRR procedures concerning grant selection, the peer review process, and negotiated postaward grant management activities (National Institute on Disability and Rehabilitation Research, 2010). The evaluation of grant proposals includes rating such elements as plans for operation and evaluation, as well as the adequacy and reasonableness of the budget

[1]The committee conducted interviews with NIDRR and ED management in four sessions during summer 2010 and one session in spring 2011.

and resources. Within 30 days of an award, NIDRR project staff conduct a postaward conference with the grantee (U.S. Department of Education, 2009). The purpose of this conference is to

- establish a mutual understanding of the expected project outcomes;
- establish a mutual understanding of the measures to be used for assessing the project's progress and results;
- clarify the frequency of and methods for project monitoring and ongoing communication between NIDRR and the grantee;
- discuss other technical assistance to be provided by NIDRR or other service providers;
- review and clarify relevant regulatory or statutory requirements; and
- review and clarify project activity and/or budget issues and concerns.

NIDRR staff generally conduct the conference via telephone, but the conference may also take place in person or via e-mail or written communication. Staff use a standard checklist to conduct the conference that covers such items as the grant award notification; the content of the initial award letter; the content of the proposal; peer reviewers' comments and concerns; progress toward Institutional Review Board (IRB) approval, where applicable; relevant performance measures; expectations regarding NIDRR's online APR; and planning and reporting of outcomes. NIDRR staff document the content of the conference and all subsequent contacts with the grantee in the official grant file.

NIDRR's Grant Monitoring

NIDRR's written procedures call for establishing working partnerships with grantees to monitor projects for performance and financial compliance (U.S. Department of Education, 2009). Following the postaward conference, periodic monitoring takes place as appropriate in accordance with a basic set of monitoring procedures to ensure the achievement of results specific to the application and any revisions, as well as progress against established performance measures that were discussed in the conference. Monitoring tools include electronic quarterly fiscal reporting and annual monitoring reports on activities undertaken during the previous fiscal year. Recipients of multiyear discretionary awards must complete an APR and submit it to NIDRR.

Fiscal monitoring As part of the monitoring process, NIDRR project officers pay particular attention to grantees' fiscal activities (U.S. Department of Education, 2009). The project officers review grantees' cash drawn down on an annual basis (or more frequently if a grantee experiences performance problems). They generally use the G5 system to determine whether actual cash draws are consistent with expected expenditures based on a project's scope of work and milestones.

Annual Performance Report The APR that recipients of multiyear discretionary awards must submit to their project officer provides data that relate progress based on the scope and objectives of the approved application or any approved revisions (U.S. Department of Education, 2009). NIDRR has developed the APR as a web-based online reporting system (National Institute on Disability and Rehabilitation Research, 2009). The APR system contains sections on general information, award abstract, budget, funding, descriptions of research and development projects, output summaries, and descriptions of the most important outputs. Grantees also report on their progress in implementing their disability-focused research, development, training, technical assistance, and knowledge translation. Grantees use the APR as well to report on the results or accomplishments of this work. According to NIDRR documentation, the APR system exceeds the minimum ED requirements for reporting (National Institute on Disability and Rehabilitation Research, 2010). Project officers use their grantees' APRs for monitoring and tracking progress and results. The APR is maintained by an external contractor who also performs analyses of the data for management and reporting purposes according to specifications provided by NIDRR.

Formative reviews Formative reviews with individual grantees are occasionally convened (two to three times a year) to give grantees who have been identified as needing additional assistance the opportunity to discuss their research methodology with experts in their field. A formative review is typically conducted after the project officer has tried other means of assisting the grantee. Experts from the original peer review panel are invited if available; if not, other experts in the grantee's topic area are invited. The experts generally conduct the review by teleconference or webinar and provide suggestions to the grantee for improving the research plan.

Monitoring of at-risk grants The processes described above pertain to routine monitoring of grants. In response to a recent ED initiative, NIDRR is instituting a new process for identifying grants at risk of failure to comply with program requirements, reach performance goals, comply with grant administration and financial management requirements, and/or account for past performance (National Institute on Disability and Rehabilitation Research, 2010). At-risk grants may be identified at different points. One point may be during the peer review process. Although a grant application may receive a fundable score in peer review, there may be concerns about certain elements of the application (e.g., feasibility of achieving the projected sample size). At-risk grants may also be identified at the postfunding conference, through routine teleconferences, or through a grantee's APR. Criteria for identifying grants that may be at risk for not reaching performance goals include prior performance; peer reviewer concerns; concerns raised during the site visit; staff concerns regarding feasibility with respect to staffing, resources, or design; slow startup; failure to hire key staff; slow enrollment of subjects; loss of a key collaborator; or failure to report progress. Administrative and financial criteria for identifying at-risk grants include failure to draw down funds, excessive drawdown, or some other financial disclosure or deviation that demonstrates failure to adhere to ED guidelines. Strategies for monitoring at-risk grants, used as needed and in consultation with NIDRR management, include conducting formative reviews; establishing performance targets; scheduling regular, frequent written or oral updates; conducting site visits; changing the status of a grant to a cooperative agreement; and delaying continuation awards (National Institute on Disability and Rehabilitation Research, 2010).

Grantee Perspectives on Their Grant Management Processes

To obtain grantees' perspectives on their grant management processes, the 30 grantees who participated in the summative evaluation were asked to complete a set of written questions asking them to describe what types of planning, project management, and budgetary processes were used to promote high-quality outputs. They were asked to consider the following questions when crafting their statements:

- Which processes you used were helpful and how? How could they be improved?
- Did you dedicate funds for quality assurance activities?
- How did you track progress and spending against your original plans for the grant?
- If grants or projects were jointly funded by NIDRR and other extramural or intramural sources, how did you ensure that NIDRR resources were used exclusively for NIDRR-funded activities?
- How do NIDRR grant management processes influence the quality of outputs?

This set of questions on grant management was asked at the end of a longer questionnaire on which the grantees described the outputs that were to be reviewed by the committee in the summative evaluation. Principal investigators of 28 of the 30 grantees that participated in the summative evaluation responded to this set of questions. Because respondents did not necessarily answer all the questions or answer the questions the same way, the number of respondents for each answer varies. Narrative data were analyzed using standard qualitative analysis techniques (see Chapter 2 for a description of these techniques). The number of grantees that responded to each set of questions is noted in the section headings below.

Consensus Views

Except for new product development projects and complex multicenter studies, grantees reported that the current NIDRR requirements for planning, project management, and budgeting generally helped ensure quality outputs. Several commented on the positive trend in changes to the requirements over the years. For example, one grantee cited the changes made during the grant under study:

> In Years 1 and 2 of the grant they were required to report more of an "output count" methodology. In year 3 a different reporting method was introduced focused on the development of short-term and long-term goals. Then "accomplishment nuggets" were to be nominated, with rigorous reporting for each nomination, relating back to one of the outcome goals. Finally, in Years 4 and 5 NIDRR stabilized on a somewhat less rigorous, more easily understood reporting of "most important" outputs, tied to one of up to four outcome oriented goals. . . . NIDRR has been making good progress in recent years on stabilizing its evaluation protocols and procedures.

Planning (N = 14)

The bulk of planning for the full range of projects was done in the proposal-writing stage, for which NIDRR has detailed requirements. As one respondent explained:

> The NIDRR requirements are quite detailed and extensive. . . . In the sense that the plans are well developed, the NIDRR grants make planning and management fairly routine since we are carrying out the commitments made in the proposal.

It was also noted that having an evaluation plan was particularly helpful, as was having a quality assurance plan.

In addition to up-front planning, continuous planning was carried out for more complex grants through regular planning meetings and consultation with other researchers as needed. Although the many requirements were off-putting for some in the beginning, they proved to be helpful (except for new product development). One respondent noted:

> NIDRR built in the development of outputs into planning. This made us more thoughtful.

Respondents attributed success in implementing their plans to a number of factors—including not having overly ambitious goals, having a high degree of oversight by the project director, using feedback from multisite study investigators, and including the development of outputs in planning.

Respondents also noted difficulties in creating and maintaining an adequate plan, which may be instructive in designing and implementing changes to the process. Examples given for difficulties encountered included the following:

- Projects deviating from more standard NIDRR research projects. For example, new product development was viewed as a fundamentally different type of project than other academic research efforts around which NIDRR processes were developed, so many requirements and metrics did not fit these projects.
- A complex, multisite project for which there were no planning models or in which fidelity of implementation over large numbers of sites caused management and budget issues.
- Projects may have been adequately planned under procedures in effect at the start of the grant, but plans had to be changed when NIDRR implemented process changes mid-project, such as imposing new reporting requirements.
- Cases were cited in which unpredictable events impacted staffing. In one case, for example, project staff were jointly funded by funds for another project. When they lost the funds for the other project, the staff left the NIDRR project as well.

Project Management (N = 24)

The variety of the projects resulted in a range of management complexity, from a single action on small individual grants (e.g., Switzer)—writing one check to the university that oversaw the dispersal of salary funds—to highly complex protocols for larger center grants requiring complex management and fidelity in implementation across many sites for success. Key project management elements specified by one or more respondents included the following:

- the APR was noted as particularly helpful in "keep[ing] to both the budget and the timeline," although the APR may not reflect accomplishments, such as journal articles, not in the original plan and delayed until the end of the project;
- quarterly meetings with the NIDRR project officer;
- the quality of NIDRR project officers;
- weekly, monthly, and annual meetings of project staff;

- specification of the quality assurance responsibilities and tasks of project staff and committees;
- annual meetings of project advisory boards;
- online project planning tools, such as a commercial project management reporting system used by another research center or an online management tool provided by the institution;
- task analytic project management;
- sufficient training and supervision for complex, multisite grant implementers;
- use of institutional grant management and budget management services where available;
- frequent and consistent project monitoring; and
- the quality of investigators and technical staff.

Dedicated Quality Assurance Funds (N = 14)

Of the 14 respondents who addressed this issue, only 8 reported separating out quality assurance activities from the rest of their budget. Quality assurance activities were generally an integral part of the planned project. To the extent that oversight was part of staff responsibilities, salary for those staff was obligated for quality assurance activities. A few respondents mentioned dedicating quality assurance funds for bringing in external experts on their oversight committee, for funding audio taping and ongoing data reports during the study, for monitoring implementation visits, for conducting conference calls, and for traveling to NIDRR and principal investigator meetings. One comment noted that the respondent's institution would not allow budgeting for quality assurance activities; however, it was not clear how the institution defined quality assurance activities.

Budgetary Processes (N = 20)

Monitoring of expenditures and budgets often was done by institutional grant management or accounting divisions or through the use of project management software. Others tracked the budget as part of the project director's monitoring. When asked specifically about what procedures grantees used to ensure that only NIDRR funds were used to fund NIDRR activities in jointly funded projects, only three grantees indicated the use of joint funding. One grantee reported working with the NIDRR project officer to ensure that there was no double billing of time. Another stated that the principal investigator and project director identified for the university financial office how NIDRR resources were used exclusively to support NIDRR-funded activities and to track in-kind and other funding.

How NIDRR Grant Management Processes Influence Results (N = 18)

When respondents were asked how NIDRR grant management processes influence grant results, topics cited most frequently with regard to fostering successful grants and high-quality outputs related to interactions with NIDRR project officers, reporting requirements, flexibility in management and budgeting, and timing of the grant application process. Following are some of the points made:

- **Interactions with NIDRR project officers**
  —The attitude (high standards and emphasis on quality) of the NIDRR project officer has the greatest impact on quality (based on experience with three project officers).
  —One grantee stated that it would have been useful to have more regular contacts or reporting opportunities earlier in the final design and proceduralization stages of the study.
- **Reporting requirements**
  —The APR requires that budget information be provided by the accounting department, which has been very useful.
  —The detailed tracking requirements of the online APR, although quite time-consuming and burdensome, provide motivation to keep focused on the overall project goals for high-quality products.
  —Quarterly reports are helpful as a quality assurance mechanism.
  —One grantee praised NIDRR for its recently implemented goal- and objective-oriented reporting scheme, which was viewed as far superior to previous schemes. The grantee did note, however, that the new scheme limits reporting of accomplishments, meaning some good work is not being reported.
  —One grantee suggested that reports should focus more on how the work of the grant is either succeeding or failing at bringing effective and practical new services and/or devices to the market.
  —Another commented that methods should be developed for capturing outputs produced at the end, or shortly after the end, of a project.
- **Flexibility in management and budgeting**
  —One grantee commented that NIDRR needs more flexibility to extend its research and development grants and adapt budgets not only to fit the initial scope of a project but also to accommodate discoveries and opportunities encountered during the course of the project.
  —Different management tools are needed for projects involving new product development rather than academic research.

—The level of funding of Model System grants is disproportionate to what is expected of grantees. For example, the insufficient funding is a major limiting factor for collaborative research efforts, which need to be well planned if scientifically rigorous treatment and intervention studies with adequate sample sizes are to be carried out.

- **Timing of the grant application process**
  —Standard deadlines are needed for grant applications. Having predetermined dates for application submissions would improve timely notification of grant availability and give principal investigators more time to prepare and consequently submit higher-quality plans and applications.
  —Applications submitted in January should receive notification of application status and award in the spring to avoid inadequate staffing at the start of the project and subsequent protracted timelines.

NIDRR Staff Perspectives on Grant Monitoring and Grantee Management

NIDRR project officers provide an important bridge between ED's and NIDRR's policies and procedures on grant management and the grantees' management of their grants. They carry out the grant monitoring functions, described in the first section of this chapter, that are aimed at identifying issues related to performance and fiscal compliance with grant requirements.[2] NIDRR procedures emphasize that monitoring activities are conducted in working partnerships with grantees. Comments made by grantees cited above referred to some of the ways in which NIDRR's procedures and processes assist grantees in managing their grants and influence the grant results (e.g., APRs help in keeping grantees focused on goals and products, quarterly reports serve as a quality assurance mechanism, and some project officers promote high standards and an emphasis on quality).

To learn more about this important interface between NIDRR's grant monitoring processes and grantees' management of their grants, 16 NIDRR project staff were interviewed in person and asked a series of open-ended questions about their activities and specific questions that related to grantee

[2] In addition to grant monitoring, project officers have duties related to peer review and priority setting (covered in other chapters of this report). Depending on their own areas of expertise, some also have responsibilities for coordinating activities for certain grant programs, such as the Field Initiated Project or Model System grants, and for developing special initiatives in such areas as knowledge translation. There are currently 14 project officer positions within NIDRR (National Institute on Disability and Rehabilitation Research, 2011), but 4 were vacant at the time of this writing. In fiscal year 2009, there were a total of 230 grants funded by NIDRR (U.S. Department of Education, 2011).

planning and budgeting processes designed to improve quality. Not all of the interviewees were project officers; some were in supervisory and other management roles. The discussion of these qualitative data is organized into issues and initiatives that could relate to the processes used by grantees to ensure quality.

Issues Related to Time

One issue that may be tangentially related to the amount and quality of grantee processes to promote high-quality outputs is the NIDRR staff time spent in monitoring activities. Staff reported a wide variation in the amount of time spent in monitoring grants—from 35 to 80 percent of their time. As stated above, NIDRR staff have other responsibilities to different degrees in addition to grant monitoring, which accounts for this wide variation. However, staff commented that the large workload of project officers (approximately 20 to 25 grants) often does not allow for as much attention to grantees as is needed. Also as reported in the *NIDRR Fiscal Year 2011 Grant Monitoring Plan*, NIDRR has seen a 25 percent reduction in staff over the last 6 years (National Institute on Disability and Rehabilitation Research, 2010), which would impact caseload size.

Issues Related to Type and Frequency of Communications with Grantees

Staff reported that the type and frequency of communications with grantees also vary, depending largely on grantee needs and issues related to performance and fiscal compliance. A variety of monitoring procedures are used, including periodic telephone conversations, e-mails that ask questions or provide consultation information, teleconferences, quarterly written reports, and the APR. It was commented that NIDRR's forms and reporting requirements are not easy for grantees because of the complexity of federal rules, which staff often must spend time translating for new grantees. Staff reported that the structured postaward teleconference has been helpful in establishing expectations for grantee performance and preventing potential problems in complying with these federal rules. They commented that limited travel funds have not permitted sufficient on-site monitoring for grants that require higher levels of technical assistance. This observation is confirmed in the *NIDRR Fiscal Year 2011 Grant Monitoring Plan* (National Institute on Disability and Rehabilitation Research, 2010), which states that the number of on-site monitoring visits and formative reviews is affected by the budget.

Issues Related to Budget

One issue mentioned by several respondents was that grantees often underspend their budgets, especially during startup; this issue is not uncommon with research grants in general. This underspending extends their grants and changes the time frame for output development and project completion. One suggestion made was that staff might be able to identify potential problems and work more with grantees on this issue if they had project-level budget data in addition to grant-level data, especially for larger grants that have multiple projects starting and ending at different points. A related comment was that there is a need for improved ongoing communication between project officers and other NIDRR planning staff who have access to all of the relevant financial information. Another suggestion was that it would be helpful to have standard forms for requesting no-cost extensions.

Issues Related to Consistency

Although it was stated that the frequency of reporting depends on grantee needs, it was suggested that greater consistency is needed across project officers in the schedule for grantee reporting between APRs. It was also suggested that new project officers need more training to foster greater consistency in grant monitoring across grantees.

Initiatives

Staff mentioned that several initiatives are ongoing to improve and facilitate the grant monitoring process. A data group is working on developing new management reports on grant status to help project officers. Efforts are being made to help train new project officers by sharing experiences and providing advice informally. In addition, staff commented that parts of their regular staff meetings are being used to consult about grants that present special monitoring challenges.

Conclusions and Recommendations Related to Grant Management Processes

To address the key study question of what planning and budgetary processes are used by grantees to promote high-quality outputs, the committee considered these grantee-level processes in the larger context of NIDRR's structure and processes that support grant management. With regard to the larger agency context, the *NIDRR Fiscal Year 2011 Grant Monitoring Plan* stemmed from initiatives within ED related to grant monitoring. In 2009, the U.S. Government Accountability Office (GAO) reported on a study of grant monitoring within ED, which included OSERS. The report recommended that ED:

- Develop department-wide guidance on risk assessment, continue efforts to develop new grantee risk assessment tools, . . . and work with the program offices to ensure these tools are implemented.
- Implement a strategy to ensure each program office has staff with sufficient financial monitoring expertise to conduct or assist other program specialists in conducting financial compliance reviews . . .
- Develop an easily accessible mechanism for sharing information across offices about grantees' past and present performance, and an accessible forum for sharing promising practices in grant monitoring to ensure all program offices are able to effectively and efficiently perform all of their duties and responsibilities. (U.S. Government Accountability Office, 2009, p. 19)

In the context of this larger department initiative, NIDRR has developed new risk management assessment and monitoring procedures for grants at risk of failure to comply with program requirements, to reach performance goals, or to comply with grant administration and financial management requirements (National Institute on Disability and Rehabilitation Research, 2010). A follow-up interview with NIDRR executives in April 2011 showed that they are enthusiastically incorporating a risk management approach that will assist them in determining how much and what type of monitoring may be needed. To identify grants at risk, NIDRR is using an ED-recommended rubric with information tailored for NIDRR grantees and drawn from the peer review, the APR, and project monitors.

NIDRR appears to have a good plan and momentum in place for upgrading its routine monitoring and for identifying and monitoring grants that are at risk of noncompliance with the new monitoring plan. On the whole, it appears that grantees appreciate aspects of NIDRR's grant management processes that facilitate their own grant management strategies. Grantees commented that NIDRR's detailed proposal requirements facilitate their planning, that NIDRR builds output development into the planning by means of the postaward conference, that the APR helps grantees adhere to both the budget and the time frame for a project, that the quarterly reports facilitate quality assurance, and that NIDRR project officers with high standards and an emphasis on quality contribute to successful grant results. While grantees generally commented that NIDRR grant management processes were effective in helping them in their own grant management processes, they offered some suggestions for improvement.

Suggestions for improvement from NIDRR staff focused on strengthening their capacity to monitor grants and to help their grantees stay on course in implementing their grants and meeting performance expectations. Among other suggestions, they expressed the need for more workable grant caseloads, additional travel funds for on-site monitoring of grants that require higher levels of technical assistance, more training for new project officers to promote consistency and quality in their monitoring processes, and a freer flow of communication between project officers and NIDRR planning staff in relation to financial information.

Recommendation 5-1: NIDRR should continue to focus efforts on improving its grant monitoring procedures and specific elements of its overall grant management system that impact grantee-level planning, budgets, and the quality of outputs.

Particular emphasis should be placed on continuing to implement the new procedures for monitoring at-risk grants. Given the budgetary constraints on the number of on-site monitoring visits and formative reviews referred to earlier in the section on staff interviews, there will of course be challenges in this area. However, allocation of limited resources for effectively monitoring grantees' planning, budgeting, and outcomes should be a critical consideration in overall resource allocation decisions.

Attention should also be given to grantee and staff suggestions for improving elements of NIDRR's overall grant management system that could impact grantee planning and budgeting and the quality of outputs. In particular, NIDRR should consider the following:

- how the timing of grant applications and notification impact the planning and quality of grant implementation and indirectly the quality of outputs subsequently produced;
- methods NIDRR staff can use when monitoring large multiproject grant budgets to identify project-level variation that could be impacting the overall grant budget (e.g., personnel costs);
- the need for improved communication between project officers and other NIDRR planning staff who have more access to financial information;
- more focused reporting in the APR on new product development, stages of output development, and how the work of grants is bringing effective and practical new services and/or devices to the field or to the market;
- methods for capturing information on outputs produced at the end, or shortly after the end, of grants so the quality and impact of these products can be assessed;
- the need for more consistency across project officers in the schedule of grantee reporting between APRs; and
- the extent to which new project officers are trained to promote consistency in expectations regarding standards of quality.

From the grantee questionnaires, the committee also learned that some grants that are developing innovations in new technologies may not fit well with a management template that calls for strict up-front planning and adherence to original designs and timetables. Similarly, grants funding large, multisite studies may require more or different supervision, monitoring, and technical assistance than more focused or limited studies. These grantees expressed the need for a greater degree of flexibility in management to allow them to stay on the cutting edge of technology or adapt more easily to changing needs of multisite research projects.

Recommendation 5-2: NIDRR should review the requirements placed upon technical innovation grants and large multisite studies to ensure that planning, reporting, supervisory, and technical assistance requirements fit their particular circumstances.

USE OF GRANT RESULTS/OUTPUTS TO INFORM FUTURE PROJECTS

In its logic model, NIDRR depicts its short-term outcomes as the array of outputs generated by grantees, which in turn are expected to inform and generate new projects (National Institute on Disability and Rehabilitation Research, 2006). The fifth main study question of this evaluation was: To what extent are the results of the reviewed research and development outputs used to inform new projects by both the grantee and NIDRR? To address this question, the committee gathered information from NIDRR management about how they use the results of their grantees' research. The principal investigators of the grants reviewed for the summative evaluation provided supplemental information on this subject on the questionnaire they completed in submitting their outputs for review by the committee (see Appendix B).

The specific question asked of grantees was: Have the results of the research and development outputs from this grant, or your prior NIDRR grants, been used to inform the development of new grant applications or other kinds of projects? The objective was not to assess grantees' individual or aggregate productivity, but to determine the extent to which NIDRR grants generate new projects and products. In this vein, the committee asked not only about respondents' present grants but also about what was generated from prior NIDRR grants because of the length of time it takes, for example, to get technology products through various stages of development to commercialization or to develop collaborations that evolve into new projects. The information gathered from grantees is presented first.

Use of Research and Development Results/Outputs by Grantees

Twenty-eight of the 30 grantees that participated in the summative evaluation responded to this specific question. Of the 28 respondents, 24 indicated that the results of their current or prior NIDRR grants had been used to inform the development of new grant applications or other kinds of projects, funding opportunities, or collaborations. Table 5-1 summarizes the approximate number and type of new projects reported.

In some cases, grantees indicated that multiple grant applications or other project types were generated, without providing specific numbers. In these cases, a "1" was entered as the quantity so as not to overcount the number of projects generated.

As can be seen in the table, these 24 grants generated funding from more than 50 other sources for new projects stemming from the original grant. Nineteen of the new projects were NIDRR-funded, but 13 were funded by other federal agencies. In open-ended remarks, one principal investigator praised NIDRR for encouraging and funding innovative work that is often taken up and expanded by other federal research agencies. Annex 5-1 at the end of this chapter contains a table with more detail about the nature of the new projects generated from existing NIDRR grants. That table is organized by type of NIDRR program mechanism and separates the grants into rows within the program mechanisms. As an example, the table shows new projects that were generated from one Rehabilitation Research and Training Center grant and the various funding sources for those projects, which included NIDRR, the National Institute for Occupational Safety and Health (NIOSH), the Centers for Disease Control and Prevention (CDC), and a private foundation. Table 5-1 above also shows that these 24 grants generated more than 19 new collaborations. The table in Annex 5-1 shows examples of these, such as participants in a Burn Model System project being invited to participate in another university study, networking among NIDRR-funded centers, and collaboration with national-level organizations. Table 5-1 shows that another type of spin-off project involved applying specific outputs—data, instruments, or models—to other projects. Examples included transferring newly gained knowledge on stroke rehabilitation interventions to hip and knee replacement rehabilitation in different types of treatment settings, translating and testing surveys in other languages, and studying the efficacy and effectiveness of a telephone-based problem-solving treatment for a different population of service members after deployment. Commercialization of technology products is a concrete example of grant outputs that have generated new types of outputs and projects, illustrated by the evolution of assistive technology devices.

TABLE 5-1 Number[a] and Type of New Projects Resulting from 24[b] Grants

Type of New Project	Successful Applications	Pending Applications	Other
New Grant (source):			
Centers for Disease Control and Prevention	1		
Department of Defense	4	1	
Department of Labor	2		
Department of Health and Human Services	1		
National Institute on Disability and Rehabilitation Research	19	1	
National Institutes of Health	3	3	
National Institute for Occupational Safety and Health	1		
Social Security Administration	1		
Foundations	2		
Other (university, state, corporation)	17	1	
Collaboration with other researchers and organizations			19
Application of data/instruments/models to other projects			19
Commercialization of technology products			5
Used as basis for convening a major conference or defining and supporting a larger agenda			7
TOTAL	51[a]	6[a]	50[a]

[a]Some respondents indicated that "multiple" projects of a certain type were generated, rather than giving a specific listing or number. Therefore the totals given are approximate.
[b]The 4 other grantees (out of the 28 that responded to this question) indicated that their results were not used to inform the development of new grant applications and other kinds of projects. Two respondents stated that their grants had come to an end point because on one a long-standing question had been successfully addressed, and on the other that there was no opportunity to propose further work in his specific line of research as an independent researcher. A third respondent stated that the study was still in the grant cycle but was fully expected to inform the development of new grant applications and projects; the fourth offered no explanation.
SOURCE: Generated by the committee based on data from the grantee questionnaire.

Use of Research and Development Results by NIDRR

NIDRR management informed the committee during early interviews about how the agency uses the results of its grantees' work. Results are used for performance monitoring, for priority setting, and for dissemination, all of which in some way inform new projects, such as by shaping priorities and funding decisions. As stated in the first section of this chapter, NIDRR's APR system collects routine information from grantees on their outputs and accomplishments. In addition to monitoring grantee performance, this information is used for NIDRR's Government Performance and Results Act (GPRA) performance reporting and in annual reports to Congress through ED. These reports, among other considerations, may influence the funding of new projects.

In its annual priority-setting process, NIDRR considers the knowledge that has been gained from the products of its various program mechanisms as one key input. This information is obtained from NIDRR project officers, from the APR system, from state-of-the-science conferences organized by center grants, and from other grantee meetings during the year.

Knowledge dissemination and transfer is at the core of NIDRR's logic model. Accordingly, the agency has incorporated requirements in grant applications for grantees to disseminate knowledge and information about outputs they have produced. Dissemination is accomplished in various ways, such as through publications, conferences, workshops, and websites.

Conclusions on the Use of Results and Outputs of NIDRR Grants

The key study questions for the external evaluation of NIDRR and its grantees were phrased in terms of the extent to which NIDRR's key processes (i.e., priority setting, peer review, and grant management) are conducted in such a way as to enhance the quality of final results. Final results can be viewed in several different ways—as the quality of a research portfolio resulting from the priority-setting process; as the quality of grants resulting from peer review; or as the quality of outputs resulting from multiple influences, such as the scientific characteristics of the researchers and the key agency processes of priority setting, peer review, and grant management. This section examines final results in terms of NIDRR's intermediate or short-term outcomes (i.e., the extent to which grants and their products generate new projects and/or are used to inform NIDRR priorities).

From the information gathered from grantees and presented at the beginning of this section, the committee found that the results of the reviewed research and development projects have been used to generate new projects by grantees to a great extent. That 24 grants generated twice as many new projects is evidence of "adoption and use of knowledge," which is a core tenet of NIDRR's mission.

Of course the projects that were generated vary in purpose, scope, and funding levels. For the present evaluation, the committee was able to take only a brief snapshot of this type of short-term outcome (i.e., generation of new projects). Grantees were asked to describe briefly in writing what new projects or products were generated by their current grants after they had completed a long questionnaire asking for detailed information about the quality of their outputs. The volume and substance of the information they provided call for further exploration—for example, to examine more deeply the pathway and evolution of knowledge/product development for individual grants and for sets of grants in different NIDRR portfolios. Tracing the pathway of grants and outputs would be helpful in answering questions about NIDRR's impact.

REFERENCES

National Institute on Disability and Rehabilitation Research. (2006). Department of Education: National Institute on Disability and Rehabilitation Research—Notice of Final Long-Range Plan for Fiscal Years 2005–2009. *Federal Register, 71*(31), 8,166-8,200.

National Institute on Disability and Rehabilitation Research. (2009). *Briefing book for The National Academies.* Unpublished document. Washington, DC: National Institute on Disability and Rehabilitation Research.

National Institute on Disability and Rehabilitation Research. (2010). *NIDRR fiscal year 2011 grant monitoring plan.* Washington, DC: National Institute on Disability and Rehabilitation Research.

National Institute on Disability and Rehabilitation Research. (2011). *NIDRR organizational chart.* Unpublished document. Washington, DC: National Institute on Disability and Rehabilitation Research.

U.S. Department of Education. (2009). *Handbook for the discretionary grant process.* Washington, DC: U.S. Department of Education.

U.S. Department of Education, Office of Special Education and Rehabilitative Services, Rehabilitation Services Administration. (2011). *Annual report on federal activities under the Rehabilitation Act, fiscal year 2011.* Washington, DC: U.S. Department of Education.

U.S. Government Accountability Office. (2009). *Department of Education could improve its processes with greater focus on assessing risks, acquiring financial skills, and sharing information.* GAO-10-57. Washington, DC: U.S. Government Accountability Office.

ANNEX 5-1
SUMMARIES OF NEW GRANTS OR OTHER TYPES OF PROJECTS GENERATED BY NIDRR GRANTEES

Grantees were asked to describe briefly what new grant applications, other projects, funding opportunities, or collaborations have resulted from the grant that was reviewed by the committee or prior NIDRR grants. The following table corresponds to Table 5-1 in the main text of the chapter and provides additional detail about the new projects for each of the 24 grantees who provided this information. The table is organized by program mechanism and grantee. Under "New Grant," "X" refers to funded grants; "X*" refers to grant applications/proposals that have not, or not as yet, been funded. An X or X* may refer to more than one grant.

TABLE A5-1

Grant (Program Mechanism)	Nature of New Projects
Grant 1 (Burn Model System)	• New NIDRR grant to evaluate a social skills training program to overcome social anxiety during community reentry • A study evaluating the effects of skin grafting on the ability of individuals to improve temperature regulation • A Burn Research State-of-the-Science Conference under the leadership of Model System and the American Burn Association • Funding from an institute in the Midwest and the American Burn Association to hold a consensus meeting on a social skills training program • Participants in the NIDRR longitudinal database have participated in another study at a medical center in the South • Video led to strengthened collaborations with national-level organizations • Burn survivor support groups
Grant 2 (Disability and Rehabilitation Research Project-General [DRRP])	• Proposal for a project on seniors with sensory loss with a university in Canada • Proposed Field Initiated Projects (FIPs) in 2005/6/7 on low-vision service delivery models for older blind and dual sensory impaired seniors • Rehabilitation Research and Training Center (RRTC)-funded project on employment for persons who are blind or visually impaired • Contacted the National Eye Institute and National Institutes of Health (NIH) about the need to have videos developed on various eye conditions, presented in American Sign Language; they were responsive to the need, but nothing has developed as yet • Good interactions and brainstorming with a Rehabilitation Engineering Research Center (RERC) and several veteran centers • Collaboration with a national center on visual and auditory impairment on one project
Grant 3 (DRRP)	• Led to successful application and awards to translate and test surveys in Spanish and to conduct a field test with California Medicaid plans and a home- and community-based waiver program • Principal investigator serving on two federal advisory panels
Grant 4 (DRRP)	• Department of Defense (DOD) funding to study the efficacy and effectiveness of a telephone-based problem-solving treatment in service members after deployment; the study uses a detailed, scripted, and modular intervention focusing on problem-solving treatment and behavioral activation and involves collaborating with two military bases and a separate data center • Use of lessons learned from this study and successful single-center studies

Types of Projects				
New grant	Basis for conference or new agenda	Collaboration	Application of output to other projects	Commercialization
X				
X		X		
	X			
	X			
		X		
		X		
			X	
X*				
X*				
X				
		X	X	
		X		
		X		
			X	
		X	X	
X		X		
			X	

continued

TABLE A5-1 Continued

Grant (Program Mechanism)	Nature of New Projects
Grant 5 (DRRP)	• Preliminary support by NIDRR has led to annual funding from major private corporate foundations to continue the grant's work • A preliminary research framework on advancing economic self-sufficiency for people with disabilities led to the development of curriculum and training programs in six states and funding from state developmental disability councils and Medicaid Infrastructure grants • On an annual basis, the $300,000 from NIDRR was leveraged to support program development, additional research, expansion of financial service options, and an inclusive economic empowerment model in more than 100 cities • A newsletter, which is received by more than 20,000 individuals in the disability community monthly, has received additional support from multiple private foundations to help expand its reach • NIDRR funding has led to new funding from the Social Security Administration, the Department of Labor, the Department of Health and Human Services, the Assets for Independence Act, and the Department of the Treasury • The principal investigator on the project has become the chair of a work group within an important consortium that involves more than 750 community groups, financial institutions, government agencies, and businesses that are working together to advance new options for financial stability and mobility for working-age adults with disabilities
Grant 6 (Field Initiated Project [FIP])	• New NIDRR grant for a Rehabilitation Research and Training Center • Collaboration across the university and with professional associations to provide new knowledge about differences in employer practices in hiring, retaining, and advancing individuals with disabilities and the relationship between these practices and employment outcomes, leading to the design of targeted interventions
Grant 7 (FIP)	• Small Business Innovation Research (SBIR) funding by one of the grantee's strategic partners • The project has helped define and support a larger long-range development agenda for applications that support self-management and community living

Types of Projects

New grant	Basis for conference or new agenda	Collaboration	Application of output to other projects	Commercialization
X				
X				
X			X	
X				
X				
		X		
X				
		X		
X				
	X			

continued

TABLE A5-1 Continued

Grant (Program Mechanism)	Nature of New Projects
Grant 8 (FIP)	• NIH grant on training methods for improving the intelligibility of speech in a noisy environment • A grant submitted to NIH on methods of noise reduction in hearing aids is in review
Grant 9 (FIP)	• Opened a whole new line of research in the United States on the relationship between multifocal lenses and falling and related crises • Many possibilities for new lines of research regarding worker safety, falling prevention, and other related health issues • Led to support for university intramural research • NIH applications regarding safety, falling prevention, and the health of individuals related to the optics and brain function of adapting to multifocal lenses • NIDRR proposals regarding safety, falling prevention, and the health of individuals related to the optics and brain function of adapting to multifocal lenses
Grant 10 (FIP)	• Help in editing a special 12-article supplement to the original study • Help in funding a research utilization conference • Leveraged a Fulbright Scholar grant for an international data analysis • Applied the approach to other issues, such as a comparative effectiveness study of hip and knee replacement rehabilitation in skilled nursing facilities and inpatient rehabilitation facilities • Used the same study design for a new NIDRR-funded study
Grant 11 (FIP)	• This grant application arose as part of a Traumatic Brain Injury Model System (TBIMS) grant; the grantee expanded on the methodology as well as the theoretical concepts addressed in that first NIDRR-funded project
Grant 12 (Rehabilitation Engineering Research Center [RERC])	• Building on the results of the first grant, RERC was refunded

Types of Projects				
New grant	Basis for conference or new agenda	Collaboration	Application of output to other projects	Commercialization
X				
X*				
	X			
	X			
X				
X*				
X*				
		X		
	X			
X				
			X	
X				
X				
X				

continued

TABLE A5-1 Continued

Grant (Program Mechanism)	Nature of New Projects
Grant 13 (RERC)	• This grant's work has informed the work of a wide range of both commercial and research projects involving more than 100 different partners in more than a dozen countries totaling more than $50 million • The virtual assistive technology work has evolved into an international collaborative effort involving more than 40 partners on every continent except Antarctica and has influenced grants from the National Science Foundation (NSF), NIDRR, the Canadian government, and the European Commission, among others • The work on accessibility guidelines has influenced policy throughout the world and led to a large number of research and development projects internationally • The work on interfaces was used to inform the development of one of the project areas in the current RERC • The cross-disability interface work has influenced both federal regulations and commercial product design • The user needs work has influenced international policy and standards design • The grant's work led to follow-up work, including an invention that allows people with "locked in" syndrome (which paralyzes the body, except for the eyes, but leaves the mind alert) to communicate; this invention was recognized as one of *Time* magazine's 50 best inventions of 2009
Grant 14 (Rehabilitation Research and Training Center [RRTC])	• A new RRTC was funded by NIDRR based on the work of this grant • DOD funding for two projects based on the work of this grant • This project was used to support a funded application for a Model System grant
Grant 15 (RRTC)	• NIDRR funding to continue the center as an RRTC to support three research areas; the NIDRR grant resulted in two articles • National Institute for Occupational Safety and Health (NIOSH) funding for collaboration to study injury among workers • CDC contract to report on training and health promotion for the workforce • Multiple Kaiser Family Foundation grants
Grant 16 (RRTC)	• Successful RRTC proposals for three subsequent RRTC grants • 2009 technical assistance grant • Data from one RRTC project used by another project to inform disability advocacy and policies • A state agency replicated a reporting model developed under this grant for use in a different grant

Types of Projects				
New grant	Basis for conference or new agenda	Collaboration	Application of output to other projects	Commercialization
X		X		X
X		X		
X			X	
			X	
			X	X
			X	
X			X	
X				
X				
X				
X				
X				
X				
X				
X				
X				
			X	
X			X	

continued

TABLE A5-1 Continued

Grant (Program Mechanism)	Nature of New Projects
Grant 17 (Small Business Innovation Research II [SBIR-II])	• Work has informed public access improvements at locations around the country • Ongoing work with SBIR to develop a virtual collection of scientific, technical, economic, and mathematical images such as the periodic table; a scientific calculator; the Sodoku game; and classic science images, such as cells and machinery—all designed to work in conjunction with the assistive technology designed as part of this grant
Grant 18 (SBIR-II)	• Results have provided the opportunity for commercialization of the device • Results have provided opportunities for new research in transportation
Grant 19 (Spinal Cord Injury Model System [SCIMS])	• Two collaborative research projects • The Model System increased visibility and has provided the infrastructure for conducting research, allowing the grantee to partner with a Department of Veterans Affairs medical center; networking efforts resulted in a wider range of patient and physician and other clinician participation • Secured a comprehensive network of collaborative partnerships resulting in a successful NIH R-01 application
Grant 20 (SCIMS)	• Small funding ($50,000) to do more with testosterone research
Grant 21 (Switzer Fellowship [Switzer])	• NIDRR FIP grant • Three separate grants from separate funders using prospective data to test social network analysis • NIH R24 pilot award and collaborations with three specialists in three different institutions
Grant 22 (Switzer)	• Using the lessons learned from this study, the grantee has been funded for a follow-up study by DOD, and is working with two military bases and a separate data center
Grant 23 (Traumatic Brain Injury Model System [TBIMS])	• Applied for DOD funding; awaiting reply but still collaborating with TBIMS and Spinal Cord Injury Model System (SCIMS) centers on this study
Grant 24 (TBIMS)	• Formed the basis for the primary local research project being advanced in the current TBIMS cycle

SOURCE: Generated by the committee based on data from the grantee questionnaire.

Types of Projects

New grant	Basis for conference or new agenda	Collaboration	Application of output to other projects	Commercialization
			X	X
			X	X
				X
	X			
X		X		
		X	X	
X		X		
X				
X				
X				
X		X		
X		X	X	
X*		X		
X			X	

6

Summative Evaluation

This chapter addresses the following key study question:

Key Question #4. To what extent are the final outputs from NIDRR grants of high quality?

The chapter answers this central question and also provides an assessment of the methods used by the committee to conduct the summative evaluation. The scope and methods used to conduct the External Evaluation of the National Institute on Disability and Rehabilitation Research (NIDRR) and its Grantees were described earlier in Chapter 2. The first section of this chapter elaborates on the methods to evaluate the quality of outputs. The second section describes the results of the assessment of grant outputs and provides recommendations for improving the quality of outputs. The final section presents the committee's self-assessment of the methods and recommendations for future evaluations.

SUMMARY OF METHODS DEVELOPED FOR ASSESSING THE QUALITY OF OUTPUTS

The methods and procedures developed by the committee for assessing the quality of outputs involved first determining the criteria and dimensions to be used for the assessment. Second, a questionnaire was developed to assist grantees in nominating outputs for review and to elicit supplemental descriptive information about those outputs. Third, a sampling plan was developed for selecting grantees who would be invited to participate in the evaluation. Fourth, the committee and staff worked with grantees who agreed to participate in the evaluation, and gathered and cataloged the outputs and supplemental information submitted for the committee's review. Finally, the committee assessed the outputs through an expert review process.

Development of Quality Criteria

A key element of the summative evaluation was the response to NIDRR's request to develop criteria for assessing the quality of its grantees' outputs. In developing these criteria, the committee drew on its own research expertise, recommendations of the external advisory group convened by NIDRR in the course of planning this evaluation (National Institute on Disability and Rehabilitation Research, 2008), and methods used in other National Research Council (NRC) and international studies that have evaluated federal research programs (Bernstein et al., 2007; Chien et al., 2009; Ismail et al., 2010; National Research Council and Institute of Medicine, 2007; Panel on Return on Investment in Health Research, 2009; Wooding and Starkey, 2010; Wooding et al., 2009).

Quality Criteria

Four criteria were developed for the evaluation of grantee outputs: (1) technical quality, (2) advancement of knowledge or the field, (3) likely or demonstrated impact, and (4) dissemination.

Technical quality The technical quality of outputs was assessed using dimensions that included the application of standards of science and technology, appropriate methodology (quantitative or qualitative design and analysis), and the degree of accessibility and usability.

Advancement of knowledge or the field (e.g., research, practice, or policy as relevant) The dimensions used to assess this criterion included scientific advancement of methods, tools, and theory; the development of new information or technologies; closing of an identified gap; and use of methods and approaches that were innovative or novel.

Likely or demonstrated impact This criterion was used to assess the likely or demonstrated impact of outputs on science (impact, citations), consumers (health, quality of life, and participation for people with disabilities), provider practice, health and social systems, social and health policy, or the private sector/commercialization.

Dissemination Dimensions of dissemination assessed included the identification and tailoring of materials for reaching different audience/user types; collaboration with audience/users in identifying content and medium needs/preferences; delivery of information through multiple media types and sources for optimal reach and accessibility; evaluation of dissemination efforts and impacts; and commercialization/patenting of devices, if applicable.

Scale Developed for Rating the Criteria

For the output ratings, the quality scale used by the committee was substantively different than the opinion scale used in the evaluation reported in earlier chapters for surveys of stakeholder organizations and peer reviewers. A 7-point scale was used to rate the criteria at varying levels of quality, where 1 indicated poor quality, 4 indicated good quality, and 7 indicated excellent quality. The committee deliberated at length in determining what the midpoint score (4) would represent on the quality scale and decided that the midpoint should be "meeting expectations for good quality." This midpoint anchor description was operationalized for assessing the technical quality of publications, which made up 70 percent of the outputs reviewed. For publications, a rating of 4 was generally assigned to journal articles that were published in peer-reviewed journals based on the fact that they had already been peer reviewed and met the scientific standards of their respective fields of research or development. However, articles could be rated higher or lower than 4 if, after review, their quality was determined to be higher or lower than "good." For other output categories (tools, devices, or informational products), there was no such common way to operationalize the midpoint anchor, but the committee applied its expert judgment in determining ratings for these other outputs relative to the standard applied to the publications category.

Box 6-1 provides examples of quality indicators considered by committee members in determining scores for each criterion. These examples are not intended to be exhaustive but to illustrate the attributes of outputs that were considered in their review. In rating the outputs, committee members drew on their scientific expertise to consider the outputs' quality with respect to the dimensions within each criterion (see the above discussion). (More information on the review procedures is presented later in this section; the review procedures guide and output rating sheet used by committee members are included in Appendix B.)

Grantee Questionnaire

NIDRR supplied the committee with information gathered from grantees in their Annual Performance Reports (APRs) (Research Triangle Inter-

BOX 6-1
Examples of Quality Indicators Considered in Determining Output Scores

Technical Quality

- Strength of literature review and framing of issues
- Competence of design, considering the research question and other parameters of the study
- Quality of measurement planning and description
- Analytic methods and interpretation; degree to which recommendations for change are drawn clearly from the analysis
- Description of feasibility, usability, accessibility, and consumer satisfaction testing

Advancement of Knowledge or the Field

- Degree to which a groundbreaking and innovative approach is presented
- Application of a formal test of a hypothesis regarding a technique used widely in the field to improve practice
- Level of advancement and improvement of current classification systems
- Usefulness of descriptive base of information about factors associated with a condition
- Novelty of ways of studying a condition that can be applied to the development of new models, training, or research

Likely or Demonstrated Impact

- Degree to which the output is well cited or has promise to be (for newer articles)
- Potential to improve the lives of persons with disabilities by increasing accessibility
- Possibly transformative clinical and policy implications
- Potential for building capacity, lowering costs, commercialization, etc.
- Influence on the direction of research, use in the field, or capacity of the field

Dissemination

- Method and scope of dissemination
- Description of the evidence of dissemination (e.g., numbers distributed to different audiences)
- Level of strategic dissemination to target audiences when needed
- Evidence of reaching the target audience
- Degree to which dissemination used appropriate multiple media outlets, such as webinars, television coverage, Senate testimony, websites, DVDs, and/or social network sites

SOURCE: Generated by the committee.

national, 2009). Grantees are required to complete an APR annually to report on their progress. At the end of a grant, they must complete a final report. To supplement the APR information provided by NIDRR, the committee developed a grantee questionnaire (see Appendix B). The first part of the questionnaire asked grantees to list all projects under the grant and nominate the top two outputs from each project that reflected their grant's best achievements. The questionnaire specified that outputs were to be drawn from the four categories defined in NIDRR's APR (Research Triangle International, 2009):

- *publications* (e.g., research reports and other publications in peer-reviewed and nonpeer-reviewed publications);
- *tools, measures, and intervention protocols* (e.g., instruments or processes created to acquire quantitative or qualitative information, knowledge, or data on a specific disability or rehabilitation issue, or to provide a rehabilitative intervention);
- *technology products and devices* (e.g., industry standards/guidelines, software/netware, inventions, patents/licenses/patent disclosures, working prototypes, product(s) evaluated or field tested, product(s) transferred to industry for potential commercialization, product(s) in the marketplace); and
- *informational products* (e.g., training manuals or curricula, fact sheets, newsletters, audiovisual materials, marketing tools, educational aids, websites or other Internet sites produced in conjunction with research and development, training, dissemination, knowledge translation, and consumer involvement activities).

The instructions for the questionnaire indicated that the committee would prefer to review one publication and one other type of output for each project within their grants, but that grantees could select two publications if that was the only type of output for a project. The questionnaire asked the grantees to submit the actual outputs for the committee's review. If the output was a website, a tool, or a technology device that had to be demonstrated, grantees were asked to provide descriptive information, pictures, or links to websites for the committee's direct review.

The second part of the questionnaire included a series of questions designed to elicit more in-depth description of an output when needed and to provide supplemental information on the output's technical quality, how it advanced knowledge or practice, its likely or demonstrated impact, and how it was disseminated. This type of information, needed for a comprehensive assessment of the output, would not always be apparent in reviewing the output in isolation. For *technical quality*, grantees were asked to describe examples, such as the approach or method used in an output's development; relevant peer recognition; receipt of a patent, approval by the Food and Drug Administration, or use of the output in standards development; and evidence of the output's usability and accessibility. For *advancement of knowledge or the field*, grantees were asked to discuss the importance of the original question or issue and describe how the output advanced knowledge in such arenas as making discoveries; providing new information; establishing theories, measures, and methods; closing gaps in the knowledge base; and developing new interventions, products, technology, and environmental adaptations. For *likely or demonstrated impact*, grantees were instructed to describe the output's potential or actual impact on science, people with disabilities, provider practice, health and social systems, social and health policy, the private sector/commercialization, capacity building, and any other relevant arenas. Under *dissemination*, grantees were asked to describe the stage and scope (e.g., local, regional, national) of dissemination efforts, specific dissemination activities, any identification and tailoring of materials for particular audiences, efforts to collaborate with particular audiences or user communities to identify content and medium needs and preferences, and the delivery of information through multiple media types. Grantees were also asked to provide information from evaluations of their dissemination efforts and impacts that they may have conducted (e.g., results of audience feedback or satisfaction surveys).

The committee piloted the questionnaire on one NIDRR grant that had ended in 2008 and was outside the sampling pool (described below). Subgroups of the committee assessed five outputs of this grant, which consisted of two publications, an assessment package, a working prototype, and a fact sheet; discussed results; and adapted the questionnaire by collapsing some of the dimensions from an original set of six criteria into the four final criteria.[1]

To supplement the grantee questionnaire in assessing the likely impact of published articles, the committee used such sources as Scopus and the Web of Science to determine the journal impact factor and the number of citations of a particular article.

Sampling

NIDRR provided the committee with a data set of grantee information that consisted of all grants ending in years 2006 to 2010 (N = 248). Included in that data set was extensive information on all of the outputs produced by

[1] An original criterion on output usability was collapsed into the final technical quality criterion. Another original criterion on consumer and audience involvement was restructured as dimensions of the other criteria. For example, the technical quality criterion now includes a dimension on "evidence of usability and accessibility"; the impact criterion includes a dimension on "impact on people with disabilities"; and the dissemination criterion includes a dimension on "tailoring materials to audiences" and "collaboration with users."

all NIDRR grantees, which NIDRR routinely collects. The committee sampled from that larger data set with no involvement of NIDRR staff in which grants were selected. The committee was directed by its charge to draw a sample of 30 grants ending in 2009 that was representative of NIDRR's 14 program mechanisms. As shown in Table 6-1, there were 107 grants that ended in 2009. As displayed in the table, however, a number of program mechanisms did not have at least 2 grants ending in 2009: Burn Model System (BMS), Spinal Cord Injury Model System (SCIMS), Traumatic Brain Injury Model System (TBIMS), Disability and Business Technical Assistance Center (DBTAC), Knowledge Translation (KT), Advanced Rehabilitation Research Training (ARRT), and Section 21.

Because the BMS, SCIMS, and TBIMS program mechanisms support some of NIDRR's flagship programs, the committee adjusted the sampling pool to ensure that these grants would be included in the sample. The committee went back to the most recent year in which at least two grants under

TABLE 6-1 Number of NIDRR Grants Ending in 2007 to 2009, with Grants Included in Sampling Pool Highlighted

Program Mechanism	2007	2008	2009
Burn Model System (BMS)	0	5	0
Traumatic Brain Injury Model System (TBIMS)	7	8	1
Spinal Cord Injury Model System (SCIMS)	9	0	0
Rehabilitation Engineering Research Center (RERC)	0	0	8
Rehabilitation Research and Training Center (RRTC)	0	0	10
Disability and Rehabilitation Research Project-General (DRRP)	0	0	14
Field Initiated Project (FIP)	0	0	36
Small Business Innovation Research I (SBIR-I)	0	0	16
Small Business Innovation Research II (SBIR-II)	0	0	8
Disability and Business Technical Assistance Center (DBTAC)	0	1	0
Knowledge Translation (KT)	0	0	0
Advanced Rehabilitation Research Training (ARRT)	0	0	1
Switzer Fellowship	0	0	12
Section 21	0	1	1
Total Grants in Years Ending in 2007, 2008, 2009	16	15	107
Total Grants Included in Sample (N = 111)	**9**	**13**	**89**

SOURCE: Generated by the committee based on data from the NIDRR grantee database.

these program mechanisms ended, which was 2008 for BMS (N = 5) and TBIMS (N = 9, with 1 in 2009 and 8 in 2008) and 2007 for SCIMS (N = 9), and included these grants in the pool. The DBTAC, KT, ARRT, and Section 21 program mechanisms were excluded from the pool for this first evaluation cycle. Small Business Innovation Research I (SBIR-I) grants also were excluded from the sampling pool because they do not produce "outputs" and therefore did not align with the evaluation parameter of reviewing two outputs for each project within a grant. After these adjustments, the total pool consisted of 111 grants across nine NIDRR program mechanisms, shown in the highlighted cells of Table 6-1. The older grants included in the evaluation may have had an advantage over the grants ending in 2009 because of the additional time for their outputs to have had an impact.

From this pool of 111 grants, 30 grants (27 percent) were randomly selected for review in the following way. To balance the desire for the sample of grants to represent the nine program mechanisms included in the pool, the committee stratified the sampling at the program-mechanism level as a proportion of all grants in the sampling pool. For example, there were 36 Field Initiated Project (FIP) grants in the sampling pool, as shown in Table 6-1, representing 32 percent of all of the grants in the sampling pool (N = 111); therefore, 32 percent of the 30 grants in the sample (N = 10) should be FIP. The 36 FIP grants in the sampling pool were numbered 1 through 36, and 10 FIP grants were randomly selected using a website that generated random numbers. A table in the next section shows the number of grants included in the sample by program mechanism.

Once the proposed evaluation methods had been approved by the Institutional Review Board of the National Academies, the sample of 30 grants was drawn, and invitations to participate were sent to the principal investigators of those grants. The principal investigators were fully informed about the methods to be used in the evaluation and what would be required of them. Of the original 30 grantees invited, 2 declined because they did not have time to fulfill the evaluation requirements and 1 because of a change in institutions. Three additional grants were then randomly selected from the pool to bring the final sample to 30. The committee acknowledges that bias from self-selection could have caused the final sample of 30 grantees that participated in the evaluation to be less representative of the larger population of grants.

Compiling Outputs to Be Reviewed and Number of Outputs Reviewed

The questionnaire described above was sent to the 30 grantees who agreed to participate in the study. As noted, the principal investigators of the grants included in the sample were given written instructions for submitting their outputs for the evaluation and providing supplemental information about the outputs. Committee staff worked with the grantees to clarify the instructions and to encourage them to submit their output packages. Because some grants had ended several years before the evaluation (2007 and 2008 for the Model System grants), some grantees had difficulty submitting materials because the principal investigators had changed institutions or departments within the same university or had other competing priorities during the time period of our review. Staff accommodated these principal investigators by providing additional time to submit their materials and in five cases by assisting them in completing the questionnaires through telephone interviews. Two grantees did not respond to the supplemental questionnaire.

As described above, grantees received questionnaires on which they were asked to list each project under their grant and identify two outputs per project to be reviewed by the committee. They were asked to identify the "top" two outputs per project that reflected their grant's best achievements. As noted, to permit assessment of outputs beyond journal publications, grantees were asked to offer at least one non-journal publication output per project if such outputs were available. The number of projects for each grant varied by size, from 1 for small FIP to 10 for larger center grants.

A total of 156 outputs were submitted for review across the 30 grants in the sample. Eight outputs were considered highly related to other outputs, and they were reviewed together with those other outputs. This occurred when one output was a derivative or different expression of another and when the principal investigator responses to criteria questions were basically the same. Therefore, the total number of outputs for analysis was 148. Table 6-2 presents the number of grants included in the sample by program mechanism and the types of outputs that were reviewed.

To place the outputs reviewed into the larger context of the outputs produced by grantees in the sampling pool of 111 grants, Table 6-2 also shows that the proportions of publications and other outputs (tools, technology, and informational products) reviewed by the committee were relatively close to the proportions of the various output types produced by grantees in the larger sampling pool. The proportion of publications reviewed was somewhat lower at 70 percent (versus 76 percent in the sampling pool), and the proportion of informational products reviewed was somewhat higher at 18 percent (versus 11 percent in the sampling pool).

Review Process

The committee members, whose expertise encompasses social sciences, rehabilitation medicine, engineering, evaluation, and knowledge translation, were divided into three groups of five members each. The subgroups were organized to ensure that outputs would be reviewed by a group of individuals with the collective expertise necessary to judge their quality. The

TABLE 6-2 Number of Grants and Distribution of Outputs Reviewed by Program Mechanism

NIDRR Grant Category and Program Mechanism	Grants	Publications	Tools	Technology	Informational Products	Total
Model System Grants						
Burn Model System (BMS)	2	12	2	0	4	18 (12%)
Traumatic Brain Injury Model System (TBIMS)	2	12	0	0	2	14 (10%)
Spinal Cord injury Model System (SCIMS)	2	11	0	0	0	11 (7%)
Center Grants						
Rehabilitation Research and Training Center (RRTC)	3	16	0	0	12	28 (19%)
Rehabilitation Engineering Research Center (RERC)	2	16	2	5	3	26 (18%)
Research and Development Grants						
Disability and Rehabilitation Research Project-General (DRRP)	4	13	4	0	5	22 (15%)
Field Initiated Project (FIP)	10	17	1	3	1	22 (15%)
Small Business Innovation Research II (SBIR-II)	2	1	0	1	0	2 (1%)
Training Grants						
Switzer Fellowship	3	5	0	0	0	5 (3%)
Total and Proportion of Output Types in Sample	30	103 (70%)	9 (6%)	9 (6%)	27 (18%)	148
Total and Proportion of Output Types in Sampling Pool	111	1,060 (76%)	101 (7%)	84 (6%)	148 (11%)	1,393

SOURCE: Generated by the committee based on data from the grantee questionnaire and NIDRR grantee database.

subgroups were convened on three occasions—in October 2010, December 2010, and February 2011. Because of the relatively short time period available to conduct the reviews, grants were scheduled for review according to size, with the smaller grants being invited first (e.g., FIP, Switzer, SBIR-II) and the larger grants (DRRP, Model System grants, center grants) being invited to participate in the later rounds. The rationale for this approach was that the smaller grants had fewer outputs and would require less preparation time for the review than the larger grants, which had many projects and more outputs so that more preparation time was required. Therefore, the content of the grants tended to be mixed during each round of reviews, necessitating a corresponding mix of expertise in each subgroup. As noted, however, efforts were made to match the expertise of the reviewers in each subgroup with the outputs they would be reviewing (e.g., technology outputs were assigned to a subgroup with engineering expertise). The review procedures are described in detail in Box 6-2.

The committee's expert review involved consideration and assessment of the multiple quality dimensions of the outputs—a process that has been recommended as a valid method for evaluating the relevance and quality of federal research programs (National Academy of Sciences, National Academy of Engineering, and Institute of Medicine, 1999). The seven-point rating scale was used to describe the results of the output assessment more precisely in terms of the varying levels of quality. During the reviews, the committee members frequently discussed how they were applying the criteria and interpreting the anchors of the rating scale so they could calibrate their ratings. In addition, brief narrative statements were written summarizing the rationale for the subgroups' ratings of each output. These statements were reviewed after the ratings had been completed to identify attributes that particularly characterized the varying levels of quality and were helpful in further exemplifying the dimensions of the criteria.

Although the final scores used to report results of the output assessment were based on subgroups' consensus scores, the committee conducted an interrater reliability analysis of their initial independent ratings (i.e., raw scores before the subgroup discussions) to determine the extent to which the individual committee members were using and interpreting the scale in the same way. The interrater reliability analysis was conducted, using methods suggested by MacLennan (1993), for more than two raters with ordinal data. This method calculates an intraclass correlation coefficient (ICC) that represents an average correlation among raters.

The interrater reliability analyses were run on 15 grants for which at least 3 outputs were reviewed by the subgroups. The analyses could not be run with less than 3 outputs, and only 15 grants had 3 or more outputs reviewed. The ratings compared were the individual committee members' raw scores (before discussion) on each of the criteria. According to Yaffee

BOX 6-2
Committee Member Review Procedures

Each of the 30 grants was assigned to one of the three subgroups so that all outputs from a grant were reviewed by the same subgroup. To ensure consistency in approach across subgroups, the committee chair attended each subgroup meeting.

Based on direct review of the output itself and descriptive information about the output in the Annual Performance Report (APR) and grantees' questionnaire responses, each subgroup member independently rated every output assigned to that subgroup. The subgroup member assigned a score for each of the four quality criteria (technical quality, advancement of knowledge or the field, likely or demonstrated impact, and dissemination), as well as an overall score for the output and provided a rationale for their scores. Scores were assigned using a 7-point scale, ranging from 1 to 7 and anchored at 3 points: 1 = poor quality, 4 = good quality, and 7 = excellent quality.

For each output, one subgroup member was assigned as the primary reviewer. The remaining four subgroup members were secondary reviewers. The process for arriving at consensus scores was as follows:

- The primary reviewer opened discussion of each output by presenting a brief summary of the output and his or her rationale for the rating of each criterion plus the overall score.
- The secondary reviewers then presented their ratings for each output, along with a brief rationale.
- The subgroup then developed consensus ratings for each output through discussion facilitated by the subgroup chair.

Following the discussion of all outputs from an individual grant, the subgroup considered the full spectrum of the reviewed material, along with the grant's overall purpose and objectives (using the grant's APR). The subgroup then assigned an overall performance rating for the grant using the same seven-point scale.

(1998), the minimum acceptable ICC is .75 to .80. The ICC resulting from the analyses are shown for each of the 4 criteria in Table 6-3.

On the *technical quality* criterion, 13 of the 15 grants had statistically significant ICCs greater than .75; on the *impact* criterion, 11 grants had ICCs in this acceptable range; on the *advancement of knowledge or the field* criterion, 10 grants had ICCs in this range; and on the *dissemination* criterion, 9 grants had ICCs in this range. Although the ICC results show greater challenges in achieving interrater reliability on the criteria other than technical quality, the results suggest that individual members were using and interpreting the seven-point scale in a similar manner prior to

TABLE 6-3 Results of Interrater Reliability Analysis

Grant	Number of Outputs Reviewed	Technical Quality ICC	Impact ICC	Advancement of Knowledge or the Field ICC	Dissemination ICC
1	8	.64[c]	.81[c]	.91[b]	.80[b]
2	3	.96[c]	–5.6	.65	–.21
3	4	.95[b]	.33	.95[b]	.92[b]
4	8	.87[a]	.88[a]	.81[a]	.83[a]
5	10	.76[b]	.79[b]	.85[a]	.74[b]
6	10	.81[a]	.83[a]	.67[b]	.85[a]
7	9	.81[b]	.57	.93	.67[c]
8	6	.97[a]	.97[a]	.93[a]	.96[a]
9	7	.83[b]	.31	.77[c]	–1.65
10	7	.79[b]	.78[b]	.64	.88[a]
11	8	.94[a]	.92[a]	.88[a]	.72[b]
12	9	.83[b]	.81[b]	.78[b]	.86[a]
13	10	.73[b]	.76[a]	.72[b]	.45
14	9	.93[a]	.94[a]	.80[b]	.87[a]
15	16	.84[b]	.92[a]	–.48	.86[a]

[a]$p \leq .001$; [b]$p \leq .01$; [c]$p \leq .05$.
NOTES: For individual grants, not all outputs reported in column 2 could be analyzed for each criterion because of missing data, which occurred when committee members did not rate all four of the criteria for all of the outputs examined during their independent reviews prior to the subgroup discussions. ICC = intraclass correlation coefficient.
SOURCE: Generated by the committee based on data from the committee's interrater reliability analysis.

the full subgroups' discussions of the output ratings and their subsequent determination of consensus scores.

It would have been advantageous to conduct the interrater reliability analysis during the course of the evaluation and make adjustments to improve interrater reliability. However, there was insufficient time for this approach because of the short span of time in which the reviews were performed. The results of the interrater reliability analysis should be considered in designing future output evaluations.

RESULTS OF THE EVALUATION OF GRANTEE OUTPUTS

This section presents the results of the committee's quality ratings of the four types of grant outputs according to the four criteria described above. In reviewing publications, the committee also referred to well-known sources that rate journal impact factors and count the number of times published articles have been cited; these results are summarized for the publications reviewed.

Quality Assessment of Outputs Reviewed

Figures 6-1 through 6-4 illustrate the distribution of ratings for all outputs[2] on each of the four quality criteria. Percentages show the proportion of outputs that received the various ratings along the 7-point scale. Figures 6-5 and 6-6 show distributions in the aggregate for the overall ratings that were determined for each output (i.e., considering all four criteria), and for grant performance (i.e., considering all outputs submitted by a grantee). Results for each criterion are discussed below the figures. For consistency in reporting these results, the discussion refers to ratings falling into the "higher quality" range (i.e., ratings of 4 to 7 with anchors of "good" to "excellent" on the quality scale) or into the "lower quality" range (i.e., ratings of 1 to 3 with anchors of "poor" to "below good" on the quality scale).

In addition, the committee wrote brief statements summarizing the rationale for its ratings of each output. The committee reviewed these statements after completing the ratings to identify attributes that particularly characterized the ratings for the four quality criteria, thereby clarifying the dimensions of each criterion. The attributes that characterized the lower-rated and higher rated outputs are summarized for each criterion below each respective figure.

[2] Although a total of 148 outputs were reviewed, the numbers vary slightly across the criteria in the figures (N = 138 to 142). The committee was not able to rate 6 outputs because the information available was not sufficient. These included a technical workshop, a national conference, a clinic, an intervention program, a list of publications, and a training curriculum. A few other outputs could be rated on some criteria, but not all 4, for the same reason.

Technical Quality

With regard to technical quality (see Figure 6-1) the majority of outputs (69 percent) were rated in the higher quality range (4-7). However, more than a quarter of the outputs (31 percent) were rated in the lower quality range (1-3).

Several characteristics distinguished the lower ratings on technical quality (1-3) from the higher ratings (4-7). An example is *lack of information presented in the output itself or in the accompanying descriptive questionnaire*. Reviewers commented in these cases that there was an insufficient description of the output itself, that a publication was written poorly, that methods or protocols for tools were not described thoroughly, that results were not clearly presented to be able to understand how the research question was answered, that documentation was lacking on how a measure was developed, that testing results for a technology product were not presented, or that not enough substance was presented in an informational product to assess it. Another example was *lack of clarity in information that was presented*. Reviewers commented that questions on a survey did not appear to be well thought out, that weak findings were not fully explained in conclusions, that it was unclear whether adequate validation had actually been performed on a measure or technology product, or that it was unclear whether a new technology was based on scientific evidence. Outputs that were rated lower in the area of *design and methods*, included reports of studies with small sample sizes that were not representative or that used single-group design with self-reported measures, no controls, and a pretest

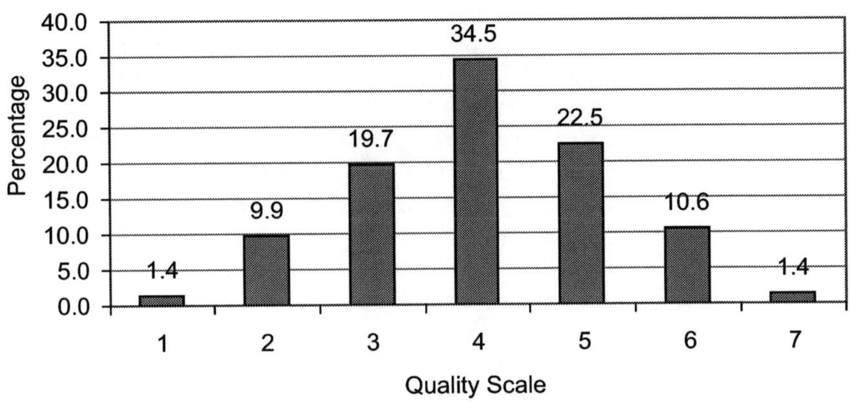

FIGURE 6-1 Distribution of quality ratings for technical quality (N = 142).
SOURCE: Generated by the committee based on data from the committee's output review.

only. These study designs and methods could still be strong if a project were treated as a pilot or feasibility study, but were seen as weak if claims were made regarding their potential for changing policy or practice. Failing to describe or address limitations in some way also was described as a weakness, particularly in cases in which there were high attrition rates or low response rates. Weaknesses in *analyses* were identified as well. These included use of obsolete data sets, failure to use standard methods of analysis, failure to fully use all of the variables available, or description of statistical analyses that appeared to be ad hoc. Informational products that were rated lower included newsletters that presented data but failed to synthesize the data for users or presented tips for practice without providing supporting evidence. They also included websites that were difficult to navigate, had missing links, or lacked interactive elements necessary to fully access or utilize the information.

In contrast, comments on outputs that were rated on the higher end of the quality scale praised attributes of *presentation and clarity*, such as careful and scholarly approach, excellent literature review and framing of issues, very systematic approach that was described well, recommendations for change drawn clearly from the analysis, and narrative descriptions of high quality that accurately represent key issues in technical and conceptual terms. Examples of positive comments on *measurement qualities* included good measurement planned and described; good description of feasibility, usability, accessibility, and consumer satisfaction testing; and use of simulator plus neurological tests. Outputs that were rated higher on *methodology and analytic techniques* were noted as being competent through use of a convenience sample with a longitudinal design, having a good sample size, using a prospective sample that was monitored across a 2-year period and used several predictors, and using analytic methods and interpretation that appeared to be sound. Attributes of tools and technology products that were rated highly were strong design and an article on a technological innovation that won a prize for technical quality from the journal in which it was published. One grantee stood out as presenting three outputs in a cohesive manner that illustrated the technical quality of the research and development: the first output described the research base, the second described the software application, and the third assessed use of the protocol. Some highly rated informational products (websites) were described as being easy to navigate, presenting evidence on consulting with and tailoring the website to users, and including data that were highly accessible and usable.

Advancement of Knowledge or the Field

The output ratings on advancement of knowledge or the field (see Figure 6-2) show that almost three-quarters of the outputs (73 percent) were

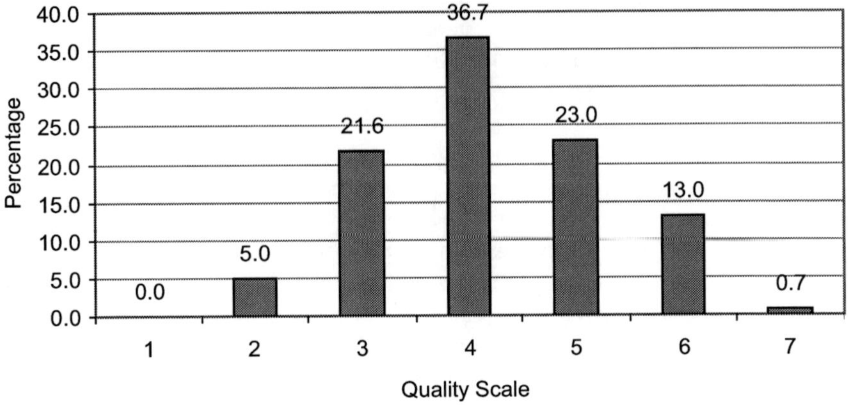

FIGURE 6-2 Distribution of quality ratings for advancement of knowledge or the field (N = 139).
SOURCE: Generated by the committee based on data from the committee's output review.

deemed to be in the higher quality range. But again slightly more than a quarter fell into the lower range.

Outputs rated lower on this criterion received comments, such as nothing new or novel presented, unclear how this work is an advancement over current knowledge, no new theory work and unclear how the output will break new ground, dated concepts in the field, unclear what the advancement is in some knowledge transfer outputs, and evolution of technology not driven by this product development.

In contrast, comments on outputs scoring at the higher end of the quality rating scale included novel and interesting topic; unique work that is a good contribution to the state of knowledge; groundbreaking and innovative; added knowledge about a practice to the field; formal test of a hypothesis regarding a clinical technique used widely in the field; randomizing to conditions was new for this technology; new indicators used to set new prevalence rates; moves the knowledge base forward by linking concepts and measures to change how measurement is done; significant advancement and clear improvement over current classification systems; provides a useful descriptive base of information about risk factors; could lead to new ways of studying a condition and developing new models that can be used for training and designing interventions or developing new study approaches; and experimental design is well conceived and well designed, with potential for moving the field forward.

Likely or Demonstrated Impact

The ratings on likely or demonstrated impact (see Figure 6-3) show that 74 percent of the outputs were determined to be in the higher quality range. But again slightly more than a quarter fell into the lower range.

Outputs rated lower on this criterion generally did not present evidence of likely or demonstrated impact, and the impact was not apparent from examining the output itself. In one case, it appeared that a paper might have had more potential for impact if it had been published in a journal more suited to the information presented, and in another case if more planning had been done to increase the likelihood of adoption of a tool.

When outputs received higher ratings, their likely or demonstrated impact was readily apparent. The outputs were published in journals that that had appropriate impact factors; they were relatively well cited or had promise to be (for newer articles), and may have been cited in national newspapers. These were outputs that had clear potential to improve the lives of people with disabilities by increasing accessibility; that had clear and possibly transformative clinical and policy implications; and whose results may hold promise for supporting new financial coverage, providing an intervention at lower cost, or being commercialized. Some of the outputs that received high ratings had demonstrated their impact by already influencing the direction of research, being widely used in the field, helping to inform and advance health care legislation, shedding light on institutional bias, or building capacity for the use of statistical products.

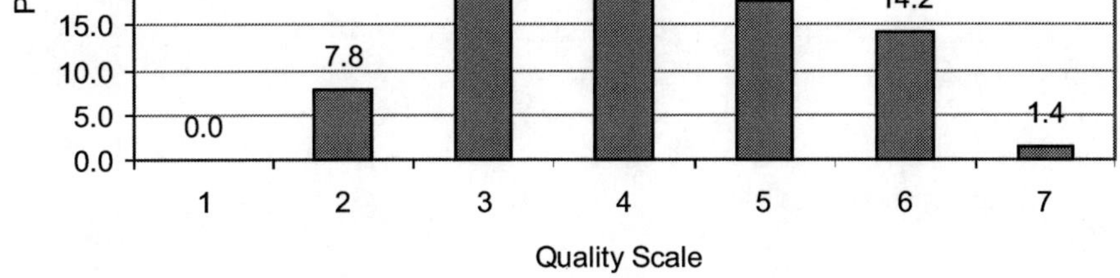

FIGURE 6-3 Distribution of quality ratings for likely or demonstrated impact (N = 141).
SOURCE: Generated by the committee based on data from the committee's output review.

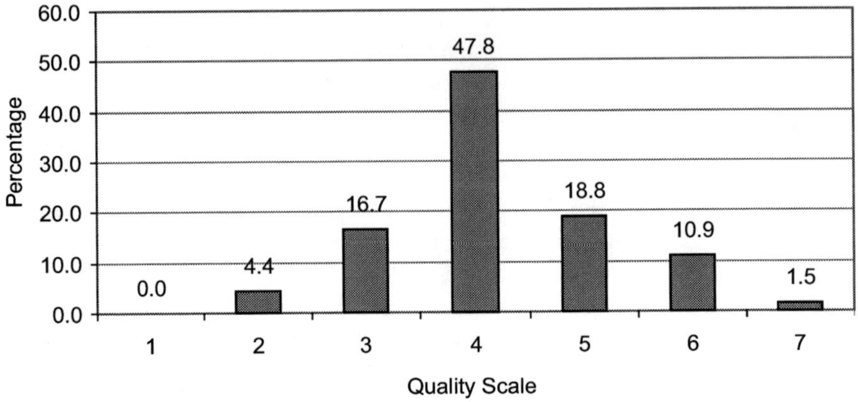

FIGURE 6-4 Distribution of quality ratings for dissemination (N = 138).
SOURCE: Generated by the committee based on data from the committee's output review.

Dissemination

Output ratings on the dissemination criterion (see Figure 6-4) are somewhat different from those on the other criteria. A higher proportion (79 percent) of the outputs were rated in the higher quality range, and less than a quarter (21 percent) fell in the lower range.

Outputs were rated low on the dissemination criterion for a variety of reasons that pertained to failure to conform to some of the basic principals of knowledge translation. For example, the target audience was unclear; the information was not targeted to the audience identified; it was unclear how the audience would use the output; or the voice, content, or format was not consumer-friendly or not of high quality. Sometimes it was unclear whether or how outputs had been disseminated and what the volume or scope of the dissemination was.

On the other hand, outputs that were rated high on this quality criterion were characterized as having extensive dissemination and a good description of the evidence for this (e.g., numbers distributed to different audiences); having an appropriate method of dissemination and format; providing evidence of reaching the target audience; being disseminated through a patent and commercialization; being widely disseminated by a federal agency; being disseminated strategically through targeting of states or associations; and using multiple media outlets for dissemination, such as webinars, television coverage, Senate testimony, websites, DVDs, and/or social network sites. One grantee was planning to disseminate a technology product through support by the grantee's university for licensing the technology for possible commercialization.

Ratings of Overall Quality of Outputs

The committee determined overall quality ratings by considering the ratings on the four criteria. Thus Figure 6-5 reflects the same overall pattern of scores skewed slightly toward the higher quality range, with 72 percent of the outputs being rated in this range and 28 percent in the lower quality range

All outputs were noted as having strengths and weakness. However, those that received lower overall scores of 1 to 3 had a preponderance of lower ratings across the individual criteria, whereas the opposite was true for the outputs that received the higher overall scores. Those outputs that received ratings of 4 had a greater mix of both positive and negative critiques, which made the products good, but not exceptional.

Ratings of Grant Performance on Outputs

After reviewing all of the outputs of an individual grant, the committee considered and rated the grant's overall performance with regard to all of the outputs reviewed for that grant. In rating grant performance, the committee also considered the fact that the outputs reviewed had been identified by the grant's principal investigators as the "top" two outputs per project, best reflecting the grant's achievements. In addition, the committee considered the grant's overall purpose and objectives (using its APR). With these considerations in mind, the committee assigned a grant performance rating using the same seven-point scale.

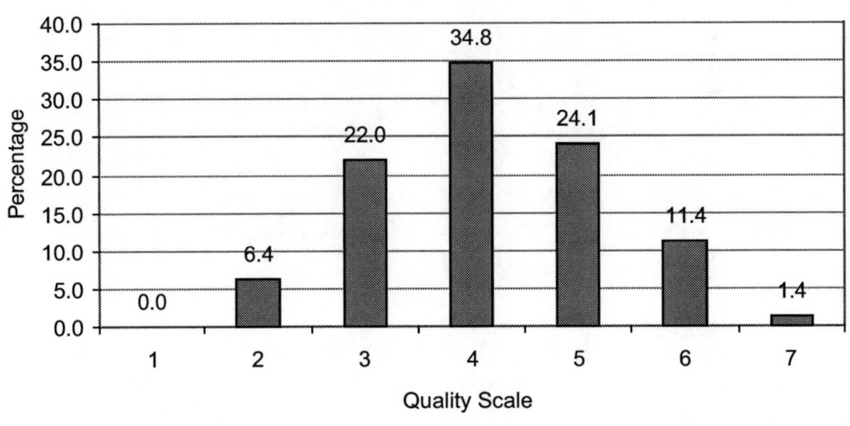

FIGURE 6-5 Distribution of overall quality ratings for each output (N = 141).
SOURCE: Generated by the committee based on data from the committee's output review.

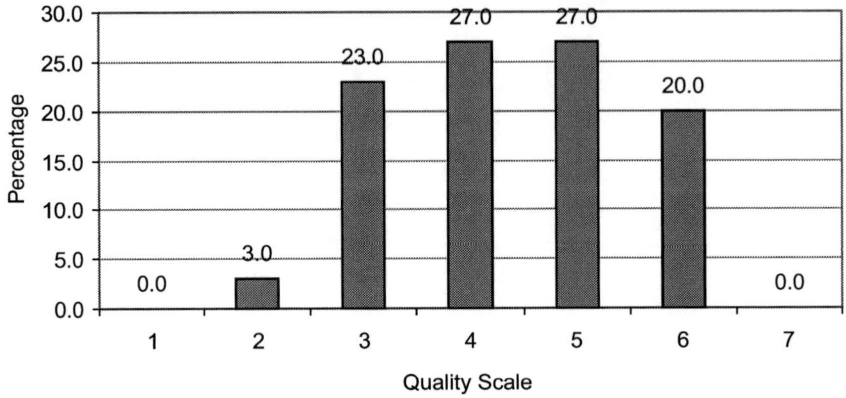

FIGURE 6-6 Distribution of quality ratings for grant performance score (N = 30).
SOURCE: Generated by the committee based on data from the committee's output review.

Figure 6-6 shows that the distribution of scores on the performance of grants is quite different from the ratings for the individual outputs. While three-quarters of the grants' overall performance was rated in the higher quality range and one-quarter as lower quality, a smaller proportion of grants were rated at the midpoint of 4 (27 percent), and larger proportions were rated on the higher end of the scale, with 27 percent receiving a rating of 5 and 20 percent scoring a 6.

This result may reflect that a grant's performance on the particular outputs reviewed was determined to be more than the sum of its outputs as considered within the context of the grant's overall purpose and objectives. However, there was great concern that the committee did not have enough information to rate grant-level performance by focusing so exclusively on outputs and not in more depth on how the outputs fit within the context of the grants' specific aims and developmental trajectories. This was particularly the case for larger, more complex projects such as those under the Rehabilitation Research and Training Center (RRTC), Rehabilitation Engineering Research Center (RERC), and Model System grants. The NIDRR APRs, which were taken into consideration, in some cases did a good job of providing this larger context, but in many cases reviewing the APR alone was not sufficient. (Issues related to rating outputs in the context of grants and program mechanisms are discussed further in the section on self-assessment of the committee's review methods later in the chapter.)

Journal Impact and Citation Analysis of Publication Outputs

Assessing the quality criterion of likely or demonstrated impact included the additional step of considering the impact factors of the journals in which articles were published, as well as the number of times specific publications reviewed by the committee had been cited in other published manuscripts. While this type of analysis has the benefit of providing quantifiable metrics, it is also fraught with many limitations that are particularly relevant to NIDRR grantees. Many NIDRR-funded researchers publish in specialty journals that may have lower impact factors because the work is in narrow fields that are not well populated with researchers. In addition, the citation half-life (the time it takes for an article to receive half of its total citations by others) can be quite lengthy. The citation half-life for the *Archives of Physical Medicine and Rehabilitation* (one of the leading journals in this field), for example, is about 8 years. Thus, it may take many years before an article's true value is revealed through this metric. Because most of the grants reviewed ended in 2009, the citation data for the publications reviewed were collected within a short time window (0-24 months).

Acknowledging these limitations, the committee used Scopus and the Web of Science to access information on the journal impact factors and number of citations for each article included in the review. Table 6-4 shows all the journals in which articles reviewed by the committee (N = 80) were published, the Scopus (SJR) and Web of Science (ISI) impact factors, and the number of articles reviewed that were published in each of these journals.

The wide variety of journals corresponds to NIDRR's broad portfolio. As can be seen in the table, the journal with the largest number of articles reviewed by the committee was the *Archives of Physical Medicine and Rehabilitation* (N = 18), followed by the *Journal of Spinal Cord Medicine* (N = 12). The Web of Science (ISI) classifies 43 journals in the subject area of rehabilitation, and the impact factors of these journals range from a low of .08 (*Athletic Therapy Today*) to a high of 3.77 (*Neurorehabilitation and Neural Repair*). The most widely cited journal in the category of rehabilitation is the *Archives of Physical Medicine and Rehabilitation*, which has an impact factor of 2.25.

The table shows that 35 percent of the 80 publications reviewed by the committee were published in journals with ISIs greater than 2.0. Only 6 of the journals in which grantees published were not listed in either Scopus (SJR) or Web of Science (ISI) databases. This could be because these journals have not applied or because they have applied and have not yet been accepted. The committee did not pursue the question beyond searching the two websites. However, the committee learned how changeable the database is. In the 2009 Web of Science journal impact factor database, there were 33 journals listed in the rehabilitation category; in 2010 there were 43.

TABLE 6-4 Journal Impact Factors of Published Articles Reviewed (N = 30 grants, 80 articles)

Journal Name	Scopus Journal Impact Factors (SJR)[a]	Web of Science Journal Impact Factors (ISI)[b]	Number of Articles Reviewed That Were Published in the Journal
Archives of Physical Medicine and Rehabilitation	0.16	2.25	18
Journal of Spinal Cord Medicine	0.12	1.44	12
Journal of Burn Care and Research	0.11	1.56	5
Disability and Rehabilitation	0.10	1.49	4
Health Affairs	0.42	3.79	3
International Journal of Telerehabilitation	NA	NA	2
Journal of Burn Care and Rehabilitation	NA	NA	2
Journal of Head Trauma Rehabilitation	0.17	2.78	2
Journal of Neurotrauma	0.36	3.43	2
Journal of Rehabilitation Research and Development	0.13	1.71	2
Rehabilitation Psychology	0.08	1.68	2
Topics in Stroke and Rehabilitation	0.10	1.22	2
AER-Journal of Research and Practice in Visual Impairment and Blindness	NA	NA	1
Assistive Technology	0.06	NA	1
Brain Injury	0.12	1.75	1
Burns	0.12	1.72	1
Developmental Neurorehabilitation	0.07	1.38	1
Disability and Health Journal	0.04	NA	1
Generations	0.03	NA	1
Hearing Journal	0.03	NA	1
IEEE Transactions on Biomedical Engineering	0.14	1.78	1
Interacting with Computers	0.04	1.19	1
International Journal of Geriatric Psychiatry	0.16	2.03	1
Journal of Aging and Social Policy	0.05	NA	1

TABLE 6-4 Continued

Journal Name	Scopus Journal Impact Factors (SJR)[a]	Web of Science Journal Impact Factors (ISI)[b]	Number of Articles Reviewed That Were Published in the Journal
Journal of Applied Rehabilitation Counseling	NA	NA	1
Journal of Behavioral Nutrition and Physical Activity	0.23	3.17	1
Journal of Cardiopulmonary Rehabilitation and Prevention	0.14	1.42	1
Journal of Occupational Rehabilitation	0.11	1.81	1
Journal of Vocational Rehabilitation	0.03	NA	1
Lecture Notes in Computer Science	0.03	NA	1
NeuroRehabilitation	0.10	1.59	1
Neurorehabilitation Neural Repair	0.31	3.77	1
Physical Medicine Clinics of North America	0.10	1.36	1
Rehabilitation Education	NA	NA	1
Spinal Cord	0.16	1.83	1
Telemedicine and E-Health	0.08	1.30	1
Total Published Articles Reviewed			80

NOTE: NA = journal not tracked by Scopus or Web of Science in the 2010 databases.
[a]SJR (Scopus): The SJR database for 2010 was used. Available: http://www.scopus.com/source/eval.url [August 29, 2011].
[b]ISI (Web of Science): These data were obtained by searching two Web of Knowledge JCR databases (editions): (1) JCR Science Edition 2010 and (2) JCR Social Sciences Edition 2010. Available: http://admin-apps.webofknowledge.com/JCR/JCR?RQ=HOME [August 29, 2011].
SOURCE: Generated by the committee based on data from Scopus (http://www.scopus.com) and Web of Science (http://apps.webofknowledge.com) (membership required for both).

As context for the results of Table 6-4, Annex 6-1 at the end of this chapter includes another table that lists the journals in which the larger pool of 111 NIDRR grantees published (the original pool of NIDRR grants from which the 30 grants in the sample for this evaluation were drawn). Thirty-six percent of these papers were published in prestigious journals (ISI >2).

Using a different metric for citation analysis, the committee was able to identify citations in Scopus for 52 of the 80 journal articles reviewed. The number of citations for these articles ranged from 1 (10 articles) to 74 (one article). The median number of citations was 7.

Limitations and Possible Biases in Rating the Quality of Outputs

As stated in Chapter 2, which describes methods used in the evaluation, several potential limitations could affect the committee's ability to draw unequivocal conclusions. First, results are not generalizable because of the small number of grants reviewed (N = 30) and the small number of outputs reviewed from each grantee's portfolio of work. Second, although the resulting distributions of ratings on all four criteria were quite similar when presented in the aggregate as in Figures 6-1 to 6-4, variation was found in post hoc comparisons of ratings by program mechanism and output type. However, the small number of grants reviewed within each program mechanism, as well as the relatively small number of outputs reviewed other than publications, made these comparisons tentative. Therefore, these comparisons are not reported here. More testing is required to assess the construct validity of the individual criteria. Third, several factors in the methods used could have biased the results in positive or negative directions and posed threats to the validity of the conclusions. These factors are discussed below with regard to the reasons for using the methods, efforts to reduce the threats when possible, and an indication of the direction and magnitude of the possible biases.

- *Reviewing only outputs that grantees nominated as their best*—The committee's decision to have grantees nominate outputs that best represented their portfolio of products was made after much debate. Alternatives such as randomly sampling outputs could have presented other challenges in determining how to accomplish this type of complex sampling across various types of grants and outputs that were produced at different times. Allowing grantees to nominate their best outputs could have biased results in a positive direction and could have had a potentially strong effect. The results were slightly skewed in a positive direction toward the "excellent" range of the scale.
- *Relying to a degree on grantees' self-reports of what was important and/or of high quality about their outputs*—As discussed later in this chapter in the committee's self-assessment of the methods used, the outputs themselves were the primary focus of the evaluation, but the supplemental information provided by grantees' self-reports could have biased the results in a strong positive direction.
- *Assessing grants potentially too soon after they ended to gain a full measure of the impact of their outputs*—This factor could have

biased results in a negative direction. To address this threat to some degree, the instructions for submitting outputs allowed grantees to submit recent outputs that may have been produced following the end of their NIDRR grants. Results did not show any notable differences in ratings for grants that had ended in 2007 and 2008 versus 2009.

- ***Excluding grantees in the original sample who declined to participate***—Self-selection could have biased results when three grantees declined to participate in the evaluation, and three more were randomly redrawn from the pool. The possible impact of this factor is judged to be fairly small, but could have made the final sample of 30 grants that participated in the evaluation less representative of the larger population of grants.
- ***Excluding the Section 21, DBTAC, KT, and AART grants from the sample***—Because NIDRR grant competitions for different program mechanisms are on different funding cycles, there were not enough grants (at least two) in these particular program mechanisms to include in the pool. This factor would not have biased results, however, because output ratings were not compared by program mechanism, and no conclusions were drawn on the entire NIDRR portfolio.

Conclusions and Recommendations Related to Output Quality

The study question addressed in this chapter was: To what extent are the final outputs from NIDRR grants of high quality? The committee found that the ratings on all of the criteria were symmetrically distributed along the quality scale with the largest proportions of scores falling at the midpoint of 4 (good quality) and most being slightly skewed toward the higher end of the scale. Although close to 75 percent of the outputs rated were found to be in the higher range of the quality scale (i.e., being rated as 4 or "good" to 7 or "excellent"), across all of the criteria a quarter of the outputs reviewed were found to be in the lower quality range (1 or "poor" to 3 or "below good").

While expert review is a widely accepted method for assessing the quality of research grant proposals, it must be emphasized that the ratings of outputs here were based on expert opinion rather than quantifiable effects. Other limitations and possible biases were discussed above. Having extensively acknowledged the limitations in conducting the summative evaluation, the committee asserts that the system developed for assessing the quality of outputs worked reasonably well, especially for publications, which made up 70 percent of the outputs reviewed. This assertion is made because the criteria used in the evaluation were based on criteria widely used in federal research programs in the United States and other countries, because expert review methods have validity (National Academy of Sciences, National Academy of Engineering, and Institute of Medicine, 1999), and because the committee did in fact find variation in ratings that was supported by descriptive rationales. Based on the evidence, a set of recommendations is offered to assist NIDRR in striving toward continuously improving the quality of their grants' outputs.

Improving Quality of Outputs

As stated earlier in this report, the quality of outputs is the product of multiple complex factors that involve the priority-setting process, funding levels, the peer review process, the grant management process, and the quality of the science/research and of the grantees. Findings presented in earlier chapters show that for grantees that are not performing optimally, NIDRR has the option of conducting ongoing formative reviews with experts to identify strategies for improvement. The committee also learned that NIDRR has begun routinely adding to its staff meetings an agenda item for project officers to consult about problems with grants, and that program officers have the flexibility to require additional reporting from grantees as needed. Chapter 5 reveals that grantees believe NIDRR's oversight and reporting functions foster successful grants and high-quality outputs by assisting them in adhering to their budget and timeline, providing an external quality assurance mechanism for their project management, and prompting them to maintain their focus on project goals for high-quality products.

> **Recommendation 6-1: Although close to 75 percent of outputs were rated as "good to excellent" (i.e., 4 or higher on the seven-point quality scale), NIDRR should make it clear that it expects all grantees to produce the highest-quality outputs.**

The intent of this recommendation is for NIDRR to encourage all of its grantees to publish in peer-reviewed journals, present at national meetings, publish/disseminate materials, and bring technology solutions to market while producing these outputs at the highest levels of quality. To this end, NIDRR should push forward by establishing clear and consistent expectations for grantees to publish in higher impact journals, which would be one indicator of higher quality. For outputs that are not publications, NIDRR should establish clear and consistent standards for quality to be achieved and adopt appropriate metrics for assessing whether grantees are meeting those standards. One way of setting the quality bar higher would be to begin to encourage grantees to use standardized reporting forms and checklists for reviewing the technical quality of their own work before subjecting it to external review. Many resources exist for reviewing different types of research manuscripts and various nonpublication outputs to ensure that the necessary technical elements have been covered. (See http://www.equator-network.org/ [November 22, 2011] for examples of standards for outputs such as publications, health information products, and clinical guidelines.) For various technologies and devices, resources such as the Principles of Universal Design (Story and Mueller, 2002) provide a good starting point for assessing quality in terms of access and usability. Although the evidence base for these types of checklists and standards may vary (testing is described in the protocols), they do provide indicators of quality for ongoing self-assessment. When grantees provided evidence of self-assessment, along with external review by consumers, academics, and other stakeholders, the committee rated their outputs higher on the quality scale. Finally, a frequent weakness noted among the tools and technology outputs in particular was that there was insufficient evidence of the science underlying their development. Relying on checklists and standards should assist in reminding developers of the need to document their evidence base.

Additionally, despite limitations of using bibliometrics as described earlier in this chapter, they are a valuable and objective set of metrics that can be used in combination with other assessment strategies. NIDRR has conducted bibliometric analyses in the past, but has not routinely incorporated use of these metrics into its performance measurement.

Recommendation 6-2: NIDRR should consider undertaking bibliometric analyses of its grantees' publications as a routine component of performance measurement.

Bibliometric analyses would take advantage of an existing data source for periodic measurement of the scientific impact of NIDRR grantees' publications, as well as the extent to which these outputs are being disseminated and used. This type of metric is being recommended for use in combination with other measures, just as it was used in this evaluation along with expert review and supplemental evidence of the impact an article may have had on consumers, practice, health and social systems, social and health policy, or the private sector and commercialization. Alternative journal quality metrics are being developed (Brown, 2011), but SJR and ISI are widely used and accepted in the field, which facilitates comparison of journal outputs of NIDRR grants and those of other federal agencies and across the diverse fields of research and development funded by NIDRR. Several technology journals in the area of rehabilitation do have journal impact factors as presented in Table 6-4 and Annex 6-1 (e.g., *Assistive Technology*, *Transactions on Biomedical Engineering*, *Telemedicine and E-health*). However, technology grantees may publish in trade journals and magazines that are not tracked by Scopus and Web of Science. Alternative metrics could be used for development projects, such as the extent of adoption and utilization of devices.

SELF-ASSESSMENT OF THE COMMITTEE'S REVIEW METHODS

As part of its charge, the committee engaged in a subjective, self-reflective appraisal of its process in developing a system for assessing the quality of grantee outputs. The committee endeavored to assess its evaluation methods informally throughout the study process. Members engaged in continuous reflection and recording of strengths and weaknesses during the rating process conducted in subgroup meetings. To facilitate this effort, the committee chair participated in all subgroup meetings to ensure that members understood how each subgroup was applying the rating methods. In addition, conference calls with the committee were held after each set of subgroup meetings to discuss the evaluation process and refine the methods. Lastly, during its final meeting, the committee devoted a half-day session to discussion of the strengths and weaknesses of the process and the development of conclusions and recommendations for future evaluations. This discussion was based on the committee's continuous reflection on the process, along with findings from an informal assessment of committee members' individual views about the review process.

Each committee member was asked about his or her level of confidence in multiple aspects of the review process and its replication. Their responses were intended to provide an indicator of each committee member's impressions of the output rating process. Individual members were generally confident in the review process and its potential replication. Aspects of the process in which the committee had the greatest confidence were the technical quality scores, the face validity of the consensus scores that were produced for outputs, and the appropriateness of a seven-point quality rating scale.

These individual impressions were consistent with those developed by the committee as a whole in reflecting on the strengths and weakness of the evaluation process over the course of its work. They also confirmed the committee's impressions regarding the challenge of rating outputs other than articles in peer-reviewed journals. The committee members indicated their lowest confidence in that aspect of the review process.

The committee's views regarding replication of the review process largely mirrored those regarding the process itself. Committee members expressed the greatest confidence in the potential ability to match appropriate reviewer expertise with outputs for review and the ability to secure knowledgeable reviewers appropriately. They expressed less confidence in the potential ability to assess the overall quality of grants by reviewing only selected outputs.

Overall, members' reflections on the summative evaluation process suggest that, based on their experience, it worked well and achieved what it was designed to do. However, the committee encountered several challenges and limitations during the course of its work that limit the generalizability of the findings from this evaluation and restrict what can be said about the totality of outputs generated by all NIDRR grantees.

CONCLUSIONS AND RECOMMENDATIONS FOR FUTURE EVALUATIONS

In this section, the committee presents its conclusions and recommendations on defining future evaluation objectives, strengthening the output assessment, and improving use of the APR to capture data for future evaluations. The goal is to address aspects of the process that might be reconsidered to improve future evaluations and to ensure that evaluation results optimally inform NIDRR's efforts to maximize the impact of its research grants.

Defining Future Evaluation Objectives

The primary focus of the summative evaluation was on assessing the quality of research and development outputs produced by grantees. The evaluation did not include in-depth examination or comparison of the larger context of the funding programs, grants, or projects within which the outputs were produced. Although capacity building is a major thrust of NIDRR's center and training grants, assessment of training outputs, such as the number of trainees moving into research positions, was also beyond the scope of the committee's charge.

NIDRR's program mechanisms vary substantially in both size and duration, with grant amounts varying from under $100,000 (fellowship grants) to more than $4 million (center grants) and their duration varying from 1 to more than 5 years. Programs also differ in their objectives, so the expectations of the grantees under different programs vary widely. For example, a Switzer training grant is designed to increase the number of qualified researchers active in the field of disability and rehabilitation research. In contrast, center grants and Model System grants have multiple objectives that include research, technical assistance, training, and dissemination. Model System grants (BMS, TBIMS, SCIMS) have the added expectation of contributing patient-level data to a pooled set of data on the targeted condition.

The number of grants to be reviewed was predetermined by the committee's charge as 30, which represented about one-quarter of the pool of 111 grants from which the sample was drawn. The committee's task included drawing a sample of grants that reflected NIDRR's program mechanisms.

The number of grants reviewed for any of the nine program mechanisms included in the sample was small—the largest number for any single program was 10 (FIP). Therefore, the committee made no attempt to compare the quality of outputs by program mechanism.

NIDRR directed the committee to review two outputs for each of the grantee's projects. A grantee with a single project had two outputs reviewed, a grantee with three projects had six outputs reviewed, and so on. Although larger grants with more projects also had more outputs reviewed, the evaluation design did not consider grant size, duration, or the relative importance of a given project within a grant.

The committee was asked to produce an overall grant rating based on the outputs reviewed. Results at the grant level are subject to more limitations than those at the output level because of the general lack of information about how the outputs did or did not interrelate; whether, and if so how, grant objectives were accomplished; and the relative priority placed on the various outputs. In addition, for larger, more complex grants, such as center grants, a number of expectations for the grants, such as capacity building, dissemination, outreach, technical assistance, and training, are unlikely to be adequately reflected in the committee's approach, which focused exclusively on specific outputs. The relationship of outputs to grants is more complex than this approach could address.

Recommendation 6-3: NIDRR should determine whether assessment of the quality of outputs should be the sole evaluation objective.

Considering other evaluation objectives might offer NIDRR further opportunities to continuously assess and improve its performance and achieve its mission. Alternative designs would be needed to evaluate the quality of grants or to allow comparison across program mechanisms. For example, if one goal of an evaluation were to assess the larger outcomes of grants (i.e., the overall impact of their full set of activities), in addition to the methods used in the current output assessment, the evaluation would need to include interviewing grantees about their original objectives to learn about how the grant was implemented and any changes that may have occurred in the projected pathway, how various projects were tied into the overall grant objectives, and how the outputs demonstrated the achievement of the grant and project objectives. The evaluation would also involve conducting bibliometric or other analyses of all publications and examining documentation of the grant's activities and self-assessments, including cumulative APRs over time. Focusing at the grant level would provide evidence of movement along the research and development pathway (e.g., from theory to measures, from prototype testing to market), as well as allow for assessment of other aspects of the grant, such as training and technical assistance and the possible synergies of multiple projects within one grant.

If the goal of an evaluation were to assess and compare the impact of program mechanisms, the methods might vary across different program mechanisms depending on the expectations for each, but would include those mentioned above and also stakeholder surveys to learn about the specific ways in which individual grants have affected their intended audiences. With regard to sampling methods, larger grant sample sizes that allowed for generalization and comparison across program mechanisms would be needed. An alternative would be to increase the grant sample size in a narrower area by focusing on grants working in specific research areas across different program mechanisms or on grants with shared objectives (e.g., product development, knowledge translation, capacity building).

NIDRR's own pressing questions would of course drive future evaluations, but other levels of analysis on which NIDRR might focus include the portfolio level (e.g., Model System grants, research and development, training grants), which NIDRR has addressed in the past; the program priority level (i.e., grants funded under certain NIDRR funding priorities) to answer questions regarding the quality and impact of NIDRR's priority setting; and institute-level questions aimed at evaluating the net impact of NIDRR grants to test assumptions embedded in NIDRR's logic model. For example, NIDRR's logic model targets adoption and use of new knowledge leading to changes/improvements in policy, practice, behavior, and system capacity for the ultimate benefit of persons with disabilities (National Institute on Disability and Rehabilitation Research, 2006). The impact of NIDRR grants might also be evaluated by comparing grant proposals that were and were not funded. Did applicants that were not funded by NIDRR go on to receive funding from other agencies for projects similar to those for which they did not receive NIDRR funding? Were they successful in achieving their objectives with that funding? What outputs were produced?

The number of outputs reviewed should depend on the unit of analysis. At the grant level, it might be advisable to assess all outputs to examine their development, their interrelationships, and their impacts. A case study methodology could be used for related subsets of outputs. If NIDRR aimed its evaluation at the program mechanism or portfolio level, sampling grants and assessing all outputs would be the preferred method. For output-level evaluation, having grantees self-nominate their best outputs, as was done for the present evaluation, is a good approach.

Although assessing grantee outputs is valuable, the committee believes that the most meaningful results would come from assessing outputs in the context of a more comprehensive grant-level and program mechanism-level evaluation. More time and resources would be required to trace a grant's progress over time toward accomplishing its objectives; to understand its evolution, which may have altered the original objectives; and to examine the specific projects that produced the various outputs. However, examining more closely the inputs and grant implementation processes that produced the outputs would yield broader implications for the value of grants, their impact, and future directions for NIDRR.

Strengthening the Output Assessment

The committee was able to develop and implement a quantifiable expert review process for evaluating the outputs of NIDRR grantees, which was based on criteria used in assessing federal research programs in both the United States and other countries. With refinements, this method could be applied to the evaluation of future outputs even more effectively. Nonetheless, in implementing this method, the committee encountered challenges and issues related to the diversity of outputs, the timing of evaluations, sources of information, and reviewer expertise.

Diversity of Outputs

The quality rating system used for the summative evaluation worked well for publications in particular, which made up 70 percent of the outputs reviewed. Using the four criteria outlined earlier in this chapter, the reviewers were able to identify varying levels of quality and the characteristics associated with each. However, the quality criteria were not as easily applied to such outputs as websites, conferences, and interventions; these outputs require more individualized criteria for assessing specialized technical elements, and sometimes more in-depth evaluation methods. Applying one set of criteria, even though broad and flexible, could not guarantee sufficient and appropriate applicability to every type of output.

Timing of Evaluations

The question arises of when best to perform an assessment of outputs. Technical quality can be assessed immediately, but assessment of the impact of outputs requires the passage of time between the release of the outputs and their eventual impact. Evaluation of outputs during the final year of an award may not allow sufficient time for the outputs to have full impact. For example, some publications will be forthcoming at this point, and others will not have had sufficient time to have an impact. The trade-off of waiting a year or more after the end of a grant before performing an evaluation is the likelihood that staff involved with the original grant may not be available, recollection of grant activities may be compromised, and engagement or interest in demonstrating results may be reduced. However, publications can be tracked regardless of access to the grantee. Outputs other than publications, such as technology products, could undergo an interim evaluation to enable examination of the development of outputs.

Sources of Information

Committee members were provided with structured briefing books containing the outputs to be reviewed. They were also provided with supplemental information on which members could draw as necessary to assign quality scores. These other sources included information submitted through the grantees' APRs and information provided in a questionnaire developed by the committee (presented in Appendix B). The primary source of information used by committee members in assigning scores was direct review of the outputs themselves. The supplemental information played a small role in assessing publications, whereas for outputs such as newsletters and websites, this information sometimes provided needed context and additional evidence helpful in assigning quality scores. However, it is important to note that the supplemental information represented grantees' self-reports, which may have been susceptible to social desirability bias. Therefore, committee members were cautious in using this information to serve as the basis for boosting output scores. Moreover, the APR is designed as a grant monitoring tool rather than as a source of information for a program evaluation, and the information it supplied was not always sufficient to inform the quality ratings.

To illustrate the limitations of the information available to the committee, the technical quality of a measurement instrument was difficult to assess if there was insufficient information about its conceptual base or its development and testing. Likewise, for conferences, workshops, and websites, it would have been preferable for the grantee to identify the intended audience so that the committee might have better assessed whether the described dissemination activities were successful in reaching that audience. For the output categories of tools, technology, and informational products, grantees sometimes provided a publication that did not necessarily describe the output. In addition, some outputs were difficult to assess when no corroborating evidence was provided to support grantees' claims about technical quality, advancement of the field, impact, or dissemination efforts.

The committee did not use standardized reporting guidelines, such as CONSORT (Schulz et al., 2010) or PRISMA (Moher et al., 2009), used by journals in their peer review processes for selecting manuscripts for publication. The committee members generally assumed that publications that had been peer reviewed warranted a minimum score of 4 for technical quality. (In some cases, peer-reviewed publications were ultimately given technical quality scores above or below 4 following committee discussion.) Had reporting guidelines been used in the review of research publications, it is possible that the committee's ratings would have changed.

Reviewer Expertise

The committee was directed to assess the quality of four types of prespecified outputs. While the most common output type was publications, NIDRR grants produce a range of other outputs, including tools and measures, technology devices and standards, and informational products. These outputs vary widely in their complexity and the investment needed to produce them. For example, a newsletter is a more modest output than a new technology or device. To assess the quality of outputs, the committee members used criteria based on the cumulative literature reviewed and their own expertise in diverse research areas of rehabilitation and disability research, medicine, and engineering, as well as their expertise in evaluation, economics, knowledge translation, and policy. However, the committee's combined expertise did not include every possible content area in the broad field of disability and rehabilitation research.

> **Recommendation 6-4: If future evaluations of output quality are conducted, the process developed by the committee should be implemented with refinements to strengthen the design related to the diversity of outputs, timing of evaluations, sources of information, and reviewer expertise.**

Corresponding to the above points, these refinements include the following.

Diversity of outputs The dimensions of the quality criteria should be tailored and appropriately operationalized for different types of outputs, such as devices, tools, and informational products (including newsletters, conferences, and websites) and should be field tested with grants under multiple program mechanisms and refined as needed.

For example, the technical quality criterion includes the dimension of accessibility and usability. The questionnaire asked grantees to provide evidence of these traits. However, the dimensions should be better operationalized for different types of outputs. For tools, such as measurement instruments, the evidence to be provided should pertain to pilot testing and psychometrics. For informational products, such as websites, the evidence should include, for example, results of user testing, assessment of usability features, compliance with Section 508 standards (regulations from the 1998 amendment to the Rehabilitation Act of 1973 requiring the accessibility of federal agencies' electronic and information technology to people with disabilities). For technology devices, the evidence should document the results of research and development tests related to such attributes as human factors, ergonomics, universal design, product reliability, and safety.

The quality criterion related to dissemination provides other clear examples of the need for further specification and operationalization of the dimensions. For example, the dissemination of technology devices should be assessed by examining progress toward commercialization; grantees' partnerships with relevant stakeholders, including consumers and manufacturers; and the delivery of information through multiple media types and sources tailored to intended audiences for optimal reach and accessibility.

Timing of evaluations The committee suggests that the timing of an output evaluation should vary by the output type. Publications would best be assessed at least 2 years after the end of the grant. However, plans for publications and dissemination and the audience for scientific papers could be included in the final report. As stated earlier, other outputs developed during the course of the grant should be evaluated on an interim basis to assess the development and evolution of products. Outputs that have the potential to generate change in practice or policy may require more time to pass before impact materializes and can be measured, and so would best be evaluated on an interim basis as well.

Sources of information A more proactive technical assistance approach is needed to ensure that grantees provide the data necessary to assess the specific dimensions of each quality criterion. As stated earlier, the information supplied in the APR and the questionnaire was not always sufficient to inform the quality ratings. (See also the above discussion of information requested on the grantee questionnaire and the discussion below of the APR.)

Reviewer expertise The committee suggests that for future output evaluations, NIDRR should consider developing an accessible pool of experts in different technical areas who can be called upon to review selected grants and outputs. In addition, it is essential that future review panels include scientists with disabilities. Consumers also could also play a vital role as review panel members by addressing key criteria related to impact and dissemination.

Improving Use of the Annual Performance Report

NIDRR's APR system has many strengths, but the committee identified some improvements the agency should consider in building greater potential for use of these data in evaluations. The APR system (Research Triangle International, 2009) includes the grant abstract, funding information, descriptions of the research and development projects, and outcome domains targeted by projects, as well as a range of variables for reporting on the four different types of grantee outputs, as shown in Table 6-5. The system is tailored to different program mechanisms as needed. All of the descriptive information listed above, plus the output-specific variables listed in Table 6-5, were utilized in the committee's evaluation. The data were provided in electronic databases and in the form of individual grant reports.

The APR data set NIDRR provided to the committee at the outset of its work was helpful in profiling the grants for sampling and in listing all of the grantees' projects and outputs. It facilitated asking the grantees to nominate outputs for the evaluation since it enabled the committee to generate comprehensive lists of all reported projects and outputs to make the task of output selection less burdensome for the grantees. If grantees had more recent outputs originating from their NIDRR grants that they wished to nominate as their top two for the committee's review, they had the option of doing so.

NIDRR also provided grantees' narrative APRs from the last year of their grants, as well as their final reports. These narratives were highly useful to the committee for compiling descriptions of the grants.[3] However, the quality of the information contained in these narrative reports varied. For example, grant abstracts were not uniform in the information they contained. Some stated the grant objectives, whereas others did not, focusing on summarizing the main grant activities. The APRs for the grants reviewed by the committee also were inconsistent in providing information useful for understanding how the outputs being reviewed fit within the overall grant or projects. The final reports in most cases did not provide a cumulative overview of the life cycle of the grants and outputs, which would have been helpful. The APR does collect information on changes in the course of a grant, yet it was not always easy to understand this information simply by viewing the last year's APR or the final report.

The APRs did not report on all of the specific outputs reviewed by the committee. Some outputs may have been reported in earlier reporting periods or have been produced after the NIDRR grant ended. However, NIDRR also provided the committee with special text reports containing some of the narrative information concerning outputs other than publications. These reports included such information as the purpose of the output, NIDRR outcome domains targeted by the output, how the output was validated, and how the output contributed to achievement of the grantee's objections.

[3]The APR is a large information technology system that is used for monitoring and tracking grantee progress and for reporting on NIDRR's performance measures under the Government Performance and Results Act (GPRA). The system was not designed to serve as the basis for grantee evaluations. A systematic evaluation of the APR was not part of the committee's charge. Although the quality and level of detail of the APRs varied, these narratives were useful in providing descriptive grant information.

TABLE 6-5 Data Elements Related to Outputs That Are Covered in the APR

Variables in APR (using APR report format for Rehabilitation Research and Training Centers as an example)	Publications	Tools	Technology	Information
Type of output	X	X	X	X
Name and full citation	X	X	X	X
Brief description of purpose		X	X	X
Brief description of how output was validated or tested		X	X	X
Whether publication was peer reviewed or not	X			
Whether the research and related activity reported in the article took place during current, immediate past, or previous (nonconsecutive) funding cycle	X			
Whether publication was sent to the National Rehabilitation Information Center (NARIC) for inclusion in REHABDATA	X			
Whether publication was produced as a direct result of receiving funding for this grant	X			
"Most important"* outputs that made the greatest contribution to achieving the outcome-oriented goals for the award	X	X	X	X
Outcome-oriented goal that corresponds to most important outputs (advances knowledge; increases capacity for research, training, or knowledge translation; or facilitates change in policy, practice, or system capacity)	X	X	X	X
NIDRR outcome arena that corresponds to most important outputs (health and function, employment, participation and community living, cross-cutting)	X	X	X	X
Whether output is described in a publication output and if so, which one		X	X	X
Key findings or lessons learned	X			
How output is contributing to outcome-oriented goal by solving a problem, closing an identified gap, or benefiting the target population	X	X	X	X
Description of "other accomplishments and contributions"	X	X	X	X

*Defined for grantees by NIDRR as "those that contributed most to achieving the outcome-oriented goals for the award by advancing knowledge; increasing capacity for research, training or knowledge translation; or facilitating changes in policy, practice, or system capacity."
SOURCE: Generated by the committee based on Research Triangle International (2009).

These reports have the potential to supply relevant information for evaluations. However, the quality of this information varied across the text reports describing the tools, technologies, and informational products reviewed by the committee. Only half contained substantive descriptive information.

> **Recommendation 6-5: NIDRR should consider revising its APR to better capture information needed to routinely evaluate the quality and impacts of outputs, grants, or program mechanisms. The agency might consider efforts such as consolidating existing data elements or adding new elements to capture the quality criteria and dimensions used in the present summative evaluation.**

According to NIDRR management, the agency's APR system has stabilized in recent years following periods of changing and improving it to make the data more usable for grantees, for grant monitoring, and for agency performance reporting. The agency currently is in the process of adding a new "accomplishments" module to the APR that will focus on the external use and adoption of NIDRR-funded outputs. In this new module, NIDRR will consolidate some data elements that are already being collected and add new ones. For up to five outputs that have been used or adopted by persons or groups external to the grant during the reporting period, grantees will be asked to provide information for each output on who adopted it (in 16 categories, such as researchers, practitioners, and service providers); how the output is being used or adopted by the target audience; the source of the evidence; and whether and how the output may be contributing to changes in policy, practice, system capacity, or other impact areas. These efforts to improve the APR will address the quality criteria used in the present evaluation for assessing the advancement of knowledge or practice and the likely or demonstrated impact of outputs.

For the technical quality criterion, the current APR system collects data on whether articles were published in peer-reviewed journals. For the technical quality of outputs other than publications, Recommendation 6-4 provides examples of ways to operationalize dimensions of accessibility and usability, such as providing evidence of testing the psychometrics of measurement instruments; assessing the usability features of informational products; and documenting the results of research and development tests of technology products that relate to human factors, ergonomics, universal design, product reliability, and safety. The APR system currently asks for information on how outputs were validated, but data elements that relate to such testing might be further specified in the system.

The APR system might also be modified to capture evidence on the quality criterion of dissemination of outputs through such data elements as target audiences for dissemination activities; media types; number of outputs disseminated; and reach of dissemination, such as number of hits on websites.

Recommendation 6-6: NIDRR should investigate ways to work with grantees to ensure the completeness and consistency of information provided in the APR.

The committee fully appreciates the need to minimize the data collection burden on grantees and acknowledges the challenges and feasibility issues related to modifying the APR system while at the same time providing continuity in the system. The committee believes that embedding evaluation data collection processes into existing processes would lead to greater efficiencies and reduce grantee burden while enhancing NIDRR's ability to evaluate quality and impact. The committee acknowledges that the suggested refinements would have to be undertaken in the context of a larger assessment of the APR system as part of NIDRR's ongoing initiatives to improve the system.

More immediately, grantees should be made aware that, in addition to being a data source for assessing individual grant performance, APRs could be a valuable data source for NIDRR's program evaluation purposes. Project officers could provide technical assistance, working with individual grantees on focusing their APRs more on the details of their findings that move their projects forward and lead to changes and improvements in policy, practice, behavior, and system capacity.

In closing, the committee developed and implemented a quantifiable expert review process that can serve as a foundation for future evaluations of the quality of outputs of NIDRR grantees. If future evaluations of output quality are conducted, the methods developed by the committee should be implemented with refinements to strengthen the design, validity, and reliability of the process. Whereas assessing grantee outputs is valuable, the committee believes that even greater value would come from assessing outputs in the context of a more comprehensive grant-level and program mechanism-level evaluation, which could yield broader implications for the value of grants, their impact, and future directions for NIDRR.

REFERENCES

Bernstein, A., Hick, V., Borbey, P., Campbell, T., McAuley, L., and Graham, I.D. (2007). A framework to measure the impacts of investments in health research. In Organisation for Economic Co-Operation and Development, *Science, technology and innovation indicators in a changing world: Responding to policy needs* (pp. 231-251). Ottawa, CA: Organisation for Economic Co-Operation and Development.

Brown, T. (2011). Journal quality metrics: Options to consider other than impact factors. *American Journal of Occupational Therapy, 65*(3), 346-350.

Chien, C.F., Chen, C.P., and Chen, C.H. (2009). Designing performance indices and a novel mechanism for evaluating government R&D project. *Journal of Quality, 19*(2), 119-135.

Ismail, S., Tiessen, J., and Wooding, S. (2010). *Strengthening research portfolio evaluation at the Medical Research Council: Developing a survey for the collection of information about research outputs*. Santa Monica, CA: RAND Corporation.

MacLennan, R.N. (1993). Interrater reliability with SPSS for Windows 5.0. *The American Statistician, 47*(4), 292-296.

Moher, D., Liberati, A., Tetzlaff, J., Altman, D.G., and The PRISMA Group. (2009). Preferred reporting items for systematic reviews and meta-analyses: The PRISMA statement. *PLoS Medicine, 6*(6), e1000097.

National Academy of Sciences, National Academy of Engineering, and Institute of Medicine. (1999). *Evaluating federal research programs: Research and Government Performance and Results Act*. Committee on Science, Engineering, and Public Policy. Washington, DC: National Academy Press.

National Institute on Disability and Rehabilitation Research. (2006). Department of Education: National Institute on Disability and Rehabilitation Research—Notice of Final Long-Range Plan for Fiscal Years 2005–2009. *Federal Register, 71*(31), 8,166-8,200.

National Institute on Disability and Rehabilitation Research. (2008, August). *Meeting report of the NIDRR External Evaluation Advisory Group*. Unpublished document. Washington, DC: National Institute on Disability and Rehabilitation Research.

National Research Council and Institute of Medicine. (2007). *Mining safety and health research at NIOSH: Reviews of research programs of the National Institute for Occupational Safety and Health*. Committee to Review the NIOSH Mining Safety and Research Program. Committee on Earth Resources and Board on Earth Sciences and Resources. Washington, DC: The National Academies Press.

Panel on Return on Investment in Health Research. (2009). *Appendices—Making an impact: A preferred framework and indicators to measure returns on investment in health research*. Ottawa, Canada: Canadian Academy of Health Sciences.

Research Triangle International. (2009). *National Institute on Disability and Rehabilitation Research. Annual Performance Report: Web-based reporting system instruction manual*. Research Triangle Park, NC: Research Triangle International.

Schulz, K.F., Altman, D.G., and Moher, D. for the CONSORT Group. (2010). CONSORT 2010 statement: Updated guidelines for reporting parallel group randomised trials. *Annals of Internal Medicine, 152*.

Story, M.F., and Mueller, J. (2002). Universal design performance measures for products: A tool for assessing universal usability. In J.M. Winters, C.J. Robinson, R.C. Simpson, and G.C. Vanderheiden (Eds.), *Emerging and accessible telecommunications, information and healthcare technologies* (pp. 19-28). Arlington, VA: RESNA Press.

Wooding, S., and Starkey, T. (2010). *Piloting the RAND/ARC Impact Scoring System (RAISS) tool in the Canadian context*. Cambridge, England: RAND Europe.

Wooding, S., Nason, E., Starkey, T., Haney, S., and Grant, J. (2009). *Mapping the impact: Exploring the payback of arthritis research*. Santa Monica, CA: RAND Corporation.

Yaffee, R.A. (1998). *Enhancement of reliability analysis: Application of intraclass correlations with SPSS/Windows v.8*. Available: http://www.nyu.edu/its/statistics/Docs/intracls.html [April 20, 2011].

ANNEX 6-1
JOURNAL IMPACT FACTORS OF PUBLISHED ARTICLES FROM GRANTS IN THE ORIGINAL POOL FROM WHICH THE SAMPLE OF 30 GRANTS WAS DRAWN (N = 111 GRANTS, 631 ARTICLES)

TABLE A6-1

Journal Name	SJR[a]	ISI[b]	Number of Times Articles Were Published in This Journal[c]
Archives of Physical Medicine and Rehabilitation	0.160	2.254	75
Journal of Spinal Cord Medicine	0.124	1.442	32
Journal of Head Trauma Rehabilitation	0.170	2.779	28
Journal of Burn Care & Research	0.109	1.563	27
Disability and Rehabilitation	0.097	1.489	24
Topics in Stroke Rehabilitation	0.099	1.224	17
American Journal of Physical Medicine & Rehabilitation	0.125	1.762	16
Rehabilitation Psychology	0.077	1.676	15
Brain Injury	0.118	1.75	10
Hearing Loss	NA	NA	10
NeuroRehabilitation	0.099	1.592	9
Assistive Technology	0.061	NA	8
Burns	0.120	1.718	7
Journal of Rehabilitation Research and Development	0.125	1.708	7
Physical Medicine and Rehabilitation Clinics of North America	0.102	1.364	7
Research and Practice for Persons with Severe Disabilities	0.031	0.484	7
Trends in Amplification	0.14	NA	7

continued

TABLE A6-1 (Continued)

Journal Name	SJR[a]	ISI[b]	Number of Times Articles Were Published in This Journal[c]
American Journal of Hospice & Palliative Medicine	0.083	0.969	6
Assistive Technology Outcomes and Benefits	NA	NA	6
Muscle & Nerve	0.263	2.302	6
Rehabilitation Counseling Bulletin	0.04	0.74	6
Respiratory Care	0.132	1.534	6
Exceptionality	NA	0.71	5
Journal of Vocational Rehabilitation	0.033	NA	5
Multiple Sclerosis	0.374	4.23	5
Topics in Spinal Cord Injury Rehabilitation	0.041	NA	5
Clinical Neuropsychologist	0.099	2.075	4
Critical Care Medicine	0.615	6.254	4
General Hospital Psychiatry	0.254	2.777	4
Health Affairs	0.424	3.792	4
Journal of Clinical and Experimental Neuropsychology	0.123	1.805	4
Neurology	0.684	8.017	4
Shock	0.37	3.203	4
Stroke	0.731	5.756	4
Annals of Biomedical Engineering	0.202	2.374	3
Career Development for Exceptional Individuals	0.032	NA	3
Developmental Disabilities Research Reviews	0.276	3.436	3
Exceptional Children	0.052	2.271	3
Exceptional Parent	NA	NA	3
IEEE Transactions on Biomedical Engineering	0.137	1.782	3
International Journal of Clinical and Experimental Hypnosis	0.068	1.842	3
Journal of Disability Policy Studies	0.04	NA	3
Journal of Early Intervention	0.048	0.694	3
Journal of Intellectual Disability Research	0.115	1.596	3
Journal of Neurotrauma	0.357	3.426	3
Journal of Rehabilitation	0.032	0.222	3
Pediatrics	0.503	5.391	3
Psychosomatic Medicine	0.354	3.974	3
Spine	0.19	2.51	3
Violence Against Women	0.057	1.215	3
ADVANCE for Directors in Rehabilitation	NA	NA	2
American Journal of Speech-Language Pathology	0.118	2.018	2
Annals of Neurology	1.415	10.746	2
Archives of Clinical Neuropsychology	0.151	2.304	2
Archives of Neurology	0.778	7.108	2
Body Image	0.1	2.109	2

TABLE A6-1 (Continued)

Journal Name	SJR[a]	ISI[b]	Number of Times Articles Were Published in This Journal[c]
Children and Youth Services Review	0.047	1.13	2
Developmental Neurorehabilitation	0.073	1.384	2
Disability and Health Journal	0.044	NA	2
Disability and Rehabilitation Assistive Technology	0.053	NA	2
Education and Training in Developmental Disabilities	0.032	0.466	2
E-Medicine	NA	NA	2
Giornale Italiano delle Disabilità [Italian Journal on Disability]	NA	NA	2
Infants and Young Children	0.038	0.6	2
Inside MS	NA	NA	2
International Journal of Telerehabilitation	NA	NA	2
Journal of Burn Care and Rehabilitation	NA	NA	2
Journal of Developmental Disabilities	0.026	0.174	2
Journal of Mine Action	NA	NA	2
Journal of Neurology Neurosurgery and Psychiatry	0.432	4.791	2
Journal of the Acoustical Society of America	0.079	1.644	2
Journal of Visual Impairment & Blindness	NA	NA	2
Journal on Developmental Disabilities	NA	NA	2
Lancet Neurology	1.977	21.659	2
Medicine and Science in Sports and Exercise	0.291	4.106	2
MS in Focus	NA	NA	2
Neuropsychological Rehabilitation	0.118	1.731	2
Pain	0.547	5.355	2
Physical Therapy	0.189	2.645	2
Progress in Brain Research	0.4	3.134	2
Prosthetics and Orthotics International	0.052	0.634	2
Rehabilitation Education	NA	NA	2
Remedial and Special Education	0.04	0.561	2
Spinal Cord	0.161	1.826	2
TASH Connections	NA	NA	2
Academic Radiology	0.191	2.195	1
ADVANCE for Managers of Respiratory Care	NA	NA	1
AER-Journal of Research and Practice in Visual Impairment and Blindness	NA	NA	1
American Annals of the Deaf	0.038	0.694	1
American Journal of Medicine	0.462	5.115	1
American Journal of Pathology	1.024	5.224	1
American Occupational Therapy Association	0.072	NA	1
Amyotrophic Lateral Sclerosis	0.293	3.397	1
Annals of Behavioral Medicine	0.249	3.984	1

continued

TABLE A6-1 (Continued)

Journal Name	SJR[a]	ISI[b]	Number of Times Articles Were Published in This Journal[c]
Annals of Surgery	0.822	7.474	1
Arthritis & Rheumatism-Arthritis Care & Research	1.158	8.435	1
Assessment for Effective Instruction	NA	NA	1
Behaviour & Information Technology	0.039	0.835	1
Brain and Language	0.187	3.162	1
Brain Injury Professional	NA	NA	1
Chest	0.61	6.519	1
Chronic Illness	0.118	NA	1
Clinical Biomechanics	0.143	2.036	1
Clinical Rheumatology	0.16	1.687	1
Communication Disorders Quarterly	0.034	NA	1
Composites Part B-Engineering	0.091	1.763	1
Connective Tissue Research	0.214	2.093	1
Critical Care	0.394	4.595	1
Current Opinion in Neurology	0.57	5.021	1
Current Treatment Options in Neurology	0.183	1.81	1
Cyberpsychology & Behavior	NA	1.803	1
Datum, Medical College of Wisconsin	NA	NA	1
Design Principles and Practices: An International Journal	NA	NA	1
Ear and Hearing	0.193	2.257	1
Exercise and Sport Sciences Reviews	0.268	3.825	1
Generations	0.032	NA	1
Hearing Journal	0.031	NA	1
Hearing Review	NA	NA	1
Hospital News (nationally syndicated)	NA	NA	1
Human Molecular Genetics	2.011	8.058	1
IEEE Engineering in Medicine and Biology Magazine	0.074	2.828	1
IEEE Transactions on Neural Systems and Rehabilitation Engineering	0.134	2.182	1
IEEE Transactions on Power Electronics	0.124	3.176	1
Intellectual and Developmental Disabilities	0.048	1.327	1
Interacting with Computers	0.044	1.192	1
International Journal of Advances in Rheumatology	NA	NA	1
International Journal of Disability, Development, and Education	0.035	NA	1
International Journal of Geriatric Psychiatry	0.160	2.029	1
International Journal of Medical Informatics	0.147	2.244	1
International Journal of MS Care	NA	NA	1

TABLE A6-1 (Continued)

Journal Name	SJR[a]	ISI[b]	Number of Times Articles Were Published in This Journal[c]
International Journal of Psychiatry in Medicine	0.097	1.055	1
International Journal of Web Engineering and Technology	0.03	NA	1
Internet Research	0.039	1.15	1
Intervention in School and Clinic	0.03	0.351	1
Journal for Vocational Special Needs Education	NA	NA	1
Journal of Aging and Social Policy	0.053	NA	1
Journal of Applied Rehabilitation Counseling	NA	NA	1
Journal of Behavioral Nutrition and Physical Activity	0.226	3.169	1
Journal of Biomedical Materials Research Part A	0.19	3.044	1
Journal of Cardiopulmonary Rehabilitation and Prevention	0.136	1.415	1
Journal of Clinical Psychology	0.088	1.612	1
Journal of Clinical Psychology in Medical Settings	0.122	1.506	1
Journal of Communication Disorders	0.107	1.433	1
Journal of Disability Policy	0.04	NA	1
Journal of Health Communication	0.116	1.5	1
Journal of Interpersonal Violence	0.065	1.354	1
Journal of Marriage and the Family	0.063	1.849	1
Journal of Neural Engineering	0.353	2.628	1
Journal of Occupational Rehabilitation	0.112	1.805	1
Journal of Orthopaedic Research	0.279	2.976	1
Journal of Pain	0.401	4.851	1
Journal of Pain and Symptom Management	0.25	2.64	1
Journal of Policy and Practice in Intellectual Disabilities	0.03	0.959	1
Journal of Positive Behavior Interventions	0.057	1.943	1
Journal of Positive Psychology	0.065	NA	1
Journal of Primary Prevention	0.059	1.09	1
Journal of Prosthetics and Orthotics	0.039	NA	1
Journal of Psychosomatic Research	0.224	2.842	1
Journal of Special Education	0.042	1.343	1
Journal of The American Geriatrics Society	0.397	3.913	1
Journal of The International Neuropsychological Society	0.209	2.91	1
Journal of Trauma-Injury Infection and Critical Care	0.155	3.129	1
Journal of Usability Studies	NA	NA	1

continued

TABLE A6-1 (Continued)

Journal Name	SJR[a]	ISI[b]	Number of Times Articles Were Published in This Journal[c]
Journal of Vocational Special Needs Education	NA	NA	1
Journal of Web Engineering	0.03	0.3	1
Kansas Public Policy Journal	NA	NA	1
L'Audition Revue D'Informations Techniques et Scientifiques	NA	NA	1
Learning Disabilities Quarterly	NA	NA	1
Lecture Notes in Computer Science	0.033	NA	1
Medical Care	0.398	3.183	1
Medical Care Research and Review	0.335	2.195	1
Mississippi Brain Injury Association Newsletter	NA	NA	1
Missouri Medicine	0.039	NA	1
Momentum	NA	NA	1
MS Exchange	NA	NA	1
Neuroimage	0.619	5.932	1
Neuromuscular Disorders	0.408	2.764	1
Neurorehabilitation Neural Repair	0.314	3.772	1
Novartis Foundation Symposium	NA	NA	1
O&P Business News	NA	NA	1
OT Practice	0.027	NA	1
Paraplegia News	NA	NA	1
Pediatric Critical Care Medicine	0.226	2.672	1
Perspectives on Neurophysiology and Neurogenic Speech and Language Disorders	NA	NA	1
Physical & Occupational Therapy in Geriatrics	0.029	NA	1
Planning	0.026	NA	1
Principal Leadership	NA	NA	1
Proceedings of IEEE Virtual Rehabilitation	NA	NA	1
Psychiatric Rehabilitation Journal	0.08	1.376	1
Psychiatric Services	0.145	2.388	1
Psychological Assessment	0.128	2.589	1
Psychology in the Schools	0.039	0.753	1
Rehabilitation Nursing	0.056	0.615	1
Rehabilitation Outlook	NA	NA	1
Seminars in Arthritis and Rheumatism	0.429	4.744	1
Seminars in Hearing	0.049	NA	1
Social Work	0.062	1.048	1
Technology and Disability	0.034	NA	1
Telemedicine and E-Health	0.081	1.297	1
The ASHA Leader	0.027	NA	1

TABLE A6-1 (Continued)

Journal Name	SJR[a]	ISI[b]	Number of Times Articles Were Published in This Journal[c]
The Journal of Special Children Education (Korea)	NA	NA	1
The Judge's Journal	NA	NA	1
The RT News, Newsletter of AER Division 11	NA	NA	1
Universal Access in the Information Society	0.036	NA	1
US-ISPO Highlights	NA	NA	1
Women's Health Issues	0.1	1.287	1
Wound Repair and Regeneration	0.35	3.443	1
Young Exceptional Children	0.026	NA	1
Total Published Articles Reviewed			**631**

NOTE: NA = journal not tracked by Scopus or Web of Science in the 2010 databases.
[a]SJR (Scopus): The SJR database for 2010 was used. Available: http://www.scopus.com/source/eval.url [August 29, 2011].
[b]ISI (Web of Science): These data were obtained by searching two Web of Knowledge JCR databases (editions): (1) JCR Science Edition 2010 and (2) JCR Social Sciences Edition 2010. Available: http://admin-apps.webofknowledge.com/JCR/JCR?RQ=HOME [August 29, 2011].
[c]The values in this column were obtained from a data set provided by NIDRR of all reported publications as of July 2010.
SOURCE: Generated by the committee based on data from Scopus (http://www.scopus.com) and Web of Science (http://apps.webofknowledge.com) (membership required for both).

Appendix A

Grant Summaries

This appendix contains individual summaries of the 30 grants that participated in the summative evaluation. Each grant summary includes (1) an abstract describing the overall work of the grant; (2) a table presenting each of the projects under the grant and listing the corresponding outputs for each project that were reviewed by the committee; and (3) a brief description of each reviewed output. Abstracts of the grants were adapted from the abstract in each grantee's Annual Performance Report (APR) or from abstracts contained in National Institute on Disability and Rehabilitation Research's (NIDRR's) National Rehabilitation Information Center (NARIC) (see: http://www.naric.com/research/ [Janauary 9, 2012]). In addition to listing the projects and reviewed outputs, the tables present the NIDRR research domains addressed by each project (see Chapter 1 for a description of NIDRR's five research domains). The output descriptions were developed by examining the outputs themselves and adapting information from the output abstracts, where available. The listing below shows each grant included in the evaluation and identifies the page in this appendix where the grant's summary can be found.

Funding Mechanism/Grant	Page Number
BURN MODEL SYSTEM (BMS)	210
Grant Title: Burn Model System/Data Coordinating Center	210
Grant Title: North Texas Burn Rehabilitation Model System	214
TRAUMATIC BRAIN INJURY MODEL SYSTEM (TBIMS)	218
Grant Title: Mayo Clinic TBI Model System	218
Grant Title: Spaulding/Partners Traumatic Brain Injury Model System at Harvard Medical School	221
SPINAL CORD INJURY MODEL SYSTEM (SCIMS)	226
Grant Title: Northern New Jersey Spinal Cord Injury System	226
Grant Title: The Missouri Model Spinal Cord Injury System	230
REHABILITATION RESEARCH AND TRAINING CENTER (RRTC)	233
Grant Title: Meeting the Nation's Needs for Personal Assistance Services: Center for Personal Assistance Services	233
Grant Title: RRTC on Disability Demographics and Statistics	237
Grant Title: RRTC on SCI: Promoting Health and Preventing Complications Through Exercise	242
REHABILITATION ENGINEERING RESEARCH CENTER (RERC)	248
Grant Title: RERC on Telerehabilitation	248
Grant Title: RERC on Universal Interface and Information Technology Access	253
DISABILITY AND REHABILITATION RESEARCH PROJECT-GENERAL (DRRP)	261
Grant Title: The Effect of Scheduled Telephone Intervention on Outcomes After TBI	261
Grant Title: Asset Accumulation and Tax Policy Project	263
Grant Title: Medicaid Quality Indicators for Individuals with Disabilities	268
Grant Title: Persons Aging with Hearing and Vision Loss	271
FIELD INITIATED PROJECT (FIP)	275
Grant Title: Efficacy of Pressure Garment Therapy After Burns	275
Grant Title: A Longitudinal Study for Hospitalization, Pressure Ulcers, and Subsequent Injuries After Spinal Cord Injuries	276
Grant Title: Black-White Disparities in Stroke Rehabilitation	278
Grant Title: Development of Intelligent Personal Activity Management and Prompting Applications for Individuals with Cognitive Disabilities	280
Grant Title: Driving After Stroke	282
Grant Title: Functional Effects of Bifocal Use: Implication for Falling Intervention	284
Grant Title: Inclusive Indoor Play	287

Grant Title: Interference in Hearing Aids from Digital Wireless Telephones: Improved Predictive Methods 289
Grant Title: Motor Training and Assessment in Adults with Hemiplegic Cerebral Palsy—The ULTrA Program 291
Grant Title: Using the U.S. EEOC Employment Discrimination Charge Data System for Research and Dissemination 293
SMALL BUSINESS INNOVATION RESEARCH II (SBIR-II) 296
Grant Title: Universal Access to Passenger Rail Cars 296
Grant Title: Web-Enabled Creation and Distribution of Audio-Tactile Maps for Use in Orientation and Mobility Training 297
SWITZER FELLOWSHIPS 300
Grant Title: A Noninvasive Surface Electromyogram Decomposition Method and Its Application in Disability Rehabilitation 300
Grant Title: Demographic Soup: Disentangling the Conceptual, Political, and Methodological Dimensions of Disability Statistics 301
Grant Title: Physical and Social Environmental Factors That Influence Health and Participation Outcomes for Chronically Ill Adults 303

BURN MODEL SYSTEM (BMS)

Grant Title: Burn Model System/Data Coordinating Center

Grant Award Number: H133A020402

Grantee: University of Colorado Denver, Colorado School of Public Health

Grant Mechanism: Burn Model System

Grant Start and End Dates: October 1, 2002, to September 30, 2008

Total Direct Cost: $1,410,621

Abstract:[1] The mission of the Burn Model System/Data Coordinating Center (BMS/DCC) was to support its respective four Burn Model System Clinical Centers by (1) serving the clinical, research, and public communities to which it is responsible; (2) serving the needs of good scientific procedure in multi-institutional outcomes research; and (3) supporting the needs for patient safety and data confidentiality as required by federal regulations when conducting collaborative clinical studies. To accomplish these objectives, researchers developed integrated systems to affect national data collection, project management, data coordination, technical support, collaborative clinical projects, scientific conduct, scientific publication, and effective dissemination. A central function of the BMS/DCC was also to accumulate and integrate a central repository of data from the four Burn Model System Clinical Centers, while being responsive to technical and analytical needs of the centers.

Research Projects and Outputs Reviewed: Grantees were asked to nominate two outputs from each of their projects for review by the committee. These outputs were identified by the study's key personnel as those that would best reflect their grant's achievements. Grantees selected the outputs to be reviewed from among the larger pool of outputs they had produced under the grant. This larger pool of outputs included six journal articles, one technical report, one fact sheet, one website, and one data dictionary. The following table shows the three projects carried out under this grant and lists the corresponding outputs that were nominated by the grantees and reviewed by the NRC committee. The reviewed outputs are briefly described following the table.

[1] Abstracts are adapted from the abstract in each grantee's Annual Performance Report, except for two, which are marked with separate footnotes.

(Note that because this grant was for a coordinating center, it was not organized by projects in the same way as the research and development grants. Therefore, for one of its main "activity areas," the grantee submitted more than two outputs for the committee's review.)

Project/*Research Domains**	**Outputs**
A. Establish and Maintain BMS Database *Health and Function* *Employment* *Participation and Community Living*	A1. Lezotte, D.C. (2008). *Model system for burn injury rehabilitation national database data dictionary* (16) [Data code listing]. Denver: Colorado School of Public Health, University of Colorado Denver. Lezotte, D.C. (2004). *Model system for burn injury rehabilitation national database data dictionary, Appendix A* (12) [Data code listing]. Denver: Colorado School of Public Health, University of Colorado Denver.
B. Develop and Implement Support Systems *Health and Function*	B1. Lezotte, D.C., and Sloan, R. (2004). *Process review of level I data center activities for burn model system/clinical sites*. Unpublished report, Department of Biostatistics and Informatics, University of Colorado, Denver.
	B2. Klein, M.B., Lezotte, D.C., Fauerbach, J.A., Herndon, D.N., Kowalske, K.J., Carrougher, G.J., deLateur, B.J., Holavanahalli, R., Esselman, P.C., San Augustin, T.B., and Engrav, L.H. (2007). The National Institute on Disability and Rehabilitation Research Burn Model System Database: A tool for the multi-center study of the outcome of burn injury. *Journal of Burn Care & Research, 28*(1), 84-96.
	B3. Lezotte, D.C., Hills, R.A., Heltshe, S.L., Holavanahalli, R.K., Fauerbach, J.A., Blakeney, P., Klein, M.B., and Engrav, L.H. (2007). Assets and liabilities of the Burn Model System Data Model: A comparison with the National Burn Registry. *Archives of Physical Medicine and Rehabilitation, 88*(12), S7-S17.
	B4. Fauerbach, J.A., Lezotte, D.C., Hills, R.A., Chromes, F.G., Kowalske, K., deLateur, B.J., Goodwin, C.W., Blakeney, P., Herndon, D.N., Wiechman, S.A., Engrav, L.H., and Patterson, D.R. (2005). Burden of burn: A norm-based inquiry into the influence of burn size and distress on recovery of physical and psychosocial function. *Journal of Burn Care & Rehabilitation, 26*(1), 21-32.
	B5. Serghiou, M.H., Rose, M.W., Pidcock, F.S., Esselman, P.C., Engrav, L.H., Kowalske, K.J., and Lezotte, D.C. (2008). The WeeFIM [R] instrument—A paediatric measure of functional independence to predict longitudinal recovery of paediatric burn patients. *Developmental Neurorehabilitation, 11*(1), 39-50.

Project/*Research Domains**	Outputs
B. Develop and Implement Support Systems *Health and Function*	B6. Lezotte, D.C. (2011). *BMS publications with DCC PI support*. Unpublished list of publications, Department of Biostatistics and Informatics, University of Colorado, Denver.
C. Implement a Dissemination Strategy for BMS *Health and Function* *Employment* *Knowledge Translation*	C1. Lezotte, D.C. (No date). *Public and secured BMS website for consumer information*. Available: http://bms-dcc.ucdenver.edu/ [January 9, 2012]. C2. Kaufman, M.S., Graham, C.C., Lezotte, D.C., Fauerbach, J.A., Gabriel, V., Engrav, L.H., and Esselman, P. (2007). Burns as a result of assault: Associated risk factors, injury characteristics, and outcomes. *Journal of Burn Care & Research, 28*(1), 21-28.

*This column also shows the key NIDRR research domain(s) that were being addressed by each project.

Brief Description of the Outputs: From the project to establish and maintain a BMS database, a data dictionary (A1) was reviewed. The data dictionary identifies what kind of data to collect and provides a coding scheme for the data. Data that should be collected include protected health information, patient status, preburn information, parts of body burned, parts of body grafted, skin-related problems, distress level, and scarring problems.

The next six outputs reviewed came from the project aimed at developing and implementing support systems. The first of these outputs was a technical report (B1), which describes site visit reviews of Burn Model System/Clinical Centers. Site visits were conducted to review data management operating procedures, review data security and privacy, seek feedback and recommendations for improving operations, and identify collaborative projects for which BMS/DCC could provide more support. Through the site visits, researchers assessed the quality of the data coming in from each site and documented effective site-specific management techniques and practices so they could be shared with other sites.

The next four outputs reviewed under this project were journal articles. Klein et al. (B2) conducted a descriptive study of both the data quality and structure of the Burn Model System database after 10 years of existence. They noted that a total of 4,600 patients had been entered into the database, with data being collected during hospitalization as well as at 6, 12, and 24 months after discharge. The structure of the database includes sections on demographics, injury complications, patient disposition, and functional and psychological surveys. It was concluded that the data and structure of the database were both of high quality and that the database is an important resource in supporting the work of Burn Model System projects. The next journal article (B3) compares the Burn Model System population with patients in the National Burn Registry. Patients from both populations were compared in terms of demographics and burn characteristics at discharge and over the course of follow up. Populations were compared in total and also broken down into groups with similar burns. Only minor and insignificant demographic variations between the Burn Model System and the National Burn Registry populations were discovered, and Lezotte et al. therefore concluded that the Burn Model System population is a representative sample, and results using Burn Model System data should be generalizable. Fauerbach et al. (B4) conducted a longitudinal study on the influence of physical and psychological burden on burn recovery. Participants included 162 adults with major burns from three burn centers. Participants were compared by level of burden and against published normative data. It was found that physical recovery was significantly slower for participants with either large physical or psychological burden. Additionally, psychosocial recovery was significantly slower for participants with large psychological burden. It was concluded that, in additional to treating the burns, clinicians must address physical and psychological burden in order to promote recovery. The final journal article (B5) was a study on the effectiveness of the WeeFIM, a standardized measure of functional performance developed for use in children 6 months to 8 years of age, in measuring the impact of burn size on functional independence and time to recovery. A total of 249 patients, ages 6 months to 16 years, participated in the 2-year study. WeeFIM measurements were taken at discharge and at 6 months, 1 year, and 2 years after burn injury. Results indicated that the WeeFIM could accurately describe the relationship among burn size, functional capacity, and recovery up to 24 months after burn injury. Serghiou et al. believe the tool should be used more widely to track recovery of burn victims.

The final output reviewed under this project (Develop and Implement Support Systems) was a list of publications (B6) from Burn Model System Clinical Centers that were produced with support from the DCC. The list includes 16 published journal articles, 1 journal article that was submitted for publication, and 1 journal article that was to be submitted for publication.

Under the project on implementing a dissemination strategy, two outputs were produced. The first, a website (C1) for the BMS/DCC, includes information about the DCC participating institutions, study group criteria, program priorities and policies, consumer products, special topics, and related links. The website also has a search function. Through the website, researchers can access Burn Model System publications, systematic reviews, consumer information, newsletters, and facts and figures, and can also contact and collaborate with DCC staff. The second output, a journal article (C2), compares victims intentionally burned as the result of an assault with victims unintentionally burned as the result of an accident. Participants included 80 intentionally burned victims and 1,982 unintentionally burned victims. Kaufman et al. discovered that intentionally burned victims were more likely to be female, black, and unemployed, and had higher rates of substance abuse, larger burns, greater mortality rates, and greater psychological distress. It is the authors' hope that understanding the characteristics of intentionally burned victims will lead to better health and social services for this population.

Grant Title: North Texas Burn Rehabilitation Model System

Grant Award Number: H133A020104

Grantee: UT Southwestern Medical Center at Dallas

Grant Mechanism: Burn Model System

Grant Start and End Dates: October 1, 2002, to September 30, 2008

Total Direct Cost: $1,190,475

Abstract: The North Texas Burn Rehabilitation Model System (NTBRMS) grant included five major research projects: (1) Barriers to Return to Work after Major Burn Injury, (2) Long-Term Outcome of Major Burn Injuries, (3) Outcome Following Deep Full Thickness Hand Burns, (4) Burn-Associated Neuropathy: Evolution over Time, and (5) The Socioeconomic Determinants of Disability in Individuals with Major Burn Injury. Each of these projects linked directly with several areas of the NIDRR Long-Range Plan. The plan of operation included clearly defined objectives, responsibilities, and timelines for model system demonstration, research, and dissemination. Additionally, researchers sought to close the loop and reassessed the progress of each activity to create intervention plans as needed to ensure that they met the proposed priorities. The NTBRMS also contributed data to the national Burn Injury Rehabilitation Model System database.

Research Projects and Outputs Reviewed: Grantees were asked to nominate two outputs from each of their projects for review by the committee. These outputs were identified by the study's key personnel as those that would best reflect their grant's achievements. Grantees selected the outputs to be reviewed from among the larger pool of outputs they had produced under the grant. This larger pool of outputs included nine journal articles, one newsletter, one seminar, one clinic, and one intervention program. The following table shows the six projects carried out under this grant and lists the corresponding outputs that were nominated by the grantees and reviewed by the NRC committee. The reviewed outputs are briefly described following the table.

Project/Research Domains*	Outputs
A. Barriers to Return to Work After Major Burn Injury—Collaborative *Employment*	A1. Esselman, P.C., Askay, S.W., Carrougher, G.J., Lezotte, D.C., Holavanahalli, R.K., Magyar-Russell, G., Fauerbach, J.A., and Engrav, L.H. (2007). Barriers to return to work after burn injuries. *Archives of Physical Medicine and Rehabilitation, 88*(12), S50-S56.
B. Long-Term Outcome of Major Burn Injuries *Health and Function*	B1. Kowalske, K.J. (2003, September). *The challenge of burn care: How to maximize outcomes—A seminar.* Seminar conducted at University of Texas Southwestern Medical Center at Dallas.
	B2. Holavanahalli, R.K., Helm, P.A., and Kowalske, K.J. (2010). Long-term outcomes in patients surviving large burns: The skin. *Journal of Burn Care & Research, 31*(4), 631-639.
C. Outcome Following Deep Full-Thickness Hand Burns—Collaborative *Health and Function*	C1. Schneider, J.C., Holavanahalli, R.K., Helm, P.A., O'Neil, C., Goldstein, R., and Kowalske, K. (2008). Contractures in burn injury part II: Investigating joints of the hand. Journal of *Burn Care & Research, 29*(4), 606-613.
	C2. Holavanahalli, R K., Helm, P.A., Gorman, A.R., and Kowalske, K.J. (2007). Outcomes after deep full-thickness hand burns. *Archives of Physical Medicine and Rehabilitation, 88*(12 Suppl. 2), S30-S35.
D. Burn-Associated Neuropathy: Evolution over Time *Health and Function*	D1. Gabriel, V., Kowalske, K.J., and Holavanahalli, R.K. (2009). Assessment of recovery from burn-related neuropathy by electrodiagnostic testing. *Journal of Burn Care & Research, 30*(4), 668-674.
E. The Socioeconomic Determinants of Disability in Individuals with Major Burn Injury *Participation and Community Living*	E1. East Texas Medical Center (ETMC) Outreach Satellite Clinic. Described to committee in grantee questionnaire.
	E2. Holavanahalli, R., Lara, C., Tollar, A., Stevens, C., Crump, D., Ellsworth, B., and Leal, D. (2006, 2008, 2009). *SOAR Annual Report.* Unpublished report, Department of Physical Medicine and Rehabilitation, University of Texas Southwestern Medical Center at Dallas and Parkland Regional Burn Center, Parkland Health and Hospital System Dallas.
F. Contribution to a Longitudinal National Database *Demographics*	F1. Holavanahalli, R.K., Lezotte, D.C., Hayes, M.P., Minhajuddin, A., Fauerbach, J.A., Engrav, L.H., Helm, P.A., and Kowalske, K.J. (2006). Profile of patients lost to follow up in the Burn Injury Rehabilitation Model Systems' longitudinal database. *Journal of Burn Care & Research, 27*(5), 703-712.

*This column also shows the key NIDRR research domain(s) that were being addressed by each project.

Brief Description of the Outputs: Under the first project, a journal article was produced addressing barriers to return to work after major burn injury. Esselman et al. (A1) followed 154 individuals who were hospitalized and met the American Burn Association criteria for major burn injury. Participants were asked to identify perceived barriers to their returning to work. Physical and wound issues, working conditions such as temperature and safety, and psychosocial factors such as flashbacks and appearance concerns all presented barriers to the return to work. The article concludes that returning to work involves treatment of both physical and psychosocial factors.

The next two outputs reviewed were associated with the long-term outcomes project. A 1-day seminar (B1) aimed to address critical issues in the treatment of individuals with burn injuries (including physical, psychological, and social outcomes) and included 14 presentations and one panel discussion on such topics as the pathophysiology of burns, wound and skin care products, neurological complications, psychological effects, community reintegration, and return to work. The seminar was intended to present relevant principles and techniques that physicians and other health care professionals could use to provide outpatient wound and skin care and rehabilitation following acute burn injuries. Holavanahalli, Helm, and Kowalske (B2) conducted a study of long-term residual skin problems in persons with severe burn injuries. They evaluated 98 individuals who had survived burns over 30 percent or more of their total body surface area. Study participants were asked to complete a patient information form and a medical problem checklist and underwent a comprehensive physical examination. The researchers identified problems that persist many years following the burn injury, such as sensory loss and itching; problems that tend to decrease over time, such as painful scars and skin rash; and problems that tend to increase over time, such as cuts and tears in fragile burns. They concluded there is a need for better long-term follow up with survivors of large burns.

Two journal articles were produced under the project assessing outcomes following deep full thickness hand burns. The first was a journal article (C1) based on a study of the incidence and severity of hand contractures after burn injury. Data were collected over 10 years from 985 adult burn survivors. Twenty-three percent of study patients developed at least one hand contracture. Schneider et al. were able to identify statistically significant predictors of both contracture development and number of contractures. Given the significant impairment hand contractures represent, the authors believe use of the identified predictors will significantly aid burn survivors. The second article (C2) was a descriptive study on measuring hand performance after deep hand burns. Thirty-two burn survivors participated. Fifty percent of participants had amputations, 40 percent had a functional range of less than 180 degrees, and 22 percent had injury to the tendons in the hand. Participants took the Jebsen-Taylor Hand Function Test (JTHFT) and Michigan Hand Questionnaire (MHQ). Holavanahalli et al. concluded that, while deep full-thickness burns did compromise hand performance, the muscles were generally still intact enough to perform a modified grasp. Training programs on this grasp could be developed to aid burn survivors.

The next output reviewed was a journal article produced under the project on burn-associated neuropathy. Gabriel et al. (D1) investigated the natural recovery from burn-related peripheral neuropathies. Thirty-six participants with burn-related neuropathy, out of 370 screened burn survivors, were repeatedly tested for improvement. Mean time between the tests was 169 days. Significant improvement between the initial and follow-up tests was found, suggesting burn-related neuropathy will naturally heal. According to the authors, the prognosis for recovery from burn-related neuropathy had not been adequately described in the literature prior to this study.

From the project on socioeconomic determinants of disability in individuals with major burn injury, two outputs were reviewed. The first, a quarterly outreach satellite clinic (E1) at the East Texas Medical Center in Tyler, Texas, cared for an average of 25 patients each quarter between 2002 and 2007. Clinic personnel included NTBRMS burn surgeons, physical medicine and rehabilitation physicians, and research personnel. In addition to receiving medical care, patients participated in NTBRMS research studies and educational programs on various burn rehabilitation topics. The clinic enabled patients living in the area to receive medical care for their burn injuries closer to their homes. The second output, Survivors Offering Assistance in Recovery Program (SOAR) (E2), provides peer support during recovery to burn patients and their families. Volunteer burn survivors and family members are trained in peer support. Each burn unit patient receives a visit at least once a week from a trained volunteer. Many burn unit patients have reported that the opportunity to speak with a recovered peer made them more optimistic about their own recovery.

The final output reviewed was part of the project focused on contributions to a longitudinal national database. Holavanahalli et al. (F1) describe common characteristics among burn survivors lost to follow up at 6, 12, or 24 months after injury. Participants were tracked over 2 years through the Burn Injury Rehabilitation Model System database, and characteristics related to both increased and decreased likelihood of attending follow-up sessions with physicians were identified. This study was reported to be the first of its kind for burn survivors, and the authors hope these findings will lead to strategies for reducing attrition in burn survivors.

TRAUMATIC BRAIN INJURY MODEL SYSTEM (TBIMS)

Grant Title: Mayo Clinic TBI Model System

Grant Award Number: H133A020507

Grantee: Rehabilitation Hospital of Indiana

Grant Mechanism: Traumatic Brain Injury Model System

Grant Start and End Dates: October 1, 2002, to March 31, 2009

Total Direct Cost: $1,402,265

Abstract: The Mayo Clinic Traumatic Brain Injury Model System (TBIMS) grant was focused on three local research projects: (1) decision making and outcomes of inpatient and outpatient rehabilitation pathways, (2) very long-term (5-15+ years postinjury) process and outcome for people with TBI identified through the Rochester Epidemiology Project, and (3) telehealth-based (Internet) cognitive rehabilitation. These projects were developed with careful attention to sample size; rigorous methodology; practical issues of data acquisition; and the needs of and feedback from people with TBI, their families, and significant others. The Mayo Clinic TBIMS also continued to contribute substantially to the TBIMS National Database and was involved in other collaborative projects using this database.

Research Projects and Outputs Reviewed: Grantees were asked to nominate two outputs from each of their projects for review by the committee. These outputs were identified by the study's key personnel as those that would best reflect their grant's achievements. Grantees selected the outputs to be reviewed from among the larger pool of outputs they had produced under the grant. This larger pool of outputs included 13 journal articles, one classification system, one inventory, one guide, one set of audiovisual materials, and one curriculum. The following table shows the four projects carried out under this grant and lists the corresponding outputs that were nominated by the grantees and reviewed by the NRC committee. The reviewed outputs are briefly described following the table.

Project/*Research Domains**	Outputs
A. Factors and Effects on Outcome of Clinical Decision Making in Selecting Rehabilitation Pathways After Traumatic Brain Injury *Health and Function*	A1. Malec, J.F., Mandrekar, J.N., Brown, A.W., and Moessner, A.M. (2009). Injury severity and disability in the selection of next-level care following acute medical treatment for traumatic brain injury. *Brain Injury, 23*(1), 22-29.
	A2. Malec, J.F., Brown, A.W., Leibson, C.L., Flaada, J.T., Mandrekar, J.N., Diehl, N.N., and Perkins, P.K. (2007). The Mayo classification system for traumatic brain injury severity. *Journal of Neurotrauma, 24*(9), 1,417-1,424.
B. Process and Outcome of TBI in the Very Long Term *Participation and Community Living*	B1. Brown, A.W., Leibson, C.L., Malec, J.F., Perkins, P.K., Diehl, N.N., and Larson, D.R. (2004). Long-term survival after traumatic brain injury: A population-based analysis. *NeuroRehabilitation, 19*(1), 37-43.
	B2. Flaada, J.T., Leibson, C.L., Mandrekar, J.N., Diehl, N., Perkins, P.K., Brown, A.W., and Malec, J.F. (2007). Relative risk of mortality after traumatic brain injury: A population-based study of the role of age and injury severity. *Journal of Neurotrauma, 24*(3), 435-455.
C. The Feasibility and Efficacy of Telehealth-Based Cognitive Rehabilitation *Health and Function* *Technology*	C1. Bergquist, T.F., Gehl, C., Lepore, S., Holzworth, N., and Beaulieu, W. (2008). Internet-based cognitive rehabilitation in individuals with acquired brain injury: A pilot feasibility study. *Brain Injury, 22*(11), 891-897.
D. Minnesota Advocacy Project *Participation and Community Living*	D1. Malec, J.F. (2008). *Minnesota advocacy project curriculum.* Unpublished curriculum materials, Rehabilitation Hospital of Indiana, Indianapolis.
	D2. Malec, J.F., Brown, A.W., and Moessner, A.M. (2010). Two new measures for assessing advocacy activities and perceived control after acquired brain injury. *Disability and Rehabilitation, 32*(1), 33-40.

*This column also shows the key NIDRR research domain(s) that were being addressed by each project.

Brief Description of the Outputs: Two journal articles were produced under the first project, Factors and Effects on Outcome of Clinical Decision Making in Selecting Rehabilitation Pathways After Traumatic Brain Injury. Malec et al. (A1) analyzed the association of demographic factors, posttraumatic amnesia, and ability limitations with clinical decisions for next level of care following moderate to severe TBI. Participants included 159 individuals suffering from posttraumatic amnesia who were also rated for ability limitations. The authors discovered that posttraumatic amnesia and certain ability limitations were associated with the decision to admit versus discharge a patient in 93 percent of cases. Age was found to be the only demographic factor associated with the decision. A more standardized measure of ability limitations was developed, which the authors believe should lead to more consistency in rehabilitation decision making for patients with TBI. The second journal article (A2) reviewed discusses a test of the Mayo Classification System for Traumatic Brain Injury Severity. The Mayo system can classify TBI from consideration of a number of factors and unlike other systems is not dependent on a single factor. Malec et al. classified a sample of 1,501 individuals with history of TBI, concluding that the Mayo classification system is accurate and superior to other, single-indicator systems and can be used both in retrospective research and for planning care.

Under the project analyzing the process and outcome of TBI in the very long term, another two journal articles were produced. The first article (B1) describes a population-based retrospective cohort study of 1,448 Olmsted County, Minnesota, residents who developed TBI from 1935 to 2000. Analysis of the case fatality rates showed (1) mild TBI to be associated with a small but significant reduction in long-term survival compared with the general population, (2) moderate to severe TBI to be associated with a very high fatality rate, but (3) 6-month survivors of moderate to severe TBI to be associated with long-term survival rates similar to those of patients with mild TBI. Brown et al. believe the similarity in long-term survival rates between patients with mild TBI and 6-month survivors of moderate to severe TBI is a new finding that could lead to new community services for TBI survivors. The second article (B2) describes a study on whether observed versus expected mortality of individuals with TBI differs by age. From residents of Olmsted County, Minnesota, with any diagnosis suggestive of TBI between 1985 and 1999, Flaada et al. randomly sampled 7,800 and reviewed records to confirm the event. Confirmed cases were divided into three age groups—pediatric (<16), adult (16-65), and elderly (>65)—and observed versus expected 6-month and 10-year mortality rates for each age group were compared. It was found that within 6 months, more individuals died from TBI than was expected for all age groups, with the elderly group showing the greatest difference and the pediatric group the smallest difference. After 10 years, observed mortality for the pediatric and elderly groups matched expected rates, but a larger percentage of the adult group had died than was expected. The authors believe these findings will help clinicians target and better care for the most vulnerable populations suffering from TBI based on age.

The next journal article (C1), from the project The Feasibility and Efficacy of Telehealth-Based Cognitive Rehabilitation, assessed whether individuals with brain injury including memory impairment could learn to use an Internet-based cognitive rehabilitation program. Ten participants were trained in using an instant messaging system and participated in weekly therapy sessions. Bergquist et al. report that only two participants missed a few of the sessions, demonstrating that individuals with memory impairment can participate in telerehabilitation.

Two outputs were produced from the Minnesota Advocacy Project. The Minnesota Advocacy Project Curriculum (D1) serves to train individuals with TBI and their families/significant others in three contiguous Midwest states in effective self and system advocacy skills. The four sessions of the curriculum include presentations on advocacy, lessons in civics, presentations on community organizing, and a mock hearing during which participants can practice applying what they have learned. Creators hope the curriculum will lead to more independence for individuals with TBI. The second output, a journal article (D2), aimed to evaluate two questionnaires: the Advocacy Activities Scale (AAS) and the Perceived Control Scale for Brain Injury (PCS-BI). These questionnaires were mailed to individuals with acquired brain injury and the responses analyzed. Malec, Brown, and Moessner determined that both the AAS and the PSC-BI showed satisfactory internal consistency and concurrent validity with other measures and concluded that survey researchers should use both questionnaires where appropriate.

Grant Title: Spaulding/Partners Traumatic Brain Injury Model System at Harvard Medical School

Grant Award Number: H133A020513

Grantee: Spaulding Rehabilitation Hospital

Grant Mechanism: Traumatic Brain Injury Model System

Grant Start and End Dates: October 1, 2002, to September 30, 2008

Total Direct Cost: $1,410,621

Abstract: The Spaulding TBI Model System (TBIMS) provided a comprehensive spectrum of care for people with traumatic brain injury (TBI) through the collaborative efforts of three hospitals that are part of Partners Health Care System, Inc. and three organizations that operate a variety of post-acute rehabilitation programs. Studies completed under the grant resulted in published articles on regional cerebral activation on functional magnetic resonance imaging (fMRI) as a predictor of outcome for a memory rehabilitation program following TBI, the ability of the size of cerebral structures associated with memory to predict the outcome among people with TBI who participate in a memory rehabilitation program, the effect of use of strategies during memorization of words on brain activation on fMRI, the efficacy of a group memory rehabilitation program emphasizing semantic strategies, the test-retest reliability of the VIrtual Planning Test (VIP), families'/caregivers' emotional status and support systems (lead center: Virginia), racial differences in employment outcomes after TBI (lead center: Virginia), and the risk of progressive cognitive deterioration in aged survivors of TBI (lead center: Texas). The Spaulding TBIMS enrolled an average of more than 50 subjects in the national database annually during the 5 years of the grant cycle from October 1, 2002, to September 30, 2007.

Research Projects and Outputs Reviewed: Grantees were asked to nominate two outputs from each of their projects for review by the committee. These outputs were identified by the study's key personnel as those that would best reflect their grant's achievements. Grantees selected the outputs to be reviewed from among the larger pool of outputs they had produced under the grant. This larger pool of outputs included 10 journal articles, one diagnostic instrument, one field-tested product, and one newsletter. The following table shows the six projects carried out under this grant and lists the corresponding outputs that were nominated by the grantees and reviewed by the NRC committee. The reviewed outputs are briefly described following the table.

Project/*Research Domains**	Outputs
A. Regional Cerebral Activation on fMRI as a Predictor of Outcome Following TBI *Health and Function*	A1. Strangman, G.E., O'Neil-Pirozzi, T.M., Goldstein, R., Kelkar, K., Katz, D.I., Burke, D., Rauch, S.L., Savage, C.R., and Glenn, M.B. (2008). Prediction of memory rehabilitation outcomes in traumatic brain injury by using functional magnetic resonance imaging. *Archives of Physical Medicine and Rehabilitation, 89*(5), 974-981.
	A2. Glenn, M.B. (2008). The TBI newscaster. In Spaulding Rehabilitation Hospital, *TBI Newscaster: A publication of Spaulding/Partners Traumatic Brain Injury Model System at Harvard Medical School* (winter edition). Boston, MA: Spaulding Rehabilitation Hospital TBI Model System.
B. Test-Retest Reliability of the VIrtual Planning Test (VIP): Subjects with Brain Injury *Health and Function*	B1. O'Neil-Pirozzi, T.M., Goldstein, R., Strangman, G.E., Katz, D.I., and Glenn, M.B. (2010). Test-retest reliability of the virtual planning test in individuals with traumatic brain injury. *Brain Injury, 24*(3), 509-516.

Project/*Research Domains**	Outputs
C. Risk of Progressive Cognitive Deterioration in Aged Survivors of Moderate to Severe Brain Injury: A Collaborative National Database Project *Health and Function*	C1. Marquez de la Plata, C.D., Hart, T., Hammond, F.M., Frol, A.B., Hudak, A., Harper, C.R., O'Neil-Pirozzi, T.M., Whyte, J., Carlile, M., and Diaz-Arrastia, R. (2008). Impact of age on long-term recovery from traumatic brain injury. *Archives of Physical Medicine and Rehabilitation, 89*(5), 896-903.
D. Family Members' and Survivors' Emotional Well Being: A Collaborative Module Project *Health and Function*	D1. Kreutzer, J.S., Rapport, L.J., Marwitz, J.H., Harrison-Felix, C., Hart, T., Glenn, M., and Hammond, F. (2009). Caregivers' well-being after traumatic brain injury: A multicenter prospective investigation. *Archives of Physical Medicine and Rehabilitation, 90*(6), 939-946.
E. Efficacy of a Group Memory Intervention: A Pilot Study *Health and Function*	E1. O'Neil-Pirozzi, T.M., Strangman, G.E., Goldstein, R., Katz, D.I., Savage, C.R., Kelkar, K., Supelana, C., Burke, D., Rauch, S.L., and Glenn, M.B. (2010). A controlled treatment study of internal memory strategies (I-MEMS) following traumatic brain injury. *Journal of Head Trauma Rehabilitation, 25*(1), 43-51.
F. TBI Model Systems National Database *Health and Function* *Employment* *Demographics*	F1. Arango-Lasprilla, J.C., Ketchum, J.M., Williams, K., Kreutzer, J.S., Marquez de la Plata, C.D., O'Neil-Pirozzi, T.M., and Wehman, P. (2008). Racial differences in employment outcomes after traumatic brain injury. *Archives of Physical Medicine and Rehabilitation, 89*(5), 988-995.

*This column also shows the key NIDRR research domain(s) that were being addressed by each project.

Brief Description of the Outputs: The first two outputs reviewed were associated with the project on regional cerebral activation on fMRI as a predictor of outcome following TBI. Strangman et al. (A1) assessed whether fMRI can be used to predict rehabilitation outcomes for TBI patients. Participants included 54 individuals who had suffered from TBI for at least 1 year. While being scanned, participants performed a word memorization task. They then participated in a 6-week memory rehabilitation group program emphasizing semantic strategies. Imaging analysis connected fMRI results with gains in memory testing following the memory rehabilitation program. The authors believe further research will clarify the relationship and allow fMRI to be used as a predictor of outcomes. The second output reviewed was an annual newsletter of the Spaulding/Partners TBIMS (A2). This newsletter was developed in a format accessible to research scientists, clinicians, people with disabilities, and their families. Its intent was to provide a general audience with information about TBI and the center's work. Study progress and findings to date were discussed.

From the project aimed at assessing the test-retest reliability of the VIP for individuals with TBI, a journal article was produced. O'Neil-Pirozzi et al. (B1) administered the VIP to 75 individuals with TBI. Participants each took the VIP twice, with 6-8 weeks separating the tests. The study concluded that the VIP had moderate overall test-retest reliability for individuals with TBI, with some elements of the test showing high reliability but other elements low reliability. The authors state that the VIP is now the first such "ecologically valid" test with demonstrated test-retest reliability for persons with TBI.

Another journal article was produced under the project on progressive cognitive deterioration. The longitudinal cohort study (C1) addressed whether functional decline after TBI was more likely for older individuals. Participants included 428 individuals with TBI enrolled in the Traumatic Brain Injury Model Systems national data set. Participants were divided into three age groups—youngest (16-26 years), intermediate (27-39 years), and oldest (≥40 years). Data from the first 5 years after the injury were examined for each age group. Marquez de la Plata et al. found that the greatest improvement over the first 5 years occurred in the youngest group and the greatest decline over the first 5 years in the oldest group. They believe these finding suggest changes in TBI treatment practice are warranted for older individuals with TBI.

From the project on emotional well being of survivors and family members, a journal article (D1) assessing the emotional distress and life satisfaction of caregivers was produced. Participants included 273 caregivers who took the Brief Symptom Inventory-18, an 18-item self-report instrument designed to quantify psychologic distress. Kreutzer et al. discovered that 1 in 5 caregivers showed significant depression, anxiety, and/or somatic symptoms. Higher distress was associated with caring for individuals with worse functional status, individuals needing more supervision, individuals who were less satisfied with life, and those who used alcohol in excess. The authors believe these findings reinforce the need to support caregivers as well as patients.

Within the project on the efficacy of a pilot study on group memory intervention, O'Neil-Pirozzi et al. (E1) described the effects of a memory group intervention on persons with TBI. Participants included 94 adults with TBI and resulting memory impairment at least 1 year postinjury at the time of study. The authors found that participation in the intervention did improve memory for those with mild, moderate, and severe TBI compared with controls (although there was less improvement in cases of severe TBI), and the improvement was maintained 1 month after the intervention. They believe further research can build on this finding to increase use of such a memory group intervention.

The final article relates to the project on contribution to the Traumatic

Brain Injury Model Systems National Database. Arango-Lasprilla et al. (F1) performed a retrospective study examining racial differences in the employment and occupation of individuals with TBI 1 year after injury. Data for this study were taken from the Traumatic Brain Injury Model Systems National Database on 3,486 white and 1,791 minority individuals hospitalized with TBI between 1989 and 2005. It was concluded that whites were 2.17 times more likely to be employed 1 year after TBI than minority individuals, although race did not have an impact on occupation. The authors believe this finding suggests more assistance should be given to minorities seeking work after TBI.

SPINAL CORD INJURY MODEL SYSTEM (SCIMS)

Grant Title: Northern New Jersey Spinal Cord Injury System

Grant Award Number: H133N000022

Grantee: KMRREC (now Kessler Foundation)

Grant Mechanism: Spinal Cord Injury Model System

Grant Start and End Date: September 1, 2000, to August 31, 2007

Total Direct Cost: $1,361,714

Abstract: The Northern New Jersey Spinal Cord Injury System (NNJSCIS) was established as a Spinal Cord Injury Model System in 1990 by NIDRR and serves the Northern New Jersey catchment area, a 13-county, ethnically diverse region of 10.2 million persons. It is a cooperative effort of the Kessler Medical Rehabilitation Research and Education Center (KMRREC), the University of Medicine and Dentistry of New Jersey University Hospital, and the Kessler Institute for Rehabilitation (KIR). For the original funding cycle, the NNJSCIS model system focused on six research projects and one demonstration project. The subsequent funding cycle focused on dissemination efforts, validation of the consumer index of accessibility demonstration project, and continued recruitment and data collection for the database.

The six research projects addressed one of the most common medical problems faced by persons with spinal cord injury (SCI) (urinary tract infections), common health issues among individuals with SCI (obesity and upper-limb overuse), and promotion of health and wellness in individuals with SCI (health literacy and the identification of health and psychosocial risk factors). The researchers developed an instrument for assessing outcomes and care specified by the Consortium for Spinal Cord Medicine's clinical practice guidelines (which was used to collect data and determine the validity of these guidelines). The consumer accessibility demonstration project tested the feasibility of an innovative methodology for expanding community access for individuals with SCI.

Research Projects and Outputs Reviewed: Grantees were asked to nominate two outputs from each of their projects for review by the committee. These outputs were identified by the study's key personnel as those that would best reflect their grant's achievements. Grantees selected the outputs to be reviewed from among the larger pool of outputs they had produced under the grant. This larger pool of outputs included 14 journal articles, one book chapter, two interventional protocols, and one newsletter. The following table shows the five projects carried out under this grant and lists the corresponding outputs that were nominated by the grantees and reviewed by the NRC committee. The reviewed outputs are briefly described following the table.

Project/*Research Domains**	Outputs
A. Health Promotion and Disease Prevention among Individuals with SCI *Health and Function*	A1. Diab, M.E., and Johnston, M.V. (2004). Relationships between level of disability and receipt of preventative health services. *Archives of Physical Medicine and Rehabilitation, 85*(5), 747-757.
	A2. Johnston, M.V., Diab, M.E., Chu, B.C., and Kirshblum, S. (2005). Preventative services and health behaviors among people with spinal cord injury. *Journal of Spinal Cord Medicine, 28*(1), 43-54.
B. Health Literacy: Its Relationship to Educational Materials and to Health-Related Outcomes among Individuals with SCI Living in the Community *Health and Function*	B1. Johnston, M.V., Diab, M.E., Kim, S.-S., and Kirshblum, S. (2005). Health literacy, morbidity, and quality of life among individuals with spinal cord injury. *Journal of Spinal Cord Medicine, 28*(3), 230-240.
C. Empiric Antibiotic Treatment for Urinary Tract Infections in Persons with SCI *Health and Function*	C1. Linsenmeyer, T.A., and Oakley, A. (2003). Accuracy of individuals with spinal cord injury at predicting urinary tract infections based on their symptoms. *Journal of Spinal Cord Medicine, 26*(4), 352-357.
	C2. Lisenmeyer, T.A., Bodner, D.R., Creasey, G.H., Green, B.G., Groah, S.L., Joseph, A., Lloyd, L.K., Perkash, I., and Wheeler, J.S. (2006). Bladder management for adults with spinal cord injury: A clinical practice guideline for health-care providers. *Journal of Spinal Cord Medicine, 29*(5), 527-573.
D. Changes in Shoulder Pain Intensity During Upper Extremity Exercise in Individuals with Spinal Cord Injury *Health and Function*	D1. Dyson-Hudson, T.A., Sisto, S.A., Bond, Q., Emmons, R., and Kirshblum, S.C. (2007). Arm crank ergometry and shoulder pain in persons with spinal cord injury. *Archives of Physical Medicine and Rehabilitation, 88*(12), 1,727-1,729.
	D2. Dyson-Hudson, T.A., and Kirshblum, S.C. (2004). Shoulder pain chronic spinal cord injury, Part I: Epidemiology, etiology, and pathomechanics. *Journal of Spinal Cord Medicine, 27*(1), 4-17.

Project/*Research Domains**	Outputs
E. Studies Based on Data Submitted to National SCI Statistical Center Database *Health and Function*	E1. Kirshblum, S., Millis, S., McKinley, W., and Tulsky, D. (2004). Late neurologic recovery after traumatic spinal cord injury. *Archives of Physical Medicine and Rehabilitation, 85*(11), 1,811-1,817.
	E2. Cardenas, D.D., Hoffman, J.M., Kirshblum, S., and McKinley, W. (2004). Etiology and incidence of rehospitalization after traumatic spinal cord injury: A multicenter analysis. *Archives Physical Medicine and Rehabilitation, 85*(11), 1,757-1,763.

*This column also shows the key NIDRR research domain(s) that were being addressed by each project.

Brief Description of the Outputs: All outputs from this grant reviewed by the NRC committee were publications. The first two journal articles, produced under the health promotion and disease prevention project, analyze the receipt of preventative services among people with SCI. Both analyze survey items from the Behavioral Risk Factor Surveillance System (BRFSS) (1998 and 2000). Diab and Johnston (A1) examined the relationships between level of disability and receipt of certain preventative services. The severity of disabilities was found to be related to the receipt of certain preventative services but not necessarily in a simple or unidirectional way. Regardless of disability, receipt of a checkup was an important determinant of receipt of preventative health services. The Johnston et al. article (A2) documents receipt of understudied preventative services and health behaviors in SCI patients compared with the general population. Surprisingly, although deficiencies in the provision of preventative services were found, they were similar to those in the general population. However, these deficiencies could be particularly problematic in SCI patients given the narrower margin of health. It is therefore recommended that preventative care needs and safety factors be routinely assessed and provided for people with SCI.

The third output reviewed, under the health literacy project, was a journal article (B1) aimed at describing levels of health literacy in SCI patients and to investigate the possible associations with morbidity, health-related quality of life, functional independence, community participation, and life satisfaction. A total of 107 community-living people with SCI were recruited from a private New Jersey outpatient SCI center and surveyed using measures from the Test of Functional Health Literacy in Adults (TOFHLA), standard questions about morbidity from the BRFSS, the Craig Handicap Assessment and Reporting Technique (CHART), the Short Form-12, and the Diener's Satisfaction with Life Scale. In this study, only 14 percent of people with SCI were found to have limited health literacy. Health literacy was found to be independently related to physical health morbidity, but associations with other outcomes were limited, intertwined with education, and affected by severity of injury.

The outputs produced under the third project (Empiric Antibiotic Treatment for Urinary Tract Infections in Persons with SCI) address one of the most common medical problems faced by persons with SCI, urinary tract infection (UTI). Linsenmeyer and Oakley (C1) describe a study aimed at evaluating the accuracy of people with SCI in determining whether they had a UTI based on signs and symptoms. The authors undertook a 9-month prospective case review of 147 persons with SCI who presented to an outpatient urology clinic with symptoms they attributed to a UTI. They found that 39 percent of SCI patients were not accurate in predicting a UTI based on signs and symptoms. This finding supports the importance of performing a urinalysis before prescribing antibiotics for UTI treatment, in addition to having high suspicion of other medical conditions. The other output from this project was a set of published guidelines (C2) for health providers on bladder management for adults with SCI. These guidelines were developed by the Consortium of Spinal Cord Medicine, led by a steering committee made up of one representative with clinical practice guideline experience from each of the consortium's 17 member organizations.

The next two outputs were journal articles from the project focused on analyzing shoulder pain in persons with SCI. Dyson-Hudson et al. (D1) examined whether a primary fitness program for people with SCI, which used arm cycle ergometry, resulted in increased shoulder pain. A comparison of 23 persons with chronic SCI participating in a weight loss program of diet alone versus diet plus arm crank ergometry found that shoulder pain did not increase in SCI subjects who used wheelchairs and performed moderate-intensity arm crank ergometry. Dyson-Hudson and Kirshblum (D2) reviewed the epidemiology, etiology, and pathomechanics of shoulder pain in persons with SCI in order to aid in the evaluation, treatment, and prevention of this disorder.

The final two outputs reviewed were journal articles produced as part of the project to conduct studies based on the National SCI Statistical Center Database. The first article (E1) presents and analyzes Spinal Cord Injury Model System (SCIMS) data on late neurologic recovery after 1 year post-SCI. Analysis of data on 987 patients with traumatic SCI admitted to an SCIMS center between 1988 and 1997 with 1- and 5-year follow up found a small degree of recovery after traumatic SCI. In addition, late conversion from complete to incomplete recovery occurred in 5.6 percent of cases. This knowledge may be useful for future surgical and pharmacological intervention studies aimed at enhancing recovery. Cardenas et al. (E2) performed an analysis of cross-sectional data to determine the frequency of and reasons for rehospitalization in person with acute SCI during follow-up years. They also examined the association between rehospitalization and demographics, injury severity, payer sources, length of stay, functional status at discharge, and discharge residence. The authors believe this information is important for the development of preventive strategies and management for persons with SCI to reduce rehospitalizations.

Grant Title: The Missouri Model Spinal Cord Injury System

Grant Award Number: H133N000012

Grantee: University of Missouri

Grant Mechanism: Spinal Cord Injury Model System

Grant Start and End Date: October 1, 2000, to September 30, 2007

Total Direct Cost: $1,504,487

Abstract: The primary Missouri Model Spinal Cord Injury System (MOMSCIS) research study focused on the effect of a consumer-directed personal assistance services training intervention on consumer satisfaction, independent living, and community integration. The MOMSCIS study involved developing, implementing, and evaluating the in-person Individualized Management of Personal Assistant/Consumer Teams (IMPACT) workshop. The IMPACT workshop participants received information on preventing and treating secondary medical conditions; topics included pressure sores, urinary tract infections, bowel and bladder management, autonomic dysreflexia, pain management, chronic fatigue, and thermoregulation. The participants also received information on relationship issues, such as hiring and managing of personal assistants, communication styles and strategies, assertiveness, and team building. The objectives of the study were (1) to determine the effect of the IMPACT workshop on consumer satisfaction, the incidence of secondary conditions, activity, and participation; (2) to determine the effect of the IMPACT workshop on personal assistants' job satisfaction, job stress, and attrition; and (3) to provide online resources to the disability community, including an online personal assistant training manual for consumers and assistants and an online resources database. A total of 99 consumers and 98 assistants participated in this study. Activity and participation were measured by the Participation Survey for Persons with Mobility Limitations (PARTS/M). To leverage NIDRR's previous investment in developing the PARTS/M, the study included collaboration with Washington University and the University of Pittsburgh to combine data with which to validate the PARTS/M among a large sample of persons with spinal cord injury (SCI). These data will provide valuable information for future studies seeking to document changes in personal independence and community integration.

In a secondary research project, surveys were sent to 16 Spinal Cord Injury Model System centers to assess which centers screen for total testosterone level among men with SCI during rehabilitation admission. A study was also conducted to document the prevalence of low testosterone among men with SCI. The study, which included 100 men with SCI, found that the prevalence of low testosterone was high. Specifically, 75 percent of participants had low testosterone levels (under 300 ng/dl). In addition, testosterone level was significantly associated with age and years since injury and with medical variables, including AST, ALT, hemoglobin, hematocrit, and albumin level.

Research Projects and Outputs Reviewed: Grantees were asked to nominate two outputs from each of their projects for review by the committee. These outputs were identified by the study's key personnel as those that would best reflect their grant's achievements. Grantees selected the outputs to be reviewed from among the larger pool of outputs they had produced under the grant. This larger pool of outputs included nine journal articles. The following table shows the main project carried out under this grant and lists the corresponding outputs that were nominated by the grantees and reviewed by the NRC committee. The reviewed outputs are briefly described following the table.

Project/*Research Domains**	Outputs
A. Individualized Management of Personal Assistant/Consumer Teams (IMPACT) *Health and Function*	A1. Schopp, L.H., Clark, M.J., Hagglund, K.J., Sherman, A.K., Stout, B.J., Gray, D.B., and Boninger, M.L. (2007). Life activities among individuals with spinal cord injury living in the community: Perceived choice and perceived barriers. *Rehabilitation Psychology, 52*, 82-88.
	A2. Clark, M.J., Hagglund, K.J., and Sherman, K.J. (2008). A longitudinal comparison of consumer-directed and agency-directed personal assistance service programmes among persons with physical disabilities. *Disability and Rehabilitation, 30*(9), 689-695.

*The column also shows the key NIDRR research domain(s) that were being addressed by each project.

Brief Description of the Outputs: The first output reviewed was a journal article by Schopp et al. (A1) exploring perceived choice over life activities and perceived barriers to engaging in life activities by persons with SCI. The authors state that this is the first study to use the International Classification of Functioning, Disability and Health (ICF) model developed by the World Health Organization with a community-based, multisite sample of community-dwelling persons with SCI. A total of 255 participants from two urban sites and one rural site were surveyed or interviewed using items from PARTS/M. In addition, an inferential approach was used to examine relationships among personal assistance services and perceived choice in, satisfaction with, and barriers to employment. Approximately half of the participants reported little or no perceived choice with employment, and the majority reported low satisfaction with choice with employment. High percentages of participants had experienced physical accessibility and transportation barriers to accessing employment. Physical impairment, pain, and fatigue were also barriers. The article therefore suggests improvements in workplace and transportation accessibility, increased vocational supports, and interventions to decrease pain and fatigue to engage persons with SCI in life activities such as employment.

The Clark et al. (A2) article describes a longitudinal comparison of outcomes for persons who were enrolled in agency-directed personal assistance services (PAS) programs and changed to consumer-directed PAS programs. In-home interviews of a convenience sample of 26 participants revealed more satisfaction and fewer unmet needs after receiving consumer-directed PAS rather than agency-directed PAS. This finding suggests that consumer-directed PAS enhances outcomes for many persons with disabilities.

REHABILITATION RESEARCH AND TRAINING CENTER (RRTC)

Grant Title: Meeting the Nation's Needs for Personal Assistance Services: Center for Personal Assistance Services

Grant Award Number: H133B031102

Grantee: University of California, San Francisco

Grant Mechanism: Rehabilitation Research and Training Center

Grant Start and End Dates: July 1, 2003, to June 30, 2009

Total Direct Cost: $3,913,045

Abstract: The University of California, San Francisco (UCSF) proposed establishing a Rehabilitation Research and Training Center (RRTC) for personal assistance services (PAS). UCSF conducted four large research projects. The first project addressed the relationship between formal and informal PAS and caregiving support and the role of assistive technology (AT) in complementing PAS. The second project dealt with home and community PAS, including state and federal policies and programs, impediments to and new models for eliminating barriers to formal and informal PAS, and best practice models in states and in the home and community. The third project studied the PAS workforce and workforce development that reflects geographic diversity and addresses PAS workforce recruitment, retention, compensation, and benefits; professional training, development, and networking for PAS providers; and crossover issues between disability and aging providers. The fourth project focused on workplace PAS and models for eliminating barriers to formal and informal PAS and AT in the workplace and best practice models in the workplace. In addition, UCSF provided training, dissemination, and technical assistance relative to PAS.

The UCSF faculty are among the nation's leading researchers in disability and PAS, with more than 15 years of research and policy experience, numerous academic publications, a previous track record of NIDRR funding for a national center for disability statistics, and teaching experience in disabilities studies. The RRTC collaborated with faculty members at the University of Maryland, the University of Michigan, and West Virginia University, as well as with the Topeka Independent Living Resource Center, InfoUse, and the Institute for the Future of Aging Services. A Blue Ribbon Advisory Committee of PAS users, disability advocates, business leaders, independent living center leaders, and academics provided guidance to the project.

Research Projects and Outputs Reviewed: Grantees were asked to nominate two outputs from each of their projects for review by the committee. These outputs were identified by the study's key personnel as those that would best reflect their grant's achievements. Grantees selected the outputs to be reviewed from among the larger pool of outputs they had produced under the grant. This larger pool of outputs included 28 journal articles, three websites, and one fact sheet. The following table shows the four projects carried out under this grant and lists the corresponding outputs that were nominated by the grantees and reviewed by the NRC committee. The reviewed outputs are briefly described following the table.

Project/*Research Domains***	**Outputs**
A. Conduct Research on Formal and Informal PAS and Caregiving Support and the Role of Assistive Technology and Evaluate Models to Eliminate Barriers *Health and Function* *Demographics*	A1. LaPlante, M.P., Kaye, H.S., and Harrington, C. (2007). Estimating the expense of a mandatory home and community-based personal assistance services benefit under Medicaid. *Journal of Aging and Social Policy, 19*(3), 47-64.
	A2. Harrington, C. (2004-2011). *PAS Center for Personal Assistance Services.* Available: http://www.pascenter.org [January 9, 2012].
B. Identify, Develop, Evaluate, and Disseminate PAS in Home- and Community-Based Settings *Health and Function* *Participation and Community Living*	B1. Kitchener, M., Ng, T., Miller, N., and Harrington, C. (2005). Medicaid home- and community-based services: National program trends. *Health Affairs, 24*(1), 206-212.
	B2. Kaye, H.S., Laplante, M.P., and Harrington, C. (2009). Do noninstitutional long-term care services reduce Medicaid spending? *Health Affairs, 28*(1), 262-272.
C. Conduct Research on the PAS Workforce and Workforce Development *Employment* *Participation and Community Living*	C1. Kaye, H.S., Chapman, S., Newcomer, R.J., and Harrington, C. (2006). The personal assistance workforce: Trends in supply and demand. *Health Affairs, 25*(4), 1,113-1,120.
	C2. Center for Personal Assistance Services and PHI. (2008, July). *State chart book on wages for personal and home care aides, 1999-2006.* Available: http://www.pascenter.org/publications/publication_home.php?id=857&focus=PAS%20Center%20Publications [January 9, 2012].

Project/*Research Domains**	**Outputs**
D. Identify, Develop, Evaluate, and Disseminate Best Practices for PAS in the Workplace to Facilitate Employment for Individuals with Disabilities	D1. Stoddard, S., and Kraus, L. (2006). Arranging for personal assistance services and assistive technology at work: A report of the rehabilitation research and training center on personal assistance services. *Disability and Rehabilitation: Assistive Technology, 1*(1-2), 89-95.
Employment	D2. Orselene, L., Batiste, L.C., Fullmer, C., Gamble, M., and Stoddard, S. (2010). *JAN personal assistance services in the workplace*. Morgantown, WV: U.S. Department of Labor. Available: http://www.jan.wvu.edu/media/pas.html [January 9, 2012].

*The column also shows the key NIDRR research domain(s) that were being addressed by each project.

Brief Description of the Outputs: The first two outputs were produced under the project focused on PAS support and technological support. LaPlante et al. (A1) provide an estimate of the cost of a mandatory PAS benefit under Medicaid for persons with low incomes, low assets, and significant disability. According to the article, the resulting estimate is one-tenth that of the Congressional Budget Office (CBO) because CBO did not restrict its estimate to persons with the required institutional level of need. The authors conclude that creation of a mandatory PAS benefit is a fiscally achievable policy strategy. The other output reviewed for this project was the website for the PAS Center (A2), specifically the pages on disability statistics and Medicaid home- and community-based services (HCBS) waiver information. This website has hosted the only historical database on waiver programs (1992-2007) and personal care and home health services (1999-2007) that includes types and numbers of participants, service expenditures, and total expenditures. This waiver information has been used by the Centers for Medicare & Medicaid Services (CMS), MedStat, AARP, the National Council of State Legislators, the Government Accountability Office (GAO), and other national and federal organizations to help describe the breadth and depth of Medicaid HCBS programs more fully.

The next two outputs were journal articles from the project aimed at identifying, developing, evaluating, and disseminating PAS in home and community-based settings. Kitchener et al. (B1) conducted a descriptive analysis of the latest national program trends in Medicaid HCBS and reported on a national survey of cost control policies used in waiver programs in 2002. The analysis revealed new information on the growth of Medicaid HCBS over 1992-2001. Waivers represented the majority of total HCBS spending. Wide variations in HCBS spending and access to services were found across states, with most states using cost controls and having limited numbers of waiver slots. The study revealed trends across states showing growth in access to services but still suggested that there was a large unmet need among those wait-listed for services. Published in *Health Affairs*, this article was intended to publicize this information beyond the long-term care audience to reach an audience of health policy makers and state officials. Kaye et al. (B2) analyzed whether noninstitutional long-term care services reduce Medicaid spending in the long term. Analysis of state spending from 1995 to 2005 showed that for two distinct population groups receiving long-term care services, growth in spending was greater for states offering limited noninstitutional services than for those with large, well-established noninstitutional programs. The authors therefore concluded that although expansion of HCBS causes a short-term increase in spending, that increase is followed by a reduction in institutional spending and long-term costs.

Under the PAS workforce and workforce development project, the two outputs reviewed were a journal article and a chart book. Kaye et al. (C1) used data from two federal U.S. population surveys to assess the size of the workforce providing paid PAS and the relative growth of that workforce compared with the population needing such services. They found that the workforce providing noninstitutional personal assistance and home health services tripled between 1989 and 2004, growing at a much faster rate than the population needing such services. Medicaid spending for such services increased dramatically, but both workforce size and spending for similar services in institutional settings remained relatively stable. The article also confirms earlier findings of low wage levels and contributes an additional comparison of wage growth compared with that for other occupations. These low wage levels, scarce health benefits, and high job turnover rates highlight the need for attention to policy to ensure a stable and well-trained PAS workforce to meet the growing demand. Also produced under this project, a *State Chart Book on Wages for Personal and Home Care Aides* (C2) provides information on the wages received by personal and home care aides in all 50 states and the nation over a 7-year period.

The final two outputs reviewed were a journal article and a resource document produced as part of the project to identify, develop, evaluate, and disseminate best practices for PAS in the workplace to facilitate employment for individuals with disabilities. Stoddard and Kraus (D1) conducted structured telephone interviews with 20 workplace PAS users, 21 employers familiar with workplace PAS, and 19 employment organizations to learn about how workplace PAS and AT were arranged for in the workplace and what issues arose. Organizations were found to construct approaches that fit their needs, abilities, and constraints. The interview respondents identified a number of practices that are succeeding, including establishing policies arranging for PAS, centralizing accommodation budgets to remove work unit disincentives, and providing a shared personal assistant for interpreting or for task-related and personal care activities. The final output reviewed was a document on PAS in the workplace (D2) (available online), produced to provide resources and information for Job Accommodation Network (JAN) users. JAN is a service of the Office of Disability Employment Policy, U.S. Department of Labor, whose users include employers, employees with disabilities, people with disabilities attempting to secure PAS, and others.

Grant Title: RRTC on Disability Demographics and Statistics

Grant Award Number: H133B031111

Grantee: Cornell University

Grant Mechanism: Rehabilitation Research and Training Center

Grant Start and End Dates: December 1, 2003, to November 30, 2009

Total Direct Cost: $3,607,885

Abstract: The Cornell Rehabilitation Research and Training Center (RRTC) on Disability Demographics and Statistics sought to bridge the divide between the sources of disability data and the users of disability statistics. Research explored (1) the reliability of existing data sources and collection methods and (2) the potential to improve current and future data collection efforts. A set of related applied activities also was conducted, including (1) utilizing existing data sources to provide a comprehensive and reliable set of disability statistics, (2) increasing access to and understanding of the effective use of these statistics to support decision making, and (3) working with key organizations to determine their needs and help them maximize the use of disability statistics in their ongoing efforts to improve the lives of people with disabilities and their families. The deliverables, resources, and services developed under this grant provided (1) tests of key hypotheses regarding the demographics of disability; (2) a best practices guide for surveying people with disabilities; (3) a set of users' guides to existing data sources; (4) options for improvement in the national disability data system, an extensive but highly fragmented effort of the federal government to collect disability data and produce disability statistics; (5) a comprehensive set of disability statistics; (6) annual Disability Report Cards (also called annual Disability Status Reports); (7) comprehensive disability and demographic statistics (see http://www.disabilitystatistics.org [January 9, 2012]); (8) online user-directed Disability Statistics Templates; (9) a Disability Statistics Syllabus, reflecting an extensive training curriculum; (10) an On-Call Technical Assistance Service and a targeted On-Call Disability Statistics Estimation Service; (11) a set of trainings targeting key audiences; and (12) a state-of-the-science conference and an edited volume on the current status of the national disability data system, recent advances, and high-priority options for improvement.

Research Projects and Outputs Reviewed: Grantees were asked to nominate two outputs from each of their projects for review by the committee. These outputs were identified by the study's key personnel as those that would best reflect their grant's achievements. Grantees selected the outputs to be reviewed from among the larger pool of outputs they had produced under the grant. This larger pool of outputs included three journal articles, two reports, one book, four annual Disability Status Reports, one users' guide series, and two websites. The following table shows the five projects carried out under this grant and lists the corresponding outputs that were nominated by the grantees and reviewed by the NRC committee. The reviewed outputs are briefly described following the table.

Project/*Research Domains**	Outputs
A. Analysis of Existing Data *Demographics*	A1. Cornell University. (2010). *Users' guide series.* Available: http://www.ilr.cornell.edu/edi/disabilitystatistics/sources-userGuides.cfm [January 9, 2012].
	A2. Stapleton, D., Honeycutt, T., and Schechter, B. (2010). Closures are the tip of the iceberg: Exploring the variation in state vocational rehabilitation program exits after service receipt. *Journal of Vocational Rehabilitation,* 32(1), 61-76.
B. Data Collection Methods *Demographics*	B1. Weathers, R.R. II (2009). Chapter 2: The disability data landscape. In A.J. Houtenville, D.C. Stapleton, R.R. Weathers II, and R.V. Burkhauser (Eds.), *Counting working-age people with disabilities: What current data tell us and options for improvement* (pp. 27-68). Kalamazoo, MI: W. E. Upjohn Institute for Employment Research. Stapleton, D.C., Wittenburg, D.C., and Thornton, C. (2009). Chapter 9: Program participants. In. A.J. Houtenville, D.C. Stapleton, R.R. Weathers II, and R.V. Burkhauser (Eds.), *Counting working-age people with disabilities: What current data tell us and options for improvement* (pp. 299-352). Kalamazoo, MI: W. E. Upjohn Institute for Employment Research.
	B2. Stapleton, D.C., Livermore, G.A., and She, P. (2009). Chapter 11: Options for improving disability data collection. In. A.J. Houtenville, D.C. Stapleton, R.R. Weathers II, and R.V. Burkhauser (Eds.), *Counting working-age people with disabilities: What current data tell us and options for improvement* (pp. 381-418). Kalamazoo, MI: W. E. Upjohn Institute for Employment Research.

Project/*Research Domains**	Outputs
C. ICF *Demographics*	C1. Bruyère, S.M., Van Looy, S., and Peterson, D. (2005). The International Classification of Functioning, Disability, and Health (ICF): Contemporary literature overview. *Rehabilitation Psychology, 50*(2), 113-121.
	C2. Bruyère, S.M. (2005). Using the International Classification of Functioning, Disability, and Health (ICF) to promote employment and community integration in rehabilitation. *Rehabilitation Education, 19*(2-3), 105-117.
D. Resource Center *Demographics*	D1. Erickson, W., Lee, C., and von Schrader, S. (2009). *2008 disability status reports: The United States.* Ithaca, NY: Cornell University Rehabilitation Research and Training Center on Disability and Demographics and Statistics.
	D2. Cornell University. (2010). *Disability statistics: Online resource for U.S. disability statistics.* Available: www.disabilitystatistics.org [January 9, 2012].
E. Technical Assistance and Training *Demographics*	E1. Cornell University and InfoUse. (no date). *Local disability data for planners: A planning resource for county and state data.* Ithaca, NY: Cornell University Employment and Disability Institute Available: http://www.disabilityplanningdata.com [January 9, 2012].
	E2. Bruyère, S.M., Houtenville, A., Ruiz-Quintanilla, S., and Weathers, R.R. II (2006). *National disability statistics for research practice and consultation (master training module on disability statistics).* Curriculum presented at the Cornell Summer Institute on Disability and Employment Policy, Ithaca, NY.

*The column also shows the key NIDRR research domain(s) that were being addressed by each project.

Brief Description of the Outputs: The first two outputs reviewed stemmed from the project on analysis of existing data. The disability statistics users' guide series (A1), a set of nine documents focused on nationally representative survey or administrative data sources such as the American Community Survey (ACS), Current Population Survey, and Panel Study of Income Dynamics, allows researchers, analysts, and other users of disability statistics to access complex data in an effective and efficient manner. The content of each guide was developed by subject experts and includes background, methodology, and definitions, as well as strengths, limitations, and implications of the data. Each guide also provides extensive documentation of the original data sources. The creators believe that such a usable and thorough resource on disability statistics did not previously exist. The second output reviewed was a journal article (A2) resulting from a study on the receipt of vocational rehabilitation services by individuals with disabilities by demographics, education, and disability type (mental, physical, or sensory) and across states. The study combined data on vocational rehabilitation services from the Rehabilitation Services Administration-911 public use file for fiscal year 2007 with data on people with disabilities by state and demographic group from the 2007 ACS Public Use Microdata Sample. Stapleton, Honeycutt, and Schechter discovered that a national average of 1.3 out of every 100 working-age adults with a disability receive vocational rehabilitation services, with significant variation by state, demographics, and disability type. They concluded that the differences suggest that vocational rehabilitation services benefit some groups in certain areas of the country more than others.

The outputs produced under the project focused on data collection methods were book chapters. The first output was Chapters 2 and 9 (B1) from the book *Counting Working-Age People with Disabilities: What Current Data Tell Us and Options for Improvement*. The book describes the kinds of valuable information current statistics and data on working-age people with disabilities can provide; these are areas in which current statistics and data are lacking, and ways in which statistics and data can be improved. Chapter 2 provides a foundation for the book, including definitions of disability, descriptions of major national surveys, and comparisons of prevalence estimates from these data sources. Chapter 9 describes the available data and statistics on working-age people with disabilities who participate in major federal programs. The authors summarize, compare, and integrate data on participation from major federal surveys, administrative data and statistics from federal agencies, and state-level participation statistics from employment service programs. The second output was Chapter 11 (B2) from *Counting Working-Age People with Disabilities: What Current Data Tell Us and Options for Improvement*. In Chapter 11, Stapleton, Livermore, and She present major limitations of the current national disability data and statistics system based on the information contained in the book and additional interviews with producers and consumers of disability statistics. The authors then present and discuss relatively inexpensive options for improving the system, as well as recommendations for expanding the system.

Two journal articles were reviewed from the project on the International Classification of Functioning, Disability and Health (ICF). The first article (C1) reviews the literature on the ICF produced in the 3 years following its endorsement by the World Health Organization. The review includes literature from the fields of rehabilitation, psychology, and health and human services. Bruyère, Van Looy, and Peterson conclude that the ICF is being applied in many governmental, health care, and rehabilitation clinical and research settings in the United States and abroad, although ongoing work is needed to further implement and support the ICF. The second article (C2) reviews selected rehabilitation literature on applications of the ICF to medical rehabilitation, employment, and community participation for persons with disabilities. It first describes the ICF and the need for a common classification system to inform data gathering and policy. The article then seeks to demonstrate the ICF's potential as a common system through a review of the literature describing its relevance and application to rehabilitation and health care delivery practice. The article goes on to state that the ICF could also potentially improve rehabilitation counseling practice in the areas of employment and environmental factors. Bruyère suggests next steps for implementing the ICF and integrating it into rehabilitation service delivery, counselor education, and research.

The next two outputs were developed as part of the grant's Resource Center. The 2008 Disability Status Reports (D1) consist of 53 individual reports produced annually, including a national-level report and reports on each state, Washington, DC, and Puerto Rico. The reports are based on analysis of the U.S. Census Bureau's ACS Public Use Microdata Sample. They provide a summary of the previous year's statistics on noninstitutionalized people with disabilities and are written such that anyone can understand and use the statistics. They contain information on disability prevalence based on population size, employment, earnings, and household income across demographic subpopulations. The disabilitystatistics.org website (D2) is a single, user-friendly, accessible resource for disability statistics from the three major national representative surveys that include disability measures: the ACS Public Use Microdata Sample, the Census Bureau's decennial Census 2000 detailed disability data tables, and the Current Population Survey. Data are available at the national, state, county, congressional district, or metropolitan area level, as well as for American Indian/Alaska Native/Hawaiian home areas. The site provides statistics on disability prevalence, employment, income, and poverty status by disability type and by demographic characteristics. It also includes an interactive search tool, and technical assistance is available to users experiencing problems.

The final two outputs were produced under the project aimed at technical assistance and training. The disabilityplanningdata.com website (E1) serves as a community planning tool, providing information on the disability population to aid urban, community, and service planners in making decisions that will affect or determine community access for people with disabilities. The website provides housing tables and population tables at the county level. The information in the tables consists of combined data from several years of the ACS. The website also includes a Data Guide that describes the ACS and other significant national surveys and provides links to further information on the surveys. Planners have generally used information such as age, gender, and race or ethnicity in planning, and this website allows them to also use information on disability. A master training module (E2) is aimed at training researchers and students to (1) understand available, existing data on people with disabilities; (2) understand, access, and utilize existing descriptive statistics; (3) identify instances in which descriptive statistics on disability can and should be meaningfully used; and (4) discuss and apply disability statistics using a personally relevant case study. The first section of the module provides a definition of disability and a description of how surveys identify disability. The second section includes an overview of the four major national survey disability data sources. The final section provides cases studies and examples in which trainees can apply the information from the first two sections. The module was created to improve the use of data and statistics in research and practice.

Grant Title: RRTC on SCI: Promoting Health and Preventing Complications Through Exercise

Grant Award Number: H133B031114

Grantee: National Rehabilitation Hospital/Medstar Research Institute

Grant Mechanism: Rehabilitation Research and Training Center

Grant Start and End Dates: December 1, 2003, to November 30, 2009

Total Direct Cost: $3,607,885

Abstract: Persons with spinal cord injury (SCI) have long been ranked at the lowest end of the physical activity spectrum. Studies published over the past decades have addressed the need for persons with SCI to adopt habitual exercise as part of a healthy lifestyle. Benefits of exercise for people with SCI mirror positive multisystem health benefits documented for those without paralysis. However, despite ample documentation of these benefits, no current exercise guidelines for people with SCI exist. NIDRR's Long-Range Plan Priorities 1 and 2 and the National Institutes of Health's (NIH's) National Center for Medical Rehabilitation Research (NCMRR) Research Priorities focus specifically on the development of clinical guidelines for identifying individuals at risk for secondary conditions and involving consumers in exercise regimens to prevent secondary conditions.

In response to these priorities, this Rehabilitation Research and Training Center (RRTC) systematically and comprehensively addressed the role and impact of physical activity in the prevention of secondary conditions in people with SCI. The RRTC was a collaborative effort of clinical and disability researchers, SCI consumer organizations, and independent living advocates. Consumers were involved in the planning, implementation, analysis, and dissemination of all research and training activities. Critical physiological responses to exercise in SCI were established, and risk for cardiovascular disease in individuals with SCI was examined comprehensively, applying accepted guidelines used in the able-bodied population. Exercise formats specifically designed according to severity and chronicity of SCI were developed to address the prevention of and knowledge regarding osteoporosis and other secondary conditions. It was determined whether regular exercise is related to fewer secondary conditions. These research findings fed into four training activities that included a peer mentoring program for newly injured people with SCI, a consumer-driven education curriculum for physical therapy and medical students, a state-of-science and training conference, and the development of a virtual resource network on exercise and prevention.

Research Projects and Outputs Reviewed: Grantees were asked to nominate two outputs from each of their projects for review by the committee. These outputs were identified by the study's key personnel as those that would best reflect their grant's achievements. Grantees selected the outputs to be reviewed from among the larger pool of outputs they had produced under the grant. This larger pool of outputs included 14 abstracts, 14 journal articles, one book chapter, one diagnostic instrument, two training manuals, one fact sheet, one educational aid, and one set of audiovisual materials. The following table shows the five projects carried out under this grant and lists the corresponding outputs that were nominated by the grantees and reviewed by the NRC committee. The reviewed outputs are briefly described following the table.

Project/*Research Domains**	**Outputs**
A. Cardiovascular Disease Risk Stratification Across Injury Levels After Spinal Cord Injury: Assessment of Need for Intervention and Its Predictors *Health and Function*	A1. Groah, S.L., Nash, M.S., Ward, E.A., Libin, A., Mendez, A.J., Burns, P., Elrod, M., and Hamm, L.F. (2010). Cardiometabolic risk in community-dwelling persons with chronic spinal cord injury. *Journal of Cardiopulmonary Rehabilitation and Prevention, 31*(2), 73-80.
	A2. RRTC on Spinal Cord Injury. (2005). *Coronary heart disease and SCI* [Cardiometabolic education package]. Available: http://www.sci-health.org/RRTC/edupackage/CHD_Final.pdf [January 9, 2012]. RRTC on Spinal Cord Injury. (2010). *Research highlights obesity and heart disease after spinal cord injury* [Cardiometabolic education package]. Available: http://sci-health.org/RRTC/edupackage/Obesity_Research_Highlights.pdf [January 9, 2012].

Project/*Research Domains**	**Outputs**
B. Effect of an Acute Intensive Exercise Intervention on the Prevention of Bone Mineral Density Loss in Individuals with Spinal Cord Injury *Health and Function*	B1. Groah, S.L., Lichy, A., Libin, A., and Ljungberg, I. (2010). Intensive electrical stimulation attenuates femoral bone loss in acute spinal cord injury. *Physical Medicine and Rehabilitation, 2*(12), 1,080-1,087.
	B2. RRTC on Spinal Cord Injury. (2005). *Osteoporosis and SCI* [Bone health and osteoporosis education package]. Available: http://www.sci-health.org/RRTC/edupackage/CHD_Final.pdf [January 9, 2012]. Lichy, A., Libin, A., Ljungberg, I., and Groah, S.L. (2007, November). *Preserving bone health after acute spinal cord injury: Differential responses to a neuromuscular electrical stimulation intervention.* Paper presented at the 12th Annual Conference of the International FES Society, Philadelphia, PA. Available: http://sci-health.org/RRTC/edupackage/IFESS2007_Lichy.pdf [January 9, 2012].
C. Effect of Robotic Body-Weight Supported Treadmill Training on Bone Mineral Density and Selected Secondary Conditions in Individuals with SCI *Health and Function*	C1. Hidler, J., Hamm, L.F., Lichy, A., and Groah, S.L. (2008). Automating activity-based interventions: The role of robotics. *Journal of Rehabilitation Research and Development, 45*(2), 337-344.
	C2. Lichy, A., Groah, S.L., Hamm, L.F., and Field-Fote, E. (2007). *Cardiac and metabolic benefits of robotic-assisted gait training after spinal cord injury.* Poster presented at the Annual Meeting of the American Spinal Cord Injury Association and Rehabilitation. Available: http://sci-health.org/RRTC/edupackage/Lichy_ASIA%202008%20poster.pdf [January 9, 2012]. Badday, H., Pineda, C., Lichy, A., and Groah, S. (2010). *Asymmetric bone mineral density loss in an ambulatory individual with spinal cord injury: A case report.* Poster presented at the Annual Meeting of the American Academy of Physical Medicine and Rehabilitation. Available: http://sci-health.org/RRTC/edupackage/BaddayAAPMR2010.pdf [January 9, 2012].
D. Comparison of Exercise Training Formats in Individuals with Spinal Cord Injury *Health and Function* *Participation and Community Living*	D1. Kroll, T., Kehn, M., Ho, P.S., and Groah, S.L. (2007). The SCI Exercise Self-Efficacy Scale (ESES): Development and psychometric properties. *The International Journal of Behavioral Nutrition and Physical Activity, 4*(34).
	D2. RRTC on Spinal Cord Injury. (2005). *Exercise and SCI* [Exercise and self-efficacy package]. Available: http://sci-health.org/RRTC/edupackage/Exercise_Factsheet.pdf [January 9, 2012].

Project/*Research Domains**	Outputs
E. Exercise and Secondary Conditions: A National Survey of Individuals with Spinal Cord Injury	E1. Kroll, T., Neri, M.T., and Ho, P.-S. (2007). Secondary conditions in spinal cord injury: Results from a prospective study. *Disability and Rehabilitation*, *29*(15), 1,229-1,237.
Health and Function *Participation and Community Living*	E2. National Rehabilitation Hospital's RRTC on SCI. (2006, November). *State of science video package*. Presented at the State-of-the-Science Conference, Bethesda, MD. Available: http://www.sci-health.org/sos/toc.html [January 9, 2012].

*The column also shows the key NIDRR research domain(s) that were being addressed by each project.

Brief Description of the Outputs: Each pair of outputs reviewed corresponds to a project and includes a journal article and a consumer education/informational package.

The first two outputs correspond to the project on cardiovascular disease risk assessment. The Groah et al. article (A1) describes cardiometabolic risk factors and risk clustering in people with SCI. It is based on a large-scale cross-sectional study that assessed 121 individuals with motor complete SCI, which according to the authors makes it one of the largest nonveteran studies of this type. The authors also report that the scope of the cardiopulmonary assessments was much broader than that of assessments previously performed and reported in the literature. The article indicates that cardiometabolic risk clustering in people with SCI differed by degree of injury. A preponderance of overweight/obesity was found in the entire population with SCI. Ten percent of the population with SCI had moderate to high 10-year risk of myocardial infarction or death. The consumer cardiometabolic education package (A2) included a coronary heart disease and SCI fact sheet, research highlights on obesity and heart disease after SCI, and an obesity trends animation piece.

The next two outputs correspond to the project focused on the effects of acute intensive exercise interventions on the prevention of bone mineral density loss in persons with SCI. Groah et al. (B1) investigated the effects of intensive electrical stimulation (ES) on femoral bone mineral density loss in acute SCI. They found that an intensive lower extremity ES program may attenuate bone mineral density loss after acute motor complete SCI, although it remained unknown whether these benefits would be maintained in the long run. The authors claim the study is one of the few randomized controlled trials investigating bone health in people with acute SCI. The consumer bone health and osteoporosis education package (B2) included an osteoporosis and SCI fact sheet resulting from an abstract on interim findings on osteoporosis in SCI presented at the 2007 American Spinal Cord Injury

Annual Meeting (awarded third-best presentation), as well as at the 2007 International Functional Electronic Stimulation Society Annual Meeting.

In an article produced under the project focused on the effect of robotic body-weight supported treadmill training on bone mineral density and selected secondary conditions in individuals with SCI, Hidler et al. (C1) review the use of robotic devices in delivering intense, activity-based therapies, which could result in significant exercise benefits for people with SCI. In the manuscript, they also present preliminary data from studies investigating the metabolic and cardiac responses during and after 6 months of lower-limb robotic training. The early evidence suggested that interventions, such as robotic-assisted gait training, may improve gait as well as metabolic and cardiovascular performance. The findings from this project did not result in a consumer education package; rather, the informational outputs targeted physicians and physical therapists. The robotics package (C2) therefore consisted of two posters, "Cardiac and Metabolic Benefits of Robotic-Assisted Gait Training after Spinal Cord Injury" and "Asymmetric Bone Mineral Density Loss in an Ambulatory Individual with Spinal Cord Injury: A Case Report," invited for presentation at the Annual Meeting of the American Spinal Cord Injury Association in 2007 and the Annual Meeting of the American Academy of Physical Medicine and Rehabilitation in 2010, respectively. Knowledge from this project, however, was able to be incorporated into consumer materials A2 and B2.

The journal article (D1) produced under the project comparing exercise training formats in individuals with SCI describes the development and psychometric properties of the Exercise Self-Efficacy Scale (ESES), a major outcome of the RRTC. Self-efficacy has wide application in studies on exercise and other health promotion activities. However, few efforts had been carried out to assess self-efficacy in people with SCI. The article's preliminary findings indicate that the ESES is a reliable instrument with high internal consistency and scale integrity. Consumer materials (D2) dealing with the prevention of secondary conditions through exercise and promotion of healthy lifestyles incorporate knowledge resulting from the ESES scale development. The materials provided for the output included the ESES questionnaire itself and a fact sheet on exercise and SCI.

The final two outputs reviewed were produced as part of the project on exercise and secondary conditions. Kroll et al. (E1) present findings from a prospective mail survey study aimed at determining significant predictors of pressure ulcers and urinary tract infections (UTIs) in adults with SCI over 2 years. The findings suggest that experience of a pressure ulcer at time 1 as well as not being married or cohabitating with a partner and lack of access to primary care services are significantly associated with the occurrence of a pressure ulcer at time 2. Reporting previous UTI, having greater functional limitations in activities of daily living, and not engaging in exercise were associated with UTI at time 2. The State-of-the-Science Conference and associated dissemination materials (E2) included multidisciplinary speakers and panel participants interested in the health and well-being of persons with SCI and in research focused on understanding the impact of exercise and physical activity on the prevention of secondary conditions in people with SCI.

REHABILITATION ENGINEERING RESEARCH CENTER (RERC)

Grant Title: RERC on Telerehabilitation

Grant Award Number: H133E040012

Grantee: University of Pittsburgh

Grant Mechanism: Rehabilitation Engineering Research Center

Grant Start and End Date: June 1, 2005, to May 31, 2009

Total Direct Costs: $3,046,093

Abstract: The vision of this Rehabilitation Engineering Research Center (RERC) was to serve people with disabilities by researching and developing methods, systems, and technologies that support remote delivery of rehabilitation and home health care services for individuals who have limited local access to comprehensive medical rehabilitation outpatient and community-based services. Research and development activities included (1) Remote Wheeled Mobility Assessment: determining whether individuals with mobility impairments can obtain appropriate prescriptions for wheeled mobility devices through the use of a telerehabilitation system based on information and telecommunication technologies; (2) Remote Accessibility Assessment of the Built Environment: determining the effectiveness of a remote accessibility assessment system in evaluating the built environment of wheeled mobility device users; (3) Telerehabilitation Infrastructure and Architecture: developing an informatics infrastructure and architecture that build on existing programs and technologies of the University of Pittsburgh Medical Center's e-Health System, supports the RERC's research and development activities, meets Health Insurance Portability and Accountability Act (HIPAA) requirements, provides a test bed for third-party telerehabilitation applications, and can be used as a model for future telerehabilitation infrastructure; (4) Telerehabilitation Clinical Assessment Modeling: developing a conceptual model for matching consumers with telerehabilitation technology. The model is user-oriented and driven by consumer experiences regarding satisfaction, simplicity, and reimbursability of telerehabilitation; (5) Teleassessment for the Promotion of Communication Function in Children with Disabilities: developing a web-based teleassessment infrastructure that links therapists and child participants, allowing therapeutic content to be adapted to a child's individual progress and abilities; and (6) Behavioral Monitoring and Job Coaching in Vocational Rehabilitation: researching technologies for conducting remote delivery of rehabilitation services to individuals with limited access to rehabilitation services that are necessary to participate in and achieve education and employment outcomes in their community.

Research Projects and Outputs Reviewed: Grantees were asked to nominate two outputs from each of their projects for review by the committee. These outputs were identified by the study's key personnel as those that would best reflect their grant's achievements. Grantees selected the outputs to be reviewed from among the larger pool of outputs they had produced under the grant. This larger pool of outputs included six abstracts, two book chapters, five journal articles, 36 proceedings, one intervention protocol, two field-tested products, one piece of software, one fact sheet, one training manual, one set of audiovisual materials, one e-journal, and one website. The following table shows the six projects carried out under this grant and lists the corresponding outputs that were nominated by the grantees and reviewed by the NRC committee. The reviewed outputs are briefly described following the table.

Project/*Research Domains*	**Outputs**
A. Evaluation of Remote Wheelchair Prescription *Health and Function*	A1. Schein, R.M., Schmeler, M.R., Brienza, D., Saptono, A., and Parmanto, B. (2008). Development of a service delivery protocol used for remote wheelchair consultation via telerehabilitation. *Telemedicine and e-Health, 14*(9), 932-938.
	A2. Schein, R.M., Schmeler, M.R., Holm, M.B., Saptono, A., and Brienza, D. (2010). Telerehabilitation wheeled mobility and seating assessments compared with in person. *Archives of Physical Medicine and Rehabilitation, 91*(6), 874-878.
B. Remote Accessibility Assessment of the Built Environment for Individuals Who Use Wheeled Mobility Devices *Participation and Community Living*	B1. Kim, J.B., and Brienza, D.M. (2006). Development of a remote accessibility assessment system through three-dimensional reconstruction technology. *Journal of Rehabilitation Research and Development, 43*(2), 257-272.
	B2. Kim, J., Brienza, D.M., Lynch, R.D., Cooper, R.A., and Boninger, M.L. (2008). Effectiveness evaluation of a remote accessibility assessment system for wheelchair users using virtualized reality. *Archives of Physical Medicine and Rehabilitation, 89*(3), 470-479.

Project/*Research Domains**	Outputs
C. Information Infrastructure and Architecture *Health and Function*	C1. Parmanto, B., Saptono, A., Pramana, G., Pulantara, W., Schein, R.M., Schmeler, M.R., McCue, M.P., Brienza, D.M. (2010). VISYTER: Versatile and Integrated System for Telerehabilitation. *Telemedicine and e-Health, 16*(9), 939-944.
	C2. *VISYTER (Version 2) [computer software].* Pittsburgh, PA: RERC on Telerehabilitation, Department of Rehabilitation Science and Technology. Available: http://him1.shrs.pitt.edu/LinkClick.aspx?fileticket=mwI2LqrS4HI%3d&tabid=39 [January 9, 2012].
D. Development of a Model for Clinical Assessment and Use of Telerehabilitation Services *Health and Function*	D1. Pramuka, M., and van Roosmalen, L. (2009). Telerehabilitation technologies: Accessibility and usability. *International Journal of Telerehabilitation, 1*(1), 85-97. Available: http://telerehab.pitt.edu/ojs/index.php/Telerehab/issue/view/227 [January 9, 2012].
	D2. Rehabilitation Engineering Research Center on Telerehabilitation. (2010). *World wide rehab* (online telerehab resource tool). Available: http://www.rerctr.pitt.edu [January 9, 2012].
E. Development and Implementation of a Teleassessment Architecture for the Promotion of Communication Function in Children with Disabilities *Health and Function*	E1. Speech-Language Telerehabilitation System based on Cosmobot—as described in: Parmanto, B., Saptono, A., Murthi, R., Safos, C., and Lathan, C.E. (2008). Secure telemonitoring system for delivering telerehabilitation therapy to enhance children's communication function to home. *Telemedicine and e-Health, 14*(9), 905-911.
	E2. Store and Forward Telemonitoring Protocol—as described in: Parmanto, B., Saptono, A., Murthi, R., Safos, C., and Lathan, C.E. (2008). Secure telemonitoring system for delivering telerehabilitation therapy to enhance children's communication function to home. *Telemedicine and e-Health, 14*(9), 905-911.
F. Behavioral Assessment and Job Coaching *Employment*	F1. McCue, M., Fairman, A., and Pramuka, M. (2010). Enhancing quality of life through telerehabilitation. *Physical Medicine Clinics of North America, 21*(1), 195-205.
	F2. Schmeler, M., Schein, R.M., McCue, M., and Betz, K. (2009). Telerehabilitation clinical and vocational applications for assistive technology: Research opportunities and challenges. *International Journal of Telerehabilitation, 1*(1), 59-72.

*The column also shows the key NIDRR research domain(s) that were being addressed by each project.

Brief Description of the Outputs: The first four outputs reviewed were all journal articles. The first two were produced under the Evaluation of Remote Wheelchair Prescription project. The Schein et al. article (A1) describes the development of a service delivery protocol that connects rural wheelchair users with urban specialists via telerehabilitation technology. To evaluate the protocol, a repeated measure study design was used. Effectiveness was evaluated through pre and post scores of the Functioning Everyday with a Wheelchair (FEW) outcome measure tool. Since many rural areas lacked qualified specialists, the protocol and study were launched at one initial site and then subsequently replicated at several additional sites. In the second journal article, Schein et al. (A2) report on a comparative assessment of wheeled mobility and seating in person at a clinic versus remotely via telerehabilitation. They used a prospective, multicenter controlled nonrandomized design at five wheelchair clinics in Western Pennsylvania. Participants included 50 individuals assessed at a clinic and 48 individuals assessed remotely. The study used the FEW outcome tool to gauge whether both sets of participants were assessed equally well. Results showed no significant differences in the quality of the assessment, indicating that such assessments can be completed adequately via telerehabilitation.

The next two journal articles stemmed from the project on remote accessibility assessment of the built environment for individuals who use wheeled mobility devices. Kim and Brienza (B1) describe an accuracy assessment of the ability of their Remote Accessibility Assessment System (RAAS) to create a 3-D reconstruction of a wheelchair user's environment for a clinician. Since the camera and 3-D reconstruction software chosen for the system can affect its overall reliability, they analyzed the accuracy of dimensional measurements in a virtual environment and compared the measurement accuracy of 3-D models created with four cameras/settings. The assessment led Kim and Brienza to identify which digital camera and software package available to consumers were capable of running the system. Using the camera and software, researchers conducted a successful field test of the system. In the next article, Kim et al. (B2) compare assessments of home environment based on the RAAS image reconstruction with assessments of home environment based on in-person inspection. The comparison was performed in three different homes of people who use wheeled mobility devices. For each home, assessments by each method were performed by a different specialist. Results indicated that assessments of the three homes by the two methods were in agreement 94 percent of the time. The authors believe these results demonstrate that the system could provide adequate service to wheelchair users in remote areas.

Under the Information Infrastructure and Architecture project, two outputs were produced. VISYTER (C1), a software platform for developing various telerehabilitation applications, includes high-quality videoconferencing, stimuli presentation, remote multiple camera control, remote control of the display screen, an eye contact teleprompter, and access to electronic health records. Since its development, the VISYTER system has been used to evaluate remote wheelchair prescriptions, support adult autistic assessments, and facilitate international physical therapy teleconsultations. The Telerehabilitation Portal (C2) supports telerehabilitation services such as remote wheelchair assessment and remote assessment of built environments. It also assists the grantee research team in managing clinical workflow and increases their ability to collaborate.

The project aimed at development of a model for clinical assessment and use of telerehabilitation services produced two outputs. The Pramuka and van Roosmalen article (D1) discusses the strengths and weaknesses of various telerehabilitation technologies. It highlights a conceptual framework that can be used to match telerehabilitation technologies, clinical applications, and user capabilities. The authors also suggest some methods of using the technology to improve the effectiveness of telerehabilitation versus in-person rehabilitation. The online tool World Wide Rehab (D2) is a resource database for information related to telerehabilitation services, such as technologies, disability types, and population types. It contains more than 800 resources (case studies, journal publications, reports, etc.) in the area of telerehabilitation, as well as a compilation of state (Medicaid) policies and clinical licensure policies related to telerehabilitation. The tool is available for all to use, and users are able to add new resources or update the information in the database. Creators envision the World Wide Rehab site resulting in better-informed clinicians and better-informed patients.

The next two outputs were pieces of netware created as part of the project on development and implementation of a teleassessment architecture for the promotion of communication function in children with disabilities. The first was a speech-language telerehabilitation system (E1) adapted from an existing stand-alone speech therapy system called Cosmobot. Researchers were able to add a secure, usable two-way telemonitoring system to Cosmobot, creating a more dynamic and valuable telerehabilitation system. They believe these efforts provide both an example of and a methodology for converting existing stand-alone rehabilitation systems into telerehabilitation systems. Converting existing systems is potentially more cost-effective for both clinicians and patients than developing and distributing new systems. The second output was a secure store-and-forward telemonitoring protocol (E2) for use in telemonitoring systems such as output E1. The protocol was new technology developed by the grantee that has wide application as more telerehabilitation systems are developed.

The final two outputs were journal articles produced under the project focused on behavioral assessment and job coaching. McCue, Fairman, and Pramuka (F1) review the literature on the history of telerehabilitation, which they describe as still a developing field. However, evidence from the literature suggests that the expressed advantages of telerehabilitation—lowering costs while increasing access and performing interventions in a patient's comfortable, natural environment—are being seen in the results of rehabilitation and in the quality of life of patients. The authors conclude that telerehabilitation has been largely successful over the course of its existence, but improvements still can be made, and further research is needed. Schmeler et al. (F2) summarize the clinical and vocational applications of telerehabilitation. As presented by the authors, these applications include pressure ulcer prevention, virtual reality applications, speech-language pathology applications, seating and wheeled mobility applications, vocational rehabilitation applications, and cost-effectiveness. The authors also provide a discussion of clinical and policy issues related to telerehabilitation and of some of the external influences on telerehabilitation.

Grant Title: RERC on Universal Interface and Information Technology Access

Grant Award Number: H133E030012

Grantee: University of Wisconsin–Madison, Trace Center

Grant Mechanism: Rehabilitation Engineering Research Center

Grant Start and End Date: October 1, 2003, to March 31, 2009

Total Direct Cost: $3,685,031

Abstract: The focus of this Rehabilitation Engineering Research Center (RERC) was on both access to information in its various forms and access to interfaces used by information technology and by electronic technologies in general. The research and development program was carefully designed to provide an interwoven set of projects that together advanced accessibility and usability in a fashion that took into account, and supported, the full range of access strategies used by manufacturers and people with disabilities. These strategies ranged from enhancing the design of mainstream products so they can be used by individuals with different ability sets to enhancing the ability of users to deal with information and interfaces as they encounter them. The program focused on advances that would have both short- and long-term outcomes related to assistive technologies (AT), interoperability, and universal design. It also included research with the potential to completely rewrite the basic precepts and approaches for accessibility and usability of information and interface technologies by people with disabilities, and may even impact the definitions and concepts of AT and universal design. Key to these projects was the development of new models and approaches for characterization of the functional requirements of current and future interfaces and a better understanding of the type, diversity, and similarity of functional limitations across etiologies and disabilities.

Research Projects and Outputs Reviewed: Grantees were asked to nominate two outputs from each of their projects for review by the committee. These outputs were identified by the study's key personnel as those that would best reflect their grant's achievements. Grantees selected the outputs to be reviewed from among the larger pool of outputs they had produced under the grant. This larger pool of outputs included five journal articles, four proceedings, four technical reports, one book chapter, two diagnostic instruments, one checklist, two miscellaneous tools, two industry standards, one working prototype, one patent, one product transferred to industry, three educational aids, and one website. The following table shows the eight projects carried out under this grant and lists the corresponding outputs that were nominated by the grantees and reviewed by the NRC committee. The reviewed outputs are briefly described following the table.

(Note that the grantee submitted more than two outputs for the committee's review for one of its projects, as reflected in the table below.)

Project/*Research Domains**	Outputs
A. Tools to Facilitate Built in Cross-Disability Access *Employment* *Participation and Community Living* *Technology* *Knowledge Translation including Technology Transfer*	A1. Vanderheiden, G.C. (2009). Accessible and usable design of information and communication technologies. In C. Stephanidis (Ed.), *The universal access handbook* (pp. 31-56). Boca Raton: CRC Press.
	A2. Vanderheiden, G.C. (2006-2009). *EZ access guidelines for implementers: Version 1.6.* Unpublished User's Guide, Trace Center, University of Wisconsin–Madison.
B. Tools for Incorporation of Interoperability Features in Mainstream Products *Employment* *Participation and Community Living* *Technology* *Knowledge Translation including Technology Transfer*	B1. Zimmermann, G., and Vanderheiden, G. (2008). Accessible design and testing in the application development process: Considerations for an integrated approach. *Universal Access in the Information Society,* 7(1-2), 117-128.
	B2. ISO/IEC 24752-1:2008(E): *Information technology—user interfaces—universal remote console—Part 1: Framework*. Available: http://www.iso.org/iso/iso_catalogue/catalogue_tc/catalogue_detail.htm?csnumber=42309 [January 10, 2012].

Project/*Research Domains**	**Outputs**
C. Server-Assisted and Virtual AT *Employment* *Participation and Community Living* *Technology*	C1. Vanderheiden, G.C. (2008). Ubiquitous accessibility, common technology core, and micro assistive technology. *ACM Transactions in Accessible Computing, 1*(2), 10.1-7.
D. Support of National and International Standards and Guidelines Efforts *Employment* *Participation and Community Living* *Technology*	D1. Cladwell, B., Cooper, C., Reid, L.G., and Vanderheiden, G. (2008). *Web Content Accessibility Guidelines (WCAG) 2.0 W3C recommendation.* Available: http://www.w3.org/TR/2008/REC-WCAG20-20081211/ [January 10, 2012]. Supporting Materials: Cladwell, B., Cooper, C., Reid, L.G., and Vanderheiden, G. (2008). *A guide to understanding and implementing Web Content Accessibility Guidelines 2.0.* Available: http://www.w3.org/TR/2008/NOTE-UNDERSTANDING-WCAG20-20081211/ [January 10, 2012]. Cladwell, B., Cooper, C., Reid, L.G., and Vanderheiden, G. (2008). *Techniques and failures for Web Content Accessibility Guidelines 2.0.* Available: http://www.w3.org/TR/2008/NOTE-WCAG20-TECHS-20081211/ [January 10, 2012].
	D2. *Photosensitive epilepsy analysis tool (PEAT)—with live capture* [computer software]. Madison: The Board of Regents of the University of Wisconsin System. Available: http://trace.wisc.edu/peat/ [January 10, 2012].
	D3. Vanderheiden, G. (2008). *HFES 200 software accessibility guidelines/ISO 9241-171 software accessibility standard*. Santa Monica, CA: Human Factors and Ergonomics Society.
	D4. ISO/IEC TC JTC1 N-888:2007: *Information technology—accessibility considerations for people with disabilities—Part 1: User needs summary.* Available: http://www.iso.org/iso/iso_catalogue/catalogue_tc/catalogue_detail.htm?csnumber=45161 [January 10, 2012].
	D5. Trace Center. (2008). *Report to the access board: Refreshed accessibility standards and guidelines in telecommunications and electronic and information technology.* Unpublished report to the Access Board, University of Wisconsin–Madison.

Project/*Research Domains**	Outputs
E. Disability and Interface Characterization Study *Health and Function* *Technology*	E1. Irwin, C.B., Meyer R.H., Yen, T.Y., Kelso, D.P., and Setso, M.E. (2008, September). *Force and impulse production during the use of a touch screen by individuals with motor control disabilities.* Paper presented at the Human Factors and Ergonomics Conference, New York, NY.
	E2. Irwin, C.B., Yen, T.Y., Meyer, R.H., Vanderheiden, G.C., Kelso, D.P., and Sesto, M.E. (2011). Use of force plate instrumentation to assess kinetic variables during touch screen use. *Universal Access in the Information Society*, 1-8.
F. Abstract User Interfaces and Interface Sockets *Participation and Community Living* *Technology*	F1. Trewin, S., Zimmermann, G., and Vanderheiden, G. (2004). Abstract representations as a basis for usable user interfaces. *Interacting with Computers, 16*(3), 477-506.
	F2. Zimmermann, G., and Vanderheiden, G. (2007). The universal control hub: An open platform for remote user interfaces in the digital home. In J. Jacko (Ed.), *Human-computer interaction: Interaction platforms and techniques* (vol. 4,551; pp. 1,040-1,049; Book Series-Lecture Notes in Computer Science). Heidelberg, Germany: Springer. Available: http://www.springerlink.com/content/x60015150w13g116/?p=4e776fc25dbf416fb05aa70120ac8664&pi=1 [January 10, 2012].
G. Technology Watch and State-of-the-Science Conference *Participation and Community Living* *Technology*	G1. National Council on Disability. (2006). *Over the horizon: Potential impact of emerging trends in information and communication technology on disability policy and practice.* Washington, DC: Author. (Written by Gregg Vanderheiden for NCD.)
	G2. Trace Center. (2007). *Emerging technology overview.* Available: http://trace.wisc.edu/tech-overview/ [January 10, 2012].
H. Direct Brain Interface Study *Health and Function* *Participation and Community Living* *Technology*	H1. Felton, E.A., Radwin, R.G., Wilson, J.A., and Williams, J.C. (2009). Evaluation of a modified Fitts law brain–computer interface target acquisition task in able and motor disabled individuals. *Journal of Neural Engineering, 6* 056002. Available: http://iopscience.iop.org/1741-2552/6/5/056002/pdf/1741-2552_6_5_056002.pdf [January 10, 2012].

*The column also shows the key NIDRR research domain(s) that were being addressed by each project.

Brief Description of the Outputs: The first two outputs were produced by the project involving the development of tools to facilitate built in cross-disability access. The first, a book chapter (A1), describes the changing nature of accessible interfaces to information and communication technologies (ICT). The chapter includes discussion of AT interfaces, pluggable user interfaces, universal design, how the meaning of these terms has changed and continues to change, demographic information, tables summarizing the known approaches to accessibility both within and across disabilities, and strategies for prioritizing. The chapter also includes a discussion of future challenges and opportunities related to ICT interfaces. The second output, the EZ Access Techniques Package and Checklist (A2), is a system of design techniques and hardware components to be used in conjunction with existing interactive electronic products to make the products more usable and accessible. According to the creators, EZ Access provides access for people with low vision; blindness; hearing impairment; deafness; physical disabilities of reach and motor control; and many cognitive, language, and learning disabilities. It also allows use of touchscreen kiosks via touchscreen or a keypad alone; has been shown to provide access for individuals with most single disabilities and most combinations of disabilities; and has been adopted by organizations, such as the U.S. Postal Service for its automated postal stations, the Phoenix Airport for its communication stations, Amtrak for its ticket kiosks, IBM for its airport checking kiosk designs, the Department of Homeland Security for its airport security kiosks, the Federal Deposit Insurance Corporation (FDIC) for its kiosk, and the World War II Memorial, among others.

Under the project focused on tools for incorporation of interoperability features in mainstream products, two outputs were produced. Zimmermann and Vanderheiden (B1) believe accessible design principles should be applied throughout any product development cycle and describe an integrated approach to accessible design. They suggest using "personas" to model the user base and derive design guidelines that would form the basis for the accessibility evaluation. From this point, iterative testing could be used to finalize the design. These principles are all in agreement with existing best practices of software engineering. The next output was a five-part International Standards Organization (ISO) standard for universal remote consoles (B2), encompassing a framework, user interface socket description, presentation template, target description, and resource description. The standard is intended for industry developers and manufacturers of electronic ICT products and systems. It directs network technology product design to expose an "interface socket" that allows users to control the new products with a previously existing interface. Creators believe the ability to use a known interface will allow users with disabilities to access more products. As reported by the grantees over 200 institutions are working directly or indirectly with these URC standards.

Associated with the project on server-assisted and virtual assistive technologies, the next output reviewed was an invited commentary article

(C1). Vanderheiden comments on changes in accessibility of computing since publication of a landmark article by Glinert and York in 1992. Changes include awareness of the need to design for accessibility and increased and improved accessibility features built into every operating system. Areas that have not changed include the prohibitive cost and limited availability of AT and the lag between new technology and necessary accessibility features. Vanderheiden introduces several new concepts that he believes researchers should be exploring to further improve AT, such as ubiquitous accessibility, a common technical core, and micro AT. As reported by the grantees, these concepts are now part of international efforts to build a Global Public Inclusive Infrastructure.

The next five outputs were all developed under the project Support of National and International Standards and Guidelines Efforts. The *Web Content Accessibility Guidelines* (WCAG 2.0) (D1), cover methods for making web content more accessible to people across disabilities, including blindness and low vision, deafness and hearing loss, learning disabilities, cognitive limitations, limited movement, speech disabilities, photosensitivity, and combinations of these. The Photosensitive Epilepsy Analysis Tool (PEAT) (D2) is a diagnostic instrument that captures video of a website in action and then analyzes the video for website content that may induce seizures in people with photosensitive seizure disorders. The analysis includes details of the severity of the risk associated with the content and suggestions for modifications that could eliminate the risk. PEAT is now a free, downloadable resource for web developers. According to the creators, the tool is cited in the support materials for both the World Wide Web Consortium (W3C) Web Accessibility Initiative (WAI) WCAG and Section 508 refresh materials. The next output involved bringing a set of software accessibility standards into alignment (D3). The Human Factors and Ergonomics Society (HFES) guidelines are the American standard, and the ISO standard is the European counterpart. The purpose of each standard is to provide guidance for designing accessibility into human-system software interfaces, but over time, the American and European standards had diverged. As reported by the developers, this effort created two new, harmonized standards that were used by the Access Board Advisory Committee in developing recommendations for revision of Section 508 of the Rehabilitation Act and Section 255 of the Communications Act. The last two outputs developed under this project were technical reports. The first was a technical report (D4) on the user needs of people with disabilities. The report was intended for standards developers, developers of information technology products, and accessibility advocates. The report describes the needs of users with a wide range of disabilities, identifies the common problems these users face when interfacing with technologies, and can be used to analyze whether accessibility measures will be effective. According to the grantee, the report was adopted by the ISO/International Electrotechnical Commission (IEC) Joint Technical Committee 1 (JTC1) Special Working Group on Accessibility as its user needs summary and processed into an ISO technical report (ISO/IEC TR 29138-1). The second technical report (D5) contains recommended standards and guidelines for updating regulations that implement two laws regarding accessible ICT: Section 508 of the Rehabilitation Act and Section 255 of the Communications Act of 1996. These two laws represent the core of all U.S. accessibility policy regarding ICT. The recommended updates will create guidelines that will work better across all technologies and devices, will be agile enough to provide guidance for technology that will be created in the near future, and will also be more in line with international standards.

Produced under the Disability and Interface Characterization Study were two publications. Irwin et al. (E1) describe touch screen use by individuals with motor control disabilities, citing a lack of such research. The authors examined how well participants with cerebral palsy and multiple sclerosis were able to use a touch screen. Kinetic variables and dwell time were measured. The study confirmed that button size is a key variable in allowing users with motor control disabilities to use devices with touch screens more easily up to a point, but that increasing the size of buttons beyond a certain level may not increase accessibility for those with severe motor impairments as is often believed. A proceedings article (E2) describes the development of instrumentation to measure the force applied to a touch screen. Irwin and colleagues designed a touch screen force plate to measure force applied to a touch screen by different users. A pilot study of the force plate included both participants with motor control disabilities and nondisabled participants. Results of the pilot study indicated that the plate was successful in measuring force for all users. The authors believe the instrumentation is the first of its kind, and the force plate was used by the study described as output E1.

The next two outputs were associated with the project on abstract user interfaces and interface sockets. Trewin, Zimmermann, and Vanderheiden (F1) examined four standards for abstract description of user interfaces. They describe a universal remote console scenario in which a personal device could easily connect with and operate any other local relevant device or service. They conclude that the technologies XForms and URC have the greatest potential to support a universal remote console scenario. The authors also identify two research challenges related to tagging and authoring. The Universal Remote Console Hub (F2) is a technology output that accesses the user interface of multiple electronic devices and provides access to all of them through one interface. It is intended to greatly improve access for persons with disabilities through the creation of one easy-to-use interface that can operate many devices. It also allows multiple devices to be controlled simultaneously and reduces the number of controllers and controls needed to operate the devices.

Under the project Technology Watch and State-of-the-Science Conference, two outputs were produced. A technical report (G1) provides an overview and analysis of the trends in technology and their impact and potential impact on various dimensions of accessibility and disability policy. The report includes such topics as trends and technological advances that are changing the rules; new opportunities, barriers, and concerns; and seven general recommended actions to be taken on a research and development and policy basis. This report was adopted and distributed by the National Council on Disability as part of its report series. The Emerging Technology Overview website (G2) is an online review, compiled in 2007, of selected emerging ICT. The website presents the information as a series of slides with images and links to further information. Its intent was to provide a sense of how future ICT could impact access by users with disabilities. The technology selected was intended to illustrate significant changes. The purpose of the overview was not to be exhaustive but to promote awareness of advances in interface technologies over the last decades that many disability (and mainstream) researchers were unaware of, and that could impact access to technologies and provide new approaches to meeting the needs of users with disabilities.

The final output reviewed was produced under the Direct Brain Interface Study. Felton et al. (H1) explored whether Fitts' law (a model of psychomotor behavior) applies when nondisabled and disabled individuals are moving a cursor on a computer screen through neural signals. Participants included eight nondisabled and five motor-disabled participants who moved a cursor on a computer screen through use of an electroencephalogram (EEG). Comparisons were made between nondisabled and disabled participants and between EEG and joystick cursor movement in nondisabled participants. Analysis of the results showed that Fitts' law did apply to the cursor movement by neural signals by both the nondisabled and disabled participants. The researchers believe this work has implications for the future design of devices controlled by neural signals.

DISABILITY AND REHABILITATION RESEARCH PROJECT-GENERAL (DRRP)

Grant Title: The Effect of Scheduled Telephone Intervention on Outcomes After TBI

Grantee: University of Washington

Grant Award Number: H133A040004

Grant Mechanism: Disability and Rehabilitation Research Project-General

Grant Start and End Dates: June 1, 2005, to May 31, 2010

Total Direct Cost: $3 million

Abstract: About 80,000 survivors of traumatic brain injury (TBI) are discharged from the hospital with long-term disabilities. Few interventions for persons with moderate to severe TBI have been shown to improve outcomes. This project examined the effect of a low-cost, easily implemented intervention on functional and health outcomes for these individuals. A randomized controlled trial was carried out in three widely disparate sites (Seattle, Washington; Philadelphia, Pennsylvania; and Jackson, Mississippi) to examine the effect of scheduled telephone intervention (STI) on function and quality of life for persons with TBI at 1 and 2 years after discharge from the hospital. The study randomized survivors of TBI into an experimental group and a control group upon discharge from inpatient rehabilitation. Both groups received the usual care, but the experimental group additionally received STI. Specific Aim 1 evaluated the effect of STI at weeks 1-2, 4, 8, and 12 and months 5, 7, and 9 on functional level, health and emotional status, community integration, and perceived quality of well-being over 1 year after TBI. Specific Aim 2 evaluated the effect of additional STI at months 15, 18, and 21 on the same variables and employment at 2 years after TBI. Specific Aim 3 evaluated whether the effects of such an intervention are similar in multiple sites over a wide geographic area and in demographic subgroups. Specific Aim 4 examined the differential impact of the intervention in demographic subgroups, with particular attention to minority versus nonminority racial and ethnic populations.

This study was based on a successful pilot single-site study carried out at the principal site, Seattle. This extension allowed cross-validation of the original results and determined whether the treatment and its results could be generalized to other disparate sites. Additionally, continuing STI through the second year allowed meaningful evaluation of its effect on return to work. Timely intervention to identify problems after TBI, to teach patients and their families coping techniques within their own communities, and to support their independent decision making would effectively decrease the need for expensive and often inaccessible services and improve the quality of life for survivors of TBI. A successful multicenter demonstration of this technique would have convincing implications for health care policy and provision of services to persons with TBI.

In addition to the original purpose, a validation study of the Community Participation Indicators, a measure being developed by Heinemann under NIDRR auspices, was carried out. Responses from persons with TBI and those from participant-identified significant others were compared to determine the validation of proxy responses for this instrument.

Research Projects and Outputs Reviewed: Grantees were asked to nominate two outputs from each of their projects for review by the committee. These outputs were identified by the study's key personnel as those that would best reflect their grant's achievements. Grantees selected the outputs to be reviewed from among outputs they had produced under the grant. These included one journal article and one workshop. The following table shows the project carried out under this grant and lists the corresponding outputs that were nominated by the grantees and reviewed by the NRC committee. The reviewed outputs are briefly described following the table.

Project/*Research Domains**	Outputs
A. The Effect of Scheduled Telephone Counseling on Outcome After TBI *Health and Function*	A1. Hart, T., Sherer, M., Temkin, N., Whyte, J., Dikmen, S., Heinemann, A.W., and Bell, K. (2010). Participant-proxy agreement on objective and subjective aspects of societal participation following traumatic brain injury. *Journal of Head Trauma Rehabilitation, 25*(5), 339-348.
	A2. Bell, K. (2010). *An experience-based discussion of challenges to conducting multicenter clinical trials in rehabilitation.* Presentation at the 2010 American Congress of Rehabilitation Medicine-American Society of Neurorehabilitation Joint Educational Conference, October 20-23, Montreal, Quebec, Canada.

*The column also shows the key NIDRR research domain(s) that were being addressed by each project.

Brief Description of the Outputs: This DRRP did not find a significant difference between treatment groups receiving STI and control groups. Secondary analyses were planned to see whether any subgroups within the intervention group had a differential response and whether there were any effects of intervention dosage. The intervention did not achieve its goals as it was applied in the study. Therefore, the outputs reviewed by the committee address some of the challenges and lessons learned in carrying out the study. The first output was a journal article (A1) examining agreement between participants and proxies (significant others) when reporting societal participation in three objective domains (economic, community, and social activities) and subjective satisfaction with participation at 1 year after TBI. The article concludes that proxy report may be an acceptable substitute for missing participant report on productivity and community activity outcomes, but should be used with caution for questions about social activities and degree of satisfaction with participation.

The second output was a workshop presentation, An Experience-Based Discussion of Challenges to Conducting Multicenter Clinical Trials in Rehabilitation (A2), held in Montreal, Canada. The objective of the workshop was to analyze the project to identify experimental factors that may have contributed to its unexpected outcome, including framing of the research question, use of pilot data, study design, recruitment and consenting of subjects, protocol management and treatment fidelity, data collection and quality monitoring, data analysis, effective dissemination, grant management, and institutional review board (IRB) concerns.

Grant Title: Asset Accumulation and Tax Policy Project

Grant Award Number: H133A031732

Grantee: University of Iowa

Grant Mechanism: Disability and Rehabilitation Research Project-General

Grant Start and End Date: June 1, 2007, to April 9, 2009

Total Direct Cost: $1,438,795

Abstract: The Asset Accumulation and Tax Policy Project (AATPP) adopted a team-based participatory approach to research, training, education, and technical assistance activities to bring to bear expertise in multiple disciplines—law, economics, community development, finance, disability studies, and public policy—and the real-world experience of persons with disabilities and their families, financial service providers, and community developers. Over a 5-year period, the Law, Health Policy, and Disability Center (LHPDC) at the University of Iowa College of Law and its strategic partners systematically examined the relationship between tax policy and asset accumulation for persons with disabilities and resultant improvements in economic and community integration. The AATPP investigated the impact of multiple intervention strategies—including financial education, matched savings accounts, expanded financial services, and increased use of state and federal tax incentives for asset and community economicdevelopment—on youth in transition and adults with disabilities in six states and 10 pilot demonstration sites nationwide. The AATPP used triangulated quantitative and qualitative techniques and a multimethod design (e.g., structured and open-ended interviews, archival analyses, policy and systems analysis, and survey techniques) to enhance the scientific rigor, policy relevance, and real-world usefulness of the research to key stakeholders, including persons with disabilities, policy makers, financial service providers, and community-based organizations.

The AATPP's knowledge transfer activities included 12 complementary methods for reaching target audiences through such avenues as publications, electronic communication, training, open forums, leadership institutes, and technical assistance activities. The AATPP partners' dissemination networks extended to the disability community and the asset accumulation and community development sectors in all 50 states. The collaborators brought a unique combination of expertise and experience as researchers, policy analysts, and practitioners in asset development (at the individual and systems levels) and economic development (at the local and state levels) to enhance knowledge transfer and impact nationwide.

Research Projects and Outputs Reviewed: Grantees were asked to nominate two outputs from each of their projects for review by the committee. These outputs were identified by the study's key personnel as those that would best reflect their grant's achievements. Grantees selected the outputs to be reviewed from among the larger pool of outputs they had produced under the grant. This larger pool of outputs included three journal articles, two technical reports, one book, one web journal, one intervention protocol, one tour, one online distance education series, one industry standard, one piece of software, two training manuals, and two newsletters. The following table shows the four projects carried out under this grant and lists the corresponding outputs that were nominated by the grantees and reviewed by the NRC committee. The reviewed outputs are briefly described following the table.

Project/*Research Domains**	**Outputs**
A. Survey of Community Development Credit Unions *Participation and Community Living*	A1. Harrison, V., Ratigan, T., and Apfel, D. (2008). Community development credit unions respond to the needs of the disability community. In *Building a better economic future: A progress report for individuals with disabilities & their families in America* (pp. 99-108). Manchester, NH: Community Economic Development Press. Available: http://realeconomicimpact.org/data/files/reports/building_better_future.pdf [January 10, 2012].
	A2. World Institute on Disability. (2006). *National Federation of Community Development Credit Unions "each one, teach many." Facilitator's guide. Disability access concepts and practice: Building bridges and breaking barriers.* Oakland, CA: World Institute on Disability. Available: http://www.natfed.org/files/public/NFCDCUDisabilityModule.pdf [January 10, 2012].
B. Tax Facts and Family Disability Survey *Employment* *Demographics*	B1. Hartnett, J. (2006). *Educating and democracy: Tax and financial service needs of working Americans with disabilities.* Washington, DC: National Disability Institute. Available: http://www.realeconomicimpact.org/data/files/reports/ford_report.pdf [January 10, 2012].
	B2. Hartnett, J.T., Morris, M., and Stengel, J. (2008). Real economic impact tour. In *Building a better economic future: A progress report for individuals with disabilities & their families in America* (pp. 85-98). Manchester, NH: Community Economic Development Press. Available: http:/ /realeconomicimpact.org/data/files/reports/building_better_future.pdf [January 10, 2012]. National Disability Institute. (2010). *Real Economic Impact Tour, 2009-2010 annual progress report.* Washington, DC: National Disability Institute. Available: http://www.realeconomicimpact.org/UploadedDocs/Documents/2010REITourReport.pdf [January 10, 2012].

Project/*Research Domains**	Outputs
C. Volunteer Income Tax Assistance and Financial Education Project *Employment*	C1. Volunteer Income Tax Assistance and Financial Education Study Intervention Protocol—as described in: Partch-Davies, T., and Rivera, J. (2008). Everyday heroes: How taxpayers with significant disabilities are building assets. In *Building a better economic future: A progress report for individuals with disabilities & their families in America* (pp. 45-62). Manchester, NH: Community Economic Development Press. Available: http:/ / realeconomicimpact.org/data/files/reports/building_better_future.pdf [January 10, 2012].
	C2. Hartnett, J., and Davies, T. (2010). Disability-inclusive asset building: New strategies for achieving real economic impact for Americans with disabilities. In *Opportunities for community development finance in the disability market* (pp. 39-53). Boston, MA: Federal Reserve Bank of Boston. Available: http://www.realeconomicimpact.org/data/files/reports/outside%20reports/draft%201-21-10.pdf [January 10, 2012].
D. IDA Project Demonstration for Self-Employment *Employment*	D1. Individual Development Account Protocol—as described in: Partch-Davies, T., and Rivera, J. (2008). Everyday heroes: How taxpayers with significant disabilities are building assets. In *Building a better economic future: A progress report for individuals with disabilities & their families in America* (pp. 45-62). Manchester, NH: Community Economic Development Press. Available: http:/ / realeconomicimpact.org/data/files/reports/building_better_future.pdf [January 10, 2012].
	D2. Hartnett, J. (2008). *Making financial connections* training brochures. Unpublished brochures, Center for Community Economic Development and Disability, Southern New Hampshire University School of Community Economic Development.

*The column also shows the key NIDRR research domain(s) that were being addressed by each project.

Brief Description of the Outputs: The first two outputs reviewed under the Survey of Community Development Credit Unions project were a book chapter and a facilitator's guide for an education training module. The book chapter (A1) summarizes and identifies how the members of the National Federation of Community Development Credit Unions are serving people with disabilities and improving services and products for this community. The facilitator's guide (A2) provides an overview and training on disability access concepts and practice. The distribution of this publication to organizations nationwide provided background on the need for and importance of serving the financial needs of disabled people. As reported by the grantee, the efforts resulted in 1,400 credit union accounts being opened by members with disabilities.

Under the Tax Facts and Family Disability Survey project, two publications of a technical nature were produced. The first, a report on the tax and financial service needs of working Americans with disabilities (B1), provides a profile of the utilization and demographics of use of tax filing and financial services for eligible workers with disabilities. This work provided a foundation for further research and led to 2007 and 2010 Internal Revenue Service (IRS) benchmark reports on the characteristics and profiles of taxpayers with disabilities. The project's second output, the Real Economic Impact (REI) Tour (B2), is described in two documents. The REI Tour is a public and private partnership of federal, state, and local organizations that promotes self-determination and full inclusion of Americans with disabilities in building a healthy economic future for themselves. The grantee reported that since 2004, the REI Tour has increased the number of taxpayers with disabilities accessing free tax services from 6 percent to 14 percent, representing more than 1 million taxpayers with disabilities and more than $1 billion in returns.

The next two outputs, produced under the Volunteer Income Tax Assistance and Financial Education Project, were a study intervention protocol and a paper. The Volunteer Income Tax Assistance and Financial Education Study Intervention Protocol (C1) is a comprehensive protocol for financial coaching designed to improve financial management behaviors of persons with disabilities consistent with financial security and asset holdings. The paper (C2) was published by the Federal Reserve Bank of Boston to raise awareness of the existing market of people with disabilities among community development, nonprofit, and private financial institutions. The paper uses the REI Tour and Volunteer Income Tax Assistance and Financial Education Project as examples of partnerships between community development and disability service organizations and implementation strategies that enhance the economic and social well-being of low-income taxpayers with disabilities. These efforts are providing the private sector with a snapshot of persons with disabilities as an emerging market segment and have engaged the Federal Reserve Banks in hosting annual meetings on economic empowerment and disability.

The final two outputs reviewed were another study intervention protocol and training brochures produced as part of the IDA Project Demonstration for Self-Employment. The Individual Development Account Protocol (D1) was intended to aid persons with disabilities in saving money from earnings for home ownership, postsecondary education, and business development, and to be used by community development entities in making their programs more universally accessible and adapting some of their program parameters for persons with disabilities. The *Making Financial Connections* training brochures (D2) targeted community development and rehabilitation specialists in an effort to build a more comprehensive, disability-inclusive infrastructure linking the two sectors. The brochures provide introductory, interdisciplinary training and information on assistance programs and resources (*Making Financial Connections*), returning to work (*Back to Work*), available tax credits and services (*Taking Your Credit*), effects of financial decisions (*Your Money, Your Choices*), and asset-building programs and ways of reaching financial goals (*Building a Strong Future*).

Grant Title: Medicaid Quality Indicators for Individuals with Disabilities

Grant Award Number: H133A040016

Grantee: George Mason University

Grant Mechanism: Disability and Rehabilitation Research Project-General

Grant Start and End Dates: January 1, 2005, to June 30, 2009

Total Direct Cost: $1.2 Million

Abstract: Nearly every state (43) operates at least one managed care plan for people with disabilities, and many Medicaid beneficiaries with disabilities have a choice of health plans. However, existing Medicaid report cards are not specifically geared to the interests of people with disabilities. The purpose of this 5-year study was to develop and test the use of comparative measures of quality, access, and satisfaction for people with disabilities and the general population. The study was designed as a joint project of George Mason University (Virginia), the Delmarva Foundation for Medical Care (Maryland), Kaiser-Permanente Center for Health Research (Oregon), and Baylor University (Texas).

The first component of the study was intended to refine a computer program that mines state Medicaid claims data to identify people who are very likely to face challenges in receiving the care they need as the result of a disability. The researchers planned to verify the accuracy of the computer program by surveying Medicaid beneficiaries in California about their ability to participate in community activities, live independently, and visit the doctor. The objective of the second study component was to review the two most widely used health plan quality indicators—the Consumer Assessment of

Healthcare Providers and Systems (CAHPS®) survey on consumer-reported quality of care and the Healthcare Effectiveness Data and Information Set (HEDIS®) Medicaid measures—to identify questions and measures (such as rates of preventive care) that are especially appropriate for people with disabilities and are statistically valid even when a relatively small number of people are being considered. The intent of the third component of the study was to interview working-age adults with disabilities in Oregon, California, and Baltimore-Washington, DC, to learn what types of information they would like to have when selecting a health plan and how they would like to obtain that information.

The overall aim of the study was to improve the field's ability to help people make informed choices among health plans, help health plans compare their performance against benchmarks and measure the progress of their quality improvement programs, and help states monitor health plan performance.

Research Projects and Outputs Reviewed: Grantees were asked to nominate two outputs from each of their projects for review by the committee. These outputs were identified by the study's key personnel as those that would best reflect their grant's achievements. Grantees selected the outputs to be reviewed from among the larger pool of outputs they had produced under the grant. This larger pool of outputs included seven publications, four measures, a software program, and a patent application for the software program. The following table shows the three projects carried out under this grant and lists the corresponding outputs that were nominated by the grantees and reviewed by the NRC committee. The reviewed outputs are briefly described following the table.

Projects/*Research Domains**	**Outputs**
A. Case Identification *Health and Function*	A1. Palsbo, S.E., Sutton, C.D., Mastal, M.F., Johnson, S., and Cohen, A. (2008). Identifying and classifying people with disabilities using claims data: Further development of the Access Risk Classification System (ARCS) algorithm. *Disability and Health Journal, 1*(4), 215-223.
	A2. Palsbo, S.E., and Mastal, M.F. (2006). *U.S. Patent application no. GMU-06-017U*. Washington, DC: U.S. Patent and Trademark Office.

Projects/*Research Domains**	Outputs
B. Assessment of Health Plans and Providers by People with Activity Limitations (AHPPPAL) and Administrative Measures *Health and Function*	B1. Palsbo, S.E., Hurtado, M.P., Levine, R.E., Barrett, K.A., and Mastal, M.F. (2011). Enabling a survey of primary care to measure the health care experiences of adults with disabilities. *Disability and Rehabilitation, 33*(1), 73-85.
	B2. Palsbo, S.E., and Mastal, M.F. (2008). *Quality indicators for individuals with disabilities in managed care.* Unpublished administrative measures, grey paper, Center for the Study of Chronic Illness and Disability, George Mason University, Fairfax, VA.
C. Comparative Reporting Tool (Plan-Reported Indicators, Comparative Reporting Tools and Consumer-Reported Indicators) *Health and Function*	C1. Palsbo, S.E., Diao, G., Palsbo, G.A., Tang, L., Rosenberger, W.F., and Mastal, M.F. (2010). Case-mix adjustment and enabled reporting of the health care experiences of adults with disabilities. *Archives of Physical Medicine and Rehabilitation, 91*(9), 1,339-1,346.

*The column also shows the key NIDRR research domain(s) that were being addressed by each project.

Brief Description of the Outputs: In an article produced under the first project, Palsbo et al. (A1) describe the results of an initiative to "refine and revalidate a software algorithm, the Access Risk Classification System (ARCS), using automated claims data to classify people into one of four categories based on the probable need for care coordination or health system accommodations." Using and combining existing sources of data, the ARCS identifies individuals needing extra medical assistance, such as those with disabilities. The authors evaluated the algorithm's sensitivity and specificity by comparing the predicted classification against self-report. Results showed the overall classification range to be from good to fair. The second output, a patent application for the algorithm (A2), was under review by the U.S. Patent and Trade Office as of this writing.

The next two outputs were produced under the project Assessment of Health Plans and Providers by People with Activity Limitations (AHPPPAL). Palsbo and colleagues (B1) field-tested adapted items from the CAHPS to assess whether this adapted instrument could capture the health care experiences of adults living with disabilities. Cognitive testing revealed problems with several items in the existing survey when answered by or about people with disabilities. Thirty-eight percent of respondents reported learning disabilities, which can interfere with access to health care services. Eight content areas in primary care were identified that are particularly important to maximize the functioning and well-being of people with disabilities. Palsbo et al. concluded that the study demonstrated the feasibility of adapting an existing instrument for use with persons with mixed functional limitations and severity of limitations. Data gathered with such an instrument could be used to identify and improve specific practices so as to provide better quality medical care for people with disabilities. The second output reviewed, Quality Indicators for Individuals with Disabilities in Managed Care (B2), resulted from an initiative to develop and field test quality measures derived from administrative and survey data sources, building on the CAHPS and HEDIS. Collection of these measures created a foundation for further exploration and testing of their relevance for individuals with disabilities. Palsbo and colleagues themselves were able to develop five peer-reviewed articles from this foundation.

The final output, reviewed under the project focused on comparative reporting tools, was a journal article (C1). It reports results of a study aimed at developing activity limitation clusters for case-mix-adjustment measures of health care processes and acting as a population profiler. Using the same respondent database as in output B1, a principal components analysis created four clusters of activity limitations. An analysis of scores of the adapted version of the CAHPS with the case-mix adjustment showed that disability caused a greater bias on health plan ratings than did demographic factors. According to Palsbo and colleagues, the new AHPPPAL is superior to the CAHPS for assessing individuals with disabilities.

Grant Title: Persons Aging with Hearing and Vision Loss

Grant Award Number: H133A020701

Grantee: Mississippi State University

Grant Mechanism: Disability and Rehabilitation Research Project-General

Grant Start and End Dates: November 1, 2002, to October 31, 2009

Total Direct Cost: $2,505,000

Abstract: The Rehabilitation Research and Training Center (RRTC) on Blindness and Low Vision at Mississippi State University (MSU), in collaboration with San Diego State University and the Helen Keller National Center for Deaf-Blind Youths and Adults in Sands Point, established a consortium Disability and Rehabilitation Research Project-General (DRRP) on Persons Aging with Hearing and Vision Loss. The collaborative effort focused on exploring strategies to improve outcomes for persons who are blind or visually impaired or deaf or hard of hearing and are now additionally experiencing a secondary onset of hearing loss or vision impairment as a result of the aging process. The 5-year project had the following priorities: (1) investigating the prevalence of age-related onset of deafness among older American blind individuals and age-related onset of blindness among older American deaf individuals and the impact on employment and community integration options, including more viable communication systems for each population; (2) identifying and evaluating technology and service delivery options, such as transportation, housing, and community integration activities, for individuals with early-onset deafness or blindness and late-onset hearing or vision loss and their effectiveness with persons experiencing secondary sensory loss resulting from aging; (3) identifying and evaluating access to use of technologies, including assistive devices and telecommunication or other existing communication systems, such as tactile interpreter support, needed to assist persons with early-onset deafness or blindness and late-onset hearing or vision loss and their effectiveness with persons experiencing secondary sensory loss resulting from aging; and (4) using available dissemination mechanisms, with appropriate assistive technical modification, and disseminating findings, and developing strategies to educate both consumers and providers, especially vocational rehabilitation workers, in the use of these techniques.

Research Projects and Outputs Reviewed: Grantees were asked to nominate two outputs from each of their projects for review by the committee. These outputs were identified by the study's key personnel as those that would best reflect their grant's achievements. Grantees selected the outputs to be reviewed from among the larger pool of outputs they had produced under the grant. This larger pool of outputs included 11 journal articles, one newsletter, and one website. The following table shows the four projects carried out under this grant and lists the corresponding outputs that were nominated by the grantees and reviewed by the NRC committee. The reviewed outputs are briefly described following the table.

Project/*Research Domains**	Output
A. Prevalence of Hearing and Vision Loss in Seniors and the Impact on Employment and Community Integration	A1. Capella-McDonnall, M., and LeJeune, B.J. (2008). Employment among older adults with combined hearing and vision loss. *Journal of Applied Rehabilitation Counseling,* 39(3), 3-9.
Employment *Participation and Community Living* *Demographics*	A2. Sansing, W.K. (2010). *An overview of hearing, vision and dual sensory impairment prevalence in the U.S.* Unpublished paper, RRTC on Blindness and Low Vision, Mississippi State University.

Project/*Research Domains**	Output
B. Technology and Service Delivery Options *Participation and Community Living*	B1. LeJeune, B.J. (2005). *Persons Aging with Hearing and Vision Loss (PAHVL) newsletter*. Issue 3.Available: http://www.blind.msstate.edu/pahvl/project/summary/PAVHL_Newsletter_3.pdf [January 10, 2012].
	B2. LeJeune, B.J. (Fall 2010). Aging with dual sensory loss: Thoughts from consumer focus groups. *AER Journal of Research and Practice in Visual Impairment*, 3(4), 146-152.
C. Identification and Evaluation of Access to Technology *Technology*	C1. LeJeune, B.J., Steinman, B., and Mascia, J. (2003). Enhancing socialization of older people experiencing loss of both vision and hearing. *Generations, 27*(1), 95-97.
	C2. Capella-McDonnall, M.E. (2005). The effects of single and dual sensory loss on symptoms of depression in the elderly. *International Journal of Geriatric Psychiatry, 20*(9), 855–861.
D. Dissemination *Participation and Community Living*	D1. LeJeune, B.J. (2010). *Persons Aging with Hearing and Vision Loss (PAHVL) newsletter series*. Available: http://www.blind.msstate.edu/pahvl/project/summary/ [January 10, 2012].
	D2. Rehabilitation Research and Training Center on Blindness and Low Vision and Helen Keller National Center for Deaf-Blind Youths and Adults. (2006). *Creating roads to independence for persons aging with hearing and vision loss.* Conference held in Atlanta, GA, February 8-10.

*The column also shows the key NIDRR research domain(s) that were being addressed by each project.

Brief Description of the Outputs: The first two journal articles produced under the Prevalence of Hearing and Vision Loss in Seniors and the Impact on Employment and Community Integration project analyze employment and prevalence of hearing and vision impairment among older adults. Capella-McDonnall and LeJeune (A1) performed an exploratory study in which they compiled data on the employment status and experiences of a group of older adults with combined hearing and vision loss. Data were obtained from two sources: primary data were collected through a survey and secondary data from a nationally representative sample. The study's results indicate that many of these adults do work or want to work and that accommodations, assistive technology, higher education levels, and changes in job or type of work are associated with continued employment. The second article (A2) is a literature review on the prevalence of hearing, visual, and dual sensory impairment among seniors in the United States. It reports that nationally representative survey estimates produce varied prevalence totals, but all demonstrate increased numbers of people aged 55 and over with all types of sensory loss.

Under the Technologies and Service Delivery Options project, the NRC committee reviewed two outputs. The first was a newsletter (B1) updating research participants, service providers, and stakeholders on the project, including survey status and results. The second was a journal article (B2) on the issues concerning services and access to technology that consumer focus groups (nine groups of 68 older adults self-identified with both hearing and visual impairments) reported having experienced. There appeared to be a perceived lack of accommodation related to hearing loss in programs for older blind adults and a lack of knowledge about visual impairment among the deaf or hard of hearing who acquired vision loss later in life.

The next two outputs were journal articles produced under the third project, Identification and Evaluation of Access to Technology. The LeJeune et al. (C1) article focuses on enhancing socialization of older people experiencing both vision and hearing loss, particularly through suggestions for improved communication, including assistive technologies. Capella-McDonnall (C2) analyzed the effects of single and dual sensory loss on symptoms of depression in the elderly. She performed secondary analyses of 2001 National Health Interview Survey data from 9,832 people age 55 and older living in community settings. Results showed that elderly individuals with dual sensory loss were not significantly more likely than those with vision loss, but were significantly more likely than those with hearing loss, to experience symptoms of depression.

The final two outputs reviewed, produced under the Dissemination project, were a newsletter series and a national conference. The *Persons Aging with Hearing and Vision Loss* (*PAHVL*) newsletter series (D1) was distributed to research participants, service providers, and stakeholders. The newsletters contained updates, preliminary research results, and helpful information. The national conference, entitled Creating Roads to Independence for Persons Aging with Hearing and Vision Loss (D2), attracted 117 participants. A variety of new information was presented on such topics as the basics of sensory loss, use of support service providers, communication strategies, assistive technology, and psychosocial adjustment. Evaluations were positive and led organizers to hold a second conference.

FIELD INITIATED PROJECT (FIP)

Grant Title: Efficacy of Pressure Garment Therapy After Burns

Grant Award Number: H133G050022

Grantee: University of Washington

Grant Mechanism: Field Initiated Project

Grant Start and End Dates: October 1, 2005, to September 30, 2009

Total Direct Cost: $450,000

Abstract: The objective of this project was to determine the efficacy of custom-fit pressure garment therapy in the prevention of hypertrophic scarring in healed burns through a randomized controlled trial. Pressure garments are the common therapy used today to minimize hypertrophic scarring, one of the most devastating outcomes following burn injury. However, these garments are unattractive, expensive, and uncomfortable, and their use needs to be validated by rigorous research.

Research Projects and Outputs Reviewed: Grantees were asked to nominate two outputs from each of their projects for review by the committee. These outputs were identified by the study's key personnel as those that would best reflect their grant's achievements. Grantees selected the outputs to be reviewed from among the larger pool of outputs they had produced under the grant. Under this grant, an instrument and a journal article were produced. The following table shows the project carried out under this grant and the corresponding output that was nominated by the grantees and reviewed by the NRC committee (the grantee chose to nominate only one output for review). The reviewed output is briefly described following the table.

Project/*Research Domains**	Outputs
A. Efficacy of Pressure Garment Therapy After Burns *Health and Function*	A1. Engrav, L.H., Heimbach, D.M., Rivara, F.P., Moore, M.L., Wang, J., Carrougher, G.J., Costa, B., Numhom, S., Calderon, J., and Gibran, N.S. (2010). 12-year within-wound study of the effectiveness of custom pressure garment therapy. *Burns, 36*(7), 975-983.

*The column also shows the key NIDRR research domain(s) that were being addressed by each project.

Brief Description of the Output: Engrav and colleagues (A1) describe the effectiveness of custom pressure garment therapy using a randomized within-wound comparison over a 12-year period. Data were obtained on 54 consecutively enrolled patients from 1995 to 2007. The study found that custom pressure garment therapy is effective, but clinical benefit is restricted to those with moderate or severe scarring. In addition, the article underlines the limitations that may have affected the paucity of prior randomized controlled trials confirming the effectiveness of custom pressure garment therapy. The authors state that theirs is the first study to utilize a within-wound protocol.

Grant Title: A Longitudinal Study for Hospitalization, Pressure Ulcers, and Subsequent Injuries After Spinal Cord Injuries

Grant Award Number: H133G050165

Grantee: Medical University of South Carolina

Grant Mechanism: Field Initiated Project

Grant Start and End Dates: June 1, 2007, to May 31, 2010

Total Direct Cost: $449,984

Abstract: The purpose of this project was to perform a longitudinal study to identify protective and risk factors associated with the onset of multiple types of adverse health events among a large sample of individuals with spinal cord injury (SCI). The onset of SCI increases the risk for development of a number of secondary conditions that may adversely impact an individual's life and even result in early mortality.

Predictor variables were first measured over a 10-month period in 1997-1998, including biographical status, injury status, psychological status, environmental factors, and health behaviors. Several health outcome measures were also used. During follow up, multiple outcome measures were administered, with a focus on adverse events (pressure ulcers, subsequent injuries, and hospitalizations) and treatments. Structural equation modeling was performed to develop risk models for each outcome. A consumer advisory committee met to review instrumentation and made recommendations regarding all components of the project.

This project addressed important NIDRR priorities related to health and function. The ultimate goal of the study was to enhance the lives of people with SCI by identifying the risk and protective factors associated with adverse health events to serve as a foundation for prevention efforts by rehabilitation and public health professionals. Consumers will be directly empowered to improve their own health through the provision of concrete information and recommendations for promoting better health and avoiding preventable secondary health complications.

Research Projects and Outputs Reviewed: Grantees were asked to nominate two outputs from each of their projects for review by the committee. These outputs were identified by the study's key personnel as those that would best reflect their grant's achievements. Grantees selected the outputs to be reviewed from among the larger pool of outputs they had produced under the grant. This larger pool of outputs included 12 journal articles, one newsletter, and one website. The following table shows the project carried out under this grant and lists the corresponding outputs that were nominated by the grantees and reviewed by the NRC committee. The reviewed outputs are briefly described following the table.

Project/*Research Domains**	Outputs
A. A Longitudinal Study for Hospitalizations, Pressure Ulcers, and Subsequent Injuries After Spinal Cord Injuries *Health and Function*	A1. Krause, J.S., and Saunders, L.L. (2009). Risk of hospitalizations after SCI: Relationship with biographic, injury, educational, and behavioral factors. *Spinal Cord, 47*, 692-697.
	A2. Krause, J.S., Reed, K.S., and McArdle, J.J. (2010). A structural analysis of health outcomes after spinal cord injury. *The Journal of Spinal Cord Injury, 33*(1), 22-32.

*The column also shows the key NIDRR research domain(s) that were being addressed by each project.

Brief Description of the Outputs: The two outputs reviewed by the NRC committee were journal articles. The first (A1) was intended to identify variables and individual health behaviors associated with hospitalization after SCI. Through a cross-sectional mail survey of 1,386 persons with SCI, two biographical and injury characteristics were found to be associated with hospitalization: race and SCI severity. After controlling for these characteristics, three behavioral factors were found to be significantly associated with hospitalization: use of prescription medications, greater engagement in smoking behaviors, and more SCI-specific health behaviors. The authors hope these findings will establish target behaviors for prevention and intervention strategies and will encourage more conservative practices regarding prescribing of medications.

In the second journal article (A2), Krause et al. describe a measurement model developed through both exploratory and confirmatory factor analysis of health domains and a latent model linking basic biographical, injury, and educational characteristics with health outcomes for persons with SCI. Survey data were obtained from 1,388 adult patients with traumatic SCI of at least 1 year's duration. The study used structural equation modeling in identifying common factors for health outcomes, distinct factors relating to secondary conditions, and factors relating to health impact. Six health outcome domains (the best overall solution) were identified in the study and were found to have a significant relationship with biographical, injury, and educational status. The authors conclude that the composite scores generated from multiple indicators provide more informative and stable outcome scores than the use of single indicators.

Grant Title: Black-White Disparities in Stroke Rehabilitation

Grant Award Number: H133G050153

Grantee: National Rehabilitation Hospital/Medstar Research Institute

Grant Mechanism: Field Initiated Project

Grant Start and End Date: October 1, 2005, to September 30, 2009

Total Direct Cost: $396,165

Abstract: The purpose of this 3-year study was to examine (1) how black and white stroke rehabilitation patients differ in terms of their clinical profiles, the care they receive, and their outcomes; and (2) how rehabilitation care and outcomes can be optimized for both groups. The goal was to translate these findings into an actionable quality improvement plan that would enhance care and outcomes for all black and white stroke rehabilitation patients.

The study capitalized on a unique comprehensive stroke rehabilitation database (N = 1,161) containing detailed patient, intervention, and outcome data assembled from 2001 to 2003 under the auspices of the NIDRR-sponsored Post-Stroke Rehabilitation Outcomes project. This database contains extraordinarily detailed data on rehabilitation care processes and treatments that allowed investigators to examine the practice of stroke rehabilitation care and to dissect the processes of care that might be different for whites and blacks. This practice-based evidence method ensured clinical buy-in and ownership of the study's findings. The project team also proposed an evaluation protocol for confirming the effectiveness and predictive validity of any suggested practice changes.

Research Projects and Outputs Reviewed: Grantees were asked to nominate two outputs from each of their projects for review by the committee. These outputs were identified by the study's key personnel as those that would best reflect their grant's achievements. Grantees selected the outputs to be reviewed from among the larger pool of outputs they had produced under the grant. This larger pool of outputs included five journal articles and one statistical technique. The following table shows the project carried out under this grant and lists the corresponding outputs that were nominated by the grantees and reviewed by the NRC committee. The reviewed outputs are briefly described following the table.

Project/*Research Domain**	**Outputs**
A. Black-White Disparities in Stroke Rehabilitation *Health and Function*	A1. Horn, S.D., Deutscher, D., Smout, R.J., DeJong, G., and Putnam, K. (2010). Black-white differences in patient characteristics, treatments, and outcomes in inpatient stroke rehabilitation. *Archives of Physical Medicine and Rehabilitation*, *91*, 1,712-1,721. Deutscher, D., Horn, S.D., Smout, R.J., DeJong, G., and Putnam, K. (2010). Black-white disparities in motor function outcomes taking into account patient characteristics, nontherapy ancillaries, therapy activities, and therapy interventions. *Archives of Physical Medicine and Rehabilitation*, *91*, 1,722-1,730.

*The column also shows the key NIDRR research domain(s) that were being addressed by each project.

Brief Description of the Output: The two journal articles reviewed by the NRC committee were considered as a pair (one output) since all the information provided for the first article applied to the second article. The articles apply a practice-based evidence approach in analyzing disparities in rehabilitation services and outcomes. They capitalize on the unique comprehensive stroke rehabilitation database assembled from 2001 to 2003 under the NIDRR-sponsored Post-Stroke Rehabilitation Outcomes project. The first article focuses on black-white differences in characteristics and factors in patient stroke rehabilitation, and the second regresses these variables on motor function outcomes. Racial differences were found in certain aspects of service receipt and outcomes, with both blacks and whites benefiting in different ways. However, it was not race itself that made a difference in outcomes, but the interventions. This project thus shows the importance of using a practice-based evidence approach in studying the processes of care and dealing with issues related to bias in observational studies.

Grant Title: Development of Intelligent Personal Activity Management and Prompting Applications for Individuals with Cognitive Disabilities

Grant Award Number: H133G050313

Grantee: Eugene Research Institute

Grant Mechanism: Field Initiated Project

Grant Start and End Dates: October 1, 2005, to September 30, 2009

Total Direct Cost: $499,852

Abstract: This project built on the successful development of the Picture Planner icon-driven personal activity management application, supported in part by previous NIDRR funding. One of the conclusions derived from the field testing that led to the development and testing of that application was the need for intelligent activity planning and prompting applications that combine cognitively accessible software design with innovative artificial intelligence approaches to provide smart applications for life management and decision making. The goal of this project was to use a consumer-driven, participatory design process to build on that foundation and develop a prototype smart planning and prompting software package for implementation on desktop and handheld platforms. Major objectives included the following:

1. Year 1—Needs assessment focus groups comprising 20 individuals with disabilities and 10 care providers, with the goal of surveying priorities from the consumer and assistant perspectives for features of a smart management system;
2. Years 1-2—Development of a proof-of-concept design and validation process to guide the subsequent development of smart features;
3. Years 2-3—Prototype application development, emphasizing integration of intelligent prompting elements into the desktop Picture Planner application and subsequent implementation on handheld systems;
4. Year 3—Comparison study of smart versus standard methods of activity planning using random assignment of 20 Consumer Development Group members; and
5. Year 3—Preparation of a final strategic white paper addressing technical challenges and directions for further development of smart life skills applications incorporating artificial intelligence methods.

The primary outcome of this project was a field-tested and experimentally evaluated intelligent life skills management system enabling people with cognitive disabilities to improve their competence in daily activity management and enhance their community integration. In addition to a commercially viable desktop and handheld application, the white paper produced under Objective 5 provided source material for submission of at least three papers to refereed journals and conference presentations and for written and electronic products targeting a variety of audiences, including consumers, families, researchers, educators, and developers.

Research Projects and Outputs Reviewed: Grantees were asked to nominate two outputs from each of their projects for review by the committee. These outputs were identified by the study's key personnel as those that would best reflect their grant's achievements. Grantees selected the outputs to be reviewed from among the larger pool of outputs they had produced under the grant. This larger pool of outputs included one journal article, one proceedings, three audiovisual materials, one prototype, one netware product, one product in the marketplace, and one website. The following table shows the project carried out under this grant and lists the corresponding outputs that were nominated by the grantees and reviewed by the NRC committee. The reviewed outputs are briefly described following the table.

Project/*Research Domains**	**Outputs**
A. Development of Intelligent Personal Activity Management and Prompting Applications for Individuals with Cognitive Disabilities *Technology*	A1. Keating, T. (2009). *Picture Planner: Icon-based personal organizer* [software]. Eugene, OR: Cognitopia Software, LLC. Available: http://www.cognitopia.com/ [January 10, 2012].
	A2. Keating, T. (2006). Picture Planner: A cognitively accessible personal activity scheduling application. In S. Keates and S. Harper (Eds.), *Proceedings of the 8th International Association for Computing Machinery, Special Interest Group on Accessible Computing (ACM SIGACCESS) Conference on Computers and Accessibility* (pp. 239-240). Available: http://www.nationaltechcenter.org/conference2010/content/Tom_Keating/tom_keating_2.pdf [January 10, 2012].

*The column also shows the key NIDRR research domain(s) that were being addressed by each project.

Brief Description of the Outputs: The first output, Picture Planner (A1), is a personal organizer application designed for individuals who either have limited or no reading ability or need a simplified and graphically driven user interface. It functions as an icon-based scheduling system that assists in planning and viewing activities by individual activity, day, week, or month. Icons can come from the stock library of images in Picture Planner, or the user can import pictures from any source. Picture Planner also uses synthesized speech to provide feedback and aid in accessibility. The target population for this application is individuals with significant cognitive disabilities, such as mental retardation or autism. The heterogeneity of this population, the challenge of representing complex concepts in graphical form, and the lack of standards or a universally understood icon system make the development of this sort of cognitively accessible application difficult. Despite the preponderance of visual scheduling applications, the developers believe there previously existed no similarly capable and cognitively accessible application.

In the second output, Keating (A2) describes the design elements and field test results that advanced the cognitive accessibility of the icon-driven Picture Planner. Field tests included more than 25 individuals with significant cognitive disabilities, ranging in age from 16 to 20 and with IQ and adaptive behavior scores that would place them in the moderate to mildly disabled range. Tested individuals were shown to be able to learn to use and benefit from an accessible computer-based self-management application such as Picture Planner.

Grant Title: Driving After Stroke

Grant Award Number: H133G050134

Grantee: Wayne State University

Grant Mechanism: Field Initiated Project

Grant Start and End Date: October 1, 2005, to May 31, 2009

Total Direct Cost: $330,474

Abstract: A variety of factors influence resumption of driving after stroke, only some of which accurately reflect the ability to drive safely. Although current methods can enhance accuracy in predicting fitness to drive, decisions about driving often are made independently of this information. Moreover, little research has focused on unwarranted barriers to driving or the consequences of having stopped. No study has examined the bases on which survivors make decisions about resumption of driving as it relates to objective driving fitness and community integration.

This study sampled pairs of survivors and their significant others recruited at inpatient discharge from the outpatient clinic of an urban rehabilitation hospital and from the metropolitan community. Barriers to driving, driving status, and community integration were assessed 6 months poststroke. A subsample also underwent a comprehensive driving evaluation. The objectives were to identify the barriers to driving after stroke and the extent to which these barriers influence driving status (i.e., decision to drive), actual driving risk, and community integration. The long-term goal was the development of interventions that maximize independence and community integration while protecting public and survivor safety. The study of barriers to driving facilitates valid evaluation of fitness to drive and the psychoeducation of survivors and their significant others regarding decisions to resume or cease driving after stroke.

Research Projects and Outputs Reviewed: Grantees were asked to nominate two outputs from each of their projects for review by the committee. These outputs were identified by the study's key personnel as those that would best reflect their grant's achievements. Grantees selected the outputs to be reviewed from among the larger pool of outputs they had produced under the grant. This larger pool of outputs included five journal articles. The following table shows the project carried out under this grant and lists the corresponding outputs that were nominated by the grantees and reviewed by the NRC committee. The reviewed outputs are briefly described following the table.

Project/*Research Domains**	Outputs
A. Driving After Stroke *Participation and Community Living*	A1. Griffen, J.A., Rapport, L.J., Bryer, R.C., and Scott, C.A. (2009). Driving status and community integration after stroke. *Topics in Stroke Rehabilitation, 16*(3), 212-221.
	A2. McKay, C., Rapport, L.J., Bryer, R.C., and Casey, J. (in press). Self-evaluation of driving simulator performance after stroke. *Topics in Stroke Rehabilitation 18*(5), 549-561.

*The column also shows the key NIDRR research domain(s) that were being addressed by each project.

Brief Description of the Outputs: Griffen et al. (A1) investigated the effects of driving cessation on community integration after stroke and assessed gender and social support as potential moderators of these effects. The authors state that most prior research had examined a single subjective outcome rather than assessing community integration as a multidimensional outcome including subjective and objective domains. The study found that driving status had a substantial influence on community integration after stroke and that social support facilitated this integration but did not buffer the effects of driving cessation. Men and women were found to resume driving at equal rates, but driving cessation showed differential effects for men and women with regard to community integration, with women experiencing adverse effects that were less strong. The authors believe that these findings identify and emphasize the need for specific follow up regarding cessation of driving, especially as it relates to the risk of detrimental outcomes for quality of life, participation, and occupation.

McKay et al. (A2) examined self-awareness of driving simulator and neuropsychological performance among stroke patients compared with healthy controls. Despite the potential dangers associated with premature return to driving after stroke, very little prior research had examined the relationship between impaired self-awareness and driving. The driving simulators enabled evaluation of driving fitness in challenging situations without the risk of accident, the novel application of metacognitive self-evaluations in prediction and postdiction of performance, and insight into the impact of experience on accurate self-awareness of deficits. The study findings support the potential use of driving simulators as a useful and safe method for assessing and improving stroke survivors' impaired self-awareness.

Grant Title: Functional Effects of Bifocal Use: Implication for Falling Intervention

Grant Award Number: H133G050340

Grantee: University of Wisconsin–Milwaukee

Grant Mechanism: Field Initiated Project

Grant Start and End Dates: October 1, 2005, to September 30, 2009

Total Direct Cost: $320,631

Abstract: This project directed an integrated set of research activities to address a seriously underconsidered factor in falls research, the use of bifocal lenses. It focused on new users of bifocal glasses, typically individuals in their fourth or fifth decade of life, and targeted a better understanding of falls intervention strategies related to eyeglass wear. The five primary goals of the study were to (1) measure outcomes of bifocal use; (2) understand the process of adaptation to new bifocals; (3) explore brain function as a potential explanatory variable; (4) draft recommendations for clinical practice and design; and (5) disseminate scientific papers and presentations to inform research, device development, and practice. In Phase 1 of the study, researchers studied longitudinally how adaption to multifocal lenses affected depth perception, edge contrast, and functional mobility. In Phase 2, researchers took functional magnetic resonance imaging (fMRI) scans of new users during adaptation. Study recommendations were articulated not only for multifocal lens wearers, but also for the producers of lenses and biomedical engineers.

Research Projects and Outputs Reviewed: Grantees were asked to nominate two outputs from each of their projects for review by the committee. These outputs were identified by the study's key personnel as those that would best reflect their grant's achievements. Grantees selected the outputs to be reviewed from among the larger pool of outputs they had produced under the grant. This larger pool of outputs included a diagnostic instrument, two technical reports, one manuscript in preparation, and four national/international presentations. The following table shows the three projects carried out under this grant and lists the corresponding outputs that were nominated by the grantees and reviewed by the NRC committee. The reviewed outputs are briefly described following the table.

Project/*Research Domains**	Outputs
A. Functional Adaptation in New Wearers of Multifocal Lenses *Health and Function*	A1. Smith, R.O. (no date). *The DGI-M, Dynamic Gait Index-Modified* [overview and protocol]. Unpublished document, Rehabilitation Research Design and Disability Center, University of Wisconsin–Milwaukee.
	A2. Smith, R.O., Tomashek, D., and Stalberger, K.J. (2010). *The effects of new multifocal lens eyeglasses on contrast edge sensitivity, depth perception and functional gait for middle aged users.* Unpublished manuscript, Rehabilitation Research Design and Disability Center, University of Wisconsin–Milwaukee.
B. Brain Response to Upper and Lower Lens Conditions, fMRI Analysis of Bifocal Wearers *Health and Function*	B1. Smith, R.O. (no date). *The upper and lower visual field depth perception performance measure* [overview and protocol]. Unpublished document, Rehabilitation Research Design and Disability Center, University of Wisconsin–Milwaukee.
	B2. Vandenbush, K.J. (2009). *The effect of multifocal lenses on visual attention and its interaction on motor performance.* Unpublished paper, Rehabilitation Research Design and Disability Center, University of Wisconsin–Milwaukee.

Project/*Research Domains**	Outputs
C. fMRI Analysis of Bifocal Wearers *Health and Function*	C1. Smith, R.O., and Tomashek, D. (2010). *Failure of adaptation to multifocal lenses: Longitudinal evidence and implications on falling.* Poster presented at the American Congress for Rehabilitation Medicine (ACRM) Conference, Montreal, QC Canada.
	C2. Smith, R.O. (no date). *Preliminary output data from functional magnetic resonance imaging (fMRI) brain scans.* Unpublished data, Rehabilitation Research Design and Disability Center, University of Wisconsin–Milwaukee.

*The column also shows the key NIDRR research domain(s) that were being addressed by each project.

Brief Description of the Outputs: The first two outputs were produced under the project focused on functional adaptation in new wearers of multifocal lenses. The Dynamic Gait Index-Modified (DGI-M) tool (A1) is a modification of the original DGI, a well-regarded tool for measuring functional gait in older adults, used to discriminate between performance with and without wearing multifocal lens glasses. The modifications included increasing the scoring scale, adding tasks targeted to wearers of multifocal lenses, redesigning the walkway and obstacles involved in the tasks, and adding a subjective response questionnaire to gauge discomfort. According to its creators, the DGI-M improves on the original by also effectively measuring functional gait in younger (ages 40-59) participants. A technical report (A2) explores how visual and functional gait performance was affected when middle-aged users of single lens glasses transitioned to multifocal lenses. Participants used single lens glasses and had been prescribed multifocal lenses but had not worn them prior to the study. Participants were tested using the Howard-Dohlman Depth Perception apparatus, the Melbourne Edge Test, and the DGI-M. The authors found significant differences between users of single lenses and multifocal lenses in depth perception, contrast edge sensitivity, and functional gait. They concluded that the transition to multifocal lenses significantly degraded visual and functional gait performance in middle-aged adults, but did not appear to increase the risk of falling.

Under the project Brain Response to Upper and Lower Lens Conditions, fMRI Analysis of Bifocal Wearers, two technical reports were produced. The first (B1) describes how researchers developed a new three-dimensional (3-D) depth perception paradigm. The paradigm involves a set of four two-color 3-D circles, one of which appears either closer to or farther away from the participant. Researchers also developed an apparatus to control participants' heads in order to divide images between upper and lower lenses. Testing of the final paradigm showed significant differences for lens type (single versus multifocal) and wearer group (multifocal versus nonmultifocal wearers). This measure allowed for the creation of a software-based data collection scheme that could be transferred to an fMRI. The creators believe this measure may lead to better understanding of depth perception and better intervention designs to prevent falls. The second technical report (B2) resulted from a study of differences in single lens versus multifocal lens use while users were (1) responding to targets in the upper versus lower visual field and (2) responding to targets with the presence of a visual distracter. Using both single and multifocal lenses, participants identified a circle, in either their upper or lower visual field, that was closer or farther away than other circles. At times participants made judgments while discriminating against a visual distracter. Statistical analysis of the data demonstrated significant performance differences between single and multifocal lenses. Results of this study suggest a difference in the attentional capability of single lens and multifocal lens users, which may be exacerbated by distraction.

The final two outputs were produced under the project focused on fMRI analysis of bifocal wearers. A presentation (C1) of a summary of output A1 at the 2010 annual meeting of the American Congress of Rehabilitation Medicine included background, goals, methods, results, conclusions, and implied future research directions. During the presentation, researchers highlighted the potential implications of their work for improving understanding of the relationship between use of multifocal lenses and falling for people with disabilities. The last output reviewed was a technical report (C2) resulting from an exploratory study of different attentional patterns for upper and lower visual fields in long-time users of multifocal versus nonmultifocal lenses. Using fMRI, maps of participants' brains were created; participants then completed a nonattentional task and an attentional task. The areas of the brain activated by each task were recorded. Results indicated that the long-time multifocal lens users had different attentional patterns for upper and lower visual areas, while nonmultifocal lens users did not have different patterns.

Grant Title: Inclusive Indoor Play

Grant Award Number: H133G040324

Grantee: Tech Research Corp, Georgia Tech

Grant Mechanism: Field Initiated Project

Grant Start and End Date: August 1, 2005, to December 31, 2009

Total Direct Cost: $293,324

Abstract:[2] This study's intent was to learn about the needs for indoor play among children with and without disabilities so universal playthings that can benefit all children can be designed. The project encompassed researching indoor play environments, developing universal design play guidelines, and designing models of play environments that are safe and accessible to all children. It included researching play and the play environment through a literature review; examining existing products, play environments, and children's play designs; conducting focus group interviews with participants; consulting with experts; and testing full-scale simulated play environments. The second year of the project focused on the development of design concepts, construction of refined design in full scale, and testing with users. The final year of the project was dedicated to prototype construction and testing.

Research Projects and Outputs Reviewed: The pool of outputs that were developed under this grant included 13 conference proceedings articles, one journal article, three assessment tools (each consisting of rating scales for measuring different aspects of play), six technology products called "playthings," and one play space known as a "Playscape." The following table lists the two outputs that were reviewed by the NRC committee. These are briefly described following the table.

Project/*Research Domains**	Outputs
A. Inclusive Indoor Play *Participation and Community Living*	A1. Endicott, S., Kar, G., and Mullick, A. (2009). Inclusive indoor play: Children at play. *Human Factors and Ergonomics Society Annual Meeting Proceedings*, *53*(19), 1,527-1,531.
	A2. Mullick, A., and Grubbs, R. L. (2009). Inclusive indoor play: Play and playthings. *Human Factors and Ergonomics Society Annual Meeting Proceedings*, *53*(19), 1,537-1,540.

*The column also shows the key NIDRR research domain(s) that were being addressed by each project.

Brief Description of the Outputs: The two outputs reviewed were both included in the 2009 Human Factors and Ergonomics Society conference proceedings. Because of their focus on able-bodied children, indoor playthings are underutilized as tools for social education of children with disabilities. The first proceedings publication (A1) identifies and analyzes five aspects of play that took place while children with and without disabilities interacted with a variety of playthings in a full-scale indoor play environment. The study was intended to provide information about the

[2]This abstract was adapted from the project abstract found on http://www.naric.com [January 10, 2012].

needs for indoor play among children with and without disabilities. A total of 18 children participated, 15 of whom had disabilities. Results suggested that a correlation exists among independence in play, level of assistance needed, and effort required to play. Observations regarding the level of difficulty and fun experienced in playing with different things were used to determine plaything components that contribute to inclusive indoor play for children with disabilities.

The second proceedings publication (A2) summarizes the results of the focus-group interview aspect of the project. The researchers convened two focus groups to investigate inclusive indoor play and playthings. The first focus group served an exploratory role and probed inclusion in indoor play, while the second had two purposes—to learn more about inclusion in indoor play and to validate information offered by the first group. A total of 15 people participated in the two focus groups, including parents of children with and without disabilities, teachers, therapists, daycare providers, and toy designers. The results of the focus group interviews produced a comprehensive list of design and evaluation criteria for inclusive playthings.

Grant Title: Interference in Hearing Aids from Digital Wireless Telephones: Improved Predictive Methods

Grantee: Advanced Hearing Concepts

Grant Award Number: H133G050228

Grant Mechanism: Field Initiated Project

Grant Start and End Dates: November 1, 2005, to October 31, 2009

Total Direct Cost: $447,600

Abstract: Digital wireless telephones (commonly referred to as cellular phones) have opened up vast new opportunities for electronic communication that could be of substantial benefit to people with hearing loss. Unfortunately, digital cellular telephones generate electromagnetic (EM) interference in hearing aids, and many hearing aid wearers cannot use these telephones. In this study, experiments were performed to develop a basic understanding of this new form of interference and to develop ways of predicting its effects on speech perception and the usability of cellular telephones by hearing aid wearers. The results of this study not only benefit consumers in helping them select a hearing aid and/or cellular telephone but also provide industry with the basic theoretical underpinnings needed to allow for the development of improved wireless telephones (and other digital wireless devices) that produce substantially less interference in hearing aids, thereby increasing the accessibility of modern digital communication systems for people with hearing loss.

Research Projects and Outputs Reviewed: Grantees were asked to nominate two outputs from each of their projects for review by the committee. These outputs were identified by the study's key personnel as those that would best reflect their grant's achievements. Grantees selected the outputs to be reviewed from among the larger pool of outputs they had produced under the grant. This larger pool of outputs included five journal articles, two industry standards, and one tutorial. The following table shows the project carried out under this grant and lists the corresponding outputs that were nominated by the grantees and reviewed by the NRC committee. The reviewed outputs are briefly described following the table.

Project/*Research Domains**	Outputs
A. Interference in Hearing Aids from Digital Wireless Telephones: Improved Predictive Methods	A1. Levitt, H. (2007). Historically, the paths of hearing aids and telephones have often intertwined. *Hearing Journal, 60*(11), 20-24.
Health and Function	Supporting Materials: Levitt, H. (2007). A historical perspective on digital hearing aids: How digital technology has changed modern hearing aids. *Trends in Amplification, 11*(1), 7-24.
	A2. Levitt, H. (2007). *American national standard methods of measurement of compatibility between wireless communications devices and hearing aids, ANSI c63.19-2007*. New York: Institute of Electrical and Electronics Engineers, Inc.

*The column also shows the key NIDRR research domain(s) that were being addressed by each project.

Brief Description of the Outputs: The first output reviewed by the NRC committee was an invited paper (A1) stemming from the Clinical Research Summit on Hearing Aids and Wireless Technology. The purpose of the summit was to identify needs for the future development of hearing aids and wireless technology. In the paper, Levitt traces the historical development and interconnectedness of hearing aids and telephones. The paper was published in a journal widely read by hearing aid engineers, telephone engineers, and audiologists, reaching its intended audience and encouraging cooperation among the three groups.

The second output is a standard method (A2) for measuring interference in a hearing aid produced by wireless communication devices such as cellular telephones. Data, methods of data analysis, and theoretical predictions developed under the project were incorporated in the standard. Standard procedures are needed for these measurements to allow researchers, telephone companies, hearing aid manufacturers, and other interested groups to have a common basis for comparing experimental results and for complying with regulations of the Federal Communications Commission.

Grant Title: Motor Training and Assessment in Adults with Hemiplegic Cerebral Palsy—The ULTrA Program

Grantee: University of Michigan

Grant Award Number: H133G050151

Grant Mechanism: Field Initiated Project

Grant Start and End Dates: December 1, 2005, to November 30, 2009

Total Direct Cost: $446,964

Abstract: Although cerebral palsy (CP) is considered a nonprogressive condition, many adults with the disease experience declines in functional performance beginning as early as late adolescence. Since current understanding and treatment of motor deficits in CP have been derived almost exclusively from pediatric populations, very little is known regarding the nature of motor declines that may occur across the life span.

This project was designed to implement an 8-week Upper-Limb Training and Assessment Program (ULTrA Program) for adults with hemiplegic CP. The Motor Control Laboratory at the University of Michigan found that motor training leads to improved upper-limb coordination during functional tasks in children with hemiplegic CP. These observations, based on the notion of brain plasticity, supported the view that movement training can lead to functional improvement despite years of limited limb use. This project targeted a growing yet neglected segment of the CP community—adults. The project was home based but linked to the research laboratory through the Internet.

Prior to and following the intervention, upper-limb sensorimotor function was assessed quantitatively using established motor control techniques. Each participant received a computer-based upper-limb training unit including high-speed connectivity. A 40-minute intervention program was performed 5 days a week. During three of these training sessions, participants were assisted by a student coach via webcam Internet connection. Data were recorded and uploaded to a central website that serves as a resource for consumers and researchers in the area of mobility in CP across the life span. Recruitment took place locally and from two other areas in Michigan, thereby demonstrating increased access to Internet-based motor training programs. This project addressed several future research priorities of NIDRR. By targeting older individuals with CP, it directly addressed the issue of aging with a disability. By developing an intervention program that is accessible through Internet technology, it addressed the issue of improved, cost-effective delivery of rehabilitation services and expansion of evaluation approaches. Lastly, this project combined a community-based, theory-driven model of upper-limb rehabilitation with a strong education component for consumers and pre-health professional students.

Research Projects and Outputs Reviewed: Grantees were asked to nominate two outputs from each of their projects for review by the committee. These outputs were identified by the study's key personnel as those that would best reflect their grant's achievements. Grantees selected the outputs to be reviewed from among the larger pool of outputs they had produced under the grant. This larger pool of outputs included five journal articles, two working prototypes, two newsletters, one website, one intervention protocol, and a field-tested product. The following table shows the two projects carried out under this grant and lists the corresponding outputs that were nominated by the grantees and reviewed by the NRC committee. The reviewed outputs are briefly described following the table.

Project/*Research Domains**	Outputs
A. Assessment of Sensorimotor Function in Adults with Hemiplegic Cerebral Palsy *Health and Function*	A1. Langan, J., Doyle, S.T., Hurvitz, E.A., and Brown, S.H. (2010). Influence of task on interlimb coordination in adults with cerebral palsy. *Archives of Physical Medicine and Rehabilitation, 91*(10), 1,571-1,576.
	A2. Brown, S.H., Langan, J., Kern, K.L., and Hurvitz, E.A. (2010). Remote monitoring and quantification of upper limb and hand function in chronic disability conditions. In P.M. Sharkey and J. Sanchez (Eds.), *Proceedings of the 8th International Conference on Disability, Virtual Reality and Associated Technologies* (pp. 147-155). Available: http://www.icdvrat.org/2010/papers/ICDVRAT2010_S05_N05_Brown_etal.pdf [January 10, 2012].
B. Sensorimotor Training in Adults with Hemiplegic Cerebral Palsy *Health and Function*	B1. Brown, S.H., Lewis, C.A., McCarthy, J.M., Doyle, S.T., and Hurvitz, E.A. (2010). The effects of Internet-based home training on upper limb function in adults with cerebral palsy. *Neurorehabilitation Neural Repair, 24*(6), 575-583.

*The column also shows the key NIDRR research domain(s) that were being addressed by each project.

Brief Description of the Outputs: All outputs reviewed by the NRC committee for this grant were journal articles. The first two were produced under the project aimed at assessment of sensorimotor function in adults with hemiplegic CP. Langan et al. (A1) describe changes in upper-limb reaching performance in adults with CP. They performed a quantitative study using between-group (four men with hemiplegic CP and four age-matched controls) repeated-measure analyses. The study concluded that bilateral sequential movements were more conducive to faster movement time compared with unilateral and bilateral simultaneous movement. According to the authors, this finding has implications for the development of more effective movement-based therapies and suggests training that includes bilateral sequential movements may be beneficial to adults with hemiplegic CP. Brown et al. (A2) describe the ULTrA Program, a home-based telerehablitation system designed to improve upper-limb and hand function in adults with CP. The program delivers exercise modules to the patient's home and is able to transmit performance-related data back to the laboratory.

The third journal article (B1), produced under the Sensorimotor Training in Adults with Hemiplegic Cerebral Palsy project, describes the improvement, detected through increased movement speed and enhanced hand manipulation, achieved and monitored through the ULTrA Program. Home-based telerehabilitation programs such as ULTrA make task-based movement training more accessible to individuals with disabilities while providing clinicians with quantitative feedback via remote monitoring, which in turn facilitates adaptation of the training program throughout the intervention period. The creators believe the ability to generate and transmit quantitative measures throughout the intervention period provides an advantage over other rehabilitation approaches that rely on pre- and postintervention assessments to conduct evaluations and make changes.

Grant Title: Using the U.S. EEOC Employment Discrimination Charge Data System for Research and Dissemination

Grant Award Number: H133G040265

Grantee: Cornell University

Grant Mechanism: Field Initiated Project

Grant Start and End Dates: October 1, 2004, to September 30, 2009

Total Direct Cost: $450,000

Abstract: This project was designed to analyze trends in employment discrimination charges related to the Americans with Disabilities Act (ADA) and other laws, using data from the Equal Employment Opportunity Commission's (EEOC's) Charge Data System (CDS). The CDS collects data on employment discrimination charges covered under Title I of the ADA, as well as data on such charges related to other laws. It contains information on (1) the demographic characteristics of charging parties, such as gender, racial and ethnic status, age, location, and type of disability (e.g., back impairment, depression); (2) the type of discriminatory behavior, such as refusal to hire, failure to provide reasonable accommodation, unfair discharge, and harassment; and (3) charge outcomes, such as withdrawal with benefits and settlements. These data were used to explore trends over time and across the states and to investigate whether these trends were related to changes in the composition of the population with disabilities and in labor market conditions. Using regression analysis, the researchers explored the relationship of the ADA-related charge rates to state-level economic conditions, statistics on participation in government programs by people with disabilities, and other state-level characteristics. Also examined were changes in the composition of charges over time with respect to the characteristics of charging parties, the size and industry of employers, and the types of alleged discriminatory treatment; differences in claims between the EEOC and the Fair Employment Protection Agency (FEPA); differences in trends and types of charges between the ADA and other statutes (specifically the Age Discrimination in Employment Act [ADEA]); and, where relevant, the potential impact of Supreme Court decisions on trends in these compositional changes. To achieve a better understanding of patterns in ADA-related charges, collaboration and input were sought from the EEOC and selected disability advocacy organizations, such as selected state FEPAs; state protection and advocacy agencies; and as needed, AARP, the American Association of Persons with Disabilities, the National Disability Rights Network (formerly called the National Association of Protection and Advocacy Systems), and the law firm of Powers, Pyles, Sutter, and Verville.

Research Projects and Outputs Reviewed: Grantees were asked to nominate two outputs from each of their projects for review by the committee. These outputs were identified by the study's key personnel as those that would best reflect their grant's achievements. Grantees selected the outputs to be reviewed from among the larger pool of outputs they had produced under the grant. This larger pool of outputs included one journal article, one technical report, one chartbook, and one website. The following table shows the project carried out under this grant and lists the corresponding outputs that were nominated by the grantees and reviewed by the NRC committee. The reviewed outputs are briefly described following the table.

Project/*Research Domains**	**Outputs**
A. Using the U.S. EEOC Employment Discrimination Charge Data System for Research and Dissemination	A1. Bjelland, M.J., Bruyère, S.M., von Schrader, S., Houtenville, A.J., Ruiz-Quantanilla, A., and Webber, D.A. (2010). Age and disability employment discrimination: Occupational rehabilitation implications. *Journal of Occupational Rehabilitation,* 20(4), 456-471.
Employment	A2. von Shrader, S., Bruyère, S., and Bjelland, M. (2010). *Americans with Disabilities Act (ADA) charge data chartbook.* Unpublished data chartbook, Employment and Disability Institute, ILR School, Cornell University, Ithaca, NY.

*The column also shows the key NIDRR research domain(s) that were being addressed by each project.

Brief Description of the Outputs: Bjelland et al. (A1) investigated the nature of employment discrimination charges that cite the ADA or ADEA individually or jointly. The authors found that employment discrimination charges originating from older or disabled workers are concentrated within a subset of issues that include reasonable accommodation, retaliation, and termination. Based on analyses of the discrimination charges filed under the ADA and ADEA, the authors discuss issues relevant to rehabilitation and human resource practitioners, including strategies for improving employment outcomes among older workers and those with disabilities and chronic health conditions as the labor force evolves to include more members of these communities.

The second output, a chartbook (A2), was the result of a request by the EEOC Office of Research, Information, and Planning for a product based on ADA charges to post on the EEOC website. The chartbook is intended to provide basic statistics on ADA charges for a wide variety of audiences that access the EEOC website.

SMALL BUSINESS INNOVATION RESEARCH II (SBIR-II)

Grant Title: Universal Access to Passenger Rail Cars

Grant Award Number: H133S050136

Grantee: Marshall Elevator Company/LINC Design LLC

Grant Mechanism: Small Business Innovation Research II

Grant Start and End Dates: October 1, 2005, to September 30, 2009

Total Direct Cost: $499,750

Abstract: Since freight rail cars often share train tracks with passenger rail cars, differences in car width result in horizontal gaps between passenger rail cars and boarding platforms. The grantee proposed a compact device—the RailRamp—that can be retrofitted to existing rail cars or integrated into new rail car designs. The device extends out from the rail car boarding area onto the station platform to provide quick, safe, easy, and independent boarding access for all possible rail passengers. The proposed boarding device is expected to eliminate the need for rail personnel assistance for individuals with disabilities and others with extra boarding needs when boarding and exiting trains. A motorized version of this device would increase passenger independence for all train riders and personnel; the manual version would reduce personnel involvement and train delays. The design was evaluated by members of the rail transit industry. Support for this research and development effort came from industry. The project built on Phase I activities during which the feasibility of the device was demonstrated.

Research Projects and Outputs Reviewed: Grantees were asked to nominate two outputs from each of their projects for review by the committee. These outputs were identified by the study's key personnel as those that would best reflect their grant's achievements. Grantees selected the outputs to be reviewed from among the larger pool of outputs they had produced under the grant. This larger pool of outputs included two descriptive publications about the RailRamp, an *Installation and User's Guide*, a powered RailRamp, the prototype and two subsequent prototype versions of the RailRamp, a patent disclosure, a manual boarding ramp device, a pamphlet, an instructional brochure, and two websites on the RailRamp. The following table shows the project carried out under this grant and lists the corresponding outputs that were nominated by the grantees and reviewed by the NRC committee. The reviewed outputs are briefly described following the table.

Project/*Research Domains****	**Outputs**
A. Development of a Powered Ramp Device for Use in Commuter Rail	A1. *The RailRamp: Installation and user's guide RailRamp II version 1.0* [apparatus]. (2009). Verona, PA: LINC Design for Human Use.
Technology Knowledge Translation	A2. van Roosmalen, L., Glogowski, F.S., Heiner, D.A., Jamison, R.S., Horvath, P.D., and Walker, S. (2010). *U.S. Patent no. 7,802,337 B2*. Washington, DC: U.S. Patent and Trademark Office.

*The column also shows the key NIDRR research domain(s) that were being addressed by each project.

Brief Description of the Outputs: The RailRamp *Installation and User's Guide* (A1) describes the need for the device, explains how it works, and provides the system components and requirements. Instructions are provided for transporting the ramp, installing it, and integrating it with automated doors and exiting controls. The *Guide* also details operation of the ramp, including deploying and stowing it both mechanically and manually, and provides general troubleshooting instructions. Finally, the *Guide* describes how to maintain the ramp and provides information on the testing and certification of ramp components. The *Guide* was intended to be used by rail car manufacturers and railroad operators.

The second output reviewed was the RailRamp patent disclosure (A2). The inventors submitted a patent application on December 22, 2007. The patent provides an abstract, as well as 13 figures illustrating and describing the ramp from multiple perspectives, including not installed and installed and not extended and extended. Figures also show the ramp broken down into components and how the components are assembled. The text of the patent contains background information on the invention, including the need for a more effective ramp that is also compliant with the ADA and the UK Code of Practice. The patent, approved on September 28, 2010, will allow the designer to market the device and potentially improve rail car access.

Grant Title: Web-Enabled Creation and Distribution of Audio-Tactile Maps for Use in Orientation and Mobility Training

Grant Award Number: H133S060105

Grantee: Touch Graphics, Inc.

Grant Mechanism: Small Business Innovation Research II

Grant Start and End Dates: October 1, 2006, to March 30, 2009

Total Direct Cost: $499,852

Abstract: This Small Business Innovation Research II (SBIR-II) project called for the development of a system for providing talking tactile neighborhood maps on demand for use by individuals who are blind, have low vision, or are otherwise print disabled. Files downloaded from a website are used to create raised-line maps from standard Braille embossers or by other methods. The finished maps are placed on a Talking Tactile Tablet, a computer peripheral device. The user interacts with a map by exploring it through touch sense and pressing down on streets and other features to hear names and descriptions of map entities of interest. The system, known as TMAP Reader, includes a web service for requesting maps of any location in the United States, a software application for outputting downloaded map files to a standard Braille embosser, an application that facilitates user interaction with the maps, and a map production and delivery service for unsophisticated users or users without access to equipment for outputting maps. Two stages of user testing were carried out to evaluate the efficacy of the planned system in orientation and mobility training.

Research Projects and Outputs Reviewed: Grantees were asked to nominate two outputs from each of their projects for review by the committee. These outputs were identified by the study's key personnel as those that would best reflect their grant's achievements. Grantees selected the outputs to be reviewed from among the larger pool of outputs they had produced under the grant. This larger pool of outputs included three technical reports, one survey, one piece of software, one website, and two automated systems. The following table shows the project carried out under this grant and lists the corresponding outputs that were nominated by the grantees and reviewed by the NRC committee. The reviewed outputs are briefly described following the table.

Project/*Research Domains**	**Outputs**
A. Usability Testing of the TMAP Reader System with up to 100 Current Users of the Talking Tactile Tablet in Geographically Diverse Settings *Technology*	A1. Miele, J.A., Landau, S., and Gilden, D. (2006). Talking TMAP: Automated generation of audio tactile maps using Smith-Kettlewell's TMAP software. *The British Journal of Visual Impairment, 24*(2), 93-100.
	A2. Landau, S. (Producer). *Touchgraphicresources* [video for TMAP software]. New York: Touch Graphics Inc. Available: https://sites.google.com/site/touchgraphicsresources/ [January 10, 2012].

*The column also shows the key NIDRR research domain(s) that were being addressed by each project.

Brief Description of the Outputs: The TMAP software (A1) creates dynamic, interactive maps that are accessible to users with disabilities. The software works on the Talking Tactile Tablet, also developed by Touch Graphics, Inc. The tactile maps used through TMAP are intended to be explored by either touch or vision. When a user presses down on a map element, the name of the element is spoken aloud. According to the designer, the audio-tactile display used by TMAP is a significant improvement over previous attempts at tactile cartography and allows for much greater exploration and customization of the maps.

The TMAP production service (A2) is an automated system available through the Touch Graphics website that can generate multisensory maps of any neighborhood in the United States and Canada for use with the TMAP software. The service is very easy to use and delivers maps in only a few days. According to the designer, the production service represents one of the most sophisticated examples of tactile graphics production currently on the market.

SWITZER FELLOWSHIPS

Grant Title: A Noninvasive Surface Electromyogram Decomposition Method and Its Application in Disability Rehabilitation

Grant Award Number: H133F070022

Grant Mechanism: Switzer Fellowship

Grant Start and End Dates: October 1, 2007, to January 15, 2009

Total Direct Cost: $75,000

Abstract[3]: This study developed surface electromyogram (EMG) decomposition methods suitable for relatively low muscle contraction levels to replace and/or supplement traditionally used indwelling needle electrode-based decomposition approaches. Results benefit the rehabilitation community and a large population of patients by reducing pain, emotional tension, and risk of infection during EMG examination.

Research Projects and Outputs Reviewed: Grantees were asked to nominate two outputs from each of their projects for review by the committee. These outputs were identified by the study's key personnel as those that would best reflect their grant's achievements. Grantees selected the outputs to be reviewed from the pool of outputs they had produced under the grant. These outputs included one journal article and one intervention. The following table shows the project carried out under this grant and lists the corresponding outputs that were nominated by the grantees and reviewed by the NRC committee. The reviewed outputs are briefly described following the table.

Project/*Research Domains**	Outputs
A. A Noninvasive Surface Electromyogram Decomposition Method and Its Application in Disability Rehabilitation	A1. Zhou, P., Suresh, N.L., Lowery, M.M., and Rymer, W.Z. (2009). Nonlinear spatial filtering of multichannel surface electromyogram signals during low-force contractions. *IEEE Transactions on Bio-medical Engineering, 56*(7), 1,871-1,879.
Health and Function	A2. Zhou, P. (2009). *Selective surface electrode arrays* [design of surface electrode array]. Chicago, IL: Rehabilitation Institute of Chicago, Northwestern University.

*The column also shows the key NIDRR research domain(s) that were being addressed by each project.

[3]This abstract was adapted from the project abstract found on http://ww.naric.com [January 10, 2012].

Brief Description of the Outputs: Zhou et al. (A1) introduce the use of nonlinear spatial filters to identify single motor unit discharge from multiple channel surface EMG signals during low force contractions. Previously, invasive percutaneous intramuscular EMG recordings were used routinely to selectively record single motor unit activity. Such invasive recordings can be inconvenient, can induce pain, and carry the risk of damage to muscle tissue and nerves. This article investigates the advantages of a novel nonlinear spatial filtering method for enhancing surface motor unit action potentials using noninvasive surface EMG recordings. Previous methods relied on linear methods for filtering. The authors demonstrate that nonlinear spatial filtering achieves better results for single-motor unit detection during low force contractions.

The second output reviewed was a one- and two-dimensional surface electrode array (A2) developed for noninvasive motor unit activity recording. The design allows for the extraction of single motor unit information using surface EMG and the appropriate signal processing methods described in output A1. A study using these arrays won the "Best Clinical Research" award at the XVIIIth Congress of the International Society of Kinesiology and Electrophysiology in 2010.

Grant Title: Demographic Soup: Disentangling the Conceptual, Political, and Methodological Dimensions of Disability Statistics

Grant Award Number: H133F060011

Grant Mechanism: Switzer Fellowship

Grant Start and End Dates: December 1, 2006, to November 30, 2009

Total Direct Cost: $75,000

Abstract: Wide variations exist in disability research, including how disability is defined and how information on the various definitions is obtained and converted into usable data. This project compiled in one document (a book manuscript) the accumulated knowledge on defining and measuring disability in survey and census contexts. By incorporating several methodologies—including historical review; analysis of political processes and decision making; and comprehensive examination of the source, placement, and evaluation of disability measures currently in use—this book manuscript contributes to the improvement of disability statistics and serves as a reference for understanding the data that exist. The manuscript is divided into five sections: (1) examination of the political and historical context, which includes chapters on the history of disability measurement; (2) examination of the conceptualization and definition of disability, including chapters on the political definitions for programmatic purposes and theoretical definitions and models; (3) examination of the science and purpose of and relationships among the components of measurement and the special problems of measurement in specific populations (children, the elderly); (4) reviews of samples of research analyses focused on the use of data, including data sources and research questions, with special focus on measures used in specific areas of research (i.e., aging and employment); and (5) exploration of international measurement of disability and the role of the United States in its development. Recommendations for improving and standardizing the measurement and data collection process are offered.

Research Projects and Outputs Reviewed: Grantees were asked to nominate two outputs from each of their projects for review by the committee. These outputs were identified by the study's key personnel as those that would best reflect their grant's achievements. Grantees selected the outputs to be reviewed from among the larger pool of outputs they had produced under the grant. This larger pool of outputs included one journal article, one technical report, one book chapter, and one set of presentations. The following table shows the project carried out under this grant and lists the corresponding outputs that were nominated by the grantees and reviewed by the NRC committee. The reviewed outputs are briefly described following the table.

Project/*Research Domains****	**Outputs**
A. Demographic Soup: Disentangling the Conceptual, Political, and Methodological Dimensions of Disability Statistics	A1. Altman, B., and Bernstein, A. (2008). *Disability and health in the United States, 2001-2005*. Hyattsville, MD: National Center for Health Statistics. Available: http://www.cdc.gov/nchs/data/misc/disability2001-2005.pdf [January 24, 2012].
Demographics *Knowledge Translation*	A2. Altman, B. (2009). *Population survey measures of functioning: Strengths and weaknesses.* In National Research Council, *Improving the measurement of late-life disability in population surveys: Beyond ADLs and IADLs: Summary of a workshop*. Washington, DC: The National Academies Press. Available: http://www.nap.edu/openbook.php?record_id=12740&page=99 [January 24, 2012].

*The column also shows the key NIDRR research domain(s) that were being addressed by each project.

Brief Description of the Outputs: The first output reviewed by the NRC committee was a chartbook (A1) compiled using data from the National Health Interview Survey (NHIS) in an attempt to begin to uncover what the data represent and what they reveal about health care for persons with disabilities. To this end, the first part of the chartbook interprets current disability definitional approaches and translates them into measures that are available in the NHIS. The rest of the chartbook uses those measures to examine the health care experience of persons with disabilities.

The second output reviewed was a paper entitled "Population Survey Measures of Functioning: Strengths and Weaknesses" (A2). The paper was presented as the Invited Plenary Presentation at an NRC workshop and was then published as an appendix to the NRC workshop summary, *Improving the Measurement of Late-Life Disability in Population Surveys: Beyond ADLs and IADLs*. The paper addresses the measurement process and the components of measurements and breaks the process down into steps one should consider when measuring or choosing measurements that are already constructed.

Grant Title: Physical and Social Environmental Factors That Influence Health and Participation Outcomes for Chronically Ill Adults

Grant Award Number: H133F080014

Grant Mechanism: Switzer Fellowship

Grant Start and End Dates: July 1, 2008, to June 30, 2009

Total Direct Cost: $65,000

Abstract: This project explored the factors in health and participation outcomes among older adults with chronic conditions who are living in the community with or without disabilities, considering individual factors such as informal, formal, and societal supports. The research had three objectives: (1) determining the direct and indirect effects of a community's social capital on health and participation outcomes; (2) identifying the relationship between health and participation outcomes and measures of the neighborhood; and (3) assessing the relationship between the subjective measure of perceived social capital and the objective measures of the neighborhood for their collective influence on the health and community participation of older adults with and without disabilities. The project included research aimed at improving community practice, policy, and the health system in order to assist adults in achieving independence, greater participation, and social involvement.

Research Projects and Outputs Reviewed: Grantees were asked to nominate two outputs from each of their projects for review by the committee. These outputs were identified by the study's key personnel as those that would best reflect their grant's achievements. Grantees selected the outputs to be reviewed from among outputs they had produced under the grant. These outputs included one manuscript and one abstract. The following table shows the project carried out under this grant and lists the corresponding outputs that were nominated by the grantees and reviewed by the NRC committee. The reviewed outputs are briefly described following the table.

Project/*Research Domains**	Outputs
A. Physical and Social Environmental Factors That Influence Health and Participation Outcomes for Chronically Ill Older Adults	A1. Prvu Bettger, J A. (2009, November). *System of support and services and the relationship with hospital utilization.* Paper presented orally at the 137th American Public Health Association Annual Meeting, Gerontological Health Section, Philadelphia, PA.
Participation and Community Living	A2. Prvu Bettger, J.A. (2010, February). *What aspects of the social environment are associated with physical activity post-stroke?* Paper presented at International Stroke Conference, San Antonio, TX.

*The column also shows the key NIDRR research domain(s) that were being addressed by each project.

Brief Description of the Outputs: Prvu Bettger (A1) explored the relationship between hospital utilization and each level of social support and environment. The study assessed hospital utilization among 2,286 nonworking adults aged 60 or older reporting at least one chronic condition or condition requiring regular medical treatment in the 2006 Southeastern Pennsylvania Household Health Survey. Several person-level factors were found to be strongly associated with hospital utilization, such as older age, low income, poor-to-fair perception of health, and use of an assistive device. Social environment factors found to be significantly associated with hospital utilization were receipt of formal care, receipt of meal services, and absence of a regular source of care. Findings highlight the relationship between specific social supports and services and hospital utilization, but further investigation into the interaction between social factors and hospital utilization is needed.

The second output was an abstract (A2) presented at the International Stroke Conference 2010. It describes a study of stroke survivors' activity and factors that prevent them from being physically active. Prvu Bettger analyzed the responses of 214 stroke survivors who participated in the 2004 Southeastern Pennsylvania Household Health Survey. Absence of depression, good-to-excellent health status, community participation, and use of transportation services were positively correlated with physical activity. Findings highlight the need for social environmental supports to facilitate physical activity poststroke and for greater attention to environmental influences on health behavior in health promotion research and practice.

Appendix B

Rating Sheets/Questionnaires

This appendix contains the following rating sheets and questionnaires used by the committee for its external evaluation of NIDRR and its grantees:

	Page Number
1. Process Evaluation Measures	
A. Web-Based Questionnaire for NIDRR Stakeholders	306
B. Web-Based Questionnaire for NIDRR Peer Reviewers	311
2. Summative Evaluation Measures	
A. Letter to Grantees Inviting Participation	316
B. Informed Consent Form for NIDRR Grantees	318
C. Grantee Questionnaire	320
D. Committee Member Review Procedures for Summative Evaluation	326
E. Committee Member Rating Sheet of the Quality of Outputs	328

1A: WEB-BASED QUESTIONNAIRE FOR NIDRR STAKEHOLDERS

Informed Consent Form

What the study is about: An expert committee of the National Research Council, of The National Academies, in Washington, DC is conducting an evaluation of some of the activities of the National Institute on Disability and Rehabilitation Research (NIDRR). The committee will be (1) reviewing NIDRR's priority setting and peer review processes; and (2) reviewing the quality of grantee "outputs" for a sample of NIDRR grants. ["Peer review" refers to a process in which experts review grant applications and make recommendations about whether they should be funded. "Outputs" are publications, measures, intervention protocols, devices, and information resources that are produced as part of a grant.]

What we will ask you to do: We are inviting you to take part in the first part of the evaluation—specifically, the review of NIDRR's priority setting processes. We will ask you a set of questions to help us understand these processes and how they may affect NIDRR's work. The questionnaire will take about 15 to 20 minutes to complete. Your participation is completely voluntary. You can choose not to answer some of the questions or to stop at any point, and there will be no consequences.

Benefits and risks:
<u>Benefits</u>: By taking part in the evaluation you will provide information that may help NIDRR improve its research portfolio for the benefit of persons with disabilities.

<u>Risks and protections</u>: You might be concerned that the information you share will not be kept private. However, we want to assure you that all of your comments will be kept confidential. Study results will be presented only in combined form, with no individual person or organization being identified. Your name will not be attached to your answers. A research identification number will be used instead. The Study Director will keep a list linking your name with your number. This list, along with the data collected, will be stored securely at the National Research Council. Only the study personnel will have access to the master list, and only for research purposes.

Compensation: There is no compensation for taking part in the evaluation.

If you have any questions: Please contact the Senior Program Officer, Dr. Jeanne Rivard, if you have any questions about this consent form or the study. She can be contacted by phone at: 202-334-2967, or by email at: jrivard@nas.edu.

If you have any questions, comments, or concerns about taking part in this study, first contact Dr. Rivard. If for any reason you do not want to contact her, or you still have concerns after doing so, you may contact the Institutional Review Board (IRB) of the National Academy of Sciences (NAS), which reviewed and approved the study plans and this consent form. You can reach the chair of the IRB, Ronald D. Taylor, Human Protections Administrator, by telephone at 202-334-1659 or you may write to him at the National Academy of Sciences; Room 1026; 500 Fifth Street, NW; Washington, DC 20001.

Statement of Consent:

☐ I have read the above information, understand it, and agree to take part in the study.
☐ I do not agree to take part in the study.

Web-Based Questionnaire for NIDRR Stakeholders

Please respond as a representative of your organization so that your answers will reflect how your organization relates to NIDRR.

1. Although your organization has multiple functions, select from the list below the one type that most closely matches your own organization.

☐ Professional association
☐ Advocacy organization
☐ Service provider
☐ Funder of research and/or development grants
☐ Technical assistance and dissemination
☐ Commercial manufacturer/distributor
☐ Other (Please specify) ______________________________

2. To what extent is your organization familiar with the National Institute on Disability and Rehabilitation Research (NIDRR)?

1	2	3	4	5
☐	☐	☐	☐	☐
Not at all		Somewhat		Very much

3. Please check all of the ways in which your organization has interacted with NIDRR since January 1, 2005.

Information Exchange

☐ Have used NIDRR website or related information sources to search for information, tools, or resources for working with consumers (non grant information)
☐ Have used NIDRR website or related resources to search for information about grants
☐ Have spoken with NIDRR staff in person or on the phone about specific professional issues
☐ Have attended NIDRR trainings, workshops, or conferences
☐ Other (Please specify in box below)

Funding

☐ Have received funding from NIDRR for research & development grants
☐ Have received funding from NIDRR for training, knowledge transfer, or dissemination grants
☐ Have received funding from NIDRR for activities other than grants (e.g., contract or agreements to conduct an evaluation, provide expert consultation, or write a paper, etc.)
☐ Have applied for funding, but did not receive award
☐ Other (Please specify in box below)

Collaboration

☐ Have collaborated with NIDRR as a member of a consortium or professional association
☐ Have participated in general planning and special purpose meetings convened by NIDRR
☐ Have coordinated activities to support joint priorities and/or to avoid duplication
☐ Other (Please specify in box below)

☐ **Have not interacted with NIDRR on any of the above types of information, funding, or collaboration activities.**

4. Please use the space below to comment on the above, or any other types of interactions, your organization has had with NIDRR. (Click in the upper left-hand corner to enter text.)

5. Has your organization had opportunities to review and comment on NIDRR's long range plan or funding priorities?

☐ Yes
☐ No
☐ Don't know

6. How did your organization find out about opportunities to review and comment on NIDRR's long range plan or funding priorities?

☐ Federal Register
☐ Professional list serve
☐ University grants source
☐ Professional newspaper
☐ Personal invitation to our organization from NIDRR
☐ Other (please specify): ____________________
☐ Don't know

7. Since January 1, 2005, has anyone from your organization submitted comments to NIDRR about its <u>long-range plan</u>?

☐ Yes
☐ No
☐ Don't know

8. Since January 1, 2005, has anyone from your organization submitted comments to NIDRR about its <u>specific funding priorities</u> (e.g., grant announcements) published in the Federal Register?

☐ Yes
☐ No
☐ Don't know

9. In your opinion, to what extent are NIDRR's long range planning and priority setting processes (Please check the boxes beneath the responses—select only one per row):

	Not at all		Somewhat		Very Much	Don't know
Transparent	1 ☐	2 ☐	3 ☐	4 ☐	5 ☐	☐
Publicized	1 ☐	2 ☐	3 ☐	4 ☐	5 ☐	☐
Relevant to your organization	1 ☐	2 ☐	3 ☐	4 ☐	5 ☐	☐
Responsive to emerging issues in disability rehabilitation and research	1 ☐	2 ☐	3 ☐	4 ☐	5 ☐	☐
Welcoming of stakeholder feedback	1 ☐	2 ☐	3 ☐	4 ☐	5 ☐	☐
Responsive to stakeholder feedback	1 ☐	2 ☐	3 ☐	4 ☐	5 ☐	☐

10. In your opinion, how do NIDRR's long range planning and priority setting processes compare with those of other federal research agencies?

☐ NIDRR's processes are weaker than other agencies'.
☐ NIDRR's processes are about the same as other agencies'.
☐ NIDRR's processes are stronger than other agencies'.
☐ Don't know

11. How well are the grants that NIDRR funds advancing the field in a direction that is beneficial for your organization, and the members and consumers that you represent? (Please select only one response.)

1	2	3	4	5		
☐	☐	☐	☐	☐	☐	☐
Not at all		Somewhat		Very much	Don't know	Not Applicable

12. What types of grants have served your organization, and the members and consumers that you represent? (Click in the upper left-hand corner to enter text.)

13. To what extent are the products of the grants that NIDRR funds (e.g., publications, websites, training or training materials, tools, devices, measures, interventions, etc.) used by your organization? (Please select one response.)

1	2	3	4	5		
☐	☐	☐	☐	☐	☐	☐
Not at all		Somewhat		Very much	Don't know	Not Applicable

14. What are the three most important NIDRR-funded products used by your organization? (Click in the upper left-hand corner to enter text.)

15. What three things might NIDRR do to enhance its long range planning and priority setting processes? (Click in the upper left-hand corner to enter text.)

Thank you very much for taking the time to complete this questionnaire. We may be contacting some respondents later to ask additional questions. If you would be willing to take part in brief follow-up interviews, please check here.

☐ **Yes, it's okay to contact me.**

☐ **No, thank you. I'm finished!**

Contact Information
(Click on the leftmost portion of the line to enter text.)

E-mail address: ______________________________
Phone number: ______________________________

1B: WEB-BASED QUESTIONNAIRE FOR NIDRR PEER REVIEWERS

Informed Consent Form

What the study is about: An expert committee of the National Research Council, of the National Academies, in Washington, DC is conducting an evaluation of some of the activities of the National Institute on Disability and Rehabilitation Research (NIDRR). The committee will be (1) reviewing NIDRR's priority setting and peer review processes; and (2) reviewing the quality of grantee "outputs" for a sample of NIDRR grants. ["Peer review" refers to a process in which experts review grant applications and make recommendations about whether they should be funded. "Outputs" are publications, measures, intervention protocols, devices, and information resources that are produced as part of a grant.]

What we will ask you to do: We are inviting you to take part in the first part of the evaluation—specifically, the review of NIDRR's peer review processes. We will ask you a set of questions to help us understand these processes and how they may affect NIDRR's work. The questionnaire will take about 15 to 20 minutes to complete. Your participation is completely voluntary. You can choose not to answer some of the questions or to stop at any point, and there will be no consequences.

Benefits and risks:
Benefits: By taking part in the evaluation you will provide information that may help NIDRR improve its research portfolio for the benefit of persons with disabilities.

Risks and protections: You might be concerned that the information you share will not be kept private. However, we want to assure you that all of your comments will be kept confidential. Study results will be presented only in combined form, with no individual person or organization being identified. Your name will not be attached to your answers. A research identification number will be used instead. The Study Director will keep a list linking your name with your number. This list, along with the data collected, will be stored securely at the National Research Council. Only the study personnel will have access to the master list, and only for research purposes.

Compensation: There is no compensation for taking part in the evaluation.

If you have any questions: Please contact the Senior Program Officer, Dr. Jeanne Rivard, if you have any questions about this consent form or the study. She can be contacted by phone at: 202-334-2967, or by e-mail at: jrivard@nas.edu.

If you have any questions, comments, or concerns about taking part in this study, first contact Dr. Rivard. If for any reason you do not want to contact her, or you still have concerns after doing so, you may contact the Institutional Review Board (IRB) of the National Academy of Sciences (NAS), which reviewed and approved the study plans and this consent form. You can reach the chair of the IRB, Ronald D. Taylor, Human Protections Administrator, by telephone at 202-334-1659 or you may write to him at the National Academy of Sciences; Room 1026; 500 Fifth Street, NW; Washington, DC 20001.

Statement of Consent:
☐ I have read the above information, understand it, and agree to take part in the study.
☐ I do not agree to take part in the study.

Web-Based Questionnaire for NIDRR Peer Reviewers

1. On how many NIDRR peer review panels have you served since January 1, 2005? (Please state the total number, such as 0, 1, 2, 3, 4, etc.): ______

(By panel, we mean every time a group of peer reviewers is convened to conduct a review, not just membership on a given panel.)

2. Across the following program funding mechanisms, please check all of those for which you have reviewed applications since January 1, 2005 (See NIDRR website for a description of these mechanisms)

Disability and Rehabilitation Research Projects (DRRP) – General	☐
Disability Business Technical Assistance Centers (DBTAC)	☐
Traumatic Brain Injury Model Systems Centers	☐
Burn Model Systems Centers	☐
Spinal Cord Injury Model Systems Centers	☐
Rehabilitation Research and Training Centers (RRTCs)	☐
Rehabilitation Engineering Research Centers (RERCs)	☐
Field Initiated Projects – Research Grants	☐
Field Initiated Projects – Development Grants	☐
Small Business Innovation Research (SBIR) – Phase I	☐
Small Business Innovation Research (SBIR) – Phase II	☐
DRRP - Knowledge Translation	☐
DRRP – Section 21	☐
(Switzer) Research Fellowship Program	☐
Advanced Rehabilitation Research Training Projects	☐
Don't Remember	☐

3. In your experience, how would you rate the following aspects of the NIDRR peer review processes (Please check the boxes beneath the responses—select only one per row):

	Poor		Adequate		Excellent	DON'T KNOW	NOT APPLI-CABLE
Quality of the training to prepare you for the review	1 ☐	2 ☐	3 ☐	4 ☐	5 ☐	☐	☐
Adequacy of time for review of materials before the meeting	1 ☐	2 ☐	3 ☐	4 ☐	5 ☐	☐	☐
Level of expertise of the peer review panel members	1 ☐	2 ☐	3 ☐	4 ☐	5 ☐	☐	☐
Appropriateness of the evaluation criteria to applications under review	1 ☐	2 ☐	3 ☐	4 ☐	5 ☐	☐	☐
Clarity of the criteria when applying them to applications	1 ☐	2 ☐	3 ☐	4 ☐	5 ☐	☐	☐

	Poor		Adequate		Excellent	DON'T KNOW	NOT APPLICABLE
Appropriateness of scoring system to applications under review	1 ☐	2 ☐	3 ☐	4 ☐	5 ☐	☐	☐
Ease of applying scoring system to applications	1 ☐	2 ☐	3 ☐	4 ☐	5 ☐	☐	☐
Thoroughness of the deliberation (i.e., grant scoring and discussion) during the meeting.	1 ☐	2 ☐	3 ☐	4 ☐	5 ☐	☐	☐
Use of reviewers' time during the panel meeting	1 ☐	2 ☐	3 ☐	4 ☐	5 ☐	☐	☐
Support and facilitation of the review panel by NIDRR staff	1 ☐	2 ☐	3 ☐	4 ☐	5 ☐	☐	☐
Guidance in writing your reviewer comments	1 ☐	2 ☐	3 ☐	4 ☐	5 ☐	☐	☐
Integrity of the peer review process overall	1 ☐	2 ☐	3 ☐	4 ☐	5 ☐	☐	☐
Consistency in the overall quality of the peer reviews across panels (if you have served on three or more panels).	1 ☐	2 ☐	3 ☐	4 ☐	5 ☐	☐	☐

4. Any additional comments you may have on these aspects of NIDRR's peer review processes would be useful. Please use the space below. (Click in the upper left-hand corner to enter text.)

5. How has the overall quality of NIDRR's peer review processes changed since January 1, 2005 (if you have served on different panels over time)?

☐ Quality has decreased.
☐ Quality is about the same.
☐ Quality has increased.
☐ Don't know
☐ Not applicable

6. Typically, the number of applications you received for each NIDRR review panel was:

☐ More than you would like to review.
☐ About the right number.
☐ Fewer than you would like to review.

7. Typically, the amount of time you spent on each NIDRR review panel was:

☐ More time than you would like to spend.

☐ About the right amount.
☐ Less time than you would like to spend.

8. Have you participated in NIDRR peer reviews that were convened through:

	Yes	No
In-person meetings?	☐	☐
Teleconference?	☐	☐

9. In your opinion, how did the quality of a NIDRR peer review compare when conducted in person versus teleconference?

☐ Quality of peer reviews is better in in-person meetings.
☐ Quality of peer reviews is better in teleconference meetings.
☐ Quality of peer reviews via in-person meetings or teleconference is about the same.
☐ Don't know
☐ Not applicable

10. Have you served as a peer reviewer of proposals for federal agencies other than NIDRR since January 1, 2005?

☐ Yes
☐ No

11. How would you compare the following characteristics of NIDRR peer reviews with those of other federal agencies? (Please check the boxes beneath the responses—select only one per row.)

	NIDRR's are much weaker than other agencies		About the same		NIDRR's are much stronger than other agencies	Don't Know	Not Appli-cable
Expertise of the panel members	1 ☐	2 ☐	3 ☐	4 ☐	5 ☐	☐	☐
Quality of the proposals reviewed	1 ☐	2 ☐	3 ☐	4 ☐	5 ☐	☐	☐
Quality of the review process	1 ☐	2 ☐	3 ☐	4 ☐	5 ☐	☐	☐
Transparency of the review process	1 ☐	2 ☐	3 ☐	4 ☐	5 ☐	☐	☐
Fairness of the review process	1 ☐	2 ☐	3 ☐	4 ☐	5 ☐	☐	☐
Reliability of the ratings	1 ☐	2 ☐	3 ☐	4 ☐	5 ☐	☐	☐

12. What three things would you suggest to enhance NIDRR's peer review processes? (Click in the upper left-hand corner to enter text.)

Thank you very much for taking the time to complete this questionnaire. We may be contacting some respondents later to ask additional questions. If you would be willing to take part in brief follow-up interviews, please check here.

☐ **Yes, it's okay to contact me.**

☐ **No, thank you. I'm finished!**

Contact Information
(Click on the leftmost portion of the line to enter text.)

E-mail address: ______________________________

Phone number: ______________________________

2A: LETTER TO GRANTEES INVITING PARTICIPATION

THE NATIONAL ACADEMIES

Advisers to the Nation on Science, Engineering, and Medicine

Division of Behavioral and Social Sciences and Education
Committee on Human-Systems Integration

500 Fifth Street, NW
Washington, DC 20001
Phone: 202 334 2678
Fax: 202 334 2210
Email: cohsi@nas.edu
www.nationalacademies.org

October 6, 2010

Grantee Address

Dear Dr. _______:

Last week we sent you an email to inform you that you are being invited to participate in the External Evaluation of the National Institute on Disability and Rehabilitation Research (NIDRR) and its Grantees that is being conducted by an expert committee of the National Research Council of the National Academies. This independent evaluation is being sponsored by NIDRR for the purpose of: 1) assessing NIDRR's priority setting and peer review processes and 2) reviewing the quality of grantee outputs for a sample of grants that represent the NIDRR portfolio.

Your NIDRR-funded grant (Grant #__________, Grant Title:______________________________) was selected to be reviewed as part of the evaluation of grantee outputs. However, your participation is completely voluntary. If you do agree to be part of the evaluation, your participation will involve the following activities.

1. We will ask you to nominate two outputs that were produced under each project that was funded by the grant. These will be outputs that best reflect your grant's achievements. We are using the four NIDRR categories of outputs as defined in NIDRR's Annual Performance Report (APR), which include a) Publications; b) Tools, Measures, and Intervention Protocols; c) Technology Products and Devices; and d) Informational Products. The committee will assess the quality of the outputs which you identify using criteria of technical quality, the extent to which they advance knowledge, their potential impact, and their dissemination.
2. To conduct the review, we would like to examine the actual outputs and to review any documentation that you may have about the outputs.
3. We will ask you to complete a questionnaire about each output that asks you to briefly summarize evidence of their technical quality, how they advance knowledge, their potential impact, and how they were disseminated.

4. The questionnaire will also ask you to respond to a brief set of questions at the grant level about approaches you used in managing your grant, how the grant may have generated new research and projects, and about your perspectives of key NIDRR processes which may influence grant results.
5. We may also ask you to participate in a follow-up telephone or videoconference interview. If so, we would like to audio-record the discussion between you and the committee.

The attachments that follow this letter include, first, an informed consent form that explains what we will do with the results of the evaluation and what steps we will take to protect the confidentiality of the evaluation results specific to your grant. The second attachment is the Grantee Questionnaire referred to above that provides instructions for:

- identifying outputs to be reviewed,
- completing the supplemental questions for each output, and
- sending us your signed consent forms, your outputs, and your completed questionnaire.

Please note that we are sending this package to you in electronic and hard copy form.

We hope that you will decide to participate. If you have any questions please don't hesitate to contact one of us using the information below.

Sincerely,

Jeanne Rivard, Ph.D., Co-Study Director
The National Academies
National Research Council
500 Fifth Street, NW
Washington, DC 20001
Phone: 202-334-2967
E-mail: jrivard@nas.edu

Mary Ellen O'Connell, Co-Study Director
The National Academies
National Research Council
500 Fifth Street, NW
Washington, DC 20001
Phone: 202-334-2607
E-mail: moconnell@nas.edu

2B: INFORMED CONSENT FORM FOR NIDRR GRANTEES

What the study is about: An expert committee of the National Research Council of the National Academies, in Washington, DC is developing an evaluation framework that will be used to: (1) review NIDRR's priority setting and peer review processes; and (2) review the quality of grantee "outputs" for a sample of grants that represent the NIDRR portfolio. ["Peer review" refers to a process in which experts review the merits of a grant application in considering whether it should be funded. "Outputs" are publications, measures, intervention protocols, devices, or information resources that are produced as part of a grant.] The committee will also assess the design and implementation of the evaluation process and make recommendations for additional evaluation cycles that may be performed subsequent to this effort.

What we will ask you to do: We would like to invite you to participate in the evaluation.

Your participation will involve:

1. Having outputs produced under your grant peer reviewed through a quality assessment by an expert panel.
2. To conduct the review, we would like to examine a copy of the actual outputs and to review any documentation that you may have about the outputs.
3. We will ask you to complete a questionnaire about the outputs to assist in assessing their technical quality, the extent to which they advance knowledge, their potential impact, and if applicable, their dissemination.
4. We may ask you to participate in a follow-up telephone or videoconference interview where we would audio-record the discussion between you and the committee.
5. We will also ask you to respond to a brief set of questions at the grant level about your grant management, the generation of new research and projects, and about key NIDRR processes which may influence grant results.

Taking part is voluntary. Your participation is completely voluntary. You can choose not to answer some of the questions, and there will be no consequences.

Benefits and risks:

Benefits: By taking part in the evaluation you will provide information that may help NIDRR improve its research portfolio for the benefit of persons with disabilities.

Risks: Because NIDRR has funded some of your research and development activities, you may feel uncomfortable having your grant's outputs formally rated in the study, or in sharing your opinions and perspectives on NIDRR's key management processes. You might feel that this could be a risk to your future grant funding. We want you to know, however, that we will take every step necessary to protect your confidentiality and minimize this risk.

Your answers will be confidential. In the final evaluation report, we will briefly describe your grant and the outputs that were reviewed, by their titles and grantee institutions. Your name as the Principal Investigator, or other investigators on your team, will not be used. In most cases we expect that you have already placed information about the outputs in the public domain through publications, presentations at conferences, and through NIDRR's National Rehabilitation Information Center (NARIC) website.

However, distinct from these descriptions will be your responses on the Grantee Questionnaire and the committee's quality ratings of your outputs. For analysis and reporting, these narrative and quantitative data will be de-identified and aggregated across all outputs and all grants. A research identification number will be used to track grants and their specific outputs. Outputs may be analyzed by categories, such as output type (e.g., publications, tools, technology, information products); quality criteria assessed (e.g., technical quality, knowledge advancement, potential impact); or program funding type (e.g., center grant, field initiated grant, training grant, etc.). If your grant or your output represents one of a kind and there is a risk of identifying you because of this, your data will be aggregated with another larger group where identification will not be a risk.

Every effort will be made to protect the confidentiality of the information that you provide. The Study Director will keep a list linking the grant and output research ID numbers with that output's identifying information (institution, grant title). This list, along with the data collected, will be stored securely at the National Research Council, and will be accessible only by the Study personnel. If a telephone or videoconference interview is convened to gather additional follow-up information, the transcription of audio-recorded interviews will be combined in a dataset with the interviews of all of the other respondents, then analyzed for common themes across the interviews. The audiotapes, transcriptions, grantee questionnaires, committee ratings, and other raw data collected will be destroyed at the end of the study when the report is released.

Compensation: There is no compensation for participating in the evaluation.

If you have any questions: The Co-Study Director of the evaluation and contact for questions is Jeanne Rivard, Ph.D. If you have any questions about this consent form or the study, she can be contacted by phone at: 202-334-2697, or by e-mail at: jrivard@nas.edu.

If you have any questions, comments, or concerns about taking part in this study, first talk to Dr. Rivard above. If for any reason you do not want to do this, or you still have concerns after doing so, you may contact the Institutional Review Board (IRB) of the National Academy of Sciences (NAS), which reviewed and approved the study plans and this consent form. You can reach the chair of the IRB by contacting Ronald D. Taylor, Human Protections Administrator, by telephone at 202-334-1659 or you may write to him at the National Academy of Sciences; Room 1026; 500 Fifth Street, NW; Washington, DC 20001.

Statement of Consent: I have read the above information, and have received answers to any questions I asked. I consent to take parting in the study.

Your Signature____ Date__-__-__

Your Name (printed) ____

In addition to agreeing to participate, if there is a follow-up interview, I also consent to having it tape-recorded.

Your Signature____ Date__-__-__

2C: GRANTEE QUESTIONNAIRE

Grant Award Number:
Grant Title:
Grantee:
Program Mechanism:
Grant End Date:

INSTRUCTIONS TO GRANTEES

This questionnaire has been designed to obtain information to assist the Committee in assessing the quality of your grant's outputs. NIDRR has provided to the Committee and the National Research Council (NRC) staff copies of its Annual Performance Report (APR) database and your last APR and your final APR. As you will see in certain places on the questionnaire we have inserted information from your APR to facilitate your completion of the questionnaire (e.g., Table 1 lists your research and development projects, and Table 2 lists your outputs reported in the APR). Where this information is in error, we would appreciate your pointing the errors out to us and correcting it; and/or updating the information as needed.

The questionnaire is divided into the following three parts:

Part A. Nominating Outputs for Review. This section asks you to nominate, for the Committee's review, the "top 2" outputs for each of your projects that best reflect your grant's achievements (Table 1 below). The Committee would prefer to review one publication and one other type of output for each project. However if you only have publications, please nominate these as your "top 2."

To make this process easier, the NRC staff has populated a list of the outputs (Table 2 below) that were reported for your grant in the APR. You could select the top 2 outputs from this table. However you are not constrained to select from this list if there are other outputs that you think better reflect your grant's achievements.

For Committee review we are requesting materials and information regarding the actual outputs selected as the top 2 for each project.

- For publications, the material for review would be pdf copies of each article.
- For the other outputs, materials for review would include:
  - Electronic or hard copies of the measures, tools, intervention protocols, manuals; or links to websites, pictures or other graphic representations of tools or devices that have been produced.
  - An abstract or summary of each output, which briefly describes:
    - what the output is,
    - its purpose,

- o target audience,
- o methods, and
- o how the output fits into the overall goals and objectives of the project and grant

Part B. Additional Questions about Outputs. For each of the outputs you nominated for review, the Committee has a series of questions related to their technical quality, how they may have advanced knowledge, their potential impact, and their dissemination. We ask that you complete the Part B section for each output. If the answers to certain questions would be the same across different outputs, you can note this and cut and paste responses from earlier output forms to other ones. Please make your responses brief, but as specific and quantitative as possible.

Part C. Grant-level Questions. The questionnaire will also contain a few other items asking about how you managed your grants to produce the highest quality outputs, how your grant's results may have generated new projects, and how key NIDRR processes influence results.

Your complete package of materials will contain:

- **Your signed informed consent form**
- **Copies of your publications and other outputs (e.g., measures, tools, intervention protocols, manuals, links to websites, pictures or other graphic representations of devices that have been produced)**
- **Your completed Grantee Questionnaire**

Please send these materials by ___DATE___ to:

Matt McDonough
The National Academies
National Research Council
500 Fifth Street, NW
WS 1134
Washington, DC 20001

We are enclosing an addressed FedEx form that can be used when mailing your package of materials to us. We estimated a shipment cost that would cover a weight up to 10 lbs. (e.g., for large center grants or devices). If your package weighs more than this, FedEx will charge us the correct amount.

If your package is light and you want to send it electronically, you could e-mail it to Matt at mmcdonough@nas.edu. However, you would need to scan your signed consent form, and send that in a pdf document.

Part A. Nominating Outputs for Review

When referring to "outputs," we are using the four NIDRR categories of outputs as defined in NIDRR's Annual Performance Report, which include: (a) Publications; (b) Tools, Measures, and Intervention Protocols; (c) Technology Products and Devices; and (d) Informational Products.

Per the instructions for nominating outputs for review, please record your nominations for your "top 2" outputs for each of your projects in Table 1 below. (Reminder "top 2" refers to those that best reflect your grant's achievements). As you can see the NRC staff has already populated Table 1 with the names of your research and development projects from data in the APR. Table 2, which follows, contains a list of outputs from which you can cut and paste into Table 1 below. Please identify any errors in this information that we have provided from your APR and correct it as needed.

Table 1. Projects and Nominated Outputs

#	Names of R&D Projects in Grant	Names of Top 2 Outputs for Each Project *Outputs to be inserted by grantee from Table 2 below or add others as needed*
Research Projects		
R1		1.
		2.
Development Projects		
D1	Dissemination	1.
		2.

INSERT GRANTEES' PROJECTS TABLE HERE

The table below lists all of the publications and other outputs that were listed in the APR data provided by NIDRR. Please use this table below in selecting your top 2 outputs for each project. (You can cut and paste from Table 2 into Table 1.) However you are not constrained to select only from this list if there are other outputs that you think better reflect your grant's achievements.

Table 2. List of Outputs from APR

Type of Output	Title of Output
publications	(title)
tool	(title)

Part B. Additional Questions About Outputs

<u>Please use one copy of this form for each publication and each other output</u> for the "top 2" outputs that you selected for each project in Part A above, and provide the following information. Please make your responses brief, but as specific and quantitative as possible. If you consider the criterion not to be applicable to your output, please explain. (Please note that an electronic copy of the questionnaire was included in the email version of this package.)

Name of Output: ______________________________

B1. Technical Quality of Output

In the space below, please describe examples of the technical quality of your output, such as:

- The particular approach or methodology used in developing your output
- Relevant peer recognition such as peer reviews or evaluations, peer endorsements, invitations to present at professional forums or conferences, invitations to present testimony, receipt of awards or honors, etc.
- Receipt of a patent, FDA approval, or use of your output in standards development
- Evidence of the usability and accessibility of the output

B2. Advancement of Knowledge

Please use the space below to describe how this output has advanced knowledge. To structure your response, include points such as:

- What the importance of your original question or issue was
- How the output has advanced knowledge in arenas, such as:
  - making discoveries
  - providing new information
  - establishing theories, measures, and methods
  - closing gaps in the knowledge base
  - developing new interventions, products, technology, and environmental adaptations

B3. Potential Impact

In the space below, please briefly describe evidence of your outputs' potential (or actual) impact on the following audiences, as relevant to your output:

- Science (e.g., new areas of inquiry, methodology, etc.)
- People with disabilities: health, quality of life, participation
- Provider practice
- Health and social systems
- Social and health policy
- Private sector/commercialization
- Capacity building in the field of rehabilitation and disability research and development (e.g., scientists, graduate students, etc.)
- Other

Include information about how this potential impact was tested, and what the results were.

B4. Dissemination of Outputs

In the space below please provide evidence of your dissemination efforts for this output. Describe this for publications if you have made any effort beyond those of the sponsor of the publication (journal, book, proceedings, etc.). Please include important aspects of dissemination such as:

- Stage and scope (e.g., local, regional, national) of dissemination
- Dissemination activities
- Identification and tailoring of materials for reaching different audience/user types
- Collaboration with audience/users in identifying content and medium needs/preferences
- Delivery of information through multiple media types and sources for optimal reach and accessibility
- Evaluation of your dissemination efforts and impacts

Part C. Grant-level Questions

Please respond to these final questions for your overall grant, not by each output specifically as in Section B.

C1. In the space below please describe what types of planning, project management, and budgetary processes were used to promote high quality outputs. In your statement consider the following types of questions:

- Which processes were useful and how? How could they be improved?
- Did you dedicate funds for quality assurance activities?
- How did you track progress and spending against your original plans for the grant?
- If grants or projects were jointly funded by NIDRR and other extramural or intramural sources, how did you ensure that NIDRR resources were used exclusively for NIDRR-funded activities?

C2. Have the results of the research and development outputs from this grant, or prior NIDRR grants, been used to inform the development of new grant applications or other kinds of projects?

No ____
Yes____

If yes, please use the space below to briefly describe what new grant applications, other projects, funding opportunities, or collaborations have emerged.

C3. Please share any perspectives you may have about how NIDRR's key processes (e.g., priority setting, peer review, and/or grants management) influence results, such as successful grants and high quality outputs.

2D: COMMITTEE MEMBER REVIEW PROCEDURES FOR SUMMATIVE EVALUATION

A. Review Subgroups: Each subgroup that will be reviewing outputs will be composed of five Committee members. For each output one committee member will be assigned as the primary reviewer; the remaining four committee members will be secondary reviewers.

B. Output Rating Procedures:

1. All reviewers will independently rate outputs using the following quality criteria (Dimensions of these criteria are shown on the attached rating sheet.):

- Technical quality of output
- Advancement of knowledge or the field (research, practice, or policy)
- Likely impact
- Dissemination

The following scale will be used for rating the outputs:

Poor Quality			Good Quality			Excellent Quality
1	2	3	4	5	6	7

2. The rating will be based on review of hard copy and electronic materials (i.e., articles/descriptive information about output and questionnaire responses) prior to the subcommittee meeting.

3. The grantee's final summary APR, and a list of all outputs reported over the course of the project, is provided for contextual purposes. The APR also will be used to inform an overall, qualitative grant-level assessment.

4. Multiple outputs of one grant will generally be rated independently of each other. However, in some cases outputs may be rated as a pair with one score applied. This could occur when one output is a derivative or different expression of another output, and when the PI responses to criterion questions are basically the same. Examples of these include:

- A manual describing a device (1) and a patent of the device (2)
- A publication describing how a new technology for assessing a condition can be applied in disability rehabilitation (1) and a description of the technology itself (2)
- A software application (e.g., map reader for persons with visual impairments) (1) and web-based method for individualizing the software for users (2)

5. The meeting will be structured as follows:

- The primary reviewer will open discussion of each output by presenting a brief summary of the output and then his/her rationale for rating each relevant criterion (up to four) plus the overall score.
- Secondary reviewers will then present their ratings for each output and a brief rationale.
- Using the same criteria, the subgroup will then develop consensus group ratings for each output. Discussion will be facilitated by the subgroup chair. If there is a subgroup member with a significantly divergent view, his/her score and rationale will be captured separately.
- Staff will document discussion points that lead to the consensus group ratings and will record the subgroup's rationale for each criterion, the overall rating, and the grant performance rating in a brief narrative.
- At the end of the review of each output, the individual subgroup members' rating sheets will be gathered.

C. Grant Assessment

Once all outputs of an individual grant are reviewed, the subgroup will consider and rate the grant's overall performance. The outputs reviewed had been identified by the grant's Principal Investigator as the "top" two outputs per project, which best reflected the grant's achievements. Taking into consideration this designation, the consensus group ratings of the entire set of outputs, and the grant's overall purpose and objectives (using the grant's APR), the subgroup will assign a grant performance rating using the same 7-point scale. These grant-level ratings and their rationale will also be documented by staff.

2E: COMMITTEE MEMBER RATING SHEET OF THE QUALITY OF OUTPUTS

Committee Member: ____________________
Output ID: ____________________________

Grantee ID: ____

Date of Review: ____

Output to Be Reviewed:

To be completed by NRC staff

Output Title: ____

Research Output: ______ Development Output: ________

Type and Subtype of Output (marked below):

Type of Publication		Type of Tool, Measure, or Intervention Protocol		Type of Technology Product or Device		Type of Informational Product	
1. abstract		1. checklist		1. industry standards/guidelines		1. training manuals/curricula	
2. book		2. survey or interview schedule		2. software or netware		2. fact sheets	
3. book chapter		3. diagnostic or assessment instrument		3. invention		3. newsletters	
4. journal article		4. outcome measure		4. patent, license, or disclosures		4. audiovisual materials	
5. proceedings		5. intervention protocol or program		5. working prototype		5. marketing tools	
6. technical		6. statistical technique		6. product evaluated or field tested		6. educational aids	
7. web journal		7. database		7. product transferred to industry for potential commercialization		7. websites or other internet sites	
8. other		8. other		8. product in marketplace		8. other	

Quality Criteria and Dimensions

For each criterion provide one rating using the scale below:

Poor			Good			Excellent
1	2	3	4	5	6	7

Criteria and Dimensions	Score
Technical Quality of Output • Applying standards of science and technology • Appropriate methodology (quantitative or qualitative design and statistics) • Accessibility, usability, etc. **Score Rationale:**	
Advancement of Knowledge or the Field (research, practice, or policy as relevant) • Science: Establishment of methods, tools, theory • New information • Closing an identified gap • New technology • Innovative or novel **Score Rationale:**	
Likely or Demonstrated Impact On: • Science (impact factor, citations) • Consumers (people with disabilities: health, quality of life, participation) • Provider practice • Health and social system • Social and health policy • Private sector/commercialization • Other **Score Rationale:**	
Dissemination • Identification and tailoring of materials for reaching different audience/user types • Collaboration with audience/users in identifying content and medium needs/preferences • Delivery of information through multiple media types and sources for optimal reach and accessibility • Evaluation of dissemination efforts and impacts • Commercialization/patenting of devices, if applicable **Score Rationale:**	
Overall Score **Score Rationale:**	

Appendix C

Acronyms

AAS	Advocacy Activities Scale
AATPP	Asset Accumulation and Tax Policy Project
ACS	American Community Survey
ADA	Americans with Disabilities Act
ADEA	Age Discrimination in Employment Act
AHPPPAL	Assessment of Health Plans and Providers by People with Activity Limitations
AHRQ	Agency for Healthcare Research and Quality
APAER	Annual Portfolio Assessment Expert Review
APR	Annual Performance Report
ARCS	Access Risk Classification System
ARRT	Advanced Rehabilitation Research Training
AT	assistive technology
BMS	Burn Model System
BMS/DCC	Burn Model System/Data Coordinating Center
BRFSS	Behavioral Risk Factor Surveillance System
CAHPS®	Consumer Assessment of Healthcare Providers and Systems
CART	communication access realtime translation services
CBO	Congressional Budget Office
CDC	Centers for Disease Control and Prevention
CDMRP	Office of Congressionally Directed Medical Research Programs (DOD)
CDS	Charge Data System

CFDA	Catalog of Federal Domestic Assistance
CFR	Code of Federal Regulations
CHART	Craig Handicap Assessment and Reporting Techniques
CIHR	Canadian Institutes of Health Research
CMS	Centers for Medicare & Medicaid Services
CP	cerebral palsy
DBTAC	Disability and Business Technical Assistance Center
DGI	Dynamic Gait Index
DGI-M	Dynamic Gait Index-Modified
DOD	U.S. Department of Defense
DOL	U.S. Department of Labor
DRRP	Disability and Rehabilitation Research Project-General
ED	U.S. Department of Education
EDGAR	Education Department General Administrative Regulations
EEG	electroencephalogram
EEOC	Equal Employment Opportunity Commission
EMG	electromyogram
ESES	Exercise Self-Efficacy Scale
FEPA	Fair Employment Protection Agency
FEW	Functioning Everyday with a Wheelchair
FID	Field Initiated Project-Development
FIP	Field Initiated Project
FIR	Field Initiated Project-Research
fMRI	functional magnetic resonance imaging
GAO	U.S. Government Accountability Office
GPRA	Government Performance and Results Act
HCBS	home- and community-based services
HCBU	historically black colleges and universities
HEDIS®	Healthcare Effectiveness Data and Information Set
HFES	Human Factors and Ergonomics Society
HHS	U.S. Department of Health and Human Services
HIPAA	Health Insurance Portability and Accountability
ICC	intraclass correlation coefficient
ICDR	Interagency Committee on Disability Research
ICF	International Classification of Functioning, Disability and Health (World Health Organization)
ICT	information and communication technologies

IMPACT	Individualized Management of Personal Assistant/ Consumer Teams
IOM	Institute of Medicine
IRB	Institutional Review Board
ISO	International Standards Organization
JAN	Job Accommodation Network
JDF	Juvenile Diabetes Research Foundation (formerly known as the Juvenile Diabetes Foundation)
JTHFT	Jebsen-Taylor Hand Function Test
KIR	Kessler Institute for Rehabilitation
KMRREC	Kessler Medical Rehabilitation Research and Education Center
KT	Knowledge Translation
LHPDC	Law, Health Policy, and Disability Center (University of Iowa)
LRP	Long-Range Plan
MHQ	Michigan Hand Questionnaire
MOMSCIS	Missouri Model Spinal Cord Injury System
MS	Model System
NARIC	National Rehabilitation Information Center
NCMRR	National Center for Medical Rehabilitation Research
NFP	notice of final priority
NHIS	National Health Interview Survey
NIA	notices inviting applications
NIDRR	National Institute on Disability and Rehabilitation Research
NIH	National Institutes of Health
NIMH	National Institute of Mental Health
NIOSH	National Institute for Occupational Safety and Health
NNJSCIS	Northern New Jersey Spinal Cord Injury System
NORA	National Occupational Research Agenda
NPP	notice of proposed priority
NRC	National Research Council
NSF	National Science Foundation
NTBRMS	North Texas Burn Rehabilitation Model System
OMB	U.S. Office of Management and Budget
OPP	Office of Policy and Planning (NIDRR)

OSERS	Office of Special Education and Rehabilitative Services (ED)
PART	Program Assessment Rating Tool
PARTS/M	Participation Survey for Persons with Mobility Limitations
PAS	personal assistance services
PCS-BI	Perceived Control Scale for Brain Injury
PEAT	Photosensitive Epilepsy Analysis Tool
PI	principal investigator
PRS	Peer Review System
QA	quality assurance
RAAS	Remote Accessibility Assessment System
REI Tour	Real Economic Impact Tour
RERC	Rehabilitation Engineering Research Center
RRTC	Rehabilitation Research and Training Center
RSD	Research Sciences Division (NIDRR)
RTI	Research Triangle International
SBIR	Small Business Innovation Research
SCI	spinal cord injury
SCIMS	Spinal Cord Injury Model System
SOAR	Survivors Offering Assistance in Recovery Program
STI	scheduled telephone intervention
TBI	traumatic brain injury
TBIMS	Traumatic Brain Injury Model System
TOFHLA	Test of Functional Health Literacy in Adults
TRIM	U.S. Department of Education's web-based grant records management system
UCSF	University of California, San Francisco
ULTrA	Upper-Limb Training and Assessment Program
UTI	urinary tract infection
VA	U.S. Department of Veterans Affairs
VIP	VIrtual Planning Test
W3C	World Wide Web Consortium
WAI	Web Accessibility Initiative
WCAG	Web Content Accessibility Guidelins

Appendix D

Committee and Staff Biographical Sketches

COMMITTEE MEMBERS

David H. Wegman (*Chair*) is professor emeritus in the School of Health and Environment at the University of Massachusetts, Lowell. Dr. Wegman was appointed professor and founding chair of the Department of Work Environment in 1987. He served a 5-year term as dean of the School of Health and Environment (2003-2008), after which he returned to the faculty until his retirement at the end of 2009. He continues to serve as adjunct professor at the Harvard School of Public Health. Previously, he served as director of the Division of Occupational and Environmental Health at the University of California, Los Angeles School of Public Health and on the faculty at Harvard School of Public Health. Dr. Wegman has focused his research on epidemiologic studies of occupational respiratory disease, musculoskeletal disorders, and cancer and has published more than 200 articles in the scientific literature. He has also written on public health and policy issues concerning hazard and health surveillance, methods of exposure assessment for epidemiologic studies, the development of alternatives to regulation, and the use of participatory methods to study occupational health risks. He has served as chair of the National Research Council (NRC)-Institute of Medicine (IOM) Committees on Health and Safety Needs of Older Workers and the Health and Safety Consequences of Child Labor, as well as the Committee to Review the NIOSH Research Programs. He has also been a member of the NRC-IOM Panel on Musculoskeletal Disorders and Work and the IOM Committees to Review the Health Consequences of Service during the Persian Gulf War and to Review Gender Differences in Susceptibility to Environmental Factors. He also served as chair of the NRC Committee on the Role of Human Factors in Home Health Care. He received his B.A. from Swarthmore College and his M.D. and M.Sc. from Harvard University, and is board certified in preventive medicine (occupational medicine).

Thomas J. Armstrong is a professor in the Departments of Industrial and Operations Engineering and Biomedical Engineering at the University of Michigan. He is also director of the University of Michigan Center for Ergonomics and was director of the Rehabilitation Engineering Research Center on Ergonomics. His research is concerned with performance and health issues in manual work and has focused on the development of methods for analyzing physical work requirements; the development of biomechanical models of hand function; analysis of the relationship between physical work requirements and musculoskeletal disorders; the design of workstations, hand tools, and keyboards; identification of ways of facilitating the return to work of injured workers; analysis and design of jobs for accommodation of restricted workers; and the design of ergonomic programs for control of work-related musculoskeletal disorders. He has conducted research and training within the automobile, aerospace, electronics, computer, office, and food processing industries. His research has resulted in numerous articles, book chapters, and reports on upper-limb biomechanics, carpal tunnel syndrome, tendinitis, job analysis, vibration, tools, workstations, and computer-aided design. Dr. Armstrong is on the editorial boards of *Human Factors and Ergonomics*, the *Journal of Occupational Rehabilitation*, and the *Scandinavian Journal of Work Environment and Health*. He is a fellow in the American Industrial Hygiene Association, the American Institute for Medical and Biological Engineering, the Human Factors and Ergonomics Society, and the International Ergonomics Association. Dr. Armstrong served on the National Research Council committee that organized the Workshop to Evaluate Work-Related Musculoskeletal Injuries: The Research Base. Dr. Armstrong holds a B.S.E. in aerospace engineering; an M.P.H. in industrial health; and a Ph.D. in industrial health, physiology, and engineering, all from the University of Michigan.

Burt S. Barnow is the Amsterdam professor of public service and of economics at George Washington University. Prior to joining George Washington University, Dr. Barnow was associate director for research at Johns Hopkins University's Institute for Policy Studies, where he worked for 18 years. Prior to that, he worked for 8 years at the Lewin Group and nearly 9 years at the U.S. Department of Labor, including 4 years as director of the Office of Research and Evaluation in the Employment and Training Administration. As a labor economist, Dr. Barnow focuses much of his work on labor markets; over the years he has conducted a number of studies looking at whether particular labor markets have experienced shortages of workers and if so, why. He has also conducted many studies of occupational training programs, including studies of how the programs are being implemented and how effective they have been. Dr. Barnow teaches the core course on program evaluation in the public policy and public administration program at George Washington University, and he has conducted evaluations of a variety of social programs, including training, welfare, child support, and fatherhood programs. His current research includes the development and evaluation of pilot programs to test self-sufficiency strategies for welfare recipients for the U.S. Department of Health and Human Services, a study of the implementation of the American Recovery and Reinvestment Act for workforce investment programs for the U.S. Department of Labor, and an evaluation of a new approach to adult education sponsored by the Gates Foundation. Dr. Barnow has been a member of eight other National Research Council committees, most recently the Committee to Review NASA's Workforce; the Committee to Review EPA's Title 42 Hiring Authority for Highly Qualified Scientists and Engineers; the Committee on the Emerging Workforce Trends in the U.S. Mining and Energy Industries; and the Committee on Science, Technology, Engineering, and Mathematics Workforce Needs for the U.S. Department of Defense and the U.S. Defense Industrial Base. He also served two terms on the NRC Board on Higher Education and the Workforce. Dr. Barnow received a B.S. in economics from the Massachusetts Institute of Technology and a Ph.D. in economics from the University of Wisconsin–Madison.

Leighton Chan is chief of the Rehabilitation Medicine Department at the Clinical Center of the National Institutes of Health. Subsequently, he completed a Robert Wood Johnson Clinical Scholar Fellowship and was a congressional fellow for the Honorable Jim McDermott (Washington). From 1994 to 2006, Dr. Chan was on the faculty of the University of Washington's Department of Rehabilitation Medicine. From 2002 to 2006, he was associate professor. He is board certified in physical medicine and rehabilitation and in electrodiagnostic medicine. Dr. Chan's research interests include health services, quality of care given to Medicare beneficiaries, and Medicare payment policy issues. He has published more than 65 peer-reviewed articles and numerous book chapters. His awards include the Young Academician Award from the Association of Academic Physiatrists, two outstanding teacher awards from the University of Washington School of Medicine, and a Presidential Citation Award for excellence in research from the American Academy of Physical Medicine and Rehabilitation. Dr. Chan is a member of the Institute of Medicine (IOM) and is a current IOM membership section leader. He holds an M.P.H. from the University of Washington and an M.D. from the University of California, Los Angeles. Dr. Chan completed postgraduate training in physical medicine and rehabilitation at the University of Washington.

Peter C. Esselman is professor and chair of the Department of Rehabilitation Medicine at the University of Washington, as well as chief of rehabilitation medicine at Harborview Medical Center in Seattle. His clinical interests include the rehabilitation of individuals after traumatic injuries, with a focus on traumatic brain injury and burn injuries. He is also interested in quality improvement. Dr. Esselman was an intern in the Department of Medicine and a resident as well as chief resident in the Department of Rehabilitation Medicine at the University of Washington. He has published more than 50 journal articles and five book chapters and is on the editorial board of the *American Journal of Physical Medicine & Rehabilitation*. He is a member of the Health Policy Legislation Committee of the American Academy of Physical Medicine and Rehabilitation and was chair of the Association of Academic Physiatrists Task Force on Chronic Disease and Disability Education. He is a member of the American Academy of Physical Medicine and Rehabilitation, the American Burn Association, and the Association of Academic Physiatrists. In 2001, he won the Harborview Medical Center Service Excellence Award. Dr. Esselman was a member of the Institute of Medicine Committee on Traumatic Brain Injury. He received an M.D. from the University of Washington School of Medicine.

Walter R. Frontera is a professor of physical medicine and rehabilitation (PM&R) and physiology and former dean of the Medical School at the University of Puerto Rico. In 1995, he spent a sabbatical year at the Karolinska Hospital in Stockholm, Sweden, in the Department of Clinical Neurophysiology, studying the effects of aging on the biochemical and contractile properties of single human muscle fibers. In 1996, he was recruited to Harvard Medical School to establish the Department of PM&R and was appointed Earle P. and Ida S. Charlton professor and chairman of the Department of PM&R at Harvard Medical School and Spaulding Rehabilitation Hospital. He was also chief of service at the Massachusetts General Hospital and the Brigham and Women's Hospital. Dr. Frontera's main research interest is study of the mechanisms underlying muscle atrophy and weakness in the elderly and the development of rehabilitative interventions for sarcopenia. He has authored more than 200 scientific publications, including more than 80 peer-reviewed articles and 12 edited books. Currently, Dr. Frontera serves as editor-in-chief of *The American Journal of PM&R* and regional vice president of the International Society of PM&R. He has received several awards, including Best Scientific Research Paper (three times), presented by the American Academy of PM&R; the Distinguished Academician (2005) and Outstanding Service (2010) awards, presented by the Association of

Academic Physiatrists; the Harvard Foundation Award for his contributions to the field of PM&R; the Joel DeLisa award (2011), presented by the Kessler Foundation; and the Sidney Licht award, presented by the International Society of PM&R (2011). In 2008, he was elected member of the Institute of Medicine (IOM). He currently serves on the IOM Committee of Medical Experts to Assist Social Security on Disability Issues. Dr. Frontera completed his M.D. and residency in PM&R in 1983 at the University of Puerto Rico and his Ph.D. in applied anatomy and physiology at Boston University in 1986.

Glenn T. Fujiura is an associate professor of human development in the Department of Disability and Human Development and associate dean of the College of Applied Health Sciences at the University of Illinois at Chicago. Dr. Fujiura's research has focused on the fiscal structure and demography of the disability service system, family policy, evaluation of long-term care services, poverty and disability, ethnic and racial issues in disability, and the statistical surveillance of disability. In addition, he has a long-standing interest in research methodology, statistical analysis, and philosophy of science. Dr. Fujiura teaches research methods, advanced research concepts, and statistics for the graduate program at the University of Illinois at Chicago. Current major projects include analyses of family demographics, evaluation of state disability spending, cognitive testing of health surveys for persons with intellectual disabilities, evaluation of international disability statistical surveillance, health statistics and intellectual disability, and the application of knowledge utilization models in Americans with Disabilities Act technical assistance. He has worked extensively in both the creation of large national data sets on intellectual and developmental disabilities and the secondary analysis of national statistical surveillance systems. He has served as chair of the U.S. Administration on Developmental Disabilities Commissioner's Multicultural Advisory Committee, and as a member of the President's Committee on Mental Retardation during the Clinton Administration, the Cultural Diversity Advisory Committee for the National Council on Disability, and NIDRR's Long-Range Plan Steering Committee. He was 1999 recipient of the National Rehabilitation Association's Switzer Scholar award. Dr. Fujiura is the editor-in-chief of the journal *Intellectual and Developmental Disabilities*. He holds a Ph.D. from the University of Illinois at Urbana-Champaign.

Bruce M. Gans is executive vice president and chief medical officer for the Kessler Institute for Rehabilitation, based in West Orange, New Jersey. He is also national medical director for rehabilitation for Select Medical Corporation, the parent company for Kessler. In addition, Dr. Gans holds an appointment as professor of physical medicine and rehabilitation (PM&R)

at the University of Medicine and Dentistry of New Jersey–New Jersey Medical School and serves on the board of directors of the Allied Health Research Institute, a nonprofit organization focused on improving access to rehabilitation therapy. Dr. Gans has published extensively, and has held more than $10 million in research and educational grants from the public and private sectors. He is an editor of the major textbook DeLisa's *Physical Medicine and Rehabilitation: Principles and Practice* (5th ed., 2010). He also serves as an associate editor of the *American Journal of Physical Medicine & Rehabilitation*. His research has focused on pediatric trauma rehabilitation, quantitative assessment of motor performance, rehabilitation engineering, rehabilitation health services delivery, and primary care for the disabled. Dr. Gans has been honored with recognition as one of "The Best Doctors in America." He has received the American Hospital Association's prestigious Brent England Award for Excellence in Rehabilitation Management (1995) and the American Medical Rehabilitation Providers Association's INDE Service Award (2005). The Association of Academic Physiatrists awarded him its Outstanding Service Award in 2000. In 2001, he was selected to deliver the 34th Annual Walter J. Zeiter Lecture to the American Academy of Physical Medicine and Rehabilitation. In 2008, he was the recipient of that organization's Distinguished Member Award. Dr. Gans received his M.D. degree from the University of Pennsylvania School of Medicine in Philadelphia and an M.S. in biomedical electronic engineering from the Moore School of Engineering at the University of Pennsylvania. He also holds an M.S. degree from the University of Washington. He served his medical internship at the Philadelphia General Hospital and his residency in PM&R at the University of Washington, Seattle. He received his B.S. degree in electrical engineering from Union College, Schenectady, New York.

Ian D. Graham is vice president of the Knowledge Translation Portfolio at Canadian Institutes of Health Research, where he is responsible for knowledge translation, partnerships and citizen engagement, communication and public outreach, and pan institute affairs and initiatives. Dr. Graham is on leave from his positions as associate professor in the School of Nursing, University of Ottawa, and senior social scientist in the Clinical Epidemiology Program of the Ottawa Hospital Research Institute. He holds cross-appointments in the Departments of Medicine and Epidemiology and Community Medicine and is an adjunct associate professor in the School of Nursing at Queen's University, Kingston, Ontario. He is a Fellow of the Canadian Academies of Health Sciences. His research has focused largely on knowledge translation (the process of research use) and applied research on strategies to increase implementation of research findings and evidence-based practice. He has also advanced knowledge translation science through the development of two planned action models, the Ottawa Model of Research Use and, more recently, the Knowledge to Action Model. His specific research projects have related to the adaptation, implementation, and quality appraisal of clinical practice guidelines, as well as the uptake of guidelines and decision support tools by practitioners. He is co-editor of *Knowledge Translation in Health Care*, published by Wiley-Blackwell (2009) and *Evaluating the Impact of Implementing Evidence-Based Practice,* published by Wiley-Blackwell (2010). Dr. Graham obtained a B.A. in sociology from McGill University, an M.A. in sociology from the University of Victoria, and a Ph.D. in medical sociology from McGill University.

Lisa I. Iezzoni is professor of medicine at Harvard Medical School and director of the Mongan Institute for Health Policy at Massachusetts General Hospital. Dr. Iezzoni has spent more than two decades conducting health services research focused in three primary areas: risk adjustment methods for predicting cost and clinical outcomes of care, use of administrative data for assessing health care quality, and health care experiences and outcomes of persons with disabilities. She has personal experience in the latter area (having had multiple sclerosis since age 22). After spending 16 years as co-director of research in the Division of General Medicine and Primary Care at Boston's Beth Israel Deaconess Medical Center, Dr. Iezzoni joined the Institute for Health Policy as associate director in 2006. She has led numerous research grants with funding from the Agency for Healthcare Research and Quality, the National Institutes of Health, the Health Care Financing Administration, The Robert Wood Johnson Foundation (RWJF), and other private foundations. An internationally recognized expert in risk adjustment, she edited *Risk Adjustment for Measuring Health Care Outcomes*, with its fourth edition in press. Dr. Iezzoni began her disability research with a 1996 Investigator Award in Health Policy Research from RWJF, and the book summarizing this work, *When Walking Fails: Mobility Impairments of Adults with Chronic Conditions*, appeared in 2003. A book considering disability experiences more broadly, *More Than Ramps: A Guide to Improving Health Care Quality and Access for People with Disabilities*, was published in 2006. Another book, *Multiple Sclerosis*, which was published in 2010, explores the epidemiology of multiple sclerosis, describes its symptoms, reviews today's treatments and research directions, and presents the experiences of persons living with multiple sclerosis. Dr. Iezzoni has also published numerous original articles, editorials, and commentaries in major medical and health services research journals. She has been a member of many Institute of Medicine (IOM) committees, including the Committee on Identifying Priority Areas for Quality Improvement; the Committee to Evaluate Measures of Health Benefits for Environmental, Health, and Safety Regulation; and the Committee on Disability in America: A New Look. Dr.

Iezzoni is a member of the IOM. She holds an M.D. from Harvard Medical School and an MSc in health policy and management from Harvard School of Public Health.

Alan M. Jette currently directs the Health & Disability Research Institute at the Boston University School of Public Health, where he also serves as professor of health policy and management. Dr. Jette's research interests include late-life exercise; evaluation of treatment outcomes; and the measurement, epidemiology, and prevention of disability. He has published more than 180 articles on these topics in the rehabilitation, geriatrics, and public health literature. Dr. Jette is research director for the New England Regional Spinal Cord Injury Center based at Boston University Medical Center, serves on the Executive Committee of the Boston Claude Pepper Older Americans Independence Center, and directs the Boston Rehabilitation Outcome Measures Center. His current work focuses on the development and dissemination of contemporary outcome measurement instruments for evaluating the quality of health care. Dr. Jette was a member of the National Research Council (NRC)-Institute of Medicine (IOM) Committee to Review the Social Security Administration's Disability Decision Process Research, was chair of the IOM Committee on the Future of Disability in America, and was chair of the NRC Steering Committee to Design and Conduct a Public Workshop on New Survey Measures of Cognitive and Functional Disability: Going Beyond ADLs and IADLs. He received his M.P.H. and Ph.D. in public health from the University of Michigan.

Thubi H.A. Kolobe is the Jill Pitman Jones professor of physical therapy in the Department of Rehabilitation Science at the University of Oklahoma Health Sciences Center. Her research in early identification of children with or at risk for disabilities, efficacy of robotics in the early mobility of young infants, cultural and environmental influences on development, and measurement has been funded by foundations and federal agencies such as the National Institutes of Health. She is a co-developer of the Test of Infant Motor Performance for preterm infants, a norm-referenced test that is used worldwide and has been translated into several languages. Dr. Kolobe has served as chair of the Research Committee of the Section on Pediatrics, chaired a task force to develop a research agenda for the American Physical Therapy Association's Section on Pediatrics, served on a recent task force to revise the research agenda for the American Physical Therapy Association, and has been appointed to serve on the Scientific Review Committee for the National Institute of Child Health and Human Development, National Institutes of Health. Dr. Kolobe has extensive clinical experience in pediatrics and community-based interventions. Over the past 30 years, her roles in this area have ranged from direct patient care in various settings, clinical education, and staff development, to program consultation. Her consultation roles have focused largely on program evaluation and development for community-based programs that serve children and families with disabilities and on funded undergraduate and graduate training programs. She serves on the Evaluation Committee for the Oklahoma SoonerStart program, a statewide early intervention program funded through the Part C program of the Individuals with Disabilities Education Amendment Act of 2004. She holds a Ph.D. in pediatric physical therapy (with a minor in family therapy) from Hahnemann University.

Pamela Loprest is a labor economist and director of the Center on Income and Benefits at the Urban Institute. Her research focuses on low-wage labor markets and barriers to work among disadvantaged populations and on policies to address these issues. Dr. Loprest is a nationally known expert in welfare policy and research. Her recent work examines how to structure programs and policies to better support work among persons with disabilities and former welfare recipients with work-related challenges. Past studies include examination of the Family and Medical Leave Act, the role of employer accommodations, public policies to support job search and training for persons with disabilities, and the impact of the Supplemental Security Income program on young adult recipients transitioning to work. Dr. Loprest is the author of numerous journal articles and book chapters, as well as three books. She received her Ph.D. in economics from the Massachusetts Institute of Technology.

Kathryn E. Newcomer is the director of the Trachtenberg School of Public Policy and Public Administration at George Washington University. She teaches public and nonprofit program evaluation, research design, and applied statistics. She routinely conducts research and training for federal and local government agencies and nonprofit organizations on performance measurement and program evaluation, and has designed and conducted evaluations for several U.S. federal agencies and dozens of nonprofit organizations. Dr. Newcomer has published five books, including *The Handbook of Practical Program Evaluation*, and numerous articles in journals, including the *Public Administration Review*. She is a fellow of the National Academy of Public Administration and currently serves on the Comptroller General's Educators' Advisory Panel. She served as president of the National Association of Schools of Public Affairs and Administration, 2006-2007, and currently serves on the board of the American Evaluation Association. Dr. Newcomer received the Elmer Staats Award for Achievements in Government Accountability, awarded by the National Capital Area Chapter of the American Society for Public Administration, May 8, 2008. She has been a member of the National Research Council (NRC) Committee on

Approaches for an Evaluation of the NIST/NRC Postdoctoral Research Associateships Program, the NRC Review of United States Institute of Peace Senior Fellows Program, and the NRC Committee on Laboratory Security and Personnel Assurance Systems for Laboratories Conducting Research on Biological Select Agents and Toxins. She received her Ph.D. in economics from the Massachusetts Institute of Technology.

Patricia M. Owens is a senior disability expert for the U.S. Government Accountability Office. Ms. Owens has more than 30 years of experience in health- and disability-related programs and policy. She has an unusual set of qualifications, having held executive, policy development, and administrative positions in both the public and private disability sectors. Her experience serves as the basis for in-depth understanding of the multidimensional and interactive nature of health and disability in terms of social policy and risk management. She has consulted with both private- and public-sector organizations on health and disability issues, programs, and products. Organizations for which she has consulted include the Social Security Administration, the Veterans Administration, the Urban Institute, the National Academy of Social Insurance (board member), Rutgers Disability Income Studies, and the Government Accountability Office. She helped UNUM, UK (an insurance company in Great Britain) launch a study of the cost of disability in 2000-2001. Ms. Owens is a member of the board of directors of Village Care of New York, a multimillion dollar AIDS treatment network and community nursing and rehabilitation services provider for persons with impairment. She was a member of the National Research Council-Institute of Medicine Committee on Veterans' Compensation for Posttraumatic Stress Disorder. She earned an M.P.A. degree from the University of Missouri.

Robert G. Radwin is a professor and founding chair of Biomedical Engineering, and a professor of Industrial and Systems Engineering, and Orthopedics and Rehabilitation at the University of Wisconsin–Madison. Dr. Radwin has received numerous grants from government agencies, private foundations, and industry and he is a regular consultant on human factors engineering. His research is concerned with ergonomics aspects of the design, selection, installation and use of manually operated equipment and products; investigating the causes and prevention of work-related musculoskeletal disorders; developing novel measurements and methods for assessing exposure to physical stress in the workplace; and quantifying functional deficits associated with musculoskeletal and neuromuscular disorders for medical surveillance, rehabilitation, and prevention. Dr. Radwin is a Fellow of the American Institute of Medical and Biological Engineers, the American Industrial Hygiene Association, the Biomedical Engineering Society, the Human Factors and Ergonomics Society (U.S.), and the Institute of Ergonomics (U.K.). He was a member of the National Research Council (NRC)-Institute of Medicine Panel on Musculoskeletal Disorders and the Workplace and the NRC Committee on Human-Systems Integration. He earned a Ph.D. in industrial and operations engineering from the University of Michigan.

STAFF

Jeanne C. Rivard is a senior program officer with the National Academies' Division on Behavioral and Social Sciences and Education (DBASSE) and was co-study director of the project. She earned a Ph.D. in social work at the University of North Carolina at Chapel Hill, where she received a National Research Service Award from the National Institute of Mental Health to conduct her dissertation study investigating factors promoting change in interagency collaboration. While she was serving on the faculty of the Columbia University School of Social Work, her research included a developmental study examining the implementation and intermediate outcomes of a trauma-focused intervention for youth and an evaluation of the implementation and outcomes of an interagency initiative designed to integrate vocational and supportive housing services for homeless persons with mental illness, substance abuse, HIV, and other disabilities. Before coming to DBASSE, she worked at the National Association of State Mental Health Program Directors Research Institute, where she led initiatives to promote the dissemination of evidence-based practices, was a team leader for the national impact component of the cross-site evaluation of the National Child Traumatic Stress Initiative, and coordinated pilot studies to increase the utilization of multistate administrative data sets to address mental health policy questions. She has also holds an M.S.W. degree (University of South Carolina) and an M.S.Ed. (Mount St. Mary's College, Los Angeles).

Mary Ellen O'Connell is deputy director of the Board on Behavioral, Cognitive and Sensory Sciences and the Board on Human-Systems Integration, and was co-study director of the project. She has served as study director for five consensus studies at the National Research Council: on prevention of mental disorders and substance abuse, on international education and foreign languages, on ethical considerations for research on housing-related health hazards involving children, on reducing underage drinking, and on assessing and improving children's health. She also served as study director for the Committee on Standards of Evidence and the Quality of Behavioral and Social Science Research, a Division of Behavioral and Social Sciences and Education-wide strategic planning effort; developed stand-alone workshops on welfare reform and children and gun violence; and facilitated meetings of the national coordinating committee of the Key National Indicators Initiative. She came to DBASSE from the U.S. Department of Health and Human Services, where she spent 8 years in the Office of the Assistant Secretary for Planning and Evaluation, most recently as director of state and local initiatives. Previously, she worked at the U.S. Department of Housing and Urban Development on homeless policy and program design issues and for the Commonwealth of Massachusetts as director of field services. She holds a B.A. (with distinction) from Cornell University and a master's degree in the management of human services from the Heller School for Social Policy and Management at Brandeis University.

Tina Winters is an associate program officer with the Division of Behavioral and Social Sciences and Education. She returned to the National Academies to work with the Committee on the External Evaluation of NIDRR and Its Grantees. Prior to rejoining the National Academies, she worked on an initiative to spread innovative health care practices and with the coordinating center for a medical registry on islet cell transplantation. In her previous tenure at the National Academies, she worked with the Committee on Social Science Evidence for Use and supported numerous studies that produced reports, including *Scientific Research in Education*, *Knowing What Students Know: The Science and Design of Educational Assessment*, and the *National Science Education Standards*.

Matthew D. McDonough is a research associate with the Division of Behavioral and Social Sciences and Education. In 7 years of working at the National Research Council, he has staffed the Board on Life Sciences; the Board on Behavioral, Cognitive, and Sensory Sciences; the Board on Human-Systems Integration; and the Board on Children, Youth, and Families. He has supported studies that have produced such reports as *Guidelines for Human Embryonic Stem Cell Research*; *Human-Systems Integration in the Design Process: A New Look*; *Human Behavior in Military Contexts*; *Early Childhood Assessment: Why, What, and How*; *Intelligence Analysis for Tomorrow: Advances from the Behavioral and Social Sciences*; and *Intelligence Analysis: Behavioral and Social Scientific Foundations*. He is a graduate of George Washington University, with an M.A. in anthropology and a concentration in international development.

Barbara Wanchisen is director of the Board on Behavioral, Cognitive and Sensory Sciences and the Board on Human-Systems Integration. She is a long-standing member of the Psychonomic Society, the Association for Behavior Analysis, and the American Psychological Association. In January 2004, she became a fellow of Division 25 (Behavior Analysis) of the American Psychological Association. She has served on the editorial boards of the *Journal of the Experimental Analysis of Behavior* and *The Behavior Analyst* while also serving as a guest reviewer for a number of other journals. From November 2001 through April 2008, Dr. Wanchisen was executive director of the Federation of Behavioral, Psychological, & Cognitive Sciences in Washington, DC. In 2004, she was instrumental in the founding of the Federation's Foundation for the Advancement of Behavioral and Brain Sciences, a nonprofit organization that assumed the educational mission of the Federation. Previously, Dr. Wanchisen was professor in the Department of Psychology and director of the college-wide Honors Program at Baldwin-Wallace College, near Cleveland, Ohio. She received a B.A. in English and philosophy from Bloomsburg University in Pennsylvania, an M.A. in English from Villanova University, and her Ph.D. in experimental psychology from Temple University.